Readings and Cases in Sustainable Marketing
A Strategic Approach to Social Responsibility

Clare D'Souza
Mehdi Taghian
Michael Polonsky

Readings and Cases in Sustainable Marketing: A Strategic Approach to Social Responsibility
1st edition, 2nd printing

Editors
Clare D'Souza, Mehdi Taghian & Michael Polonsky

Cover designer
Christopher Besley, Besley Design.

ISBN: 978-0-7346-1085-0

Disclaimer

All reasonable efforts have been made to ensure the quality and accuracy of this publication. Tilde Publishing and Distribution assumes no responsibility for any errors or omissions and no warranties are made with regard to this publication. Neither Tilde Publishing and Distribution nor any authorised distributors shall be held responsible for any direct, incidental or consequential damages resulting from the use of this publication.

Published in Australia by:
Tilde Publishing and Distribution
PO Box 72
Prahran VIC 3181 Australia
www.tup.net.au

Contents

About the editors

Clare D'Souza, PhD (Environmental Economics), MBA, M. Com., LLB, B. Com., Dip. Tourism Mgt, is Associate Professor in the School of Management at La Trobe University in Melbourne, Australia. Clare comes from a multi-disciplinary background and has taught across an extensive range of subjects. Her primary research interests are in environmental management and marketing. She has taught in various countries across Asia and Europe. Her research has been presented at international conferences in the UK, Europe and America, and she has published in international journals and co-authored two text books. She is a member of the Editorial Review Board for Journal of Non-profit and Public Sector Marketing and has extensive consulting and policy experience.

Mehdi Taghian, BA (Econ) American U, GradDip, MBus Monash, PhD Deakin, is Senior Lecturer at the Deakin Graduate School of Business at Deakin University in Melbourne, Australia. Mehdi lectured in various marketing subjects at La Trobe University. He comes from a long industry employment background in marketing management at Gillette Australia and Ansell International. He also provides marketing consultancy services to SMEs in Australia. His research interests are in marketing strategy and environmental marketing.

Michael Polonsky, BS Towson, MA Rutgers, MA Temple, PhD ACU, is the Chair of Marketing, within the School of Management and Marketing at Deakin University in Melbourne, Australia. Michael received the Society for Marketing Advances, Elsevier Distinguished Marketing Scholar Award for 2010, for his 20 years of contributions on green marketing and best marketing practices for a global world. The award was presented at the Society's annual conference in Atlanta, November 2010. The Society for Marketing Advances is a premier marketing association that brings together marketing educators from the United States and abroad. Only one such award was given in 2010. Michael has been the Guest Editor for a number of journals, including recent issues of the *Journal of Marketing Education* (2009) on marketing education in Australia and New Zealand and *Tourism Culture and Communication* (2010) on Creative Industries and Experiences: Development, Marketing and Consumption.

About the contributors

Giuseppe E Adamo, Universidad Carlos III de Madrid, Madrid, Spain • Professor Sivakumar Alur, Delft University of Technology, The Netherlands • Dr Vanessa Apaolaza-Ibanez, University of the Basque Country, Spain • Dr Carol Brennan, Queen Margaret University, Edinburgh, UK • Associate Professor Jaime R Camino, Universidad Carlos III de Madrid, Madrid, Spain • Dr Louise Canning, University of Birmingham, UK • Professor Leslie C Carlson, University of Nebraska - Lincoln, USA • Suzanne L Conner, New Mexico State University, USA • Dr Bethany Cooper, La Trobe University, Melbourne, Australia • Associate Professor Michael J Dorsch, Clemson University, USA • Associate Professor Clare D'Souza, La Trobe University, Melbourne, Australia • Dr José Manuel Ortega Egea, University of Almería, Spain • Dr Kathryn Fahy, Lancaster University, UK • Nieves García de Frutos, University of Almería, Spain • José-Carlos García-Rosell, University of Lapland, Finland • Professor Stephen J Grove, Clemson University, USA •Professor Patrick Hartmann, University of the Basque Country, Spain • Dr Christopher S Hodkinson, La Trobe University, Melbourne, Australia • Professor Michael Hyman, New Mexico State University, USA • Dr Johan Jansson, Umeå University, Sweden • Dr S Menuka Jayaratne, La Trobe University, Melbourne, Australia • Associate Professor Lee Kaman, Chinese University of Hong Kong • Associate Professor Mark J Kay, Montclair State University, USA • Professor Agneta Marell, Umeå University, Sweden • Dr Morven McEachern, Lancaster University, UK • Professor Johanna Moisander, Aalto University, Finland • Sumesh R Nair, Monash University, Malaysia • Assistant Professor Annika Nordlund, Umeå University, Sweden • Professor Michael Polonsky, Deakin University, Melbourne, Australia • Mike Pretious, Queen Margaret University, Edinburgh, UK • Chad Renando, Brisbane, Australia • Elaine Ritch, Queen Margaret University, Edinburgh, UK • Dr Monika Schröder, Queen Margaret University, Edinburgh, UK • Principal Consultant Nicholas Shipley, DeakinPrime, Deakin University, Melbourne, Australia • Assistant Professor Alin Stancu, Bucharest Academy of Economic Studies, Bucharest, Romania • Professor Gillian Sullivan Mort, La Trobe University, Melbourne, Australia • Professor Isabelle Szmigin, University of Birmingham, UK • Professor Richard J Varey, University of Waikato, NZ • Professor Rodica Milena Zaharia, Bucharest Academy of Economic Studies, Bucharest, Romania

Introduction

The concept of corporate social responsibility has long been of interest to academics and business practitioners as well as social and environmental activists (Carroll 1979, 1991). Heightened interest in issues revolving around global warming and the consequences it has for business and society have increased the focus on the social responsibilities of firms (Svensson & Wagner 2011). This is evidenced by growing public awareness and extensive media coverage, as well as the numerous government initiatives aimed at addressing environmental problems. Increasingly, research warns of substantial changes taking place in the natural environment. The general view is that this is, at least in part, caused or accelerated by humans through growing populations, urbanisation, economic development, production inefficiencies and growing consumption, among other things. The risk of carelessness in addressing (or failing to address) the deteriorating environmental problem will be substantial. In line with these dire environmental predictions, the role of business managers as positive change agents is considerable. Management actions could include: the redesign of products to minimise environmentally harmful ingredients and components; changes in packaging design and quality; alterations to production processes to achieve cleaner methods; and adoption of more appropriate technologies. Thus, managers and marketers can make a substantial contribution towards the solution of environmental problems.

The classical economic theory argument championed by Friedman (1970) holds that the main motivation and responsibility of business is to create and maximise returns for its owners while operating within the legal rules of conduct. Thus, unfortunately, business decisions are primarily motivated by self-interest (Hunt 2011). Others believe that business activities should also be conducted with care for the safety of the environment and the society, and, where and when necessary, business should initiate activities to this end beyond the expressed legal permissions and/or limitations (Carroll 1991). Even the more traditional management theorists are increasingly acknowledging that addressing environmental issues makes good business sense (Porter & Linde 1995).

Those who support corporate social responsibility as a core tenet of business maintain that, in addition to being ethical and proper in discharging social and environmental obligations, it provides substantial direct and indirect benefits to the business, which eventually assists with the accomplishment of its main objective, generating profit. Corporate social responsibility promotes goodwill in the community and attracts consumer support. It allows business to prepare more directly and effectively for future social and environmental changes, making the business more relevant and viable over time. Further, corporate social responsibility promotes development of new technologies and may result in competitive advantages (such as emission reduction and energy saving). It is also said that this direct voluntary involvement will reduce the motivation by the government to apply additional regulation and control mechanisms on business.

This book seeks to assist in advancing these issues by discussing a range of topics related to sustainable marketing. We define sustainable marketing as an effort to create sustainable development and a sustainable economy, using marketing strategies to support sustainable economic development (Hunt 2011). This is a big task and requires substantial reorientation of business from cultural aspects to control and measurement techniques. But the interest in environmental sustainability marketing is increasing while at the same time the issues involved in promoting the interest become more complex. The influential factors driving this interest in environmental sustainability are numerous, and the debate about global warming seems to have been won. Consumers in developed countries appear to be changing behaviour and showing a desire to behave responsibly, as well as expecting that government and business initiatives also demonstrate environmental care and assume greater societal responsibility.

There are various ways businesses might become engaged in sustainability: (1) aligning their activities to stakeholder expectations and avoiding negative publicity, (2) adhering to regulatory control mechanisms (to avoid punishments), (3) seeking to undertake self-regulation and minimise the need for external governmental control initiatives, and (4) practicing ethical management actions because it is the right thing to do. Senior employees who respond to these triggers can direct and formulate the corporate strategies; they can change the organisational cultural values and establish more responsible frameworks for sustainable business activities. The framework of action can provide for the satisfaction of stakeholder expectations and at the same time optimise organisational profits while it enhances society's quality of life.

The role of marketing discipline in this process of shifting from an immediate marketing operation to a broader transformative focus on sustainability requires that firms translate strategic actions into environmental and social objectives. These activities relate to engaging with influential stakeholders and ensuring their interests are considered. The challenge is to create a market position that substantiates the application of the business theory, while responding to market fundamentals and dynamics. It brings business to the essence of sustainability by the application of marketing theory and true market orientation.

The challenge is to identify the most appropriate areas for action. Firms must be able to assess market risks and opportunities as well as costs and benefits associated with these initiatives and investments. This needs to be done in a framework that has the appropriate metrics that embrace social and environmental outcomes and which are supported by internal control systems ensuring true triple-p bottom line objectives are achieved. There is evidence that there is a relationship between proactive environmental strategies and corporate financial performance (Andersen 2011; Griffin & Mahon 1997) and an increasing number of companies are responding by integrating sustainability strategy to promote positive marketing innovation.

The debate continues

The purpose of this book is to bring together some of the recent scholarly contributions and examples from practice, related to the role of marketing in managing for environmental sustainability. The contributions are classified to address the fundamental driving forces behind the motivation to engage in sustainability marketing strategy. The understanding of the emerging environmentally sensitive consumer market segment(s) can inform the marketer's approach in environmental business strategy formulation, but sustainability also needs to be embedded as a core corporate value. Integrating sustainability into all activities can help the business to facilitate the management of corporate aggregate consumption and respond appropriately to environmentally sensitive stakeholders while creating and supporting a meaningful competitive advantage. Ultimately, this may improve business performance; however, a shift in both business management and the cultural values of consumers might be needed. Business needs to view the generation of profit as a consequence not only of serving the market, but of serving the market ethically. Business thereby must be an agent of positive change. Consumers are changing their attitudes, albeit slowly, by recognising that current prevailing lifestyles lead to unsustainable consumption patterns that cannot continue. The shift in the attitude of consumers and business leads to the broader discussion of the importance of reducing the negative societal impacts of excessive consumption. This may inspire support for a range of consumer actions such as environmentally oriented anti-consumption campaigns.

The contributions in this book discuss a range of topics contributing to the conversation on environmental marketing, with specific focus on the strategy and marketing mix elements needed to bring about change. What follows is a brief reference to the articles and cases included.

Chapter 1 Sustainability consumption and consumers

Clare D'Souza presents a paper focused on the issue of sustainability consumption and consumers. It addresses green brand management and the requirement needed for clear green market segmentation. The paper identifies four green segments and proposes how to increase brand resonance in terms of sustainable green brand values across all consumers using a multidimensional model. The model incorporates four dimensions of high and low green brand sensitivity and environmental values. The article revisits green brand anomalies in terms of core benefits including functional (disappointing performance), experiential (convenience) and symbolic (positioning) aspects and proposes a branding framework that includes environmental benefits associated with green brands.

Jose Egea and Nieves Garcia de Frutos present a paper on consumption reduction. They link environmental degradation with the western consumption-focused lifestyles that lead to unsustainable consumption patterns. They propose that consumption reduction is a way of moderating the intensity and the risk associated with climate change. The authors examine the role of three psychographics (environmental attitudes, motivations, and knowledge) for consumption reduction behaviour of European citizens. Their findings highlight the importance of both altruistic and egoistic ecological motivations for developing positive attitudes towards the environment and thus ultimately shifting behaviour. They refer to the level of knowledge about the causes, consequences and ways of fighting climate change. This contributes to both positive and negative attitudes, thus suggesting that not all types of environmental messages and information can be assumed to be equally effective in fostering consumption reduction behaviour.

Chapter 2 Goods and services

Morven McEachern talks about the un-sustainability of 'business as usual' and refers to the need to instigate substantial changes, with the provision of sustainable products being a key societal challenge. The point is that there is a need for change in business practices to develop and implement sustainable product strategies.

Patrick Hartman and Vanessa Apaolaza-Ibanez present a discussion of the role of sustainability information and propose that it is needed in order to increase consumer demand for green energy. This needs to supplement the information on sustainable product characteristics and psychological brand benefits. They refer to empirical evidence confirming the relevance of both sustainability information and psychological brand benefits that in combination assist in influencing consumer demand.

Chapter 3 Pricing

Suzanne Conner and Michael Hyman discuss the importance of pricing in motivating changes in consumer behaviour and in maximising environmental and social benefits. They propose that the pricing of environmentally sensitive products should incorporate the monetary value of externalities in influencing the level of demand to safeguard a habitable environment for future generations and to provide incentives for innovations. This may be starting to happen with the increased use of carbon taxes or carbon pricing.

Bethany Cooper discusses the water management policy failure in South Australia in a severe water shortage situation. The paper addresses the role of regulatory controls in effectively restricting water usage. Mandated restrictions over the use of water have been a common response to shortages and substantial attention has been focussed on the efficacy of different approaches available. This study identifies the variations in consumer demand and characterises the factors that need to somehow be integrated into policy development.

Chapter 4 Marketing communication

Richard Varey challenges the notion that 'people are born to produce' and highlights the importance of man being in balance with nature. He discusses how marketers can better communicate about environmental responsibility. He suggests that to do this, marketers need to address the notion of human welfare and its dependence on excessive consumption, thereby re-establishing the interdependent relationship of humans and nature, focusing on humans as members and citizens rather than consumers. This further means redefining the business from being profit-orientated to being an enterprise in harmony with humans and nature, promoting intelligent consumption (benefits that exceed the costs). This requires the changing the orientation of marketing from simple profit generation to a value focused relationship – selling values, substance, moderation and responsibility.

Leslie Carlson, Stephen Grove and Michael Dorsch also address sustainability in environmental advertising. They highlight the concept of sustainability as a component of green advertisements. Sustainability claims are investigated to determine if it is possible for consumers to distinguish sustainability claims within advertisements. They report that consumers are capable of identifying whether a message is linked to sustainability and the clarity of the information presented. From a marketing strategy point of view, it is reported that messages related to sustainability are seen as having an impact on the organisation's image, while non-sustainability related messages tend to be product specific.

Chapter 5 Distribution

Sivakumar Alur discusses the application of sustainability within the concept of physical distribution. He suggests that the entire logistical process needs to be reviewed as a holistic system, as an alternative to existing distribution procedure. Various issues should be considered such as production streamlining (scheduling), the distance the product needs to travel (location of manufacture and inventory) and the way goods are handled. Other logistical issues such as designing reusable packaging and alternative packaging design (recyclable) can be used to reduce the overall volume and weight of materials being transported, and this can be supported with energy efficient transportation. All of which factors could minimise multiple handling requirements, further assisting in reduced energy consumption.

Elaine Ritch, Monika Schröder, Carol Brennan and Mike Pretious present a paper about fashion and food ethics in production. They argue for care in the use of resources and adequate and accurate communication of information to motivate and support sustainable consumption and retail trade participation. They note the increasing consumer concern regarding the ethics of production and want retailers to provide alternative, ethically produced products for their shoppers. This move is prominent in the supermarket sector, where firms compete to be the 'greenest' as well as encouraging consumers to behave ethically by, for example, reducing packaging and providing recycling facilities. This includes, retailers promoting organic, locally produced and fair trade foods. The authors also discuss these issues within the fashion industry, which faces a slightly different situation. They identify that while consumers are increasingly concerned about the ethics of production and manufacturing impact upon the environment, they may be unprepared to change habits to accommodate environmental concerns and engage with practices that ordinary consumers cannot comprehend and from which they are physically removed. A move towards promoting consumption for the benefit of the environment is proposed.

Chapter 6 Stakeholder influence

José-Carlos García-Rosell, Johanna Moisander and Kathryn Fahy discuss the issue that commitment to environmental and social causes is usually thought to be counter to profit maximisation. They suggest that engaging and integrating multiple stakeholders in organisational marketing activities is needed to build dynamic and proactive environmental corporate strategies. The practice of engaging with multiple stakeholders, however, is a potentially challenging social endeavour as it is difficult to effectively integrate multi-stakeholder approaches into all strategy development and day-to-day business practices.

Jaime Camino and Giuseppe Adamo refer to the importance of identifying and qualifying the appropriate stakeholders who are relevant to the environmental issues of sustainability in formulating the strategy for organisational sustainability. They use European examples to highlight the links, the interactions and the bi-directional influence that exists between stakeholder pressure and management choices within the marketing strategies.

Chapter 7 Future trends

Michael Polonsky addresses the obstacles to a future associated with marketing of green goods. These challenges are related to consumer, business and regulatory processes and barriers. In focusing on consumers, there are four critical issues indicated: getting people to pay for the environment, changing how people think about the environment, communicating complex environmental information and bringing about changes in consumer behaviour. A number of business issues need to be considered and these are also briefly addressed. One example is managerial orientation to environmental issues and how this impacts on organisational behaviour. In overviewing these challenges a number of avenues for regulator action are identified, as well as opportunities for future research. Both can assist marketers in bringing about more responsible consumer and business behaviour.

Johan Jansson, Agneta Marell and Annika Nordlund discuss the adopters and non-adopters of consumer curtailment behaviours in the context of new technology. They indicate that it is important to understand the determinants of the curtailment behaviours of consumers. It is also vital to understand the factors that drive or hinder consumers to adopt innovations that are less harmful to the environment. Two types of consumer behaviours are discussed (curtailment and innovation) as part of the solution to environmental sustainability issues, and detail is provided of the marketing challenges of encouraging consumers to adopt such behaviours. The authors indicate that understanding the drivers and how to leverage them is crucial in marketing efforts that will contribute to the continuing attempts at achieving environmental sustainability.

Cases

The cases included in the book present wide coverage of the topics and provide evidence of the application of sustainability theory as well as practical use of some of the strategies discussed in the other sections of the book.

Lee Kaman presents a case based on a Hong Kong study that discusses the factors that could be used to predict the green purchasing behaviour of adolescent consumers. It is suggested that for this group of consumers green purchasing behaviour is predicted by factors including environmental information seeking, environmental involvement, environmental information processing, environmental constraint recognition and environmental problem recognition.

Chad Renaldo notes that consumers who engage in frequent activities involving convenience products may not hold strong environmental beliefs. However, consumers that do hold environmental beliefs are willing to pay higher prices and be more brand loyal to companies that support those beliefs. These green consumers are also more likely to champion the cause of the company within their community.

Nicholas Shipley examines the case of rural Cambodians and suggests that in spite of the concerted efforts of the community to provide clean water, this is still an outstanding issue. Failure of clean water programs has significant negative health outcomes, and Cambodia has one of the highest infant and under-five mortality rates in the region.

Mark Kay examines the importance of the first-mover actions for niche marketers that have been sustainably-focused. He identifies that as environmental problems arise new sustainability practices are developed, but that there are some challenges adapting to the changing business landscape dealing with these issues. The paper presents a promotional model for effective green marketing efforts to achieve competitive advantages.

Christopher Hodkinson discusses the issue of green electricity distribution. While electricity is a widely used household energy source, there is increasing concern about its contribution to household carbon footprints. Consumers appear to be at a loss as to how to reduce their electricity usage and costs, while maintaining their lifestyle. The lack of a proper feedback system contributes to a lack of consumer awareness and increased confusion. The paper identifies social and general marketing strategies that may provide household consumers with the opportunity to review and modify their consumption behaviour.

Rodica Milena Zaharia and Alin Stancu discuss building marketing communication to influence stakeholders. They highlight that the stakeholder theory suggests companies should target all their stakeholders, not only the shareholders. They argue that companies have a social responsibility that goes beyond creation of profitability, growth and added value for shareholders. This means that companies have an obligation to include all parties affected by their decision making, both directly and indirectly.

Sumesh Nair's contribution discusses the lack of a comprehensive framework for the practice of environmental actions. The paper offers a framework of sustainable marketing that will aid practitioners and academics in better understanding and developing the green marketing concept. The framework uses a systems thinking approach taking a holistic green marketing perspective. It concludes that sustainable organisational actions need to precede sustainable marketing and green practices. Therefore, the focus should be to develop sustainable organisations where marketing takes a central role in spearheading green practices within the organisation.

Louise Canning and Isabelle Szmigin discuss the interface between consumption behaviour and supply chains. They recommend that a move towards more mindful consumption can lead to reduced use of resources and less environmentally damaging behaviour. However, they propose that due to the nature of demand for some types of consumption, reducing surplus and reversing supply is less applicable, as reuse and recycling options are limited. They take an innovative approach by looking at the funeral industry and present a case study that examines the convergence of the consumer decision with key environmental issues associated with disposal of the deceased.

Finally, in *Consumer decision-making: A case for green labelling*, S Menuka Jayaratne, Gillian Sullivan Mort and Clare D'Souza explore the role of labelling products in a sustainable manner and suggest sustainable labelling as a key component for linking consumer and sustainable development. The case emphasises the critical role labelling can play, and provides directions for implementing labels as a part of sustainable marketing mix strategies.

We hope that this collection of well-informed contributions enhances the conversation on environmental issues and the role of marketing, not only participating in, but in driving society toward environmental and socially sustainable management.

References

Andersen, M.L. (2011), "Corporate social and financial performance: the role of size, industry, risk, R&D and advertising expenses as control variables," *Business and Society Review*, 116 (2), 237-256.

Carroll, A.B. (1979), "A three-dimensional conceptual model of corporate performance," *The Academy of Management Review,* 4 (4), 497-505.

Carroll, A.B. (1991), "The Pyramid of corporate social responsibility: toward the moral management of organisational stakeholders, "Business *Horizon,* 34 (4), 39-48.

Friedman, M. (1970), The social responsibility of business is to increase its profits, *The New York Times Magazine.* 15 September, 32-33, 122-126.

Griffin, J.J and Mahon, J.F. (1997), "The corporate social performance and corporate financial performance debate," *Business and Society*, 36 (1), 5-32.

Hunt, S.D. (2011), "Sustainability marketing, equity, and economic growth: a resource-advantage, economic freedom approach, *Academy of Marketing Science*, 39 (1), 7-20.

Porter, M.E. and Linde, C.V. (1995), "Toward a new conception of the environment-competitiveness relationship," *The Journal of Economic Perspective*, 9 (4), 97-118.

Svensson, G. and Wagner, B. (2011), "A process directed towards sustainable business operations and a model for improving the GWP-footprint (CO2e) on earth." *Management of Environmental Quality: An International Journal*, 22 (4), 451-462).

Chapter 1

Sustainability consumption and consumers

Sustainable consumption of green brands and segmentation of green consumers

CLARE D'SOUZA

ABSTRACT

Effective green brand management requires a thorough understanding of the brand meaning and proper positioning of the brand. Clarity in segmentation can help managers devise marketing programs to meet specific consumer needs. Research conducted by practitioners identified four green segments, 'LOHAS', 'naturalites', 'drifters', and 'conventionals'. Since this prime target market upholds green and lifestyle values, the aim of this research is to examine these segments and propose how to increase brand resonance in terms of environmental values using a multidimensional model. Thus, to serve the four market segments identified by practitioners, the article revisits green brand anomalies and proposes a branding framework that includes environmental benefits associated with green brands. The article begins with a brief description of behavioural segmentation of green consumers, noting that the scope is not exhaustive but focusing on the key literature and issues that are prominent within the context of green brands. This is followed by an attempt to reconcile the gap within an all-encompassing framework of branding for green consumers. In undertaking this, we suggest an all-inclusive dimension to capture and include environmental attributes and benefits within the meta-theoretical framework of branding that will suit the four different green consumer segments.

Introduction

Sustainability and environmental issues are recognised as sources of competitive advantage in businesses, and this has resulted in an influx of environmental green products, yet relatively only a few consumers turn their preferences towards green products (Chan 2001; D'Souza & Taghian 2008. Human behaviour can either maintain the environment or contribute to its deterioration (Kinnear, Taylor & Ahmed 1974), and while many consumers are factoring companies' environmental actions into their purchasing decisions (Lash & Wellington 2007), it has not resulted in significant behavioural change when it comes to the purchase of 'green products' (D'Souza *et al.* 2006; Roberts 1996; Schlossberg 1991). Consumers have mixed opinions and rarely is there any consistency in the purchase of green products (Kilbourne & Pickett 2008). Previous studies (Hartmann & Ibanez 2006; Kim & Choi 2005) identify gaps between concern for the environment and actual behaviour. Similarly, research shows that though consumers are increasingly concerned about the impact of environmental degradation, the gap between their attitudes and their pro-environmental purchasing behaviour is large and is not transforming into sales that would benefit the environment (Kilbourne & Pickett 2008). Thus there are two concerns that arise in the case of green products: the first is identifying green segmentation behaviour and the second is how to position green products as green brands for these segments.

Green products can be challenged from many vantage points and they have arguably generated profound controversies. Consumers want to see tangible benefits when purchasing green products, and they base their purchase decisions not only on the environmental characteristics of the product but also on a combination of the more conventional considerations of price, quality and convenience of the brand. Higher priced green products are seen as problematic, with many consumers not willing to sacrifice quality or pay a premium price despite having pro-environmental attitudes (D'Souza *et al.* 2006; Peattie 2001; Polonsky & Rosenberg III 2001; Schaefer & Crane 2005). When consuming green products, consumers do not experience immediate individual benefits (Hartmann & Ibanez 2006). Green products have dual benefits, functional and environmental, this is elaborated I the following paragraphs (D'Souza *et al.* 2006).

While green ideologies and their corresponding sustainable effects still have an impact on certain segments of the market, businesses will continue to modify or reposition their products to respond to the wellbeing of society. Businesses, in their quest for attempting to be in line with people, planet and profit (often known as the triple-p bottom line), have often poorly positioned green products, this may have resulted in diminishing sales returns or failing to understand the different profiles of a green consumer. . This concern is so crucial that it can result in important impositions on the sales of green products, such as which segments to target, and in the worst case scenario, the need to create new customers and new markets requiring clarity in the segmentation process (Doyle & Saunders 1985).

Prior research conducted in Australia, the US and the UK (Barr, Gilg & Shaw 2006; Roberts 1996; Roper Organization 1990; Said 1997) provided significant 'acid tests' or green segmentation, identifying various types of green segments. These acid tests identified that there might be a range of consumers with different environmental needs that are emerging across the continents. Using the practitioners' approach to segmentation, this research thus revises the model of D'Souza (2004) and revisits the anomalies of green branding.

Research conducted by practitioners identified four green segments, 'LOHAS', 'naturalites', 'drifters', and 'conventionals'. Since this prime target market upholds green and lifestyle values, the aim of this research is to examine these segments and propose how to increase brand resonance in terms of environmental values using a multidimensional model. Thus, to serve the four market segments identified by practitioners, the article revisits green brand anomalies and proposes a branding framework that includes environmental benefits associated with green brands. A two-dimensional segmentation model is presented to identify how green brands can create strong resonance for green consumer segments. There are two influences worthy of the attention that arises in terms for practitioners to understand green products: one is the evaluation of green segmentation and the other is the benefits the product/ brand provides consumers f. This will be discussed in the following paragraphs.

Segmentation

There are different ways consumers can be classified and segmented. Discussed here are some of the antecedents that contribute to green segmentation. How practitioners respond to diverse perspectives about a target market will depend on how they identify the segments, the characteristics of these segments and, in particular, the perceived role consumers are to assume in the decision-making process. Whether or not consumer segmentation is required for businesses would depend on the carrying capacity of the market being large enough to be serviced and profitable; and for the brands to be differentiated. The transmissive view for the definition of 'market' is best 'described in terms of a customer need in a way which covers the aggregation of all the alternative products or services customers regard as being capable of satisfying that need' (McDonald & Dunbar 1998, p. 3). While it is noted that a market expresses a customer need that would include all the alternative products or services that consumers consider capable of satisfying that need, a 'segment' identifies specific products, combined with other elements of the marketing mix (McDonald & Dunbar 1998). Researchers have coined segmentation as a creative and iterative process that closely satisfies customer needs. The success of segmentation is not about just identifying new opportunities but rather creating some brand value for the consumer.

There are numerous suggestions proposed on the theoretical constructs that comprise segmentation for green consumers. While socio-demographics (Schlegelmilch Diamantopoulos & Bohlen 1994) are used to segment green consumers, it is more likely that characteristics such as personality measures, which examine locus of control and alienation (Kinnear, Taylor & Ahmed 1974); and, socio-psychological constructs, which have focused on altruism, values, values-attitudes behaviour, and attitude-intentions behaviour, are likely to separate consumers on their pro-environmental behaviour (Dempsey 1999; Kim & Choi 2005). Considering socio-demographics alone for segmentation can amount to be poor predictions of environmental behaviour and provide a limited understanding of green brand decisions (Kinnear and Kenneth 1986).

Studies have preferred personality variables as predictors, over demographic or socioeconomic variables (Webster 1986). Consumers can be segmented on personality variables such as dogmatism, anxiety and self-esteem, and this segmentation has shown positive results (Kinnear, Taylor & Ahmed, 1974). But the more preferable personality variables, linked to pro-environmental behaviour, are 'alienation' and 'locus of control'. Consumers with an internal locus of control are likely to show positive attitudes towards green behaviour (Schwepker & Cornwell 1991). Feelings of helplessness may restrain consumers from seeing how green behaviour can help solve environmental problems. Thus consumers with an internal locus of control are likely to exhibit positive attitudes towards green behaviour (Soonthonsmai 2001).

Socio-psychological factors are internal characteristics of consumers that may cause them to have different responses to the same issues (Kim 2002), thus characterising motivations of consumers and their green behaviour. Several studies (Dunlap & Van Liere 1986; Oskamp et al. 1991) have also identified the links between environmentalism and social-psychological factors involving values, attitudes, beliefs and behavioural intentions.

The theory of altruism and the value-attitude relationship have shown that consumers who have a sense of altruism and a positive value-attitude relationship towards the environment are likely to display pro-environmental behaviour. For instance, Schwartz's (1977) theory of altruism assumes people have a general orientation toward the welfare of others (e.g. altruistic value orientation), 'they value outcomes that benefit others and can be motivated to act to prevent harm to others' (Stern, Dietz & Kalof 1993, p. 324). In addition, social altruism, biospheric altruism and egotism influence willingness to take action (Stern, Dietz & Kalof 1993). Therefore, consumers who exhibit this altruistic value orientation are likely to engage in pro-environmental behaviours. A number of studies support Schwartz's (1977) theory of altruism, in which altruistic behaviour is seen as a result of the activation of (personal) norms; can be used to predict environmental behaviour (Guagnano, Dietz & Stern 1994; Kim 2002; Stern, Dietz & Black 1986). Schwartz's norm activation theory explains that altruistic behaviour is more likely to occur when consumers develop a sense of moral obligation to operate in ways that benefit rather than harm others, and when they recognise the harmful consequences of their actions for others and undertake personally to assign responsibility for these consequences (Kim 2002).

Values, on the other hand, serve as basic standards that provide direction for human attitudes and behaviour (Grunert-Beckman & Thogersen 1997). Values are also embedded in childhood and individuals have a tendency to carry-on similar values towards adulthood. Values provide the foundation for developing individual attitudes that lead to specific decision-making behaviour based on the values that consumers uphold (Homer & Kahle 1988).

Stern and Dietz (1994) have identified that those consumers with higher environmental values have greater regard for the environment; for example, environmental attitudes can flow from a value orientation that reflects concern for the welfare of others. The motivation for environmental behaviour is consequent of egotistic, social-altruistic and bio-centric value orientations (Stern, Dietz & Kalof 1993). Conservation behaviour can be seen in eco-centric and anthropocentric value orientation (Thompson & Barton 1994) and few researchers have used psychographic variables to explain ecological behaviour.

Perceived Behavioural Control (PCB) echoes beliefs regarding access to resources, time and the situation required to perform green behaviours (Ajzen 1991; Chiou 1998). It depends how much an individual will expend in terms of resources such as money and cost and their self confidence in their ability to conduct the behaviour (Ajzen 1991; Chiou 1998). While PCB can be used to segment green consumers, it is considered a critical factor as it has both a direct effect on behaviour and an indirect effect on behaviour through intentions (Kalafatis *et al.* 1999). PCB predicts both behaviour and intention. It provides a reflection on consumer's beliefs and their likely behavioural action (Ajzen & Madden 1986).

Perceived Consumer Effectiveness (PCE), used by many researchers, refers to the extent to which individuals believe that their actions will make a difference to solving an environmental problem (Ellen, Weiner & Cobb-Walgren 1991). Consumers will act when they believe their behaviour will make a difference if it would result in a positive outcome for the environment (Kim & Choi 2005). Arguably, if PCE is believed to motivate a wide variety of behaviours, then this role may be over or understated (Kim 2002).

The above characteristics can form the basis of green segmentation, ranging from intense green consumers to weak green consumers. This is important for marketers as products are often designed to serve a particular segment. Given below is a profile of green consumers and how they can be segmented ranging from intense green generally possessing all the characteristics listed above such as perceived consumer effectiveness, personality traits, altruism, attitudes and values that support pro-environmental behaviour, to a weaker segment not fulfilling all the above characteristics.

Green profiles

For segmentation to be functional more than one level of segmentation criteria is required to identify the customer types and to categorise these consumer needs. Taking a somewhat pragmatic view based on how practitioners have shaped green segments, the research develops an emergent heuristic model that can be used closely to satisfy those customer needs.

While academics have provided useful studies within this important segmentation fabric (see Barr, Gilg & Shaw 2006; Roberts 1996; Roper Organization 1990; Said

1997), recent research by practitioners have provided a similar but smaller topography of the profile of green segments. There has been considerable work conducted by the NMI (Natural Marketing Institute) on their consumer segmentation methodology over the last several years (Cooney 2010; French & Rogers 2009). They have identified five segments 'LOHAS', 'naturalites', 'drifters', 'conventionals' and the 'unconcerned'. LOHAS (Lifestyles of Health and Sustainability) has emerged as a distinct consumer group with unique characteristics that distinguishes members from other consumer groups. They suggest that though the LOHAS consumer is the leading and foremost target for environmentally conscious, socially responsible, and healthy products, they have strong green behavioural characteristics as described above. The naturalites can also be considered within the top tier segment. Drifters and conventionals are each attracted to diverse constituents of the broader LOHAS marketplace. In this research we do not consider the unconcerned group in the matrix.

The four segments embrace values that are innate to them giving different levels of priority to decisions, opinions and beliefs based on sustainable values. The values of consumers tend to stem from their culture and the way they were brought up. While values may also be influenced by peers, the media or role models, understanding these consumers' sustainable values, characteristics, ideals and purchase criteria, allows marketers to broaden their strategic initiatives and logic on how to position their brand value. Since the prime target market upholds values on sustainability, the present research examines these segments and proposes how to increase brand resonance in terms of sustainable green brand values using a multidimensional model.

In Figure 1.1 following, the vertical axis depicts green brand sensitivity in consumers – from sensitive to non-sensitive. The horizontal axis represents the degree to which the consumer segments are likely to respond to environmental value. The four quadrants represent the four segments classified by practitioners' research as stated above using US-based consumer groups.

The LOHAS segment is committed to supporting health, environmental issues and social justice and is a growing segment in North America, Western Europe, Japan and Australia. LOHAS seminal work began in the mid-1990s in the US by sociologist Paul Ray, who undertook extensive research. He claimed that this segment should be called the 'cultural creatives', which described as innovators and leaders of cultural change. He found that LOHAS consumers don't fit neatly into traditional mainstream stereotypes. They have a sense of altruism and are strong in terms of the pro-environmental value-attitude relationship. They have a high level of perceived consumer effectiveness. Their belief is in values, a world view and how it reflects on lifestyle choice (Mobium Group 2007).

Figure 1.1 Two dimensional model for green branding

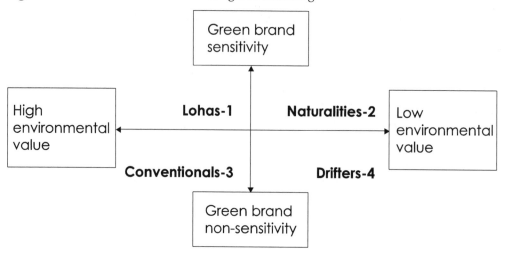

The LOHAS segment represents a huge market and it is reported that 27 per cent (around 55 million people) of the US population fall into this category (Marlow 2008). They exist in many countries; a report presented by the Mobium Group (2007) suggests that about 4 million Australians (26 per cent of adult population) fall in this category. LOHAS come from all walks of society and have unique values. Interestingly, their world view is not attached to income, geography and gender but leans largely towards lifestyle. As stated above in terms of green behaviour, there is little research on lifestyles and psychographics. The Mobium group has identified that these consumers have intentions to integrate healthier more sustainable options into all aspects of their lives. They make decisions in generally six key areas, namely:

- food and nutrition – e.g. organic and natural food, vitamin supplements

- mind and body – e.g. yoga, meditation, personal development

- home life – e.g. natural cleaning products, efficient appliances, recycled paper

- buildings and energy – e.g. water tanks, solar hot water, green energy

- transport and leisure – e.g. low impact commuting, eco-tourism

- work and money – e.g. socially responsible investing, green loans.

The Mobium group identified that in 2006 the US adult population comprised about 16 per cent (35 million) LOHAS consumers. These groups are leaders in their attitudes and values towards the environment. They are passionate about the environment and are early adopters, less price sensitive and more brand loyal. Hence this segment is placed in quadrant 1 of the model, whereby they place high value on the environment and would express greater green brand sensitivity.

The naturalities segment is by far the biggest, containing one out of every four US adults. Individuals in this segment are identified as being mainly health conscious and users of natural products. They are less committed to the notions of 'holistic sustainability' but are likely to pay a little more for eco-friendly products and services, especially if found to be healthier. They would place low value on the environment but express high sensitivity to green brands if they are natural and healthy. This segment is more likely to be placed in quadrant 2.

Conventionals make up 23 per cent of the US population and are often treated as part of the LOHAS market. They are heavy on recycling, energy conservation and waste reduction and can be termed as more behaviourally engaged. They are price sensitive and may not pay more for green brands. This segment is likely to fall in quadrant 3, their reluctance to indulge in green brands is due to their price sensitive nature.

Similar to the conventionals, drifters also comprise 23 per cent of US adults, but are mostly a younger segment. Although the group consisting of the drifter's segments are pro-environmental in their views and attitudes towards the environment, this group can consider other things more important than the environment when making decisions. They speculate about green claims and are driven by trends and fashion (Cooney 2010). They are most likely to fall in quadrant 4. The group profiled as the unconcerned segment are not against the environment but they are too engaged in other activities and yet will not act towards protecting the environment.

Segmenting and positioning green brands

The above paragraph gave an outline of the four segments that would be likely to purchase green brands. The following paragraph explains how green brands can be positioned to meet the green segment needs. Effective green brand management requires a thorough understanding of the brand meaning and proper positioning of the brand. Thus to serve the four consumer segments of the market identified above, a more comprehensive and consistent understanding of a green brand is required. This can be achieved by incorporating the branding framework to include the environmental benefits associated with green brands. The following begins with a brief description of the branding paradigms, noting that the scope is not exhaustive but focuses on the key literature. This is followed by an attempt to reconcile the gap within an all-encompassing segmentation framework. In undertaking to do so, an all-inclusive dimension to capture and include environmental attributes and benefits within the meta-theoretical framework of branding is suggested.

Consumers that are green brand sensitive appear more opportunistic in terms of fulfilling the sustainable direction, yet as suggested by the literature, green brand consumption has been slow, unethical and remains disputed across several theoretical positions. While historically green brands have shown to have problems, the slow growth could also partially contribute to lack of understanding appropriate segmentation strategies. Studies conducted on green branding effects on consumer attitudes (Hartmann, Ibanez & Sainz 2005) and positioning are seen as essential factors in the success of green strategies (Coddington 1993; Meffert & Kirchgeorg 1993). Market surveys documented and reported consumers' interest in genuine green products and their willingness to accept and pay somewhat higher prices for them (Reitman 1992). In the past, channels of distribution members reported increasing concerns by consumers about the welfare of the environment and indicated that the level of interest in the environment may influence consumer purchase behaviour (Bennett 1992), yet, historically, green brands have failed to inspire consumers or convince them of their environmental significance (Murphy 1993; Reitman 1992).

More recent surveys conducted in the US that focused on energy and the environment has shown that there is clearly a green gap between consumer expectations and green products offered in the market. The survey results suggested that there was virtually no 'green' recognition by consumers despite substantial investment made by some firms to position their products as green products. These surveys have indicated that there is still confusion over the term 'green' (Hall 2007). They also recommend that companies should work harder on their marketing communication (Cogar 2008).

Green branding strategy

In comparison to mainstream brands, conceptual analysis on green products has generally been poorly assessed given the importance of a well-defined brand identity as a prerequisite for offering brand value (Aaker & Joachimsthaler 2000; de Chernatony & Dall'Olmo Riley 1998). Should a green product be considered as a green brand then a brand gives meaning to the product beyond its functional attributes. It communicates a message so the consumer can relate to it (Knowles 2001). Although there is no universally accepted definition of brands (de Chernatony & Dall'Olmo Riley 1997), it is generally accepted that brands are a multidimensional construct incorporating functional, symbolic, legal, and strategic aspects (de Chernatony & McDonald 2003) that help consumers identify products and differentiate products from those of competitors. They can comprise names, symbols or logos (Aaker 1991; Barwise *et al.* 1990; Keller 1993). Besides, brands are viewed with ontological assumptions, making substantive, methodological and theoretical advances, thus the need to position them from a segmentation perspective would be useful. The definition of a green brand should extend to encompass the key environmental attributes of a product; this is discussed below along with two critical areas within the brand framework: brand equity and company image.

Emphasis on environmental value

A combination of the atomic framework (de Chernatony 1993) that conceptualises brands in terms of nine elements is considered below, as it serves to provide some justification required for an effective framework (Lunn 1978) that would be useful to the above segments. In light of de Chernatony and Riley's (1998) framework of the components of the brand, we draw on two elements that receive universal mention. The first is the brand's functional capabilities, such as the tangible and rational aspects as well as the performance of the brand. The second element is the symbolic features such as intangibles, emotional value of the brand personality.

A third element receives some mention and relates to the company, that is, the sign of ownership. This entails its company identity, authority, ethical stance, vision, employee policies and the staff.

This framework in terms of green brands can be challenged by introspective issues that exist within the outline of the dominant environmental or green paradigm. This has been echoed by Reinhardt (1998) who differentiates a green brand by three elements, namely:

- customers pay for environmental quality

- the brand establishes credible information about the environmental attributes of its products

- the brand should be capable of defending itself against imitation by competitors.

When individuals perceive products, their perceptions are based largely on intuition and subconscious ways or they might make generalisations based on their own interpretive prowess based and understanding or experience with the product. De Chernatony (1993) provides an illustration of branding when referring to the functioning and symbolism of a brand.

Critical to the evaluation of a brand are its core benefits. Addressed below are some of the anomalies that green brands face in terms of core benefits. A brand's core benefits can be distinguished and placed into three categories based on the motivations with which they can be associated, that is, functional, experiential and symbolic (Keller 2001; Park, Jaworski & MacInnis 1986). Orth and De Marchi, (2007) suggest that the functional benefits are largely associated with inherent advantages of the consumption status of the product and correspond to attributes of the product. While experiential benefits also relate to attributes of the product, these benefits often relate to what it feels like when using the product. This could be seen as satisfying needs that are sensory pleasurable and cognitively stimulating. Orth and De Marchi (2007) suggest that the symbolic benefits are the more extrinsic ones, corresponding to non-product related attributes, and are associated with needs for social approval, personal expression and outer-directed self-esteem.

However, green products face critical issues in terms of their functionality; they are criticised for a disappointing performance, unwarranted green claims and poor texture and appearance (Johnson *et al.* 1997; Polonsky *et al.* 1998). In terms of experiential benefits, the results also pointed to the trade-off on issues such as products for convenience; for example, disposable cups, diapers etc. appeared easier for consumers to accept and use (Reitman 1992).

Some other reasons that green products have been poorly rated are due to the quality and incompetence of environmental labelling claims (D'Souza *et al.* 2006). It also clear that the key problems green products face are in brand awareness, price, quality, environmental effectiveness, convenience and availability (D'Souza *et al.* 2006; Wasik 1992).

In terms of symbolic benefits, some studies have considered the symbolic or emotional aspects of green products indicating that, if green products can induce positive emotions in certain green groups by providing information that the product is green, just having knowledge that a product is green may satisfy customers (Hartmann & Ibañez 2006). Rooks' (2010) survey compared environmental products in terms of emotion vs. science. Operative words like carbon, CO_2, eco-friendly and carbon offset were bisected into either 'emotive' (change, progress, clean) or 'scientific' (carbon, planet, hybrid) categories. It was identified that in most cases green was used emotionally or aspirationally and not scientifically. Notably, there are some emotional benefits that can be derived from a brand, such as intrinsic values felt by consumers when using green products, often driven by the 'warm glow of giving' (Boyce *et al.* 1992; Menges 2003). Similarly, Ritov and Kahnemann (1997) opined that those consumers had a feeling of wellbeing (warm glow) associated with acting in an altruistic way. This warm glow benefit experienced by consumers rated low on measures of environmental consciousness was also reported by Hartmann and Ibáñez (2005).

The consideration of environmental values can be emphasised strongly in the functional and symbolic dimension of de Chernatony (1993) framework. This will attract particularly the two segments, LOHAS and conventionalists. The environmental considerations such as value, elements, attributes or sentiments could lead to anything from recycling claims, green product lifecycle, renewable resources, green/carbon labelling or a green image, which is intended as central rather than peripheral for this green target market. The anomalies are revealed in the failure of many green brands, and this reaction would suggest fundamental misgivings about the appropriateness of making environmentalism the focal point. This should be clearly distinct in producing and marketing a green brand, and while there is a constellation of ideas as to what a green brand might entail, the lack of consensus about the positioning prevents green branding prescriptions. Thus, to attract the two segments (LOHAS and conventionalists) the functional, symbolic, ownership framework for brands, environmental attributes and benefits are detrimental for green brands.

Conventionalists and drifters are likely to embrace the symbolic or emotional nature of the brand while naturalites and LOHAS would also consider auto-expressive benefits through the socially visible consumption of green brands, making the selection of a green brand their way of illustrating environmental consciousness to society. To attract LOHAS and naturalites, green brands would have to associate with their consumers emotionally with logical facts and rational appeals but simultaneously the need to justify the environmental attributes and benefits would appeal to this group very strongly.

Brand equity

Brand Equity is '. . . a set of brand assets and liabilities linked to a brand, its name and symbol, that add or subtract from the value provided by a product to a firm and/or that firm's customers' (Aaker 1991, p. 15). While Farquhar (1989) underscores brand equity as the value that the brand name attaches to a product, others have stated that brand equity depends on the willingness of consumers to pay a premium price for a brand depending on the perceived value attributed to the brand name (Bello & Holbrook 1995).

Consumer willingness to pay a premium for green brands has affected by the product itself – consumers are willing to pay more but will not compromise on quality (D'Souza *et al.* 2006). Keller's (2001) proposition of the ten top traits for the world's strongest brands states that a pricing strategy is essential and that, in order to derive green values, it should be in keeping with the perceptions and strength of attitude of consumers. It has, however, been suggested that for green brands pricing involves a three-way balance to create a green brand value strategy. The balance is between price, eco-performance and primary performance, and the strategy preferably attracts conventionalists – but prices may have to be kept low as this segment is highly price sensitive.

On the other hand, given that green products demonstrate quality at par with traditional brands – could a premium price be demanded for LOHAS and naturalists? This would depend on the brand equity value that has built up over a period of time. To demand a higher price for green brands that could be attractive to this consumer group, greater emphasis would be required for creating a green image, generating consumer awareness on the environmental components of a brand, establishing green perception, through proper positioning strategies and building brand loyalty.

Corporate responsibility

A corporation's responsibility towards the environment lies beyond their legal and economic obligations (Burton & Goldsby 2007; McGuire 1963). The other level of branding is based on corporate image. Should green brands only rely on corporate image?

Recent surveys have indicated that 80 per cent of consumers support purchasing green products from companies with a green image (Garcia 2007). The LOHAS category of consumers falls largely into this area. Brand functions are also fundamental to classification and can be separated into different categories depending on the function they serve (Stern 2006), for instance, as an entity or a process. This suggests that if referred to as an entity, it may be regarded as an organisational brand. Process refers to processes incorporated by the firm to make the product more meaningful (Calder & Reagan 2001).

It is evident that the nature of corporate social behaviour could contribute to overall corporate brand image, signifying corporate image as a multidimensional concept (Barich & Kotler 1991; Barich & Srinavasan 1993; Marckwill & Fill 1997; Siegel &

Vitaliano 2007). Companies with established brand names, such as Coca Cola, may still want to be perceived as an enjoyable and fun drink, but with respect to company image they would want to be thought of as socially responsible and in keeping with sustainable principles. Clearly, although this suggests that being socially responsible provides the foundation for cultivating an investment in green brands, it is likely that targeting a specific segment like the LOHAS consumer would require a company like Coca Cola to emerge as a green brand – not just ride on the company's green image. It could be argued that the company *and* the product would need to be identified as green. LOHAS consumers evaluate brands by a different bottom line; they consider not only corporate practices, but also whether brands can align with consumer values – as these values form the leading and foremost target for environmentally conscious and socially responsible brands.

Researchers who want to explore the nuances of green brands could use this integrative framework that establishes the components required for green branding by making assumptions across various epistemologies. To increase green brand value, further investigations are necessary to ascertain how brand perceptions have been formed. Further, future research should investigate brand managers' perceptions towards green products and the accuracy of green claims across product categories. This would assist in developing consumer trust towards green brands and building brand loyalty.

Conclusions

Whilst this paper identifies that consumers can be segmented based on their pro-environmental attitudes, green brands need to be appropriately positioned to target these segments. It has shown that a larger constituent of consumers form decisions, opinions and beliefs based on environmental values; thus, while branding postulates functional and symbolic attributes as key determinants for the universal acceptance of brands, it is important to include environmental considerations and benefits to support environmental effects for establishing green brands. Given that companies are embracing greener measures and there is a large segment of consumers demanding green brands, an understanding of segmentation profiles of green consumers will assist managers in positioning their brands.

Despite the unsatisfactory status and negative publicity associated with green brands, and in spite of public expressions of disappointment and scepticism, there still exists opportunities for green brands to be positioned in this niche consumer segment. Highlighting environmental value for green brands will help support companies in developing their philosophies in terms of green brands and the complexities that exist within their tangible and intangible aspects.

References

Aaker, D.A. (1991). *Managing Brand Equity.* New York, 1991, The Free Press.

Aaker, D.A. & Joachimsthaler, E. (2000). *Brand Leadership*, New York, 2000, The Free Press.

Ajzen, I. (1991). The theory of planned behavior, Organizational Behavior and Human Decision Processes, 20, 179-211

Ajzen, I., & Madden, T. J. (1986). Prediction of goal-directed behavior: Attitudes, intentions, and perceived behavioral control. *Journal of Experimental Social Psychology*, 22, 45374.

Barich, H. & Kotler, P. (1991). A Framework for Marketing Image Management, *Sloan Management Review*, Winter 32(2), 94–109.

Barich, H. & Srinivasan, V. (1993). Prioritizing Marketing Image Goals Under Resource Constraints, *Sloan Management Review*, Summer 34(4), 69–76.

Barwise, P., Higson, C., Likierman, A., & Marsh, P. (1990). Brands as 'Separable Assets' *Business Strategy Review*, Summer, 43-59.

Barr, Stewart, A., Gilg, Andrew and Shaw, Gareth (2006): *Promoting Sustainable Lifestyles: a social marketing approach*, Final Summary Report to Defra, London

Bello, D.C., & Holbrook, M.B. (1995). Does and Absence of Brand Equity Generalize Across Product Classes, *Journal of Business Research*, 34 (October), 125-131.

Bennett, S. (1992). Green commitment: Fading Out? *Progressive Grocer*, New York: 17 (12-3), 4-7

Blackwell, R., D'Souza, C., Taghian, M., Minard, P and Engel, J. (2006) *Consumer Behaviour: An Asia Pacific Approach*, Thompson Learning Australia, South Melbourne – 1st edition.

Boyce, R.R., Brown, T.C., McClelland, G.H., Peterson, G.L. & Schulze, W.D. (1992). An experimental examination of intrinsic values as a source of the WTA-WTP disparity, *American Economic Review*, Vol. 82, 1366-73

Burton, B. K. and Goldsby, M. (2007). Corporate social responsibility orientation, goals, and behaviour: a study of small business owners, *Business & Society*, 20 (10), 1-17.

Calder, Bobby J. & Reagan, S., *Brand Design*, In Kellogg on Marketing. Ed. Dawn Iacobucci. New York, 2001, John Wiley, 58-73.

Chan, R.Y.K. (2001). Determinants of Chinese consumers; green purchase behaviour, *Psychology and Marketing*, New York, 18, 4, 389

Chiou, J.S. (1998). The effects of Attitude, Subjective Norm and Perceived Behavioural Control on Consumers' Purchase Intentions: The moderating Effects of Product Knowledge and Attention to Social Comparison Information, *Proc. Natl. Sci. Counc. ROC (C)*, 9, 2, 298-308

Coddington, W. *Environmental Marketing*, McGraw-Hill, New York 1993, NY.

Cogar, D. (2008). EcoPinion: Branding green but seeing red – consumer perceptions of green brands, *Survey Report*, Issue 3 (March), EcoAlign

Cooney, S. (2010). State of the LOHAS Consumer Segment: Answers from the Natural Marketing Institute, http://www.triplepundit.com/2010/06/whats-the-state-of-the-lohas-consumer-segment-answers-from-the-natural-marketing-institute/, accessed Jan 2010

de Chernatony, L. (1993). New directions - understanding the dynamics of brands as molecules, *Admap*, February, 21-3

de Chernatony, L. & DaH'Olmo Riley, F. (1998). Modelling the components of the brand, *European Journal of Marketing*, 32 (11/12), 1074-90 de Chernatony, L. & Dall'Olmo Riley, F (1997). Brand consultants perspectives on the concept of the brand, *Marketing and Research Today*, 25 (1), 45-52

de Chernatony, L., & Riley, Francesca, (1998). Modeling the components of the brand, *European Journal of Marketing*, 32(11/12), 1074-1090

de Chernatony, L., & McDonald, M. (2003). Creating Powerful Brands in Consumer, Service and Industrial Markets, 3rd ed., Elsevier Butterworth Heinemann, Oxford

Dempsey, M. (1999). Values, Attitudes and Purchase Intentions: Indian Students as Consumers of Green Laundry Detergents", A thesis presented to the Faculty of graduate studies of the University of Guelph. ABI Inform

Doyle, P. & Saunders, J. (1985). Market segmentation and repositioning in specialized industrial markets, Journal of Marketing 49 (2), pp. 24–32

D'Souza, C (2004) Ecolabel programmes: a stakeholder (consumer) perspective, *Corporate Communications: An International Journal*, 9 (3), pp. 179-188

D'Souza, C., Taghian, M., Lamb, P. & Peretiatko, R. (2006). Green products and corporate strategy: an empirical investigation, *Society and Business Review*, 1(2), 144-157

D'Souza, C., and Taghian, M. (2008), "Key requirements for empowering green brands", Second Annual International Conference on Business & Sustainability: Designing Sustainability, proceedings in conference, held at Portland, Oregon, United States from October 14-17, 2008

D'Souza C, Taghian M, Khosla R, 2007, Examination of environmental beliefs and its impact on the influence of price, quality and demographic characteristics with respect to green purchase intention. *Journal of Targeting Measurement and Analysis For Marketing*, Vol.2, 68-78

Dunlap, R.E. (1991). Public Opinion in the 1980s Clear Consensus, Ambiguous Commitment, *Environment,* 33, 8 (October), 10-37.

Dunlap, R.E. and Van Liere, K.D. (1986), "Commitment to the dominant social paradigm and concern for environmental quality", *Social Science Quarterly*, Vol. 65, pp. 1013-28.

Ellen, P. S., Weiner J.L., and Cobb-Walgren, C. (1991). The role of Perceived Consumer Effectiveness in Motivating Environmentally Conscious Behaviours, *Journal of Public Policy and Marketing*, 10 (fall), 102-117.

Farquhar, P.H. (1989). Managing Brand Equity, *Marketing Research*, 1 (September), 24-33.

French, S., and Rogers, G. (2009). Understanding the LOHAS Consumer: The Rise of Ethical Consumerism: A Strategic Market Research Update from the Natural Marketing Institute, http://www.lohas.com/journal/consumertrends.htm, accessed Jan 2010.

Gagnon-Thompson, S. C., and Barton, M., (1994). Ecocentric And Anthropocentric Attitudes Towards The Environment, *Journal of Environmental Psychology*. 14, 149-157.

Garcia, T. (2007). Survey finds people favour green brands, *P R Week* (US ed.), 10(18), 4

Grunert-Beckmann, S.C., and Thogersen, J. (1997). Values and attitude formation, towards emerging attitude objects: from recycling to general waste minimizing behaviour, *Advances in Consumer Research*, 24, 182-189.

Guagnano, G. A., Dietz, T. & Stern, P. C. (1994). Willingness to pay for Public Goods: A test of the contribution model, Psychological Scinece, 5, 411-415

Hall, E. (2007). Want U.K. consumers to label your company 'green'? Just use PR, *Advertising Age*, May 28, 78(22), 20

Hartmann, P. & Apaolaza Ibáñez, V. (2005). Green brand associations and brand attitude: The moderating role of environmental consciousness, Proceedings of the 33rd EMAC Conference, *European Marketing Academy*, Milan.

Hartmann, P., & Ibañez, V. (2006). Green value added, *Marketing Intelligence and Planning,* 24 (7), 673-686

Hartmann, P., Ibañez, A., & Sainz, F. (2005). Green branding effects on attitude: functional versus emotional positioning strategies, *Marketing Intelligence and Planning*, 23(1), 9-29

Homer, P., and Kahle, L.R. (1988). "A structural equation test of the values-attitude-behaviour hierarchy, *Journal of Personality and Social Psychology*, 54 (April), 638-646.

Johnson, D., Ambrose, S., Bassett, T. & Bowen, N. (1997). Meaning of environmental terms, *Journal of Environmental Quality,* 26(3), 581-589

Kalafatis, S.P., Pollard, M., East, R., Tsogas, M.H (1999). Green marketing and Ajzen's theory of planned behaviour: a cross-market examination, *Journal of Environmental Education* 16, 5, 441-460

Keller, K. (2001). The Brand Report Card in Harvard Business Review on Marketing, *Harvard Business School Publishing*, Boston.

Keller, Kevin L. (1993). Conceptualizing, Measuring, Managing Customer-Based Brand Equity, *Journal of Marketing*, 57 (1), 1-21.

Kilbourne, W., and Pickett, G. (2008). How materialism affects environmental beliefs, concern, and environmentally responsible behaviour, *Journal of Business Research*, 61, 885-893

Kim, Y. (2002). The impact of personal value structures on consumer pro environmental attitudes, behaviours and consumerism – A Cross Cultural study, Michigan State University, Michigan State University, 1-171.

Kim, Y., and Choi, S.M. (2005). Antecedents of Green Purchase Behaviour: An Examination of Collectivism, Environmental Concern and PCE, *Advances in Consumer Research*, 32, 592-597

Kinnear, T.C., Taylor, R.J., and Ahmed, A. S. (1974). Ecologically concerned consumers: who are they?, *Journal of Marketing*, 38, 20

Kinnear, T. C., and Kenneth, B. L., ***Principles of Marketing*** (2nd ed.), Scott, Foresman and Company, Glenview, IL, 1986

Knowles, J. (2001) The Role of Brands in Business, in Brands, visions and values, edited by John Godchild and Clive Callow, John Wiley and Sons Ltd. West Sussex, England.

Lash, J., and Wellington, J., Australian Financial Review , http://0-global.factiva.com.alpha2.latrobe.edu.au/ha/default.aspxv.Accessed Online 8th June 2010

Lunn, T. (1978) Consumer modelling, in Worcester, R. & Downham, J. (Eds), *Consumer Market Research* Handbook, Van Nostrand Reinhold Company, New York, NY

Marckwill, N. and Fill, C. (1997) 'Towards a Framework for Managing Corporate Identity', *European Journal of Marketing*, 31(5/6): 396–409.

McDonald, M and Dunbar, I (1998) *Market Segmentation: How to do it, how to profit from it*, 2nd ed., Macmillan Press Ltd; London

Mcguire, J. B (1963), *Business and Society* (McGraw Hill, New York).

Marlow, Leigh (2008) LOHAS Lifestyles of health and sustainability, http://www.thegreendirectory.com.au/green-news-and-events/green-marketing/lohas-lifestyles-of-health-and-sustainability.html accessed Jan 2009

Meffert, H. & Kirchgeorg, M. (1993) Marktorientiertes Umweltmanagement, Schaeffer-Poeschel, Stuttgart, cited in Hartmann, P., Ibanez, A., and Sainz, F. (2005), Green branding effects on attitude: functional versus emotional positioning strategies, *Marketing Intelligence and Planning*, 23(1),.9-29

Menges, R. (2003) 'Supporting renewable energy on liberalized markets: Green electricity between additionally and consumer sovereignty', *Energy Policy*, 31, pp. 583-96

Mobium Group Pty Ltd (2007) *"Living LOHAS: Lifestyles of Health and Sustainability in Australia: Consumer Trends Report*, South Melbourne, www.mobium.com.au, accessed Jan 2010

Murphy, Claire (1993) 'Are dark greens about to fade?' *Marketing Week* (London), 16(3), 16-18

Orth, Ulrich R. and Renate De Marchi (2007) 'Understanding the Relations between Functional, Symbolic, and Experiential Brand Beliefs, Product Experiential Attributes, and Product Schema: Advertising-Trial Interactions Revisited,' Journal of Marketing Theory and Practice, 15 (3):219-233

Oskamp, S., Harrington, M.J., Edwards, T.C., Sherwood, D.L., Okuda, S.M. and Swanson, D.C. (1991), Factors influencing Household recycling behaviour, Environment and Behaviour, Vol 23, no 4 pp 494-519

Park, C. Whan, Jaworski, B. & Maclnnis, D. (1986) 'Strategic Brand Concept-Image Management', Journal of Marketing 50 (4): 135-145

Peattie, K. (2001). Golden goose or wild goose? the hunt for the green consumer. *Business Strategy and the Environment, 10*(4), 187-199.

Polonsky, M., Bailey, J., Baker, H., and Basche, C. (1998) 'Communicating environmental information: are marketing claims on packaging misleading', *Journal of Business Ethics*, 17(3): 281-294

Polonsky, M.J. and P.J. Rosenberger III (2001), "Re-evaluating to green marketing – An integrated approach", *Business Horizons*, Vol. 44, no.5, pp. 21-30.

Reinhardt, F. (1998) Environmental product differentiation: Implications for Corporate Strategy, *California Management Review*, 40(4): 43-74

Reitman, V. (1992) 'Marketing: 'Green' Product Sales seem to be wilting', *Wall Street Journal*, New York 18 May: p. B1

Ritov, I. & Kahnemann, D. (1997) *How people value the environment. Attitudes versus economic values,* in Bazermann, M.H., Messick, D.M., Tenbrunsel, A.E. and Wade-Benzoni, K.A. (Eds), Environment, Ethics, and Behaviour, The New Lexington Press, San Francisco, CA, 33-51

Roberts, J. (1996) Green consumers in the 1990s: profile and implications for advertising, *Journal of Business Research*, Vol. 36 No. 2, pp. 217-31

Rooks, J 2010, What does green language look like today? http://www.lohas.com/journal/green_language.html, accessed Jan 2010

Roper Organization (1990) *The Environment: Public Attitudes and Individual Behavior*. New York: Roper Organization

Said, D. (1997), *Green Australia: Mapping the market*, Prospect Publishing, Sydney Australia

Siegel, D. S. and Vitaliano, D. F. (2007) 'An empirical analysis of the strategic use of corporate social responsibility', *Journal of Economics & Management Strategy* 16(3): 773-792

Schaefer, Anja, and Andrew Crane. 2005. Addressing sustainability and consumption, *Journal of Macromarketing* 25 (1):76-92

Schlegelmilch, B.B., Diamantopoulos, A. and Bohlen, G.M. (1994), "The value of socio-demographic characteristics for predicting environmental consciousness", in Park, C.W. and Smith, D.C., Marketing Theory and Applications: The Proceedings of the 1994 American Marketing Association's Winter Educator's Conference, Chicago, IL, pp. 348-9.

Schlegelmilch, B.B., Diamantopoulos, A., and Bohlen, G.M. (1995). The link between green purchasing decisions and measures of environmental consciousness, *European Journal of Marketing*, 30, 5: 35-55.

Schlossberg, H. (1991). Innovation sees to elude green marketers, *Marketing News*, 25 (April 16): 16-20

Schwartz, S. H. (1977). Normative influence on altruism. In L. Berkowitz (Ed), *Advances in Experimental Social Psychology*, 221-279

Schwepker, C.H., and Cornwell, T.B. (1991). An Examination of Ecologically Concerned Consumers and Their Intention to Purchase Ecologically Packaged Products, *Journal of Public Policy and Marketing*, 10(2) (Fall), 77-101

Soonthonsmai, V. (2001) Predicting Intention and Behaviour to Purchase Environmentally Sound or Green products among Thai consumers: an Application of the Theory of Reasoned Action The Wayne Huizenga Graduate School of Business and Entrepreneurship, Nova Southeastern University. 2001

Stern, B. (2006) 'What does brand mean? Historical analysis method and construct definition', *Academy of Marketing Science* 334 (2): 216-224

Stern, P. C.,&Dietz, T. (1994). The value basis of environmental concern. *Journal of Social Issues*, 50, 65–84.

Stern, P.C., Dietz, T., and Black, J. S. (1986). Support for environmental protection: The role of morale norms, *Population and Environment*, 8, 204-222.

Stern, P.C., Dietz, T., and Kalof, L. (1993). Value orientations, gender and environmental concern, *Environment and Behaviour*, 25(3) 322-348

Thompson, S.C., and Barton, M.A. (1994). Ecocentric and Anthropocentric attitudes toward the environment. *Journal of Environmental Psychology*, 14, 149-157

Webster, F.E. (1986). Determining the characteristics of the socially conscious consumer, *Journal of Consumer Research*, 2, 188

Wasik, J. (1992) 'Green Marketing: Market is confusing, but patience will pay', *Marketing News* (Chicago), 26 (21): 16-18

Understanding European citizens' environmentally orientated consumption reduction

José Manuel Ortega Egea and Nieves García de Frutos

Abstract

Environmental degradation may be linked to the prevailing lifestyles in modern societies that often lead to unsustainable consumption patterns. Faced with the threat of climate change, many authors support the importance of reducing current consumption levels. Specifically, this work focuses on environmentally orientated anti-consumption as a means of fighting climate change. Based on social psychology theory, the authors examine the role of three psychographics (environmental attitudes, motivations, and knowledge) in the consumption reduction behaviour of European citizens. The model is moderately successful in predicting two types of anti-consumption: reducing household water and energy consumption; and anti-shopping actions. Positive and negative environmental attitudes (towards climate change) are differentiated and jointly influenced by knowledge about climate change and ecological motivations; in turn, environmental attitudes directly determine the consumption reduction of Europeans. These findings highlight the importance of both altruistic and egoistic ecological motivations for developing positive attitudes towards the environment. Interestingly, the level of knowledge of respondents about the causes, consequences and ways of fighting climate change contributes to both positive and negative attitudes. Thus, not all types of environmental messages and information can be assumed to be equally effective in fostering consumption reduction behaviour.

Introduction

Increasing levels of environmental degradation and resource depletion lead to extremely serious global-scale consequences (European Commission 2010). Climate change is probably the most challenging environmental issue of our time, owing to its magnitude, complexity and irreversible effects (European Commission 2008; Gardiner 2004). In the European Union (EU), households are responsible for as much as 20 per cent of greenhouse emissions and one third of the energy consumed (Junta de Andalucía 2010). Such data suggest that, despite continued efforts to promote more environmentally-friendly citizen and consumer behaviour, there is still much room for improvement within most EU countries (European Environment Agency 2010). In modern societies, environmental problems have been linked to prevailing unsustainable lifestyles that often lead to higher rates of consumption (Jackson 2005; Varey 2010). In fact, a common belief is that greater consumption equates to increased wellbeing (Jackson 2005). Also, people tend to construct and express their 'self' (e.g. self-image and personality) through the products and brands that they purchase and use (Rucker & Galinsky 2008; Varey 2010).

Excessive consumption leads to the depletion of natural resources (Brown & Kütting 2008) and generates huge quantities of waste (Thøgersen & Grunert-Beckmann 1997). Recycling is a major solution to solid waste problems caused by consumption (Ebreo, Hershey & Vining 1999; Thøgersen & Grunert-Beckmann 1997). Even so, recycling efforts appear to be insufficient, owing to non-recyclable materials and less than desirable recycling rates (Ebreo, Hershey & Vining 1999; European Commission 2008). In addition, recycling is a resource-intensive process that demands significant amounts of energy (Ayres 2004). Another pathway towards sustainability is based on the development of ecologically efficient new products and product substitutions; however, such incremental eco-efficiency improvements have been largely offset by substantial growth in global consumption (Maxwell & Sheate 2006; Peattie & Peattie 2009).

'Mainstream' environmental solutions place great emphasis on sustainable production and consumption practices, for example, achieving sustainability through the application of science and technology (Black & Cherrier 2010). Despite the importance of 'green' production and waste disposal, these measures fall short in preserving natural resources and fighting climate change (Thøgersen & Crompton 2009). Some authors argue that more effective solutions to environmental degradation lie in changing the dominant lifestyles and reducing current consumption levels (Jackson 2005; Peattie & Peattie 2009). Lower consumption levels will reduce pressure on natural resources, but will not necessarily have negative effects on GDP growth, as long as organisations are able to adapt effectively and take advantage of available opportunities (Peattie & Peattie 2009; Varey 2010).

Reducing current consumption rates will clearly contribute to sustainability, given that more resources will remain available for future generations. Yet, there is controversy concerning the best means of achieving the desired consumption reduction results (Burroughs 2010; Varey 2010). Radical shifts in behaviour seem unlikely for most individuals; it is more reasonable to expect gradual improvements resulting from small, step-by-step modifications in peoples' lifestyles (Huneke 2005). The present work focuses on environmentally orientated reduction behaviours (i.e. reducing household water and energy consumption, and anti-shopping actions) that do not excessively alter European citizens' habits and routines.

Specifically, this paper seeks to provide a better understanding of the factors that lead people to reduce their consumption levels for environmental reasons (i.e. fighting climate change). For this purpose, the authors examine the role of three psychographics (environmental attitudes, motivations, and knowledge) in the consumption reduction behaviour of European citizens. Based on expectancy-value models (Ajzen 1991; Fishbein & Ajzen 1975), the research model posits that environmental attitudes are important predictors of consumption reduction behaviour; respondents' ecological motivations and level of knowledge about climate change are, respectively, modelled as internal and external factors jointly influencing environmental attitudes.

Consumption reduction: Literature and hypotheses

Anti-consumption is not as uncommon as it may seem at first sight. Nowadays, various types of 'anti-consumers' exist. Some people reduce their consumption levels in a general way; whereas others selectively avoid only certain products or brands perceived as harmful to the environment (Iyer & Muncy 2009). These issues are receiving increasing attention from business scholars (Ballantine & Creery 2010). In this regard, the recent publication of special issues devoted to 'sustainability' and 'anti-consumption', in business and marketing journals such as *Journal of Business Research* (2009), *Journal of Macromarketing* (2010) or *International Journal of Consumer Studies* (2009), exemplifies the importance of discovering and investigating alternative forms of environmentally sustainable consumption, such as consumption reduction.

Nonetheless, there is still relatively little research on the factors influencing people's anti-consumption. In the developing literature on environmentally orientated consumption reduction (see Barr 2007; Fujii 2006), most studies have focused on specific kinds of household behaviour, such as reducing energy consumption (Abrahamse *et al.* 2009), saving water (Gilg & Barr 2006) or minimising waste generation (Tonglet, Phillips & Bates 2004). There is evidence that common and unique antecedents exist for each type of reduction behaviour (Fujii 2006). Given the wide range of anti-consumption manifestations, research in this field may benefit from the prediction of consumption reduction behaviours at aggregate or more general levels. Such analyses will likely lead to the identification of factors predicting anti-consumption in a wide array of domains.

Theories for environmentally orientated consumption reduction

The analysis of environmentally orientated consumption reduction, aimed at fighting climate change, justifies the value of two main (social psychology) theoretical approaches to ecological behaviour analysis. Pro-environmental behaviour is seen as a mixture of self-interest and concern for others (Bamberg & Möser 2007). Researchers viewing individual ecological behaviour as motivated by the desire to 'do good' for society often select Schwartz's norm-activation model (NAM) (Schwartz 1977) as a theoretical framework. Conversely, researchers who consider self-interest to be the most important factor underlying pro-environmental behaviour tend to rely on Ajzen's theory of planned behaviour (TPB) (Ajzen 1991). Other studies have combined these theories to provide a more complete picture of pro-environmental behaviour (e.g. Abrahamse *et al.* 2009; Bamberg & Schmidt 2003). In consumption reduction research, successful applications of the TPB and NAM frameworks can be found in the works of Taylor and Todd (1995) and Barr (2007), among others.

Consumption reduction behaviour

The differentiation of various types and domains of consumption reduction has proven useful in anti-consumption research. Two behavioural categories emerged from Barr and Gilg's (2006) analysis: home routines vs. purchasing decisions. De Young *et al.* (1993) drew a similar distinction based on location ('at home' vs. 'at a store' consumption reductions), but also differentiated between toxic and non-toxic items (i.e. the type of source reduction behaviour). Consumption reduction decisions in household and shopping domains differ not only in terms of behaviour frequency, with home activities being more habitual than purchasing ones, but also in the moment of decision making or choice (Ebreo, Hershey & Vining 1999) and the individual's ability and options for anti-consumption (De Young *et al.* 1993).

Home-based consumption reduction will depend, for the most part, on the person's commitment to act (De Young *et al.* 1993). Conversely, purchase activities are more complex, require higher effort levels (e.g. time and money) and are frequently constrained by contextual factors beyond individual control (Young *et al.* 2010). Thus, despite the willingness to engage in consumption reduction activities, several barriers may impede behaviour change, for example, diverting consumer attention away from water- and energy-efficient technologies (De Young *et al.* 1993; Young *et al.* 2010). Concerning the decision moment, anti-shopping activities will most likely differ from other environmentally orientated reduction behaviours in that purchase (or non-purchase) decisions are made in advance of the consumption stage. However, 'in-home' consumption reduction often requires decisions to be made during consumption, for example, at the stages of domestic energy or water use (Ebreo, Hershey & Vining 1999). Nonetheless, anti-consumption decisions made in the household may also affect future shopping actions in terms of quantity or frequency of purchases.

The present study aims to explain both the domestic and 'out-of-home' domains of environmentally orientated consumption reduction. The first two items measure respondents' reduction of energy and water consumption at home; the other two items are self-reported measures of anti-shopping actions (i.e. consuming fewer disposable items such as plastic bags and packaging, and avoiding products that come from far-away places). Thus, the dependent construct in the analysis (consumption reduction behaviour) is expected to be either uni- or bi-dimensional in structure.

Attitude influence

Attitude is defined as an individual's positive or negative feelings (evaluative affect) about a psychological object (Fishbein & Ajzen 1975; Kollmuss & Agyeman 2002), be it a physical entity, a person or group of people, an abstract concept or a behaviour (Ajzen & Gilbert 2008). In the environmental literature, attitude has been identified as a major determinant of pro-environmental intention and behaviour (Bamberg & Möser 2007; Kaiser, Wölfing & Fuhrer 1999). Consistent with expectancy-value models (Ajzen 1991; Fishbein & Ajzen 1975), individuals with positive attitudes towards the environment should be more likely to engage in environmentally responsible behaviour (Bamberg & Möser 2007; Bord, O'Connor & Fisher 2000; Kollmuss & Agyeman 2002). In this respect, Ebreo, Hershey and Vining (1999) argued that the 'attitude effect' is shared across most (if not all) pro-environmental actions, regardless of the specific antecedents of each class of behaviour.

Previous meta-analyses have revealed a significant, moderate correlation (approximately 0.4) between attitude and pro-environmental behaviour (Bamberg & Möser 2007; Hines, Hungerford & Tomera 1986). Consumption reduction research has assessed the effects of alternative kinds of attitudes. Attitude toward frugality (Fujii 2006) and attitude toward the community (Tonglet, Phillips & Bates 2004) have been found to positively influence certain kinds of consumption reduction intentions and behaviour. Nonetheless, environmental attitudes have been far more commonly used to predict reduction behaviours, with findings ranging from moderate to weak or marginal effects of environmental attitudes on a wide array of reduction behaviours (Abrahamse et al. 2005; Barr 2007; Barr & Gilg 2006; Barr, Gilg & Ford 2001; Gilg & Barr 2006; Poortinga et al. 2003; Poortinga, Steg & Vlek 2004; Taylor & Todd 1995).

The consistency of the attitude-behaviour link may be contingent on factors such as the consideration (or not) of intention as a potential mediator (Bamberg & Möser 2007; Fishbein & Ajzen 1975), attitude strength and certainty (Smith, Haugtvedt & Petty 1994), similarity in the degree of specificity/generality of attitude and behaviour (Fazio 1990; Kaiser et al. 1999) and situational constraints on behaviour (Ajzen 1991; Kaiser & Keller 2001). In the present study, environmental attitude should contribute significantly to the reduction behaviour of European citizens, owing to (1) the coherent level of measurement generality in attitude (attitudes towards climate change) and reduction behaviours (aimed at fighting climate change), and (2) the high degree of volitional control over consumption reduction, which is modelled as an aggregate of four specific reduction behaviours (Ajzen 1991).

Hypothesis 1 (H1)

Environmental attitudes will have a positive effect on consumption reduction behaviour.

Motivation influence

Motivation is described as the internal force guiding behaviour (Kollmuss & Agyeman 2002) or the reason for performing a given action (Moisander 2007). Previous research has examined which values underlie people's motivation for ecological behaviour (De Groot & Steg 2008; Schultz & Zelezny 1999). As a consequence of Schwartz's influence (Schwartz 1977), most researchers have distinguished between altruistic and egoistic values. Stern, Dietz and Kalof (1993) split altruistic values into social and biospheric values. In a similar fashion, Gagnon Thompson and Barton (1994) differentiated between ecocentric and anthropocentric value orientations. Ecocentrics appreciate and care about the environment for its own sake and will engage in environmentally responsible behaviour even if it requires some sacrifice (Gagnon Thompson & Barton 1994; Stern, Dietz & Kalof 1993). Anthropocentrics' behaviour will be guided more by egoistic and social values (De Groot & Steg 2008; Stern, Dietz & Kalof 1993); that is, these citizens will engage in pro-environmental actions to the extent that those actions have positive consequences for people and do not decrease their quality of life or wealth (Gagnon Thompson & Barton 1994).

An individual's motives for environmentally orientated consumption reduction have been explored from different perspectives. In general, previous work has found that reduction behaviours, much like other pro-environmental actions, are more common among people holding altruistic values (Barr 2007; Barr & Gilg 2006). Other studies have focused on the motivations for reducing consumption of 'voluntary simplifiers', that is, people adopting a frugal lifestyle; their behaviour change (consumption reduction) can be driven by different value sets − not only biospheric (ecocentric) values, but also egoistic and social ones (Bekin, Carrigan & Schmizin 2007; Huneke 2005; Nelson, Rademacher & Paek 2007). De Young *et al.* (1993) also found that both altruistic and egoistic motivations can lead to reduction behaviour, especially when both sets of values combine in a coherent manner. However, the motivational complexity of environmentally friendly consumption decisions often generates conflicts between an individual's egoistic motivations and his or her altruistic values (Moisander 2007).

Based on expectancy-value models such as TRA or TPB (Ajzen 1991; Fishbein & Ajzen 1975), which posit that attitude develops from salient beliefs about the consequences of the behaviour (i.e. altruistic vs. selfish beliefs), and considering the 'value/belief' nature of ecological motivations (Grunert & Juhl 1995), environmental attitudes (towards climate change) should mediate the effect of (altruistic and egoistic) motivations on reduction behaviour (see Barr 2007; Barr, Gilg & Ford 2001).

Hypothesis 2 (H2)

Ecological motivations will have a positive effect on environmental attitudes.

Knowledge influence

Knowledge of environmental issues is also considered to be a necessary, but insufficient, antecedent condition for pro-environmental behaviour (Bamberg & Möser 2007; Kaiser Wölfing & Fuhrer 1999; Kollmuss & Agyeman 2002). Attitudes are not innate, but evolve in response to different stimuli, such as people's access to external information (Ajzen & Gilbert 2008; Bostrom *et al.* 1994). Environmental researchers have debated the specific role of environmental knowledge and information in ecological decision making (Bostrom *et al.* 1994; Mobley, Vagias & DeWard 2010). Linear-sequential models (from environmental knowledge to ecological behaviour) have been criticised for being too simplistic and ineffective (Kollmuss & Agyeman 2002). However, meta-analytic results support the predictive value of environmental knowledge for pro-environmental behaviour (Bamberg & Möser 2007).

The level and type of environmental knowledge (and information) can affect the consistency of 'knowledge-behaviour' linkages (Hines, Hungerford & Tomera 1986; Kaiser & Fuhrer 2003; Kollmuss & Agyeman 2002). Basic knowledge is needed to properly understand environmental problems and motivate ecological action (Kollmuss & Agyeman 2002). Conversely, excessive information or very detailed technical data, concerning a complex and controversial environmental issue like climate change, can elicit feelings of confusion and frustration (Immerwahr 1999; Kollmus & Aygeman 2002). In addition, communication messages for green purchasing are frequently confusing (Moisander 2007; Young *et al.* 2010), which may lead to distrust in environmental information (Barr & Gilg 2006).

Hence, it is important to know what kind of environmental information is effective in promoting sustainable consumption patterns (Bostrom *et al.* 1994). Drawing on the distinction between 'declarative, procedural and effectiveness' types of environmental knowledge (see Kaiser & Fuhrer, 2003), knowledge about the nature and causes of environmental problems (i.e. declarative knowledge) and knowledge of ecological action strategies (i.e. procedural knowledge) tend to be particularly associated with pro-environmental behaviour (Hines, Hungerford & Tomera 1986; Kaiser & Fuhrer 2003; Kaiser, Wölfing & Fuhrer 1999). This has also been true in consumption reduction research (Abrahamse *et al.* 2005; Barr, Gilg & Ford 2001). In the present study, environmental knowledge (about climate change) is posited to influence consumption reduction behaviour indirectly through respondents' environmental attitudes (Abrahamse *et al.* 2005; Barr 2007; Barr, Gilg & Ford 2001; De Young *et al.* 1993).

Hypothesis 3a (H3a)

Environmental knowledge will have a positive effect on environmental attitudes.

Environmental knowledge will also exert a significant influence on (altruistic and egoistic) motivations for ecological behaviour (Thøgersen 1994). Based on previous research (Schultz, Oskamp & Mainier 1995), the 'knowledge-motivation' effect should be stronger for people who have lower environmental concern and lack the internal motivation to act ecologically; thus, providing high-quality information about the causes, ways of fighting and consequences of climate change should be a powerful instrument to improve the public's ecological motivations (Schultz, Oskamp & Mainier 1995). In recent work on sustainable consumption, green motivations and values are thought to be influenced by consumer knowledge of relevant environmental issues (Young *et al.* 2010). In this regard, providing environmental messages and information to enhance both egoistic and altruistic ecological motivations has shown to contribute more efficiently to consumption reduction behaviours (De Young *et al.* 1993).

Hypothesis 3b (H3b)

Environmental knowledge will have a positive effect on ecological motivations.

Methodology

Sample

The empirical analyses are based on the survey database 'Eurobarometer 69.2 N° 300 – Europeans' attitudes towards climate change'. This cross-national dataset covers a representative sample of the population (citizens aged 15 and over) of the EU-27 member states, three candidate countries (Croatia, Turkey and the Former Yugoslav Republic of Macedonia) and the Turkish Cypriot community. The fieldwork was carried out between 25 March and 4 May 2008 through face-to-face interviews in people's homes. In all member states, a stratified, multistage probability sampling design was used.

A total of 30,170 individuals participated in the survey (approximately 1,000 per country). To date, little anti-consumption research has been based on such large-scale, cross-national survey data; in this respect, the present study differs significantly from most other studies on consumption reduction (e.g. Fujii 2006). The questionnaire addressed two types of environmentally motivated anti-consumption:

- domestic (reducing household water and energy consumption) and
- out-of-home (anti-shopping actions) domains of anti-consumption.

Other measures include European citizens' attitudes, motivations and level of information about climate change, as well as socio-demographic variables such as age, country, gender, professional activity and political ideology.

Statistical methodology

First, exploratory factor analysis (EFA) is used to check the dimensional structure of the model. Next, confirmatory factor analysis (CFA) and structural equation modelling (SEM), using the EQS v6.1 statistical software, are respectively applied to examine the psychometric properties of the scales and test the proposed conceptual model and hypotheses. In addition, several statistical tests and criteria (such as Cronbach's alpha values, composite reliabilities, the average variance extracted (AVE), and chi-square difference tests) are used to analyse measurement reliability and convergent and discriminant validity.

Results

From the initial sample of 30,170 respondents, the authors selected those European citizens who 'personally have taken actions aimed at helping to fight climate change' for testing the hypotheses of the study. Individuals agreeing with that statement (57.1% of the sample; n=17,233) were asked about their consumption reduction behaviour; only these individuals were included in the SEM analysis.

Psychometric properties of scales

As expected, both exploratory and confirmatory factor analyses suggested the distinction between two subtypes of consumption reduction behaviour, which comprise the dependent factor in the research model (see Figure 1.2). The first factor (two items) covers respondents' self-reported reduction of energy and water consumption at home; the second factor comprises anti-shopping actions, that is, consuming fewer disposable items (e.g. plastic bags and packaging), and avoiding products that come from far-away places (e.g. to reduce CO_2 emissions caused by transport). The internal consistency of the second-order anti-consumption scale was satisfactory, according to the common threshold of 0.7 (Hair *et al.* 1998); the obtained Cronbach's alpha and Raykov's rho coefficients were, respectively, 0.64 and 0.76.

For the environmental attitude construct, the analyses revealed the need to separate positive (alpha=0.47; rho=0.65) from negative (alpha=0.65; rho=0.66) attitudes towards climate change. Consistent with previous literature (e.g. Thøgersen, 2009), the analyses supported a second-order factor of environmental motivations (alpha=0.56; rho=0.61), composed of altruistic and egoistic motivations. In the knowledge factor, internal consistency coefficients were well above the recommended level of 0.8 (Straub 1989). For both (positive and negative) attitudes and motivation, Cronbach's alphas were around 0.5, but all Raykov's rho coefficients exceeded the more lenient cut-off of 0.6 (Hair *et al.* 1998). These results were expected, owing to the use of Eurobarometer data with predefined indicators.

Thus, the internal consistency of the constructs may be acceptable in this study (Hair *et al.* 1998; Peter 1979).

Two separate tests were conducted sequentially to assess the discriminant validity of each pair of constructs. First, following Anderson and Gerbing's (1988) recommendations, a confidence interval test was used to assess the discriminant validity of each pair of factors. Next, chi-square difference tests were applied only to those pairs of factors showing problems of discriminant validity, according to the confidence interval test. The performed tests confirmed that discriminant validity was achieved between all analysed pairs of factors.

Explaining environmentally orientated consumption reduction

The results provided support for all the hypothesized relationships (see Figure 1.2). Both positive and negative environmental attitudes (towards climate change) were moderately predictive of environmentally orientated consumption reduction, jointly accounting for 17.35% of the variance (support for H1). However, the strength and direction of effects on the reduction behaviour of respondents were different for both types of environmental attitudes: positive attitudes had a positive (and stronger) influence on anti-consumption (std. β=0.355; p<0.01); whereas negative attitudes were negatively (and more weakly) related to behaviour (std. β =-0.185; p<0.01).

Figure 1.2 Assessment of the structural model: standardised solution

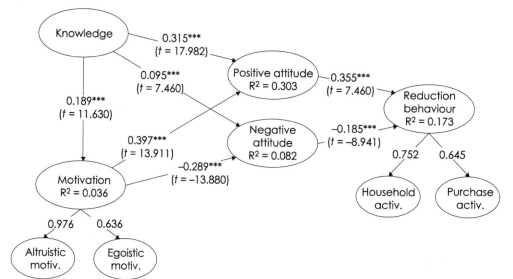

***Significant for p<0.001; T values in brackets

***Significant for p<0.001; T values in brackets

The analysis also supported the hypothesized direct paths from ecological motivations and environmental knowledge (about climate change) to respondents' environmental attitudes (support for H2 and H3a); these influences were stronger on positive attitudes than on negative attitudes (30.3% vs. 8.2% of their respective variances explained). Altruistic and egoistic ecological motivations had a slightly greater impact than environmental knowledge on positive environmental attitudes (std. β=0.397; p<0.01 vs. β=0.315; p<0.01). As expected, ecological motivations exerted a negative influence on negative environmental attitudes (std. β =-0.289; p<0.01); surprisingly, the link between respondents' level of environmental knowledge (about climate change) on negative environmental attitudes was positive, but weak (std. β =0.095; p<0.01). Consistent with H3b, environmental knowledge had a modest, positive influence on (altruistic and egoistic) ecological motivations (std. β =0.189; p<0.01).

The final model also provided a very good fit to the data. The assessment of absolute fit showed that the scaled chi-square (S-B χ^2) was significant at p<0.01. Given the sensitivity of the chi-square statistic to samples with more than 200 observations, alternative indices were examined (Hair *et al.* 1998). RMSEA (0.029) fell below the recommended level of 0.08. Incremental fit measures also indicated a good model fit with all values (NNFI, NFI, CFI, IFI and MFI) exceeding the rigorous threshold of 0.95 (Schumacker & Lomax 2004).

Discussion

The study has shed some light on environmentally orientated consumption reduction. Based on social psychology theory, the research model examined the role of three psychographics (environmental attitudes, motivations and knowledge) in explaining European citizens' anti-consumption aimed at fighting climate change. Environmental attitudes were posited to directly predict and mediate the effects of other relevant factors on reduction behaviour. Respondents' (altruistic and egoistic) ecological motivations and environmental knowledge (about climate change) were respectively selected as internal and external factors influencing environmental attitudes. Knowledge was also hypothesised to have a positive direct effect on ecological motivations. The results provided support for all the postulated relationships. However, the limited explained variance (below 20%) points to other un-modelled antecedents of environmentally orientated anti-consumption (most notably, behavioural intentions). In part, the omission of alternative factors was the result of using a secondary dataset, and the preference of parsimonious models.

In line with previous literature (e.g. Barr & Gilg 2006; De Young *et al.* 1993), the analyses supported the differentiation of 'at home' and purchasing domains of environmentally orientated consumption reduction. Household activities comprised reducing energy and water consumption at home; anti-shopping actions referred to consuming fewer disposable items (e.g. plastic bags and packaging) and avoiding products that come from far-away places (e.g. to reduce CO_2 emissions caused by transport). Instead of focusing on a specific kind of anti-consumption (e.g. Abrahamse *et al.* 2009), the aggregate prediction of consumption reduction behaviours (two types; four specific actions) leads to implications of practical relevance for fostering anti-consumption in a wider array of settings. If possible, promoting consumption reduction at greater generality will be more efficient than developing separate interventions for each reduction behaviour.

The results suggested a distinction between two attitudinal factors, that is, positive and negative environmental attitudes (towards climate change). Their links to behaviour conformed to the hypotheses, with positive attitudes contributing to and negative attitudes detracting from Europeans' consumption reduction behaviour. On the positive side, positive attitudes seem to affect anti-consumption more strongly (though moderately) than negative attitudes. The findings also highlighted the important role of (altruistic and egoistic) environmental motivations in the development of positive environmental attitudes. In addition, enhancing citizens' altruistic and egoistic ecological motivations will be helpful in lowering their levels of negative attitude towards the environment.

Based on the results, informing consumers about environmental issues such as climate change can be an effective means (external influence) of shaping both ecological motivations and positive environmental attitudes. Environmental knowledge and information may also contribute to negative attitudes, but this effect was rather weak and not all types of ecological messages and information (e.g. information about the causes, ways of fighting and consequences of climate change) can be assumed to be equally effective in fostering consumption reduction behaviour. The reasons behind the 'knowledge-negative attitudes' link are beyond the scope of this work, but may include issues such as the technical complexity of environmental problems (Immerwahr 1999; Kollmuss & Agyeman 2002), contradictory or confusing ecological messages (Moisander 2007) or lack of trust in environmental information (Barr & Gilg 2006).

Implications for policy makers and practitioners

Increased levels of environmental degradation, linked to the prevailing unsustainable lifestyles in modern societies (e.g. excessive consumption) call for action and effective environmental strategies for both policy makers and practitioners. Policy makers should be interested in reducing citizens' consumption levels as a means of fighting climate change; the costs associated with the consequences of climate change would far outweigh the costs of stopping or slowing the rate of environmental change (European Commission 2010; Junta de Andalucía 2010). Private companies and institutions have the opportunity to discover and translate environmental challenges into new ways of satisfying consumer needs, while minimising environmental degradation and depletion of natural resources (Varey 2010).

The present study provides insights for promoting consumption reduction behaviours at the individual level. The findings support the role of environmental knowledge as a necessary, but not sufficient, precondition for consumption reduction. Overall, providing information about environmental problems to citizens and consumers can be expected to contribute to environmentally orientated anti-consumption. To a lesser extent, the findings warn of unintended effects of environmental information and messages, which might also lead to negative environmental attitudes. It is not only important to inform the public about environmental issues and problems, but also to ensure that the various types of environmental messages and information (e.g. about the causes, ways of solving and consequences of environmental problems) 'work together in a convergent manner' (Kaiser & Fuhrer 2003, p. 599). Thus, environmental awareness campaigns should be carefully designed to avoid vague, contradictory and complex ecological messages. Moreover, the results suggest that environmental information and messages should appeal to both altruistic and egoistic ecological motivations if they are to foster consumption reduction. Effective promotion of anti-consumption behaviour will also require the coordination of different communications media.

Many opportunities exist for the joint promotion of environmentally orientated consumption reduction and innovative ways of doing business – such as product service systems (PSS) (Cox *et al.* 2010). The idea behind PSS is that consumers purchase a service that reduces their need to acquire physical products or equipment (e.g. laundry or garden maintenance), thus reducing the amount of time and money spent (i.e. in buying the equipment) and, over time, the quantity of generated waste (e.g. waste electrical and electronic equipment) (Cox *et al.* 2010). Consistent with the motivations for environmentally orientated consumption reduction, services like PSS could be effectively promoted as a means of preserving the environment (ecocentric motivation) and saving time and money (egoistic or self-centred motivations).

Limitations and future research

This study has several limitations that warrant further research. Probably the most important one refers to the use of Eurobarometer data. Despite its benefits, such as providing a rich and useful source of information, using these types of data had restrictive effects on research design. A social desirability effect may also bias the results of survey research focusing on ecological behaviours such as anti-consumption, that is, respondents might have exaggerated their responses to project a socially desirable image of themselves. Despite its clarity and parsimony, the proposed research model aims to explain complex and dynamic human behaviours with ethical and ecological implications. Thus, un-modelled factors will also influence the consumption reduction behaviour of European citizens.

Further research should focus on alternative antecedents of anti-consumption in order to account for more variance in environmentally orientated consumption reduction. Other potentially relevant factors include:

- behavioural intentions
- subjective norms
- perceived behavioural control (Ajzen 1991)
- attitude toward frugality (Fujii 2006)
- socio-demographics (Abrahamse *et al.* 2005; Barr 2007) or
- situational barriers (Kaiser & Keller 2001).

Additional measurement items should cover domains of consumption reduction other than household and anti-shopping actions; a third important set of anti-consumption behaviours (not studied here) might include transport decisions.

More research is needed on the most effective ways of providing information aimed at fostering citizens' engagement in environmentally orientated consumption reduction. In this regard, the quality of the arguments used has been found to have an important impact, as long as the topic is of personal relevance to the individual. On the contrary, if the topic is not relevant to people, they will be guided more by their (altruistic or egoistic) motivational orientation (Ajzen & Brown 1996). Thus, future studies should consider including measures of citizens' perceptions of self-relevance or involvement with environmental issues. Further work might also analyse the (similar or differentiated) effects of altruistic vs. egoistic ecological motivations on environmental attitudes and anti-consumption behaviour, as well as the influence of different kinds of environmental information on each of type of ecological motivation.

Finally, because of its growing importance in modern societies such as the European Union, the phenomenon of consumption reduction requires a close follow-up. Among other issues, research in this field should continue to profile different segments of 'anti-consumers' and 'consumption reducers', examine the correspondence between 'most frequent' and 'environmentally orientated' anti-consumption behaviours and identify the main drivers and barriers for anti-consumption — particularly, environmentally motivated consumption reduction.

References

Abrahamse, W., Steg, L., Gifford, R., Vlek, C. (2009). Factors influencing car use for commuting and the intention to reduce it: a question of self-interest or morality? *Transportation Research Part F*, 12(4), 317–324.

Abrahamse, W., Steg, L., Vlek, C., & Rothengatter, T. (2005). A review of intervention studies aimed at household energy conservation. *Journal of Environmental Psychology*, 25, 273–291.

Ajzen, I. (1991). The theory of planned behavior. *Organizational behavior and human decision processes*, 50(2), 179–211.

Ajzen, I., Brown, T.C., (1996). Information bias in contingent valuation: effects of personal relevance, quality of information and motivational orientation. Journal of Environmental Economics and Management, 30(1), 43–57.

Ajzen, I., Gilbert, N. (2008). Attitudes and the prediction of behavior. In Attitudes and attitude change (Eds.: W.D. Crano, R. Prislin), pp. 289–311. New York, NY: Psychology Press.

Anderson, J.C., Gerbing, D.W. (1988). Structural equation modelling in practice: a review and recommended two-step approach. *Psychological Bulletin*, 103(3), 411–423.

Ayres, R.U. (2004). Thermodynamics and economics, overview. In: *Encyclopedia of Energy, vol. 6* (91–97). Elsevier.

Ballantine, P.W., Creery S. (2010). The consumption and disposition behaviour of voluntary simplifiers. *Journal of Consumer Behaviour*, 9(1), 45–56.

Bamberg, S., Möser, G. (2007). Twenty years after Hines, Hungerford and Tomera: a new meta-analysis of psychosocial determinants of pro-environmental behavior. *Journal of Environmental Psychology*, 27(1), 14–25.

Bamberg, S., Schmidt, P. (2003). Incentives, morality or habit? Predicting students' car use for university routes with the models of Ajzen, Schwartz, and Triandis. *Environment & Behavior*, 35(2), 264–285.

Barr, S. (2007). Factors influencing environmental attitudes and behaviors: a U.K. case study of household waste management. *Environment & Behavior*, 39(4), 435–473.

Barr, S., Gilg, A.W. (2006). Sustainable lifestyles: framing environmental action in and around the home. *Geoforum*, 37(6), 906–920.

Barr, S., Gilg, A.W., & Ford, N.J. (2001). Differences between household waste reduction, reuse and recycling behaviour: a study of reported behaviors, intentions and explanatory variables. *Environmental & Waste Management*, 4(2), 69–82.

Bekin, C., Carrigan, M., & Szmigin, I. (2007). Beyond recycling: 'commons-friendly' waste reduction at new consumption communities. *Journal of Consumer Behaviour*, 6(5), 271–286.

Black, I. R., & Cherrier, H., (2010). Anti-consumption as part of living a sustainable lifestyle: daily practices, contextual motivations and subjective values. *Journal of Consumer Behavior*, 9(6), 437-453.

Bord, R.J., O'Connor, R.E, Fisher, A. (2000). In what sense does the public need to understand global climate change? *Public Understanding of Science*, 9(3), 205–218.

Bostrom, A., Morgan, M. G., Fischhoff, B., Read, D. (1994). What do people know about global climate change? 1. Mental models. *Risk Analysis*, 14(6), 959–970.

Brown, A, Kütting, G. (2008). The environment. In: *Issues in International Relations* (Eds: T.C. Salmon, M.F. Imber), pp. 153–181. New York: Routledge.

Burroughs, J. E. (2010). Can consumer culture be contained? Comments on 'marketing means and ends for a sustainable society'. *Journal of Macromarketing*, 30(2), 127–132.

Cox, J., Giorgi, S., Sharp, V., Strange, K., Wilson, D.C., & Blakey, N. (2010). Household waste prevention – a review of evidence. *Waste Management & Research*, 28(3), 193–219.

De Groot, J.I.M., Steg, L. (2008). Value orientations to explain beliefs related to environmental significant behavior: how to measure egoistic, altruistic, and biospheric value orientations. *Environment & Behavior*, 40(3), 330–354.

De Young, R., Duncan, A., Frank, J., Gill, N., Rothman, S., Shenot, R., Shotkin, A., Zweizig, M. (1993). Promoting source reduction behavior. The role of motivational information. *Environment & Behavior*, 25(1), 70–85.

Ebreo, A., Hershey, J., Vining, J. (1999). Reducing Solid Waste: Linking Recycling to Environmentally Responsible Consumerism. *Environment & Behavior*, 31(1), 107–135.

European Commission (2008). *Europeans' attitudes towards climate change*. Available as 30112009 from http://ec.europa.eu/public_opinion/archives/ebs/ebs_300_full_en.pdf

European Commission (2010). Climate Change. Available as 12042011 from http://ec.europa.eu/clima/publications/docs/factsheet-climate-change_en.pdf

European Environment Agency (2010). *Tracking progress towards Kyoto and 2020 targets in Europe.* EEA Report No 7/2010. EEA, Copenhagen, 2010. Available as 16102010 from http://www.eea.europa.eu/publications/progress-towards-kyoto/at_download/file

Fazio, R.H. (1990). Multiple processes by which attitudes guide behavior: the MODE model as an integrative framework. In: *Advances in experimental social psychology, vol. 23* (Eds.: M.P. Zanna), pp. 75–109. New York, NY: Academic Press.

Fishbein, M., Ajzen, I. (1975). *Belief, attitude, intention, and behavior: an introduction to theory and research.* Reading, MA: Addison-Wesley.

Fujii, S. (2006). Environmental concern, attitude toward frugality, and ease of behavior as determinants of pro-environmental behavior intentions. Journal of Environmental Psychology, 26(4), 262–268.

Gagnon Thompson, S., Barton, M. (1994). Ecocentric and anthropocentric attitudes toward the environment. *Journal of Environmental Psychology*, 14(2), 149–157.

Gardiner, S.M. (2004). Ethics and global climate change. *Ethics*, 114(3), 555–600.

Gilg, A., Barr, S. (2006). Behavioural attitudes towards water saving? Evidence from a study of environmental actions. *Ecological Economics*, 57(3), 400–414.

Grunert, S.C., Juhl, H.J. (1995). Values, environmental attitudes and buying of organic foods. *Journal of Economic Psychology*, 16(1), 39–62.

Hair, J.F.Jr., Anderson, R.E., Tatham, R.L., Black, W.C. (1998). *Multivariate data analysis, 5th edition.* Englewood Cliffs: Prentice Hall.

Hines, J.M., Hungerford, H.P., & Tomera, A.N. (1986). Analysis and synthesis of research on responsible environmental behavior: a meta-analysis. *Journal of Environmental Education*, 18(2), 1–8.

Huneke, M.E. (2005). The face of the unconsumer: an empirical examination of the practice of voluntary simplicity in the United States. *Psychology & Marketing*, 22(7), 527–550.

Immerwahr, J. (1999). Waiting for a signal: public attitudes towards global warming, the environment and geophysical research. *Public Agenda and American Geophysical Union.*

Iyer, R., Muncy, J.A. (2009). Purpose and object of anti-consumption. *Journal of Business Research*, 62(2), 160–168.

Jackson, T. (2005). Live better by consuming less? Is there a "Double Dividend" in sustainable consumption? *Journal of Industrial Ecology*, 9(1–2), 19–36.

Junta de Andalucía (2010). *Andalucía Innova. Especial cambio climático.*

Kaiser, F.G., Fuhrer, U. (2003). Ecological behavior's dependency on different forms of knowledge. *Applied Psychology: An International Review*, 52(4), 598–613.

Kaiser, F.G., Keller, C. (2001). Disclosing situational constraints to ecological behavior: a confirmatory application of the mixed Rasch model. *European Journal of Psychological Assessment*, 17(3), 212–221.

Kaiser, F. G., Wölfing, S., & Fuhrer, U. (1999). Environmental attitude and ecological behavior. Journal of Environmental Psychology, 19(1), 1–19.

Kollmuss A., Agyeman, J. (2002). Mind the gap: why do people act environmentally and what are the barriers to pro-environmental behavior? *Environmental Education Research*, 8(3), 239–260.

Maxwell, D., Sheate, W. (2006). Enabling Sustainable Development through Sustainable Consumption and Production. *International Journal of Environment and Sustainable Development*, 5(3), 221–239.

Mobley, C., Vagias, W.M., & DeWard, S.L. (2010). Exploring Additional Determinants of Environmentally Responsible Behavior: The Influence of Environmental Literature and Environmental Attitudes. *Environment & Behavior*, 42(4), 420–447.

Moisander, J. (2007). Motivational complexity of green consumerism. *International Journal of Consumer Studies*, 31(4), 404–409.

Nelson, M.R., Rademacher, M.A., & Paek, H.-J. (2007). Downshifting consumer = upshifting citizen? An examination of a local freecycle community. *The ANNALS of the American Academy of Political and Social Science*, 611(1), 141–156.

Peattie, K., Peattie, S. (2009). Social marketing: a pathway to consumption reduction? *Journal of Business Research*, 62(2), 260–268.

Peter, J.P. (1979). Reliability: a review of psychometric basics and recent marketing practices. *Journal of Marketing Research*, 16(1), 6–17.

Poortinga, W., Steg, L., Vlek, C., & Wiersma, G. (2003). Household preferences for energy-saving measures: a conjoint analysis. *Journal of Economic Psychology*, 24(1), 49–64.

Poortinga, W., Steg, L., & Vlek, C. (2004). Values, environmental concern, and environmental behavior: a study into household energy use. *Environment & Behavior*, 36(1), 70–93.

Rucker, D.D., Galinsky, A. (2008). Desire to Acquire: Powerlessness and Compensatory Consumption. *Journal of Consumer Research*, 35(2), 257–67.

Schwartz, S.H. (1977). Normative influences on altruism. In: *Advances in Experimental Social Psychology, vol. 10* (Ed.: L. Berkowitz), pp. 221–279. New York: Academic Press.

Schumacker, R.E., Lomax R.G. (2004). *A beginner's guide to structural equation modeling, 2nd Edition*. Mahwah, NJ: Erlbaum and Associates.

Schultz, P. W., Oskamp, S., Mainieri, T. (1995).Who recycles and when: a review of personal and situational factors. *Journal of Environmental Psychology*, 15(2), 105–121.

Schultz, P.W., Zelezny, L. (1999). Values as predictors of environmental attitudes: Evidence for consistency across 14 countries. *Journal of Environmental Psychology*, 19(3), 255–265.

Smith, S.M., Haugtvedt, C.P., Petty, R.E. (1994). Attitudes and recycling: does the measurement of affect enhance behavioral prediction? *Psychology & Marketing*, 11(4), 359–374.

Stern, P.C., Dietz, T., Kalof, L. (1993). Value orientations, gender and environmental concern. *Environment & Behavior*, 25(5), 322–348.

Straub, D.W. (1989). Validating instruments in MIS research. *MIS Quarterly*, 13(2), 147–168.

Taylor, S., Todd, P. (1995). Understanding household garbage reduction behavior: a test of an integrated model. *Journal of Public Policy & Marketing*, 14(2), 192–205.

Thøgersen, J. (1994). A model of recycling behaviour, with evidence from Danish source separation programmes. *International Journal of Marketing Research*, 11(2), 145–163.

Thøgersen, J. (2009). The motivational roots of norms for environmentally responsible behavior. *Basic and Applied Social Psychology*, 31(4), 348–362.

Thøgersen, J., Crompton, T., (2009). Simple and painless? The limitations of spillover in environmental campaign. *Journal of Consumer Policy*, 32(2), 141–163.

Thøgersen, J., Grunert-Beckmann, S.C. (1997). Values and Attitude Formation towards Emerging Attitude Objects: From Recycling to General, Waste Minimizing Behavior. In: *Advances in Consumer Research, vol. 24* (Eds.: M. Brucks, D.J. MacInnis), pp. 182–189. Provo, UT: Association for Consumer Research.

Tonglet, M., Phillips, P.S., & Bates, M.P. (2004). Determining the drivers for householder pro-environmental behaviour: waste minimization compared to recycling. *Resources, Conservation and Recycling*, 42(1), 27–48.

Varey, R.J. (2010). Marketing Means and Ends for a Sustainable Society: A Welfare Agenda for Transformative Change. *Journal of Macromarketing*, 30(2), 112–126.

Young, W., Hwang, K., McDonald, S., & Oates, C. J. (2010). Sustainable consumption: Green consumer behaviour when purchasing products. *Sustainable Development*, 18(1), 20–31.

Chapter 2

Goods and services

Sustainable goods

Morven G McEachern

Abstract

The extant literature overwhelmingly concludes that our current consumption practices are unsustainable. Therefore, it is imperative that we act immediately and that we do it with the collective global participation of government, NGOs, businesses and consumers. To help gain a multifaceted understanding of the environmental impacts for all product stages, the 'strong sustainability model' and the lifecycle assessment process provide effective measurement and analysis tools. This chapter provides a theoretical overview of these tools and, in so doing, identifies both stakeholders and issues that impact upon our ability to deliver sustainable product development. The participation of each stakeholder is clearly evident. Firstly, as product choices are often constrained by the availability of environmentally friendly products, designers, manufacturers, distributors and other relevant service sectors (e.g. retailers, waste management organisations) are urged to create products that have a longer lifespan and are easily disposed of safely by consumers. Secondly, consumers are required to change and/or alter their consumption behaviour. In particular, social marketing campaigns may help to change consumer attitudes and behaviour and subsequently help to bring about a paradigm shift whereby sustainability rather than consumerism is the 'new cultural orientation'. The 'cradle-to-cradle' approach adopted throughout this chapter would enable society members to live more sustainable lifestyles and help maintain our planet for longer.

Introduction

The World Summit on Sustainable Development in 2002 appealed to the international community to encourage and promote a societal shift towards sustainable consumption and production. 'Business as usual' is no longer an option as the future survival of the planet depends on our ability to provide goods for seven billion people without exhausting resources (Fletcher 2008; O'Brien 1999; Tucker *et al.* 2010). Soron (2010) estimates that our global footprint exceeds our capacity to regenerate by as much as 30%, meaning that in order to sustain our consumption levels over the next two decades, an entire planet is required. Therefore, the provision of sustainable products is a key societal challenge which is increasingly recognised by governments, NGOs, business and consumers. Although actionable solutions are complex, an overhaul of 'today's industries, sectors, and corporations to deliver a new generation of goods, services and value relationships for tomorrow's consumer' is called for (Krantz 2010, p. 9; Walker 2007). Similarly, by recognising the powerful role that global business plays in terms of stimulating change, new business models can help prevent further damage and instead guide society towards a more sustainable era (Assadourian 2010a). While there are already many visionary examples (see *The Global 100* 2010), most businesses will require fundamental changes to business practices and mindsets to develop and implement sustainable product strategies. Therefore, in order to help guide businesses in developing and delivering sustainable products to consumers; this chapter aims to provide a theoretical overview of measurement and analysis tools and, in so doing, identifies both stakeholders and issues (e.g. materials/resources, lean production, technology, distribution, consumption, disposal) that impact upon our ability to deliver sustainable product development. More specifically, the objectives of this chapter are:

- to define sustainable products and explain their benefits

- to evaluate sustainable measurement and analysis tools available to business managers

- to examine the trade-offs concerning sustainable material selection, manufacturing and distribution

- to examine integrated behavioural approaches designed to achieve consumer behaviour change with regards to sustainable consumption and disposal.

Sustainable products and their benefits

A sustainable product is one that has either no or little impact upon the environment and can be produced indefinitely in large quantities (Dresner 2002; Simon & Sweatman 1997). In addition, it is a product that meets consumer needs (i.e. functionality) and wants (i.e. design/style) in a cost-effective way (Maxwell & Van der Vorst 2003). However, the extant literature suggests that there is no such thing as a truly sustainable product and that all goods produced incorporate a negative environmental impact at some stage in their lifecycle (see for example

Cooper 2000; Ljungberg 2007; Peattie 1995; Simon & Sweatman 1997; Vale & Vale 2009). That is, they could deplete non-renewable resources, pollute the environment and/or damage human health. In accepting that the environmental impact of products cannot be zero, market regulation and policy as well as economic pressures play a significant role in persuading product manufacturers to comply with sustainability goals in order to minimise impact (Maxwell & Van der Vorst 2003; Waage 2007).

Two core advantages offered by sustainable business practices is that the production of sustainable products helps to attend to issues of efficiency in terms of getting the same from less resources as well as sufficiency in terms of obtaining the same benefits from fewer goods (Cooper 2000; Marchand & Walker 2008). In addition to minimising environmental effects, other benefits attributed to sustainable products is that their consumption helps to generate a better quality of life as well as proactively take into account the needs of future generations (Kilbourne, McDonagh & Prothero 1997). Thøgersen and Crompton (2009) also add that pro-environmental consumption behaviour leads consumers to think of themselves in a more positive light and therefore helps to encourage habitual sustainable behaviours which in turn act as an incentive to encourage businesses to produce more sustainable goods. Sheth, Sethia and Srinivas (2011) add that a firm's response to sustainability challenges may prove crucial in terms of market competiveness, and perhaps even the very survival, of their organizations. Consequently, sustainability theory provides a number of measurement approaches and analytical tools which companies must incorporate to help achieve greater improvements in sustainability performance.

Sustainable measurement and analysis tools

One approach to measuring the sustainability of a product is the Triple Bottom Line (TBL). Developed by John Elkington in 1995, the TBL model is used to assess and report performance against a range of economic, social and environmental factors (Figure 2.1). However, in an Australian scoping study, Vandenberg (2002) concluded that there was considerable confusion regarding the definition and philosophy underpinning TBL. SANZ (2009) also criticises the TBL for the small 'intersection of the three circles [which] represents the possibility of sustainability' and that any constraints imposed by the environment on the economy and society are ignored.

Instead, Vanclay (2004) recommends that Social Impact Assessment (SIA) and Environmental Impact Assessment (EIA) along with TBL should be used by organisations when developing sustainable products. One assessment model that incorporates this wider perspective is the Sustainability Assessment Model (SAM) created by the University of Aberdeen and Inchferry Consulting. Over the lifecycle of the product/service, resource availability, environmental protection, social progress and economic prosperity are measured and scored via 22 key indicators

Figure 2.1 The triple bottom line (TBL) model

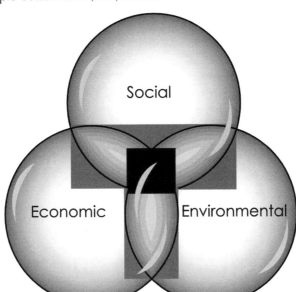

Source: Adapted from SANZ (2009, p. 8).

and then compared with best practice (Edwards 2010). However, SANZ (2009, p. 10) further argues that any incorporation of the TBL is not only wrong in regard to the actual science applied, but that it is also 'making the world less sustainable [as well as being] misleading as a framework for human policy'. As an alternative, the 'strong model' of sustainability recognises that human activity is indeed limited by the earth's capacity and therefore the economy is placed within society and society is placed within the environment (Figure 2.2). Thus, the environment is regarded as 'the most important of the three, because without it we have nothing' (Vale & Vale 2009, p. 11).

Another assessment approach is the Sustainable Product and Service Development (SPSD) framework. The aims of the SPSD are to create sustainable products and/or services that respond to consumer needs, fulfil their functionality in a cost effective way (Maxwell & Van der Vorst 2003). Although the SPSD framework is designed to offer more practical guidance, sustainability frameworks are still generally viewed as complex and there is still little agreement on a unilateral reporting standard (Hubbard 2006). However, it is often agreed throughout the extant literature that no single approach to sustainability will provide all the answers (Fletcher 2008; Walker 2007). Moreover, it is also agreed that whatever measurement approach is embraced, it is essential that a full lifecycle perspective is adopted. Consequently, it is envisaged that the 'new battleground for "competition" will arise from a shift from linear thinking toward industrial ecosystems that take a product life cycle view' (Krantz 2010, p. 7).

Figure 2.2 The Strong Sustainability Model

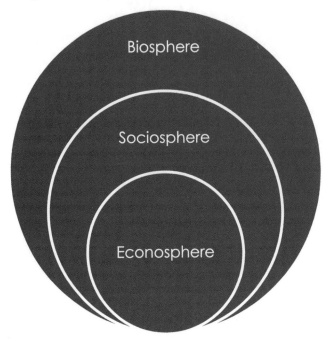

Source: Adapted from SANZ (2009, p. 8).

Lifecycle assessment methods are extensively used to measure the environmental impact of products (Kaebernick, Kara & Sun 2003). The traditional linear view of the lifecycle process is that disposal is perceived as the end of the product's life (i.e. 'cradle-to-grave'). However, in the pursuit of more sustainable practices, this view has been rejected and now extends the product lifecycle process by encouraging users to consider the product's afterlife, thus producing the term 'cradle-to-cradle' (Fletcher 2008). The cradle-to-cradle lifecycle approach (Figure 2.3) now forms the structure of this chapter as we examine the sustainability issues that need to be addressed within each stage to help strategically develop and deliver sustainable product development. As can be seen, the dotted lines indicate the potential re-use and recovery options available to product designers and manufacturers alike.

Product design and materials

Eighty per cent of the environmental and cost factors for a product are determined at the product design stage (Maxwell & Van der Vorst 2003). Therefore, functionality and efficiency of energy and material use must be maximised to ensure the supply of sustainable goods and services. Although sustainability goals must be clearly led and communicated by the organisation, much of this responsibility lies with the product designer. In fact, it is tentatively suggested by Van der Ryn and Cowan (1996) that the current environmental crisis could in some ways be described as a design crisis. Cooper (2000, p. 54) criticises designers for

Figure 2.3 Typical product lifecycle stages using a 'cradle-to-cradle' approach

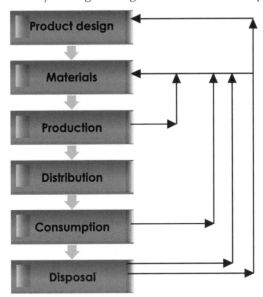

their bland 'marketing-led' design principles and urges them to incorporate greater consideration for the product's environmental impact and a move towards a 'design for society'. Traditional decision making within the product design process has generally consisted of performance assessment and cost estimates. More recently, additional decisions regarding the development speed and environmental performance have been added (Kaebernick, Kara & Sun 2003), thus generating a trade-off model for sustainable product development (Figure 2.4). Consequently, a useful starting point for designers in the development of sustainable products is to examine previous environmental assessments of the product and review data on consumer usage of the product and satisfaction concerning product functionality, cost and environmental impact (Marchand & Walker 2008; Waage 2007).

Figure 2.4 Trade-off model for sustainable design decisions

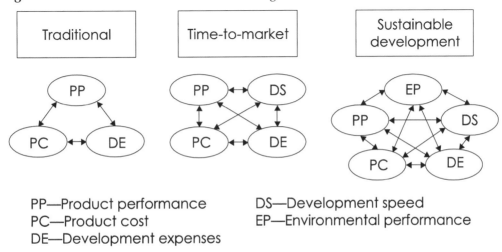

Source: Kaebernick, Kara & Sun (2003, p. 464).

Dyson is just one of many global companies that adopts such an approach, manufacturing award-winning products using fewer materials and less energy. Collaboration and input from all stakeholders is also required during this stage. Once agreement relating to characteristics and sustainable criteria is reached, designers are then in a position to consider a variety of future solutions (Waage 2007). These decision-points help businesses to define the problem; without them, there 'will be little chance of innovative green design' (Edwards 2010, p. 163). A further issue that needs to be recognised when planning any sustainable design process is the environmental regulatory trends. While a thorough overview of such trends is beyond the remit of this chapter, a useful resource to help address any regulatory uncertainty when creating product designs can be found in Noori and Chen (2003). The next design consideration is the materials required and the trade-offs that are often required to ensure sustainability throughout the remainder of the product lifecycle.

In many industrialised countries, the use of materials in the manufacturing and packaging of products has increased 20-fold per capita (Ljungberg 2007). However, while it is possible to select sustainable and recyclable materials (e.g. wood), the excessive extraction of such materials can still lead to significant environmental damage (see Table 2.1). Hence, availability of resources is also a crucial factor in influencing material selection. Such discussions usually revolve around energy supplies, metals, plastics and timber sources but equally important to such impact assessments is the sustainability of water supplies (Edwards 2010). For example in the fashion sector, the production of one kilogram of cotton can use up to 8000 litres of water. The same weight of polyester uses little or no water but consumes twice the energy needed to make the same quantity of cotton (Fletcher 2008). Such trade-offs have led fashion designers towards the use of biodegradable synthetics made from plants, but again, this material selection could still impact on the sustainability of water supplies.

Ljungberg's (2007) table clearly helps businesses to conduct a strategic analysis regarding the material trade-offs to be considered during the design process. There are also some other relevant global data sources such as ASM International for databases on alloys and materials and CAS for databases on chemical substances. However, the difficulty for many businesses is that data that could help in the evaluation of material selection are often unavailable, expensive to obtain and/or unconfirmed as a reliable source (Waage 2007).

One strategy for designers that may help to minimise the impact of materials used in the manufacturing of products is 'dematerialisation' (Dresner 2002). Dematerialisation is defined by the United Nations Environment Programme (UNEP) as:

> ... the reduction of total material and energy throughput of any product and service, and thus the limitation of its environmental impact. This includes reduction of raw materials at the production stage, of energy and material inputs at the use stage, and of waste at the disposal stage (ACCR 2011).

Table 2.1 Product material groups & sustainability classifications

The six typical product material groups, as well as examples and aspects for developing sustainable products are presented

Material group	Examples on materials	Typical advantages	Typical disadvantages	Classification of the sustainability[a]
Metals	• Steel (Fe+C) • Aluminium • Bronze (e.g., Cu+Sn)	• Durable and strong • Often plastic formable • Often cheap	• High cost for machining • Mostly corrosion sensitive	• Easy recyclable (re-meltable) 2–3
Ceramics	Synthetic materials like: • Porcelain (clay) • Mineral glass • Al_2O_3, Si_3N_4, SiC, etc.	• Non toxic • Light • Hard and durable • Corrosion resistant • High temp. resistant	• Brittle • High cost for machining when burnt • Not suitable for load in tension	• Easy to deposit (non toxic) • Possible but expensive to re-melt 2–3
Synthetic polymers	• Thermoplastics (e.g., PE, PS, PC, PP) • Two component polymers (e.g., epoxy) • Rubber(e.g., Isopren)	• Non toxic • Light • Cheap and easy forming • Often easy to recycle(e.g., by re-melting or burning)	• Sometimes very toxic when burnt • Sensitive to high temperatures	• Typically non-renewable • Often easy to re-melt or burn 1–3
Natural organic materials	• Wood • Cotton • Silk	• Renewable • Light • Cheap and easy forming • Recyclable by, e.g., burning	• Decomposes easily • Not durable • Toxic when impregnated	• Recyclable by, e.g., burning • Renewable 2–3
Natural inorganic materials	• Stone • Minerals	See ceramics above!	• Brittle • High cost for machining • Not suitable for load in tension	See ceramics above! 3
Composites	• Mixed materials, e.g.: PS+glassfibres, Cu+W-fibres, Rubber+textilfibres, asphalt(oil+stone), Wood polymer Composites (WPC)	• Optimised use of the materials • Often very strong and light	• Often expensive to produce • Very various properties for various composites	• Typically low sustainability due to separation problems for the mixed materials 1–2

Note that the advantages/disadvantages and the 'sustainability' can change due to the specific material type and the examples are not valid for all materials in a certain material group.
[a] The sustainability is estimated from a scale 1 to 3, where 3 indicates the highest (or best) sustainability and 1 the lowest.

Source: Ljungberg (2007, p. 472).

As China and India place greater demands on materials and energy (Kleindorfer, Singhal & Van Wassenhove 2005), thus raising the cost, dematerialisation may become increasingly attractive to businesses across the globe. Many businesses reject the move towards more sustainable processes because they perceive such practices as costly (O'Brien 1999), but sustainable design and dematerialisation present clear cost efficiencies for the manufacturer. Recent studies of sustainable and green office buildings demonstrate that 'over a 20-year period, the productivity benefits of green design outweigh the energy benefits by a factor of six' (Edwards 2010, p. 204). Marks & Spencer's offer a pioneering example in the fashion sector. Their Plan A strategy has transformed sourcing and material flows by prohibiting the use of certain chemicals by suppliers and pledging to extend the firm's sustainable sourcing of organic cotton, linen and wool and recycled polyester (Fletcher 2008). Marks & Spencer's aim of sending no waste to landfill and becoming carbon-neutral by 2015 will surely help to position them as a world-leading retailer when it comes to sustainable practices (Marks & Spencer 2011).

To help reduce future environmental problems, when selecting materials it is crucial that the business can facilitate recovery, re-use and recycling of their products (de Ron 1998). Fletcher (2008, p. 108) notes that 'over 90% of the resources taken out of the ground today [are] becoming waste within only three months'. Business decisions whether to recycle or re-use is also dependent upon world prices. For example, the abundance and relative cheapness of aluminium often creates little incentive to recycle, but the expensive nature and limited supply of copper ensures that 75% of copper is recycled (compared to only 40% of aluminium) (Edwards 2010). Thus, the ultimate goal is to develop a product that produces little or no waste, uses renewable resources and is entirely recyclable at the end of its lifespan (Assadourian 2010b). These practices will also be picked up again in relation to the consumption stage at the end of the chapter. A final aspect to consider here is, how complementary are the materials and overall product design with the manufacturing process?

Production

As many businesses continue to follow conventional cost-profit models, a move towards the production of sustainable products may require a fundamental shift in traditional manufacturing processes. Whilst it is unlikely that the emphasis on cost and profits will disappear, a new 'paradigm for sustainable manufacturing' is likely to take off (Kaebernick, Kara & Sun 2003, p. 461). Technology plays a significant part here as many manufacturing businesses look increasingly to more automated production systems to help achieve economies of scale. However, from a sustainability perspective, O'Brien (1999, p. 3) urges businesses to move from 'cleaning technologies to clean technologies which reduce the actual level of emissions produced and the energy and other resources used during processing'. Throughout Australia and New Zealand, Narayanaswamy and Stone (2007) note that the cleaner production debate has progressed somewhat over the last decade and that cleaner production methods and tools continue to evolve. Indeed, the regulatory environment has placed significant pressure on companies to move towards cleaner systems of production, but Delmas (2004) and Woensel, Creten & Vandaele (2001) believe that by going beyond current regulations, businesses can actually reduce the costs of changing production systems.

Sustainable and/or environmentally friendly products are often perceived as being of lesser quality and effectiveness (e.g. ecological detergents). Therefore, to help avoid any reluctance to purchase such products, it is imperative that manufacturers also continue to focus on improvements to product quality (de Ron 1998). In some cases, improvements in environmental activities have also led to improvements in quality (de Ron 1998; Pil & Rothenberg 2003). The growth of the fair trade coffee market is just one example where the commitment to environmental and social factors by coffee producers has helped to bring about improvements in product quality (Nelson & Pound 2010).

Flexibility of operations is another aspect that merits consideration at this stage; for example, how can the manufacturer maintain an extended product lifecycle and avoid the erosion of materials when creating new products (Linton, Klassen & Jayaraman 2007)? In the move towards leaner operations, it is crucial that businesses avoid the build-up of large stocks of spare parts and respond instead to such challenges by manufacturing on demand (O'Brien 1999). Also relevant here is the management of product recovery and the pursuit of closed-loop supply chains (Kleindorfer, Singhal & Van Wassenhove 2005).

Some businesses are responding to sustainability concerns by considering a shift away from producing products to the provision of a service and/or a variety of services designed to support and complement sales of the original product (Linton, Klassen & Jayaraman 2007). This strategy not only helps to decrease the quantities of products manufactured but also helps to boost profits (Maxwell & Van der Vorst 2003). From a customer satisfaction perspective, a product that incorporates service elements can help provide the requisite functionality more effectively and/or enhance perceived trust and loyalty towards the brand. One example of a small sustainable business that operates such a strategy is the Loch Fyne Oyster Bar which began as a producer and now currently operates a luxury catering arm as well as a chain of restaurants around the UK (Loch Fyne 2011).

Another factor that shapes the sustainability of the production stage is that of the place of manufacture. Certainly during the early 1900s, the majority of our household wares, clothes and tools would have been manufactured in the domestic market (Walker 2007). However, this is no longer the case, with the majority of our products imported and/or just assembled and distributed within the domestic market; thus it also impacts significantly upon the sustainability of the distribution/supply chain process.

Distribution/SCM

The supply chain can play a substantial role in reducing the sustainable impact of products (Maxwell & Van der Vorst 2003). However, in spite of the available hybrid and/or energy reducing technology, transportation accounts for a quarter of all CO_2 output and continues to have a growing impact on the environment. European business and private household resistance to embrace sustainable transport is demonstrated by the fact that between 1996 and 2006 (EEA 2009)

- Road and air freight transport continued to grow, increasing by 35%.

- Passenger car use increased by 18%.

- No improvements in particulates (PM_{10}) and nitrogen oxides (NO_x) were observed.

- Fifty-five per cent of the population were exposed to transport noise levels exceeding 55 L $_{den}$ (an EU benchmark for exceeding noise levels).

Consequently, both businesses and private households have been frequently targeted by governments to reduce transport CO_2 emissions (see *Business Link* 2011; Directgov 2011). However, a fundamental problem in meeting sustainable transport targets is that governments also have an obligation to generate economic growth (O'Brien 1999; Peattie & Collins 2009), which in turn has generally contributed to rising demand for transport (e.g. the tourism and building sectors). As sustainable supply chain management is covered in more detail elsewhere in this text, it remains outside the scope of this chapter to offer guidance on how sustainable transport targets can be developed and achieved. Therefore, this chapter now examines the final stage, that is, the sustainable consumption and disposal of products.

Consumption and disposal

Over the last five decades, consumption *per se* has significantly grown. Moreover, countless products have become progressively more disposable, as in the case of the contradictorily named consumer durables now lasting for just a few years at best (Walker 2007). As a result, up to 40% of all environmentally damaging activities can be linked to the behaviours of private households in the Western world (Hirschel, Konrad & Scholl 2003). In order to satisfy rising consumer demand for products, production using metals increased six-fold, oil consumption eight-fold and gas fourteen-fold, resulting in 60 billion tonnes of resources being extracted annually from the planet – a 50% rise since the late 1970s (Assadourian 2010b). Such statistics are also symbolic of policymakers' efforts to bolster production and promote consumption as a means of invigorating the economy (Fedrigo & Hontelez 2010). Simultaneously, many attempts have been made by heads of government to implement sustainable development priorities for the 21st century; for example, the Rio and Johannesburg Earth Summit meetings, Framework Convention on Climate Change, Agenda 21, The Commission on Sustainable Development, UNCED and The Kyoto Protocol. Despite these attempts to pursue more global sustainable policies, action plans have either not yet been fully executed due to incompatible growth policies or have been hindered by a lack of understanding surrounding household consumption behaviours (Dressner 2002). Munasinghe (2010) criticises the efforts of world leaders to date and demands that they take a more long-term approach towards promoting sustainable consumption. A widely held view is that shifts towards more sustainable business practices may only occur if 'corporate survival depends on them' (Michaelis 2003, p. 921). Similarly, others add that 'doing the same things a little differently, better or faster will not bring about the transformational changes' required to meet the sustainability challenge (Anderson, Amodea & Hartzfeld 2010, p. 101; Fedrigo & Hontelez 2010; SANZ 2009). Answers to the

> … *riddle of sustainable consumption however, are not so simple. In the search for actionable solutions, leaders must navigate a complex network of systems inter-linkages, difficult trade-offs, and powerful feedback loops within the political, business and natural environments (Krantz 2010, p. 7).*

To help businesses lead such a paradigm shift, Anderson, Amodea and Hartzfeld (2010, p. 98) propose a framework for cultural change within businesses (Figure 2.5). Here the authors describe each of the transformative stages and the accompanying changes in their belief systems. With the result that 'sustainability becomes fully embraced as the way we do things around here', thus, helping to bring about greater connectivity and trust within the marketplace.

Figure 2.5 Cultural change model

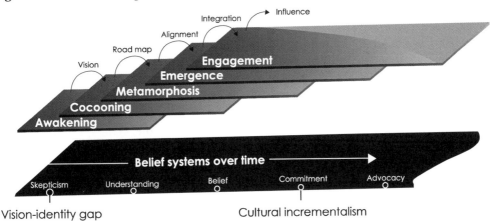

Source: Anderson *et al.* (2010 p. 98).

A number of voluntary policy tools have been implemented across Europe to aid moves towards more sustainable consumption. One example is the Red/Green Calculator which enables retailers to assess the sustainability of their products (Defra 2011). Another example is the Dutch Green Funds Scheme (GFS) which is a tax incentive instrument introduced by the Dutch government to help encourage environmentally friendly initiatives (Europa 2009). Certainly, to date, government regulation has largely been responsible for driving forward business commitment towards sustainable production and consumption (Michaelis 2003). Consequently, some businesses have been successful in improving products and technology with the result of helping the European household to decrease their energy requirements by 22 per cent. At the same time, however, due to the increasing number of appliances being purchased for the home, household energy during the same period is estimated to have increased by four per cent (Tukker *et al.* 2005). Defra's (2006) sustainable consumption and production indicators also show that while manufacturing, agriculture, river water quality, land recycling, service and public sector emissions all showed significant CO_2 emission improvements between 1990 and 1999, CO_2 emissions from households and private vehicles, water leakages and household waste all showed deterioration during the same period. Peattie (2007, p. 194) describes this as a 'disastrous lack of change and progress'.

While little progress appears to have been made regarding shifts in consumer transport usage, some inroads have been made relating to disposal and recycling targets. Particular success has been noted in the electronics, packaging and motoring sectors, again mainly driven by implementation of EU regulations such as the Waste Electronic & Electrical Equipment (WEEE) Directive 2002/96, the EC Packaging and Packaging Waste Directive and the End of Life Vehicles (ELV) Directive. However, Fletcher (2008, p. 113) criticises such targeted sector approaches as falling short of 'regulating for zero waste'. Nonetheless, many charity groups and local councils continue to use the 3R approach – Reduce, Re-use & Recycle – when targeting consumers to encourage their residents to cut back on waste. A typical website detailing the persuasive attempts to encourage consumers to reduce, re-use and recycle more is illustrated by The Royal Borough of Kingston upon Thames whose waste levels are currently three per cent above the national UK average (Royal Kingston 2011).

Other key areas of behaviour generally targeted by policymakers include the reduction and re-use of clothing, appliances/gadgets and plastic bags; the saving of energy and water (i.e. loft and cavity insulation); and the reduction of CO_2 emissions (e.g. fuel emissions, air travel). When recycling is not an option, many governments/business sectors resort to deposition. This describes a safe method to store materials and guarantees, as much as is achievable, a low environmental impact (Ljungberg 2007). This option however is sometimes viewed as 'sweeping the issue under the carpet' rather than dealing with the environmental problem – more an action than a solution. Therefore, due to the increasing need for the earth's resources to be repaired and recovered, environmentalists have added a fourth R – recover. One example of where sustainable practices have helped bring about improvements in air pollution in urban areas is the combined efforts of architects, construction companies and city councils to increase tree planting and provide more pedestrian and cycle-friendly spaces (Edwards 2010).

Throughout the last three decades however, the general public 'has remained largely disengaged' (Cooper 2000, p. 49) from government sustainability campaigns, with the result that the 'four Rs' (i.e. reduce, reuse, recycle, recover) have only been embraced by the green/ethical consumer (see Harrison, Newholm & Shaw 2005). Given that ethical consumer markets only average around two–three per cent (Berry & McEachern 2005) much more targeted efforts are required from policymakers and NGOs to persuade the majority of households to engage in such practices. While there is a significant amount of understanding regarding consumer motivations for adopting sustainable behaviour (see Jackson 2004), Peattie and Collins (2009) suggest that we require more research in this area to help make more progress towards achieving higher levels of sustainability from consumers. However, it is argued that sustainable consumer behaviour cannot be fully understood if research continues to look at sustainable consumer behaviour as a succession of isolated activities (Hirschl, Konrad & Scholl 2003). Moreover, Stern (2007) advocates that it is more about developing the right balance of measures for different population groups and behavioural goals. Therefore, if governments/businesses continue to adopt a one-size-fits-all approach to sustainable product use, they will inevitably fail.

Consequently, some governments have recently begun to implement more holistic and integrated approaches towards achieving sustainability targets. One example of a more targeted approach is Defra's (2008) pro-environmental segmentation model which defines distinct audience segments based on shared environmental attitudes and values (Figure 2.6). As can be seen, each segment profile covers socio-geodemographics, attitudes towards behaviours, current and potential behaviours, knowledge and engagement, and motivations and barriers to sustainable behaviour. Surprisingly some contradictory areas between attitudes and behaviour are apparent because committed consumers were less willing to use their cars less for short trips and/or change their diet to a lower impact one (Defra 2008). BMRB

(2007) suggests a similar anomaly in that individuals with strong pro-environmental attitudes were also the most likely to have flown recently.

Figure 2.6 Seven population segments for pro-environmental behaviours

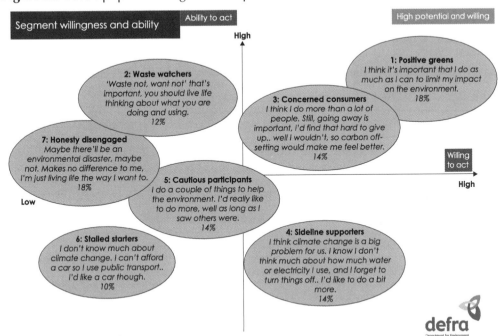

Source: Defra (2008, p. 8).

It is clear that consumers are struggling to achieve some consistency in amalgamating their values and concerns with the demands of their daily working lives and their sustainable consumption behaviours (Szmigin, Carrigan & McEachern 2009). Given this predicament, governments must move beyond 'nudges' such as voluntary eco-labelling mechanisms/policy efforts and persuade consumers to change behaviour. This will then persuade industry to produce more sustainable products (O'Brien 1999). However, as indicated above, information campaigns alone appear to have little impact upon behavioural change (Polonsky 2010). Consequently, French (2010) proposes that a better mechanism to change consumption behaviour could be social marketing techniques.

McKenzie-Mohr (2000) advocates that the first step of social marketing is to understand the barriers that prevent consumers from engaging in an activity. This stage is sometimes by-passed by policymakers/planners as they often believe they are familiar with all of the barriers. Based on the identification of this information, step 2 emphasises the importance of selecting a desired behaviour and promoting a positive vision of that behaviour to consumers. After designing a plan of action to overcome the barriers (step 3), the plan must be piloted and evaluated after implementation (step 4). One example of a recent initiative to help policymakers implement theoretical insights to their social marketing practices and help bring about population-level behavioural change is MINDSPACE (see Dolan *et al.* 2010).

The simple mnemonic, MINDSPACE, equates to the following checklist when making policy (Table 2.2). When implementing MINDSPACE, the government draws upon the 4Es framework (Enable, Encourage, Exemplify and Engage), allowing policymakers to better understand behavioural actions. Specific success stories relating to MINDSPACE are currently evident in the London borough of Southwark which is attempting to reduce littering behaviour (see Southwark Council 2011). Time will tell whether this framework will help bring about behavioural change in the sustainable consumption practices of consumers.

Table 2.2 MINDSPACE: A checklist for policymakers

Messenger	We are heavily influenced by who communicates information
Incentives	Our responses to incentives are shaped by predictable mental shortcuts such as strongly avoiding losses
Norms	We are strongly influenced by what others do
Defaults	We 'go with the flow' of pre-set options
Salience	Our attention is drawn to what is novel and seems relevant to us
Priming	Our acts are often influenced by sub-conscious cues
Affect	Our emotional associations can powerfully shape our actions
Commitments	We seek to be consistent with our public promises, and reciprocate acts
Ego	We act in ways that make us feel better about ourselves.

Source: Dolan *et al.* (2010, p. 8).

Also relevant to many international policies that focus on behavioural change (and also referred to within the MINDSPACE model – see Table 2.2) is the explicit incorporation of the normative aspects of sustainable behaviour. The aim here is to overcome motivational barriers and create an encouraging framework for collective progress (see for example Sustainable Development Commission/ National Consumer Council 2006).

Summary

There is unanimous agreement throughout the literature that continuing along the path of unsustainability will ultimately lead to disaster (Dresner 2002; Marchand & Walker 2008; Munasinghe 2010; O'Brien 1999; Tukker *et al.* 2010; Vale & Vale 2009). Therefore, in order to help assist business managers to develop and deliver sustainable products to consumers, this chapter fulfils the aforementioned objectives and, in using 'effective' (see Ljungberg 2007, p. 477) measurement and analysis tools such as the strong sustainability model and the lifecycle assessment process, identifies both stakeholders and relevant issues that impact upon our ability to deliver sustainable product development. Not only is it vital that we act now (Stern 2007) to achieve sustainable targets, but we must do it with the collective global participation of government, NGOs, businesses and consumers to successfully reduce our impact on the environment. Indeed, Dresner (2002, p. 167) agrees that 'attempting to achieve sustainability in one country is almost useless if other countries continue to act unsustainably'. The role of designers, manufacturers, distributors and other relevant service sectors is crucial to ensuring the production of products that do not need to be replaced so regularly and can be disposed of safely and easily by consumers. However, this alone will not bring about sustainable development. It is accepted that lifestyle changes and product choices are often constrained by the availability of environmentally friendly products (Marchand & Walker 2008), but consumers also have to form part of the movement towards achieving sustainable development (Cooper 2000; Jackson 2005; Vale & Vale 2009). Therefore, to help change and/or alter consumption behaviour, this chapter has discussed some examples of how this change in attitude and behaviour may be gradually introduced and therefore help to bring about a new cultural orientation which views 'sustainability – rather than consumerism – as natural' (Assadourian 2010b, p. 20; Jackson 2005; Peattie & Collins 2009). Perhaps the collective cradle-to-cradle approach described above will be perceived by many as no more than idealistic optimism or a step too far, but it is envisaged that only a collective effort will permit 'humanity to live better lives today and long into the future' (Assadourian 2010b, p. 20).

References

ACCR (2011) What is Dematerialisation? Available at http://resourcities.acrplus.org/dematerialisation/what_dematerialisation.htm

Anderson, R., Amodea, M. & Hartzfeld, J. (2010) Changing Business Cultures From Within, *State of the World, Transforming cultures: From Consumerism to Sustainability,* W.W. Norton, New York.

Assadourian, E. (2010a) Business and Economy: Management Priorities, *State of the World, Transforming cultures: From Consumerism to Sustainability,* W.W. Norton, New York.

Assadourian, E. (2010b) The Rise and Fall of Consumer Cultures, *State of the World, Transforming cultures: From Consumerism to Sustainability,* W.W. Norton, New York.

Berry, H. & McEachern, M.G. (2005) Informing Ethical Consumers, In Harrison, R., Newholm, T. and Shaw, D.S. (Eds), *The Ethical Consumer,* Sage Publications, London.

BMRB (2007) *Can Fly Will Fly,* British Market Research Bureau, London.

Business Link (2011) Information, Support and Compliance on Reducing and Recycling waste, Available at http://www.businesslink.gov.uk/bdotg/action/layer?topicId=1086048456.

Cooper, T. (2000) Product Development Implications of Sustainable Consumption, *The Design Journal,* 3(2), 46-57.

Defra (2006) *Sustainable Development Indicators in Your Pocket,* DEFRA, London.

Defra (2008) *A Framework for Pro-environmental Behaviours,* DEFRA, London.

Defra (2011) Red/Green Calculator Tool for Consumer Electronics, Available at http://www.mtprog.com/cms/retailer/.

de Ron, Ad J. (1998) Sustainable Production: The Ultimate Result of a Continuous Improvement, *International Journal of Production Economics*, 56-57, 99-110.

Delmas, M.D. (2004) Erratum to "Stakeholders and Competitive Advantage: The Case of ISO 14001", *Production and Operations Management*, 13(4), 398.

Directgov (2011) Environment and Greener Living, Available at http://www.direct.gov.uk/en/Environmentandgreenerliving/Greenertravel/Greenercarsanddriving/DG_064428.

Dolan, P., Hallsworth, M., Halpern, D., King, D. & Vlaev, I. (2010) *MINDSPACE: Influencing Behavior Through Public Policy*, Institute for Government. London.

Dresner, S. (2002) *The Principles of Sustainability*, Earthscan, London.

Edwards, B. (2010) *Rough Guide to Sustainability*, 3rd Edition, Earthscan, London.

EEA (2009) *Transport at a Crossroads: Term 2008, Indicators Tracking Transport and Environment in the European Union*, EEA Report No.3, European Environment Agency, Copenhagen.

Europa (2009) State Aid: Commission Approves Dutch Green Funds Scheme for Environmentally-Friendly Investment Projects, Available at http://europa.eu/rapid/pressReleasesAction.do?reference=IP/09/1514&format=HTML&aged=0&language=EN&guiLanguage=en.

Fedrigo, D. & Hontelez, J. (2010) Sustainable Consumption and Production: An Agenda Beyond Sustainable Consumer Procurement, *Journal of Industrial Ecology*, 14(1), 10-12.

Fletcher, K. (2008) *Sustainable Fashion & Textiles*, Earthscan, London.

French, J. (2010) *Why Nudges are not Enough and Why Social Marketing is Part of the Answer to the Current Conceptual Confusion Evident Within State Sponsored Social Improvement Programmes*, Proceedings from ISM-Open, Challenging Times, New Challenges, November, The Open University, Milton Keynes.

Harrison, R., Newholm, T. & Shaw, D.S. (Eds), *The Ethical Consumer*, Sage Publications, London.

Hirschel, B., Konrad, W. & Scholl, G. (2003) New Concepts in Product Use for Sustainable Consumption, *Journal of Cleaner Production*, 11, 873-881.

Hubbard, G. (2006) Measuring Organisational Performance: Beyond the Triple Bottom Line, *Business Strategy and the Environment*, 18(3), 177-191.

Jackson, T. (2004) *Motivating Sustainable Consumption: A Review of Evidence on Consumer Behaviour and Behavioural Change*, Centre for Environmental Strategy, University of Surrey, Guildford.

Jackson, T. (2005) Living Better by Consuming Less? Is There a "Double Dividend" in Sustainable Consumption, *Journal of Industrial Ecology*, 9(1-2), 19-36.

Kaebernick, H., Kara, S. & Sun, M. (2003) Sustainable Product Development and Manufacturing by Considering Environmental Requirements, *Robotics and Computer Integrated Manufacturing*, 19, 461-468.

Kilbourne, W., McDonagh, P. & Prothero, A. (1997) Sustainable Consumption and the Quality of Life: A Macromarketing Challenge to the Dominant Social Paradigm, *Journal of Macromarketing*, 17(1), 4-24.

Kleindorfer, P.R., Singhal, K. & Van Wassenhove, L.N. (2005) Sustainable Operations Management, *Production and Operations Management,* 14(4), 482-492.

Krantz, R. (2010) A New Vision of Sustainable Consumption: The Business Challenge, *Journal of Industrial Ecology,* 14(1), 7-9.

Linton, J.D., Klassen, R. & Jayaraman, V. (2007) Sustainable Supply Chains: An Introduction, *Journal of Operations Management,* 25(6), 1075-1082.

Loch Fyne (2011) About Us, Available at http://www.lochfyne.com/Home.aspx.

Ljungberg, L.Y. (2007) Materials Selection and Design for Development of Sustainable Products, *Materials and Design,* 28, 466-479.

Marchand, A. & Walker, S. (2008) Product Development and Responsible Consumption: Designing Alternatives for Sustainable Lifestyles, *Journal of Cleaner Production,* 16, 1163-1169.

Marks & Spencer (2011) Plan A – Doing the Right Thing, Available at http://plana.marksandspencer.com/about.

Maxwell, D. & Van der Vorst, R. (2003) Developing Sustainable Products and Services, *Journal of Cleaner Production,* 11, 883-895.

McKenzie-Mohr, D. (2000) Promoting Sustainable Behaviour: An Introduction to Community-Based Social Marketing, *Journal of Social Issues,* 56(3), 543-554.

Michaelis, L. (2003) The Role of Business in Sustainable Consumption, *Journal of Cleaner Production,* 11, 915-921.

Munasinghe, M. (2010) Can Sustainable Consumers and Producers Save the Planet? *Journal of Industrial Ecology,* 14(2), 4-6.

Narayanaswamy, V. & Stone, L. (2007) From Cleaner Production to Sustainable Production and Consumption in Australia and New Zealand: Achievements, Challenges and Opportunities, *Journal of Cleaner Production,* 15(8-9), 711-715.

Nelson, V. and Pound, B. (2010) *A Review of the Impact of Fairtrade Over the Last Ten Years,* Available at http://www.fairtrade.org.uk/resources/natural_resources _institute.aspx?

Noori, H. & Chen, C. (2003) Applying Scenario-Driven Strategy to Integrate Environmental Management and Product Design, *Production and Operations Management,* 12(3), 352-368.

O'Brien, C. (1999) Sustainable Production – A New Paradigm for a New Millennium, *International Journal of Production Economics,* 60-61, 1-7.

Peattie, K. (1995) *Environmental Marketing Management: Meeting the Green Challenge,* Pitman, London.

Peattie, K. (2007) Sustainable marketing: Marketing Re-thought, Re-mixed and Re-tooled, In Saren, M., MacLaran, P., Goulding, C., Elliott, R., Shankar, A. and Catterall, A. (Eds) *Critical Marketing: Defining the Field,* Butterworth-Heinemann, Oxford.

Peattie, K. & Collins, A. (2009) Guest Editorial: Perspectives on Sustainable Consumption, In Peattie, K. and Collins, A. (Eds) Special Issue on Sustainable Consumption, *International Journal of Consumer Studies,* 33(2), 107-112.

Pil, F.K.S. & Rothenberg, S. (2003) Environmental Performance as a Driver of Superior Quality, *Production and Operations Management,* 12(3), 404-415.

Polonsky, M. (2010) *Examining Carbon and General Environmental Information*, Proceedings from ISM-Open, Challenging Times, New Challenges, November, The Open University, Milton Keynes.

Royal Kingston (2011) Reduce, Reuse, Recycle, Available at http://www.kingston.gov.uk/browse/environment/recycling/reducing_reusing_and_recyclin g.htm.

SANZ (2009) *Strong Sustainability for New Zealand*, Sustainable Aotearoa New Zealand Inc., New Zealand.

Sheth, J.N., Sethia, N.K. & Srinivas, S. (2011) Mindful Consumption: A Customer-Centric Approach to Sustainability. *Journal of the Academy of Marketing Science,* 39, 21-39.

Simon, M. & Sweatman, A. (1997) *Products of a Sustainable Future*, Proceedings from the International Sustainable Development Research Conference, April, Manchester.

Soron, D. (2010) Sustainability, Self-Identity and the Sociology of Consumption, *Sustainable Development,* 18, 172-181.

Southwark Council (2011) Stalking Litter, Available at http://www.southwark.gov.uk/info/10111/environmental_campaigns_and_education/550/stalking_litter /1.

Stern, N. (2007) *Stern Review on the Economics of Climate Change,* Available at http://www.hmtreasury.gov.uk/independent_reviews/stern_review_economics_ climate_change/stern_review_report.cfm.

Sustainable Development Commission/National Consumer Council (2006) *I Will If You Will, Towards Sustainable Consumption,* Seacourt, London.

Szmigin, I., Carrigan, M. & McEachern, M.G. (2009) The Conscious Consumer: Taking a Flexible Approach to Ethical Behaviour. In: Peattie, K. and Collins, A. (Eds). Special Issue on Sustainable Consumption. *International Journal of Consumer Studies.* 33(2), 224-231.

The Global 100 (2010) Most Sustainable Corporations in the World, Available at http://www.global100.org/annual-reviews/2010-global-100-list.html?sort=company.

Thøgersen, J. & Crompton, T. (2009) Simple and Painless? The Limitations of Spillover in Environmental Campaigning, *Journal of Consumer Policy,* 32(2), 141-163.

Tukker, A., Huppes, G., Guinée, J., Heijungs, R., de Koning, A., Van Oers, L., Suh, S., Geerken, T., Van Holderbeke, M., Jansen, B. & Nielsen, P. (2005) *Environmental Impact of Products 9EIPRO): Analysis of the Life Cycle Environmental Impacts Related to the Final Consumption of the EU25,* IPTS/ESTO European Commission Joint Research Centre, Brussels.

Tucker, A., Cohen, M.J., Hubacek, K. & Mont, O. (2010) Sustainable Consumption and Production, *Journal of Industrial Ecology,* 14(1), 1-3.

Vale, R. & Vale, B. (2009) *Time to Eat the Dog? The Real Guide to Sustainable Living,* Thames & Hudson, London.

Vanclay, F. (2004) The Triple Bottom Line and Impact Assessment: How Do TBL, EIA, SIA, SEA and EMS Relate to Each Other? *Journal of Environmental Assessment Policy and Management,* 6(3), 265-288.

Vandenberg, M. (2002) Victoria Scoping Study - How Victorian Businesses, Governments and Non-Government Organisations Are Taking the Journey Towards the Triple Bottom Line, Available at www.ethyka.com/tbl/resources.

Van der Ryn, S. & Cowan, S. (1996) *Ecological Design,* Island Press, Washington.

Waage, S.A. (2007) Re-considering Product Design: A Practical "Road-Map" for Integration of Sustainability Issues, *Journal of Cleaner production,* 15, 638-649.

Walker, S. (2007) *Sustainable By Design: Explorations in Theory and Practice,* Earthscan, London.

Woensel, T.V., Creten, R.C. & Vandaele, N. (2001) Managing the Environmental Externalities of Traffic Logistics: The Issue of Emissions, *Production and Operations Management,* 10(2), 207-223.

Branding green energy: The roles of sustainability information and psychological brand benefits

PATRICK HARTMANN AND VANESSA APAOLAZA-IBÁÑEZ

ABSTRACT

Previous research suggests that information on sustainable product characteristics, such as reduced emissions due to renewable energy sources, should be taken into account to increase consumer demand for green energy. This paper proposes that psychological brand benefits should also be considered. The literature review identifies distinct categories of psychological benefits that may enhance the adoption of green energy brands by consumers. Empirical evidence confirms overall the relevance of both sustainability information and psychological brand benefits, and the authors discuss how findings may improve green energy branding strategy.

KEYWORDS

Environmental marketing, green energy, brand attitude, psychological benefits

Introduction

Sustainable energy supply constitutes one of the fundamental pillars of a sustainable society. Renewable energy generation technologies, besides energy saving, may hold the key to minimising environmental impact from growing energy demand. 'Green energy' or 'green power' refer to electricity generated using renewable energy resources and include technologies such as photovoltaic and thermoelectric solar energy, biomass, geothermal energy and wind farms. Salmela and Varho (2006) define with the term 'green electricity' as electricity produced from renewable sources and differentiated from other electricity products as environmentally friendly. Green energy is receiving widespread public and official support. In various regions of the world, such as many European countries, some states of the US as well as Australia, consumers are now able to exercise choice due to liberalisation of the energy markets. This allows them to choose from which energy company they receive their supply of energy and also whether or not the electricity is generated from renewable sources (Faiers, Cook & Neame 2007).

Green energy brands such as *Green Mountain Energy* in the US, *GreenChoice* in Australia, *Ecotricity* in the UK, *Lichtblick* in Germany, *NaturEnergie* in Austria and *Iberdrola Energía Verde* in Spain offer electricity from renewable sources. However, higher generation costs – and consequently higher market prices compared to conventional energy sources – constitute the principal barrier to consumer adoption of renewable energy (e.g. Salmela & Varho 2006; Zoellner, Schweizer-Ries & Wernheuer 2008). Accordingly, renewable energy generation depends mainly on subsidising government programs (Gan, Eskeland & Kolshus 2007). A market-based, customer-driven approach to renewable energy assumes that consumers will pay a premium for green electricity products (Nakarado 1996), overcoming their reluctance to pay a higher price for cleaner energies as compared to lower-priced conventional offerings (Roe, Teislb & Levy, 2001). However, whereas the share of renewable energy generation increases significantly each year and has reached already a significant proportion of total energy supply, actual market share of green energy brands remains low (Gan, Eskeland & Kolshus 2007).

The challenge for green marketing is to promote green energy to such an extent as to achieve a market-driven adoption of green energy by consumers' voluntary purchase at a price that covers actual generation costs in part or entirely (Wiser, Pickle & Goldman 1998). To promote renewable energy efficiently, behavioural aspects should be considered more deeply, because people are the initiators of change and the final consumers of energy (Schweizer-Ries 2008). Consequently, the profound understanding of consumer behaviour is a prerequisite for developing market strategies fostering consumer demand for renewable energy. In the aftermath of the oil crisis of the 1970s, the newly awakened public awareness of energy related issues drew the attention of consumer research (e.g. Hummel, Levitt & Loomis 1978; Labay & Kinnear 1981; McDougall, Claxton & Ritchie 1981). At present, a surge in behaviour research publications focusing on the adoption of green energy can be observed. Current research highlights the influences of cultural, social and psychological factors on the adoption of green energy by consumers (Faiers, Cook & Neame 2007; Yamamoto *et al.* 2008). For the marketing of green energy, most authors refer to the framework of green marketing of consumer goods (e.g. Paulos 1998). In particular, the success of green energy may depend on adequate marketing communication and branding strategy (Truffer, Markard & Wüstenhagen 2001). Since only green energy products perceived as offering more benefits than conventional energy services can compete at a premium price, using adequate branding to foster the benefit perception of consumers constitutes a critical factor for market success.

Fostering perceived brand benefits with sustainability information

Earlier research addressing advertising claims has shown that the information content of a significant number of environmental advertisements must be considered vague or even misleading (Carlson, Grove & Kangun 1993; Kangun, Carlson & Grove 1991). The difficulty of determining a product's or an organisation's true environmental stance has resulted in worldwide scepticism regarding green advertising (Kangun & Polonsky 1995). Following Carlson, Grove and Kangun's (1993) classifications, environmental claims can be considered either substantive or associative. Substantive claims present concrete, tangible benefits and provide information that enables and facilitates individual consumption decisions. Conversely, associative claims are image related or present environmental facts and merely link the organisation to an environmental cause. An international comparison found that though US advertisements tended to stress associative claims, advertisements from Australia, Great Britain and Canada appeared to emphasise process- and product-based claims (Carlson *et al.* 1996). Because of many consumers' high involvement regarding environmental issues as a consequence of growing environmental consciousness, most authors recommend providing detailed environmental product information in green advertising (e.g. Carlson *et al.* 1996; Cope & Winward 1991; Kinnear, Taylor & Ahmed 1974).

For consumers to perceive the environmental benefits of a green energy brand, they need a certain amount of information about the electricity supply and, in particular, the environmental impact of different electricity products (Salmela & Varho 2006). Research shows that consumers clearly want information on the environmental impact of products to inform adequate purchase decisions and that environmentally relevant information has an effect on these purchase decisions (Roberts 1996; Scholder-Ellen 1994). Exposure to information about energy resource issues leads to an increase in intention to pay a price-premium to support renewable energy (Zarnikau 2003), which is a fundamental condition for the consumer-driven adoption of green energy. Adequately informed consumers perceive that the adoption of green energy prevents or decelerates climate change and global warming, increases air quality and decreases energy dependence (Roe, Teislb & Levy, 2001). Since the objective of green power customers may be either to make sure that their money does not support unsustainable energy sources or to contribute to climate protection and growth of renewable energy by means of their purchasing decision (Wüstenhagen & Bilharz 2006), green advertising should provide relevant information on these issues. In particular, information on newly created renewable generation capacity and green electricity certification have been shown to correlate with price premiums actually paid on green electricity (Roe, Teislb, Levy, 2001). Eco-labelling of electricity may help consumers to identify energy products with genuine environmental benefits (Truffer, Markard & Wüstenhagen 2001). For instance, the Australian government issues the GreenPower label to certify that energy supply is from renewable sources. Research on environmental consumer behaviour shows that eco-labelling enhances consumer acceptance of environmentally sound products (D'Souza 2000, 2004). Official or third-party labelling schemes are, arguably, more credible than producers' own labels (D'Souza, Taghian & Lamb 2006; D'Souza *et al.* 2007). However, information delivered through current environmental labelling of energy products may be insufficient to inform adequate consumer choice. For example, in a recent study, purchasing decisions were shown to depend on whether consumers are exposed to energy-source-only or energy-source-plus-emissions information. Consumers may need more accurate and detailed information than offered by most current eco-labelling schemes (Johnson & Frank 2006). Green energy brand advertising should be aimed at filling this gap.

Figure 2.7 Green power label issued by the Australian government

Evoking psychological benefits

Warm glow

The purchase of green energy solely because of its environmental benefits would entail consumer altruism since individual consumers do not experience individual benefits from their contribution to environmental preservation. An improvement in relation to environmental hazards like global warming or social issues such as energy dependency could be experienced merely as a collective benefit – and only under the condition that most consumers worldwide would also adopt renewable energy. However, research shows that individuals contributing to the common good indeed experience a direct, private benefit, which Andreoni (1989, 1990) denominates the 'warm glow of giving', arising from the contribution itself. Consumers contributing to environmental conservation receive an intrinsic value – the 'warm glow' feeling of wellbeing as a consequence of moral satisfaction induced by the contribution to the common good environment (Kahneman & Knetsch 1992; Nunes & Schokkaert 2003; Ritov & Kahneman 1997). The warm glow approach is consistent with empirical research about the individual willingness to purchase green energy. People may pay a premium for green energy brands mainly because they wish to feel better with green energy and not because they are primarily interested in the objective environmental impact of their decision (Wüstenhagen & Bilharz 2006). Thus, while the environmental benefit of green energy is consumed by the society as a whole, green energy customers seem to also experience individual psychological warm glow benefits – drawing satisfaction from contributing to climate protection and energy independence (Menges, Schroeder & Traub 2005). Green energy brands are likely to be more successful when they foster the experience of warm glow by consumers evoking a sense of community and appealing to social values (Wiser 1998).

Status related benefits from conspicuous consumption

Research on conspicuous consumption suggests that consumers may also experience psychological benefits from socially visible consumption of environmentally friendly products. Costly signalling theory (Miller 2000) and research on competitive altruism (Roberts 1998; Van Vugt, Roberts & Hardy 2007) support this view, which focuses on status and reputation as motives for engaging in environmental behaviours. Signalling theory refers to the act of conveying information about oneself in an implicit fashion by engaging in behaviours that reveal one's traits and preferences to observers. Competitive altruism posits that conspicuous displays of altruism enhance pro-social reputations (Bird & Smith 2005). In addition to signalling that a person is pro-social, conspicuous altruism can simultaneously signal that one has sufficient time, energy, money or other valuable resources to afford giving away such resources without a negative impact on fitness and survival. In a recent series of experiments, Griskevicius, Tybur & Van den Bergh (2010) showed that activating status motives leads people to choose green products over non-green products. These authors argue that the consumption of green products can demonstrate to others that the individual is voluntarily willing and has sufficient resources to incur the cost of consuming a product that benefits environment and society but may be inferior for personal use (for instance, by driving a Toyota Prius hybrid vehicle). Green energy customers may experience psychological benefits as a consequence of conspicuous consumption, signalling to others their pro-social and pro-environmental orientation, as well as the capacity to incur additional costs for the sake of the environment and society. Consumers who, for instance, install rooftop solar panels may experience significant psychological benefits from signalling. However, customers of green electricity from an external provider may not experience this type of psychological benefit at all, since they do not consume electricity in a socially visible manner. Green energy marketers may overcome this limitation, in part, by providing customers with wall-certificates, stickers or other means of making green energy consumption visible from inside and outside of the customers' residences.

Associating nature imagery with the brand

In Banerjee, Gulas and Iyer's (1995) green advertising study, most of the sampled advertisements addressed the impact of the product or advertiser on the environment in general terms, using visuals depicting 'the beauty of nature'. The authors note that a typical example is an advertisement placed by a major oil company. The ad contained pictures of scenic mountains and valleys featuring the slogan 'We care about the environment'. This type of image-related claim fails to provide information that facilitates consumption decisions based on sound environmental reasoning, and Carlson *et al.* (1996) thus recommend advertisers avoid it. However, they also state that, ostensibly, when processing an ad with associative claims, consumers associate the claim with the brand to form a more benevolent perception of the organisation or product.

Figure 2.8 Nature experiences in Iberdrola's green energy advertising

Many print advertisements and commercials for green energy display pictures of pristine nature scenery. For instance, the communication campaigns of green energy brands *Meridian Energy* and *Iberdrola Green Energy* embed the brand in pleasant imagery of natural environments. Recipients' exposure to nature imagery can have two aims. On the one hand, images of unspoiled natural environments may increase the intensity of the consumer's environmental concern, and environmental concern has been shown to affect positively consumer purchase decisions for environmental products. On the other hand, the purpose may be to associate the brand with nature imagery in the consumer's perception. Extensive research from environmental psychology shows that contact with nature leads to a wide array of predominantly positive psychological and physiological responses (e.g. Cackowski & Nasar 2003; Hartig, Mang & Evans 1991; Kaplan 1995, 2001; Ulrich 1981, 1984). People seem to have an innate desire to experience nature (Wilson 1994), an emotional 'affinity with nature' (Lockwood 1999; Mayer & McPherson 2004). Kals, Schumacher & Montada (1999) or identify the human affinity toward nature such as 'loving nature' or 'feeling one with nature' as a motivational basis to protect natural environments. Contact with nature induces environmental protection behaviours (Hartig, Kaiser & Bowler 2001). The psychological effect of nature, however, is not limited to the contact with or visual exposure to 'real' nature. Photographic pictures or video recordings of nature have the capacity to evoke pleasant emotional states (e.g. pleasure feelings, relaxation) akin to those experienced in contact with actual nature (Kaplan & Kaplan 1989). The successful implementation of adequate communicational persuasion techniques (i.e. emotional conditioning or transformational advertising; Aaker & Stayman 1992; Allen & Madden 1985; Kim, Lim & Bhargava 1998; Kroeber-Riel

1984) can associate nature experiences in consumer perception with the brand. The association of a green energy brand with nature imagery may evoke additional psychological reward in consumers.

Empirical evidence

Study 1

The objective of Hartmann and Apaolaza-Ibáñez's (2007) representative personal survey of 2,020 Spanish households, carried-out together with the Spanish energy utility Iberdrola and the market research institute GfK, was to analyse brand associations, customer satisfaction and loyalty with respect to the Spanish energy providers. The results of structural equation analysis show that, among other brand associations, the perception of the brand as 'environmentally and socially committed' has a significant positive effect on satisfaction with the brand and customer loyalty (standardised regression coefficient [SRC]=.11, p=.02). In addition, one item of the questionnaire, measuring the degree to which consumers would appreciate that their energy supplier offered them the possibility to purchase renewable energy, received a 3.80 rating on a five point Likert-type scale. Less than four months after this study, the Spanish energy provider Iberdrola launched Iberdrola Green Energy, a new brand offering subscribers the possibility to purchase renewable energy. An intensive communicational branding campaign in print media, television and radio promoted the product launch.

Study 2

The data collection for Hartmann and Apaolaza-Ibáñez's (2008) study was carried out in the fourth and fifth month of the Iberdrola Green Energy branding campaign. The aim of this study was to analyse the effects of perceived sustainable product attributes and psychological brand benefits on consumer perceptions of the three principal energy brands in the Spanish market, including the Iberdrola Green Energy brand. The sample comprised 432 random street interviews. A comparison was made between the ratings of the statement 'Brand X cares about the environment' for all brands in this study and the results obtained in previous research before Iberdrola's green branding campaign (Hartmann, Apaolaza Ibáñez & Forcada-Sainz 2002). The comparison shows that the Iberdrola Green Energy brand is perceived as significantly more environmentally committed (p<.001) than the former Iberdrola corporate brand and any other of the competing brands in the study (Figure 2.9).

Furthermore, results of structural equation analysis show that subjects rating high on environmental concern showed significant and pronounced influence by evoked nature experiences (SRC=.84, p<.001) and somewhat less significant influence by perceived sustainable product attributes (SRC=.26, p=.014) on their attitude towards the analysed brands. Conversely, for environmentally unconcerned respondents, warm glow benefits (SRC=.40, p<.001) and nature experiences (SRC=.55, p<.001) have significant positive effects on brand attitude. The effect of sustainable product attributes seems to be absent in the latter case, while warm glow benefits do not seem to affect the brand attitude of concerned respondents. Also, status benefits derived from conspicuous consumption do not exert significant influences in either segment of the sample.

Figure 2.9 Perceived environmental commitment of competing energy brands before and after the Iberdrola Green Energy branding campaign

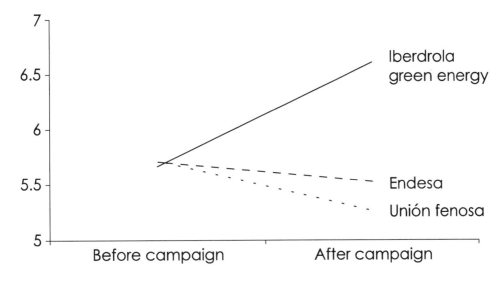

Source: Hartmann & Apaolaza-Ibáñez 2006, p. 227.

Furthermore, results of structural equation analysis show that subjects rating high on environmental concern showed significant and pronounced influence by evoked nature experiences (SRC=.84, p<.001) and somewhat less significant influence by perceived sustainable product attributes (SRC=.26, p=.014) on their attitude towards the analysed brands. Conversely, for environmentally unconcerned respondents, warm glow benefits (SRC=.40, p<.001) and nature experiences (SRC=.55, p<.001) have significant positive effects on brand attitude. The effect of sustainable product attributes seems to be absent in the latter case, while warm glow benefits do not seem to affect the brand attitude of concerned respondents. Also, status benefits derived from conspicuous consumption do not exert significant influences in either segment of the sample.

Study 3

Hartmann and Apaolaza-Ibáñez's (2009) study aimed to analyse the attitudinal effects of both the perception of environmentally friendly product attributes and the brand's association with nature imagery in the scope of a multi-product and multi-brand study. For this purpose, the authors conducted an experimental field study, which exposed 360 participants in five Spanish cities (Madrid, Barcelona, Bilbao, Vitoria and San Sebastián) to several experimental brands and print advertisements. Results of structural equation analysis show that, as hypothesized, both information on sustainable product attributes (SRC=.35, p<.001) and association with nature imagery (SRC=.45, p<.001) lead to significant positive effects on the consumer's attitude toward the brand. The exposure to pleasant nature imagery leads to the association of specific emotional experiences with the brand, which are to some extent comparable to those experienced in contact with nature (SRC=.59, p<.001). Findings confirm that the adequate association of a green brand with nature experiences leads to a significantly higher degree of brand attitude (p=.007) – as compared to the sole effect of informational claims.

Table 2.3 Influences of perceived sustainable product attributes and psychological brand benefits on consumer attitudes toward green energy brands (strong influence: ++, moderate influence: +, no significant influence: /)

	Environmentally concerned consumers	Environmentally unconcerned consumers
Sustainable product attributes	+	/
Warm glow	/	+
Conspicuous consumption benefits	/	/
Association with nature imagery	++	+

Study 4

To address the effect of different nature representations in green advertising on emotional responses and attitude toward the advertisement and brand, Hartmann and Apaolaza-Ibáñez's (2010) study exposes 750 participants randomly to different experimental green energy advertisements, each displaying a different natural landscape type. Results indicate that advertisements displaying images of pristine nature with lush green vegetation and clear water evoke the most favourable emotional responses (SRC=.19, p<.001). They lead to the highest-rated attitude toward the advertisement and the experimental green energy brand, mediated by the influence of emotional responses on attitude toward the ad (SRC=.68, p<.001) and the effect of attitude towards the ad on brand attitude (SRC=.46, p<.001).

Conclusions and implications

The wider customer-driven adoption of green energy is still in need of significant support. To foster consumer demand despite premium market prices, marketers should aim to increment perceived benefits of green energy brands with effective branding strategy. Research shows that the perception of sustainable product attributes, that is, reduced emissions due to renewable energy sources, affects the decision to adopt green energy. Therefore, brand communications should supply relevant and sufficiently detailed environmental product information. Current energy labelling schemes may prove too limited for this purpose. Green energy brand advertising should be aimed at filling this gap. Sustainability information supplied should include air emissions, energy mix and new renewable capacity installed (Johnson & Frank 2006; Salmela & Varho 2006; Truffer, Markard & Wüstenhagen 2001).

In addition to delivering utilitarian benefits to consumers, the consumption of green energy also seems to evoke psychological benefits. Empirical evidence supports the view that warm glow feelings rising from the experience of participating in the improvement of the common good environment contribute to consumer's decision for green energy (Wiser 1998; Wüstenhagen & Bilharz 2006). A major challenge is fostering the association of warm glow benefits with the green energy brand through adequate advertising. Messages should appeal to consumers' sense of community (Wiser 1998), stressing that they can 'feel good while doing good' to society and environment (Kahneman & Knetsch 1992; Ritov & Kahneman 1997).

On the other hand, the hypothetical effect of status motives and signalling derived from conspicuous consumption is not supported by the empirical research of the authors. The mainly private manner of energy consumption may hinder the perception of psychological benefits related to conspicuous consumption, which supposes the social visibility of product ownership and consumption. Findings are consistent with Griskevicius, Tybur and Van den Bergh (2010) insofar as these authors show that, in line with reputational benefits of self-sacrifice, status motives increase desire for green products only with conspicuous consumption. In addition, in line with cost-signalling theory, status motives increase desirability for green products especially if these are relatively expensive. Electricity, however, is a very basic non-expensive good, even at a significant price premium for green energy.

Finally, empirical evidence supports the authors' proposition that nature experiences can be associated with green energy brands, and that this additional psychological benefit enhances consumer attitudes toward the brand. Exposed to brand advertisements displaying photographic pictures of pleasant natural landscapes, participants in several empirical studies reported subsequently that the brand evoked feelings similar to those experienced in contact with nature. Psychological consumption experiences that share characteristics with emotions evoked by actual nature may satisfy the hypothetical human need or desire for contact with natural environments. Nature experiences as an additional psychological reward may increase perceived benefits of green energy brands and stimulate the adoption of renewable energy. Consequently, green energy branding campaigns should emphasise the relationship of the brand with nature. Advertising imagery should display photographic pictures of pristine natural landscapes with lush green vegetation and abundant clear water to evoke nature experiences as additional psychological brand benefit.

References

Aaker, D.A., Stayman, D.M. Implementing the concept of transformational advertising. Psychology & Marketing 1992; 9: 237-253.

Allen, C.T., Madden, T.J. A Closer Look at Classical Conditioning. Journal of Consumer Research 1985; 12: 301-315.

Andreoni, J. Giving with impure altruism: applications to charity and Ricardian equivalence. Journal of Political Economy 1989; 97: 1447-1458.

Andreoni, J. Impure altruism and donations to public goods: a theory of warm-glowing giving. The Economic Journal 1990; 100: 464-477.

Banerjee, B., Gulas, C.S., Iyer, E. Shades of green: a multidimensional analysis of environmental advertising. Journal of Advertising 1985; 24 (2): 21-31.

Bird, R., Smith, E.A. Signaling theory, strategic interaction, and symbolic capital. Current Anthropology 2005; 46: 221-248.

Cackowski, J.M., Nasar, J.L. The Restorative Effects of Roadside Vegetation. Environment and Behavior 2003; 35: 736-751.

Carlson, L., Grove, S.J., Kangun, N. A content analysis of environmental advertising claims: a matrix method approach. Journal of Advertising 1993; 22 (3): 27-39.

Carlson, L., Grove, S.J., Kangun, N., Polonsky, M.J. An international comparison of environmental advertising: Substantive versus Associative Claims. Journal of Macromarketing 1996; 16 (Fall): 57-68.

Cope, D., Winward, J. Information Failures in Green Consumerism. Consumer Policy Review 1991; 1: 83-86.

D'Souza, C. *Bridging the communication gap: dolphin-safe "ecolabels"*. Corporate Communications: An International Journal 2000; 5 (2): 185-190.

D'Souza, C. Ecolabel programmes: a stakeholder (consumer) perspective. Corporate Communications: An International Journal 2004; 9 (3): 179-188.

D'Souza, C., Taghian, M., Lamb, P. An empirical study on the influence of environmental labels on consumers. Corporate Communications: An International Journal 2006; 11 (2): 162-173.

D'Souza, C., Taghian, M., Lamb, P., Peretiatko, R. Green decisions: demographics and consumer understanding of environmental labels. International Journal of Consumer Studies 2007; 31 (4): 371-376.

Faiers, A., Cook, M., Neame, C. Towards a contemporary approach for understanding consumer behavior in the context of domestic energy use. Energy Policy 2007; 35 (8): 4381-4390.

Gan, L., Eskeland, G.S., Kolshus, H.H. Green electricity market development: Lessons from Europe and the US. Energy Policy 2007; 35: 144-155.

Griskevicius, V., Tybur, J.M., Van den Bergh, B. Going green to be seen: Status, reputation, and conspicuous conservation. Journal of Personality and Social Psychology 2010; 98: 392-404.

Hartig, T., Kaiser, F.G., Bowler, P.A. Psychological Restoration in Nature as a Positive Motivation for Ecological Behavior. Environment and Behavior 2001; 33: 590-607.

Hartig, T., Mang, M., Evans, G.W. Restorative Effects of Natural Environment Experiences. Environment and Behavior 1991; 23: 3-26.

Hartmann, P., Apaolaza Ibáñez, V. Effects of green brand communication on brand associations and attitude. Diehl, S., Terlutter, R. (eds) International Advertising and Communication. Current insights and empirical findings. Wiesbaden: Deutscher Universitäts-Verlag, 2006: 217-236.

Hartmann, P., Apaolaza Ibáñez, V., Forcada-Sainz F.J. El efecto del posicionamiento en la lealtad del cliente: un análisis empírico para el caso de Iberdrola. Cuadernos de Gestión 2002; 2: 103-118.

Hartmann, P., Apaolaza-Ibañez, V. Beyond savanna: An evolutionary and environmental psychology approach to behavioral effects of nature scenery in green advertising. Journal of Environmental Psychology 2010; 30 (1): 119-128.

Hartmann, P., Apaolaza-Ibáñez, V. Green advertising revisited: Conditioning virtual nature experiences. International Journal of Advertising 2009; 28 (4): 715-739.

Hartmann, P., Apaolaza-Ibañez, V. Managing customer loyalty in liberalized residential energy markets: The impact of energy branding. Energy Policy 2007; 35 (4): 2661-2672.

Hartmann, P., Apaolaza-Ibañez, V. Virtual Nature Experiences as Emotional Benefits in Green Product Consumption: The moderating role of environmental attitudes. Environment and Behavior 2008; 40 (6): 818-842.

Hummel, C.F., Levitt, L., Loomis, R.J. Perceptions of the energy crisis. Environment and Behavior 1978; 10: 37-88.

Johnson, B.B., Frank, P.G. Public understanding of environmental impacts of electricity deregulation. Energy Policy 2006; 34 (12): 1332-1343.

Kahneman, D., Knetsch, J.L. Valuing public goods: the purchase of moral satisfaction. Journal of Environmental Economics and Management 1992; 22: 57-70.

Kals, E., Schumacher, D., Montada, L. Emotional affinity toward nature as a motivational basis to protect nature. Environment and Behavior 1999; 31: 178-202.

Kangun, N., Carlson, L., Grove, S.J. Environmental Advertising Claims: A Preliminary Investigation. Journal of Public Policy & Marketing 1991; 10: 47-58.

Kangun, N., Polonsky, M.J. Regulation of Environmental Marketing Claims: A Comparative Perspective. International Journal of Advertising 1995; 14: 1-24.

Kaplan, R. The Nature of the View From Home: Psychological Benefits. Environment and Behavior 2001; 33: 507-542.

Kaplan, R., Kaplan, S. The experience of nature: A psychological perspective. New York: Cambridge University Press, 1989.

Kaplan, S. The restorative benefits of nature: Toward an integrative framework. Journal of Environmental Psychology 1995; 15: 169-182.

Kim, J., Lim, J-S., Bhargava, M. The role of affect in attitude formation: A classical conditioning approach. Journal of the Academy of Marketing Science 1998; 26: 143-152.

Kinnear, T.C., Taylor, J.R., Ahmed, S.A. Ecologically concerned consumers: Who are they?. Journal of Marketing 1974; 38: 20-24.

Kroeber-Riel, W. Emotional Product Differentiation by Classical Conditioning (with Consequences for the "Low-Involvement Hierarchy"). Advances in Consumer Research 1984; 11: 538-543.

Labay, D.G., Kinnear, T.C. Exploring the Consumer Decision Process in the Adoption of Solar Energy Systems. Journal of Consumer Research 1981; 8 (3): 271-278.

Lockwood M. Humans Valuing Nature: Synthesising Insights from Philosophy, Psychology and Economics. Environmental Values 1999; 8: 381-401.

Mayer, F.S., McPherson, F.C. The connectedness to nature scale: A measure of individuals' feeling in community with nature. Journal of Environmental Psychology 2004; 24: 503-515.

McDougall, G., Claxton, J., Ritchie, J.R.B. Consumer Energy Research: A Review. Journal of Consumer Research 1981; 8 (3): 343-354.

Menges, R., Schroeder, C., Traub, S. Altruism, Warm Glow and the Willingness-to-Donate for Green Electricity: An artefactual Field Experiment. Environmental & Resource Economics 2005; 31 (4): 431-458.

Miller, G.F. The mating mind: How sexual choice shaped the evolution of human nature. New York, NY: Doubleday, 2000.

Nakarado, G.L. A marketing orientation is the key to a sustainable energy future. Energy Policy 1996; 24 (2): 187-193.

Nunes, P.A.L.D., Schokkaert, E. Identifying the warm glow effect in contingent valuation. Journal of Environmental Economics and Management 2003; 45: 231-245.

Paulos, B. Green power in perspective: lessons from green marketing of consumer goods. The Electricity Journal 1998; 11 (1): 46-55.

Ritov, I., Kahneman, D. How People Value the Environment. Attitudes Versus Economic Values. In: Bazermann, M.H., Messick, D.M., Tenbrunsel, A.E., Wade-Benzoni, K.A., editors. Environment, Ethics, and Behavior. San Francisco: The New Lexington Press, 1997. pp. 33-51.

Roberts, G. *Competitive altruism: From reciprocity to the handicap principle.* Proceedings of the Royal Society of London B 1998; 265: 427-431.

Roberts, J.A. Green consumers in the 1990s: Profile and implications for advertising. Journal of Business Research 1996; 36 (July): 217-231.

Roe, B., Teislb, M.F., Levyc, A., Russell, M. US consumers' willingness to pay for green electricity. Energy Policy 2001; 29: 917-925.

Salmela, S., Varho, V. Consumers in the green electricity market in Finland. Energy Policy 2006; 34: 3669-3683.

Scholder-Ellen, P. Do we know what we need to know? Objective and subjective knowledge effects on pro-ecological behaviors. Journal of Business Research 1994; 30 (1): 43-52.

Schweizer-Ries, P. Energy sustainable communities: Environmental psychological investigations. Energy Policy 2008; 36: 4126-4135.

Truffer B., Markard J., Wüstenhagen R. Eco-labeling of electricity - strategies and tradeoffs in the definition of environmental standards. Energy Policy 2001; 29 (11): 885-897.

Ulrich, R.S. Natural Versus Urban Scenes. Environment and Behavior 1981; 13: 523-556.

Ulrich, R.S. View through a window may influence recovery from surgery. Science 1984; 224: 420-421.

Van Vugt, M., Roberts, G., Hardy, C. Competitive altruism: Development of reputation-based cooperation in groups. In: Dunbar, R., Barrett, L., editors. Handbook of evolutionary psychology. Oxford, England: Oxford University Press, 2007, pp. 531-540.

Wilson, R. Enhancing the outdoor learning environment of preschool programmes. Environment Education 1994; 46: 26-27

Wiser, R., Pickle, S., Goldman, C. Renewable energy policy and electricity restructuring: a California case study. Energy Policy 1998; 26: 465-475.

Wiser, R.H. Green power marketing: increasing customer demand for renewable energy. Utilities Policy 1998; 7: 107-119.

Wüstenhagen, R., Bilharz, M. Green energy market development in Germany: effective public policy and emerging customer demand. Energy Policy 2006; 34: 1681-1696.

Yamamoto, Y., Suzuki, A., Fuwa, Y., Sato, T. Decision-making in appliance use in the home. Energy Policy 2008; 36: 1679-1686.

Zarnikau, J. Consumer demand for 'green power' and energy efficiency. Energy Policy 2003; 31: 1661-1672.

Zoellner, J., Schweizer-Ries, P., Wemheuer, C. Public Acceptance of Renewable Energies: Results from Case Studies in Germany. Energy Policy 2008; 36: 4136-4141.

Chapter 3

Pricing

Adjusting prices for externalities

SUZANNE L CONNER AND MICHAEL R HYMAN

ABSTRACT

Pricing goods and services is, in and of itself, a daunting task. When organisations add externalities – the 'benefits or costs generated as an unintended by-product of an economic activity and where no compensation takes place' (Owen 2004, p. 129) – to their pricing deliberations, the task becomes even more onerous. Nonetheless, adjusting prices for externalities is critical to ensuring a habitable environment for future generations and the optimal economic incentives for eco-friendly innovation. In this chapter, we present a framework for setting prices that promotes maximum environmental and societal benefit. Our exposition proceeds as follows. We begin by examining the difficulties associated with assigning a monetary value to externalities. Next, we discuss allocating the externality cost burden to determine how, when, and who should incur it. Finally, we offer six questions – grounded in a cradle to grave pricing framework – to help structure thinking about externalities.

A complex problem

Setting a marketing-clearing price for a good or service remains a complex problem. The myriad of consumer, company and industry-related factors to consider include customers' willingness to pay, cost-benefit breakeven point, targeted profits and competitors' prices. Although its inclusion would further muddy this marketing quagmire, pricing texts typically ignore one socially and economically critical factor: externalities. Externalities may be positive or negative and are 'benefits or costs generated as an unintended by-product of an economic activity and where no compensation takes place' (Owen 2004, p. 129). Historically, marketers' externality avoidance may be an artefact of accounting systems that systematically exclude environmental costs (Herbig & Butler 1993). Regardless, many organisations are adopting eco-friendly practices.

Several mechanisms increase the likelihood that future generations will inherit a habitable environment with sufficient natural resources: government regulation/legislation, positive (e.g. subsidies, rebates) and negative (e.g. taxes, fees) incentives, moral suasion and price adjustments for major externalities. Although popular with left-leaning legislators and regulators, the imposition of science-informed environmental standards on an industry (e.g. CAFE regulations for internal combustion vehicles) exposes the satisfaction of society's needs to a political process that is warpable by special interest groups pandering to politicians and an electorate lacking foresight. In addition, such standards may stifle competition and eco-friendly production innovations by creating market entry barriers (Fullerton & Metcalf 2001).

The subsidising of eco-friendly production and consumption may direct funds to activities that, in fact, require no inducement (e.g. efforts by universities to recycle paper). The result could be short-term environmental destruction conducive to higher future subsidies and rebates (Engel, Pagiola & Wunder 2008). For example, government-sponsored rebates may entice consumers to buy more eco-friendly products, yet eco-stressing durable goods often are the most heavily promoted and enticing. In essence, such subsidies represent an inefficient expenditure of public funds.

Pollution-deterring taxes and fees, which in developed countries are often meant to fund eco-friendly public works (e.g. a light rail system), can fail in developing countries. In these countries pollution-producing exports pay for vital imports or and landowners often cannot absorb additional costs (Engel, Pagiola & Wunder 2008); thus the governments use the revenue raised to reduce poverty rather than to control pollution (Blackman & Harrington 2000). More generally, such taxes and fees on manufacturing inputs may adversely affect untargeted industries or inspire black markets (Blackman & Harrington 2000). For example, mining coal creates eco-damage in the form of pollution (e.g. water, noise and dust), acid rain, methane, subsidence, defoliation, soil degradation and harm to wildlife. Relative to other fossil fuels, burning coal produces more carbon dioxide emissions per British Thermal Unit (BTU) (Hong & Slatick 1994; NaturalGas.org 2010). However, coal is more than a fuel source; it is also a component of aspirin, dyes, cosmetics, toothpaste, soap, water, air filters and lightweight composite materials. Taxing coal to deter eco-damage would affect the manufacturers of these products.

Moral suasion – convincing people to do the right thing because to do otherwise would be wrong – may fail to foster underlying beliefs consistent with eco-friendly behaviours; specifically, changing beliefs about moral obligations may or may not influence behaviours (Hopper & Nielson 1991; Tanner & Kast 2003). Movies such as *An Inconvenient Truth* and well-publicised eco-disasters such as BP's Deepwater Horizon oil rig disaster may raise ecological awareness without reducing oil consumption because consumers often doubt the impact of their personal actions (Gupta & Ogden 2009). Even eco-conscious consumers may fail to connect their beliefs and actions (Alsmadi 2007; do Paco & Raposo 2010).

In this chapter, we present a framework for setting prices that promote maximum environmental and societal benefit. Our exposition proceeds as follows. We begin by examining the difficulties associated with assigning a monetary value to externalities. Next, we discuss allocating the externality cost burden to determine how, when, and who should incur it. Finally, we offer a basic question set – to help structuring thinking about externalities – grounded in a cradle-to-grave pricing framework.

Difficulty in assigning a monetary value to externalities

Lacking pressure to do otherwise, producers historically have minimised or ignored externalities when setting prices. In addition to economic disincentives, such as reduced profits, it remains difficult to calculate welfare loss, health impacts, opportunity costs, and eco-system degradation (Bickel *et al.* 2006; Goldman 1972). However, new legislative efforts, such as California's cap and trade allowances, India's carbon tax on coal, and New York's Electronic Equipment Recycling and Reuse Act (Baker 2010; Department of Environmental Conservation 2010; Pearson 2010), will force corporations to consider the cost of their pollution and waste.

Positive versus negative externalities

To account for the full cost of a product, including the environmental impact on current and future generations, producers must consider positive and negative externalities. Producers and government frequently focus on positive externalities, which are benefits accrued to non-payers. For example, all of society benefits when a person receives a flu shot, as that person can no longer spread the flu – thus increasing overall worker productivity and reducing health care costs. Although eco-friendly coffee farming under natural shade canopies produces lower yields, advocates tout the concomitant carbon sequestration, reduced soil erosion, flood control and preserved wildlife habitats and local cultural values (Heidkamp, Hanink & Cromley 2008; Pretty *et al.* 2001; Randall 2007). Positive environmental externalities include the benefits of open space, outdoor recreation and tourism (Randall 2007). In general, positive externalities vary by their nature, scope (e.g. local versus global) and recipients (e.g. consumers or society-at-large).

Nonetheless, non-governmental organisations, lobbyist groups and public policy makers tend to focus on negative externalities such as air and noise pollution, greenhouse gas emissions, oil dependency, urban sprawl, disposal of products, climate change, soil and water deterioration, chemical leakage and damage, and visual pollution (Bickel *et al.* 2006; Parry, Walls & Harrington 2007). Negative externalities are more noticeable (e.g. a polluted stream, a landfill) and simpler to valuate; although difficult, it is easier to calculate the cost of dredging the Chesapeake Bay for polychlorinated biphenyls (PCBs) and the value of increased seafood production (Blankenship 2002) than the value of a pristine Grand Canyon National Park. In addition, the aforementioned groups frequently leverage negative externalities into political and/or financial gains (Zilberman 2002). In 2009, The Nature Conservancy, whose mission is 'to preserve the plants, animal, and natural communities that represent the diversity of life on Earth by protecting the lands and waters they need to survive' (The Nature Conservancy 2011), spent more than $2 million on environmental lobbyists (Center for Responsive Politics 2011). Total spending for environmental lobbying that year was more than $22 million (Center for Responsive Politics 2011).

Note that producers can couch any negative externality as a positive externality and vice versa; for example, eliminating a water-polluting manufacturing process is identical to installing a non-water-polluting process. Typically, political considerations, such as marshalling public support critical to passing environmental legislation, determine the positive or negative positioning of an externality. After all, voters asked to subsidise a new production facility are more likely to be swayed by arguments for reducing unemployment (avoiding a negative) than by arguments for creating new jobs (achieving a positive) (Steinacker 2006). Regardless, avoiding a negative externality and achieving the reverse positive externality are mathematically equivalent.

Calculating net present value of externalities

The value of a resource to future generations cannot be calculated with certainty. For example, global gas production will peak within 50 years and oil production will peak sooner (Meadows, Randers & Meadows 2004). Concurrently, an expanding world economy will consume ever-greater amounts of natural gas and petroleum-based fuels unless alternatives like algae-based biofuel or solar electric plants (Howell 2009; Motavalli 2009) are developed and sold. As demand outstrips supply, prices will rise – especially given the current dependence on hydrocarbons for non-fuel purposes (e.g. plastics, roads and fertilisers) (News of the Future 2011; Oil Price 2011). However, if new transportation and power generation technologies obviate demand for gas and oil, or if consumers can avoid petrochemical-based products, then both the demand for and price of natural gas and petroleum will decrease. The uncertainty surrounding new technologies and consumer lifestyle changes illustrates one of many problems associated with calculating the future value of any natural resources.

Valuation of positive externalities is equally difficult because it entails an assessment of society's environmental preference, the benefits received and the recipients of those benefits. Fundamental assumptions include the implicit discount rate, the future value of natural resources and the desired lifestyles and habitats of future generations. To calculate the net present value of eco-resources requires suppositions about the needs and preferences of future generations. Perhaps future generations will prefer lifestyles unrelated to current eco-preferences (John & Pecchenino 1994). For example, societies may dwell in closed ecological compounds analogous to the Biosphere 2 project (Sagan 2007). Vertical hydroponic and aeroponic farming may eliminate the need for arable soil and the high-cost transporting and warehousing of crops (*Hydroponic Farming* 2010; Wikipedia 2011a). New technologies may not require feedstocks depleted by current production methods (e.g. petroleum) (Forester 1988; USC Energy Institute 2010). Voluntary simplicity or the consumption of experiences may come to dominate consumption of goods (Cave 2010). The realisation of such forecasts would dictate a high discount rate as people living in such a society would minimally value globally clean air, water and soil.

Allocating the cost burden

Assuming a price reflective of the total societal cost is calculable, is it possible to allocate the cost burden equitably? The answer requires consideration of several who, what and how questions. Industry-level profits, historical acceptance of business practices by consumers and consumer willingness to pay, all influence the allocation of costs between producers and consumers. In some cases, producers can pass all externality costs to consumers; in other cases, producers can pass only the most important costs to consumers due to the difficulty in determining and subsequently quantifying all externalities (Bickel *et al.* 2006).

Who should pay environmental costs?

Legislation often determines who should pay for environmental costs. Although many self-identifying 'green' consumers will pay more for eco-friendly goods (Laroche, Bergeron & Barbaro-Forleo 2001) or sacrifice product quality for eco-sustainability (Shrum, McCarty & Lowrey 1995), consumption trends suggest that most consumers will avoid similar trade-offs. Sans legislation, beneficiaries may prefer to forego payment for positive externalities, consumers may resist higher prices to cover the costs of negative externalities, and shareholders may be unwilling to earn reduced profits.

The beneficiaries of positive externalities may be unwilling to pay for them. Many people might believe that their enjoyment of a national park, a recreational lake or the by-product of a high-quality educational system, is an inherent right. As a result, they may oppose legislation that would assess taxes or fees on such benefits.

The 'free rider' problem is a by-product of efforts to create a positive externality. Free riders are members of a group who 'contribute little or nothing toward the cost of the good, while enjoying the benefits as fully as any other member of the group' (Kim & Walker 1984, p. 3). Although any preferred cost allocation system would eliminate free riders, current law typically precludes firms from charging recipients for unrequested benefits (Porat 2009).

Willingness to pay is a useful device for assessing consumers' valuation of environmental goods (Söderholm & Sundqvist 2003). Nonetheless, consumers who seemingly value environmental preservation may be unwilling to pay for it (Stevens *et al.* 1991). For example, consumers may opt for less expense alternative goods manufactured in countries with minimal or no eco-safeguards rather than pay more for goods produced in countries with more stringent environmental regulation.

Although some investors will accept lower returns to support eco-friendly companies (thus explaining the growth of socially responsible investing), other investors seek only to maximise profits. The latter investors will balk when companies volunteer to pay for negative externalities by reducing earnings rather than passing costs onto consumers.

Companies forced to cover the costs of negative externalities often shift a portion of these costs onto consumers through higher prices and/or decreased product availability (Keohane & Olmstead 2007). When remaining costs preclude shareholder-required profits, companies may quit production, thus reducing product assortment. Alternatively, companies can shift production to locations with laxer environmental regulations, thus perpetuating the original negative externalities and perhaps incurring additional ones associated with increased transportation costs (McGuire 1982).

When should environmental costs be paid?

After deciding 'who should pay', the next step is deciding when they should pay. Should payment be made at purchase, during usage, at disposal or some combination of these times?

A combination of payment approaches may be best for consumer products. Payment only at purchase is the most common method because it is easiest to administer; however, it cannot account properly for type of usage, length of usage or disposal. For example, assume two consumers bought the same car make and model. During the next five years, Consumer X drove 100,000 mostly inner-city miles and Consumer Y drove 50,000 mostly rural miles. As Consumer X caused more eco-damage than Consumer Y, the former should incur a larger usage penalty, but this only is assessable post-consumption (e.g. during assessment of the annual vehicle registration fee). In addition, only Consumer Y followed recommended maintenance procedures; as a result, Consumer X's car is ready for salvage while Consumer Y's car remains a useful asset. Clearly, an excise tax cannot account for usage behaviours, and usage fees cannot account for car disposal; hence, a series of payments is needed to properly capture the eco-costs of car ownership. As a positive by-product, this would motivate more careful car usage and disposal.

The ideal payment schedule would differ by consumer product. For example, an excise tax alone is appropriate to account for eco-damage caused by using rolls of paper towels; whereas a combination of fees – including congestion tolls, sales taxes, fuel taxes, road use taxes, mileage taxes, emission taxes and disposal fees – would be appropriate for gasoline-powered cars (Parry, Walls & Harrington 2007). For services, eco-damage fees should be incurred at the time of usage because, for all services, the final product is not produced until time of delivery.

Eco-payments by producers of capital goods, which are the inputs for consumer products, should not be redundant of the eco-payments of consumers, as the latter payments cover usage and disposal exclusively, not manufacturing externalities. Because capital goods 'contribute about 20% to cumulative fossil and about 50% to the cumulative nuclear demand' (Frischknecht *et al.* 2007, p. 9), their eco-impact cannot be ignored. At the appropriate stage in the green lifecycle (see section entitled 'Cradle-to-grave pricing'), producers would pay the eco-costs associated with inputs such as 'electricity, construction materials and metals, agricultural products and processes, as well as transport and waste management services' (Frischknecht *et al.* 2007, p. 4).

Payment options for reducing negative externalities and boosting positive externalities

Several payment and reimbursement options exist for consumers and producers. For producers, the options include taxes, fees, tradable emission permits, legal penalties and fines. For consumers, the options include tax credits and rebates (e.g. Cash for Clunkers), rewards for eco-friendly actions or purchases (e.g. RecycleBank), discounts for renting rather than owning, shared ownership, voluntary payments (e.g. carbon offsets) and externality-inclusive prices.

Taxes

Federal, state and local governments can impose taxes, which come in many forms. Sales, use and disposal taxes can be imposed on consumers; eco-taxes such as carbon taxes, duties, disposal taxes and pollution taxes can be borne by producers.

Pigovian taxes are 'equal to the marginal environmental damage' (Goodstein 2003, p. 402). Pigou noticed that pollution created costs for third parties who were excluded from the original transaction (Owen 2004). To overcome this limitation, his proposed tax internalised negative pollution externalities into normal market transactions. Benefits of Pigovian taxes include setting prices in accord with full societal costs and generating tax revenues that could offset less popular revenue sources (Goodstein 2003). One limitation – discouraging firms from producing goods subject to Pigovian taxes – may boost unemployment in some industry sectors and spur overproduction in other industry sectors (McKitrick & Collinge 2000).

Shifting taxes is another possibility. For example, corporate income tax rates could be lowered – thereby stimulating the economy and reducing unemployment – while taxes on resource usage, pollution and waste could be introduced. This tax incidence shift would spur firms to reduce resource usage and adopt innovative production technologies (Hawken, Lovins & Lovins 1999). Personal income and sales taxes could be lowered for consumers who buy more eco-friendly products – for example, lower registration fees for relatively eco-friendly cars – thus shifting society's overall tax burden onto companies.

Fees

Usage fees, 'feebates', could be imposed on consumers who prefer to use fewer eco-friendly products. For the auto industry, a feebate is a 'market-based alternative in which vehicles with fuel consumption rates above a certain point are charged fees while vehicles below receive rebates' (Greene *et al.* 2005, p. 757). The French attach a feebate to automobile purchases. Buyers receive a rebate if they purchase a low-emission vehicle but pay a fee if they purchase a high-emission vehicle. France may extend this program to other types of products (Green 2008). Feebates may encourage eco-friendly innovations by manufacturers as well as changes in consumption behaviour. For a commercial building or residence, the buyer would either receive a feebate or pay a fee based on the structure's relative energy efficiency (Hawken, Lovins & Lovins 1999). Minnesota has initiated a program that encourages cities to become greener; one requirement to be a GreenStep City is to use 'volume-based pricing on residential garbage and/or feebates on recycling' (Minnesota 2010).

Tradable emission permits

In 2010, California legislated the first cap-and-trade system in the US (Baker 2010). Under this system, states sell companies a permit that allows pollution at a certain level. Because companies can trade these permits among themselves, lesser polluters derive a market-rate profit from the sale of their unused pollution allowance to another company. Reducing the pollution cap over time encourages companies to develop ever-cleaner production methods.

Legal penalties and fines

Traditionally, industrialised countries have used laws and regulations – in the form of standards, bans, licensing, monitoring and non-compliance fines – to address environmental policy (Owen 2004). In essence, governments fine firms that behave outside eco-responsible norms. The US Environmental Protection Agency administers laws on hazardous air and water pollution as well as other environmental concerns (U.S. EPA 2010a, b); the EU Directorate-General for the Environment proposes environmental policies and enforcing environmental laws (European Commission 2010).

Tax credits and rebates

By lowering the net price of eco-friendly goods and services, tax credits and rebates encourage more eco-friendly consumption. For example, the US government – through the *Energy Policy Act (2005)* – gave tax credits to consumers who bought hybrid gas-electric cars, alternative-fuel vehicles, fuel-cell vehicles or select diesel vehicles. Vehicle weight, fuel efficiency and date of credit sunset determined the credit amount. Several states also offered rebates on such vehicles (e.g. Illinois gave $1,000 rebates and Pennsylvania gave $500 rebates) (Hybrid Center 2011). The US Department of Energy developed similar programs to spur energy-efficient home improvements like improved heating and cooling equipment, insulation and windows (U.S. Department of Energy 2011).

Rewards for eco-friendly actions or purchases

Companies have developed reward programs for consumers who behave in more eco-friendly ways. For example, RecycleBank offers reward points for activities such as home and electronic recycling, switching to a greener energy source and reselling items on ebay.com (RecycleBank 2010). Consumers can redeem reward points for merchandise, services and charitable donations.

Discounts for renting rather than owning and shared ownership

At the non-hedonic end of the durable goods spectrum, Zipcar – founded in 2000 and now located in the U S, UK and Canada – allows members to rent a car by the hour or day. The vehicles are available from various city locations and college campuses. The rental fee covers up to 180 miles per day, gasoline and insurance. Renters need only to reserve a car, pick it up and return it by the deadline. Relative to car owners, Zipcar members typically save more than $500 per month; in addition, each Zipcar in service removes an estimated 15–20 personally owned vehicles from roadways (Zipcar 2011).

In contrast, consumers increasingly obtain luxury goods via fractional/shared ownership, which began with residential real estate in the 1970s (Garigliano 2007). Companies such as Curvy Road offer fractional ownership of luxury cars such as Bentleys, Ferraris and Lamborghinis. For a membership fee plus a commitment to pay for either four or eight weeks of use per year, fractional owners receive a car delivered to their home or office, insurance, repairs, pre-paid tolls and a mileage allowance (Curvy Road 2010). By fractionally owning a luxury car, affluent consumers can mitigate eco-damage by eliminating the capital inputs that would have been needed to produce multiple cars that often sit idle.

Voluntary payments

Moral suasion can motivate socially responsible consumers to make discretionary payments related to the eco-repair costs concomitant with their consumption behaviour. Carbon offset restitution, which travel industry companies such as Enterprise Holding, Inc. have initiated, is an example of such payments. In this case, customers opt to pay $1.25 per rental to fund certified carbon offset projects meant to remove CO_2 from the atmosphere. '[E]very 100,000 customers who choose to take part in this program…will offset more than 30 million pounds…of CO_2' (Enterprise Holdings, Inc. 2010). Other travel companies, such as airlines and hotels, also offer voluntary carbon offset payment options to travellers. Even the wedding industry is being targeted by companies like TerraPass, which provide online carbon footprint calculators and shopping carts through which consumers can make a carbon offset payment to support an environmental project (TerraPass 2011). The Carbonfund donation program, which attempts to balance emissions created by consumer lifestyle choices, allows consumers to calculate their own carbon footprint and make a comparable tax-deductible donation; in turn, Carbonfund supports projects that reduce carbon dioxide emissions (Carbonfund 2010).

Externality-inclusive prices

Adjusting prices for externalities can account for positive and negative externalities. Eco-transparent prices would allow consumers to consider the true cost of a product or service and thus make a better-informed purchase decision. Manufacturers could adopt more eco-friendly production methods that would permit lower prices that in turn would boost sales. Because externality-inclusive pricing may be the most equitably derived method for appropriating costs across different lifestyles and consumption patterns, this method may be the most effective. The question set that follows assumes this payment option.

What are the political constraints?

Political constraints haunt all pricing efforts other than voluntary programs (e.g., rewards for eco-friendly behaviours and shared ownership) to adjust prices for externalities. Without massive election reform, the self-interests of well-heeled corporations and industry groups will guarantee a public inundated with pro-business (non-eco-friendly) advocacy advertising and politicians beholden to such business entities. After all, taxpayers typically resist tax increases regardless of merit, and if given the choice, would likely vote against politicians who support them. The development and oversight of regulatory eco-friendly programs (e.g. tradable emission permits) would shift resources from more politically popular programs. Likewise, the funds to support rebates and tax credits must be siphoned from an already overcommitted pool of tax dollars.

Thus, well-intentioned producers and consumers alone are insufficient to address eco-issues. Rather than induce the myopic self-interest-preserving actions of each stakeholder group, the political environment could facilitate the adoption of an externality-inclusive pricing scheme that properly values and encourages eco-friendly behaviours. For example, some European countries have added an eco-tax on disposable bottles and batteries (Rajah & Smith 1994).

Cradle-to-grave pricing

A green lifecycle, also called 'cradle-to-grave' or 'whole life' costing (Owen 2004), 'includes impacts along the entire continuum of a product's life from raw material extraction, through manufacturing, distribution and transportation, use, recycle, and ultimately to final disposal' (Boje 1999). These impacts include energy and resource consumption as well as environmental discharges (Hendrickson *et al.* 1998). A cradle-to-grave approach would account equitably for externalities in the pricing of products and services by assessing each externality at each stage of the production and consumption process.

Pricing questions

Although not a pricing model, our preliminary set of six questions can help structure producers' thoughts about externality-inclusive prices and serve as a basis for future models. The set includes questions, applicable at each stage of the product lifecycle, to help identify the economic costs and benefits of externalities. Once determined, the costs of positive and negative externalities should be subtracted from or added to the cost of the product so that its price reflects its total cost/benefit to society.

Question 1: In what type of economic system is the product available (i.e. free market, planned economy, mixed economy)?

This predominantly political question relates to 'who pays'—a previously addressed issue—rather than to 'total cost'. The type of government and economic system may affect the externality payment structure and process; thus, the issue is 'control' of externalities and the answer to this question will affect answers to the remaining questions.

In an unregulated market, pricing and moral suasion provide the only controls. For example, publishers may produce books in hard copy or electronic form and price each form in accord with the cost of production, distribution and disposal. Readers are free to purchase the version that provides the greatest relative value to them.

Resource overuse characterises many unregulated markets. For example, farmers may not rotate crops to maintain soil balances when a key cash crop is more profitable. When beef prices are high, ranchers may allow cattle to overgraze. Without controls, public assets may be exploited. In the *Tragedy of the Commons* (Hardin 1969), public resources such as open grazing lands and public parks are overused because each person has no incentive to moderate use. As a result, these common resources become depleted and unavailable to future generations

In a planned economy, the state would allocate externality costs among all stakeholders. As apportionment is a political and value-based process, the state – relative to producers or consumers – is likely to assign more weight to higher societal needs, such as impact on economic growth, health care costs and the like. In a regulated market, countervailing powers (Galbraith 1956) will determine apportionment.

Government control means citizens' preferences have little influence over resource usage. Eliminating personal property ownership can erase the first line of defence against environmental disruption, as individual citizens do not 'suffer losses, create restraints, or voice objections' (Goldman 1972, p. 325). Under this system, managers earn premiums for increasing production and may willingly swap pollution fines for production bonuses (Goldman 1972). When governments begin to control natural resources, 'either socialism or the privatism of free enterprise' may follow

(Hardin 1998, p. 683). Without management of the commons, the overuse of resources will reduce carrying capacity and 'ruin is inevitable' (Hardin 1998, p. 683). Even with leasing of national lands for grazing – under which some governmental control exists – ranchers continue to pressure authorities to increase head-counts, which worsens soil erosion and weed infestation in turn (Hardin 2009).

In a mixed economy, both government entities and private concerns control resource usage. Public policy makers may dictate that certain activities are cost prohibitive, like the negative health externalities associated with using lead-based paints or selling sugar-filled soft drinks in US public schools. In these two cases, producers and sellers bear the entire cost burden of now-banned products. Public policy makers also may create regulations and pass legislation that determines and allocates cost burdens; for example, the Alar (an apple pesticide) ban by the US Environmental Protection Agency or the CAFE standards for motor vehicles set by the US National Highway Traffic Safety Administration. Although producers may absorb some of the increased cost of production associated with such regulations and legislation, most of the additional cost of production is borne by consumers.

Besides governmental control, private enterprise also controls resource utilisation in a mixed economy. Managers in privately owned firms make strategic and tactical decisions (if not prohibited by government regulations), while consumer demand determines the products to be sold and their selling price. Centralised government planning of production is unnecessary.

The point is that the economic system will determine cost allocation, which has political and marketing implications. In unregulated markets, profit-driven producers have incentives to hide negative externalities. In a planned economy, the state has incentives to maximise the long-run welfare of the state, even at the expense of individual freedoms and initiatives. In mixed economies, producers have incentives to downplay negative externalities because they will bear the costs at least in part.

Question 2: What stage of the product life cycle is being considered, and what are the externalities concomitant with that stage?

There are many equitable ways to adjust prices for externalities. For example, a value-centric approach would identify the highest cost/benefit externalities and then adjust prices only for those externalities. An input-centric approach would first group inputs by type (e.g. energy, precious metals) and then calculate the total cost/benefit for each type. Instead, we advocate a lifecycle approach because it allocates costs/benefits to the proximate parties to those costs/benefits (i.e. the parties most motivated to minimise costs and maximise benefits), is widely accepted by industry for 'pollution prevention and green design efforts' (Hendrickson *et al.* 1998, p. 184) and is implementable via extant software packages (Hendrickson *et al.* 1998). In fact, both the International Standards Organisation and US Environmental Protection Agency recommend this approach (Joshi 2000).

By assessing the positive and negative externalities encountered at each stage of production, usage, and disposal – a decompositional approach – producers can calculate a societally fair price that includes eco-costs/benefits. A stage-by-stage analysis ensures prices are adjusted for most, if not all, externalities. Figure 3.1 shows the stages of a product lifecycle from raw mineral extraction through disposal/recycling. This figure serves as a reminder of the various stages and a prompt for the externalities associated with each stage. Of course, waste from some processes can be inputs for other processes; as a result, producers can pass repeatedly through the following stages.

Preproduction

For manufacturers, negative externalities in this stage include energy production and consumption, natural resource extraction and depletion, and environmental pollution (e.g. air, water, visual, noise). For example, the hydroelectric dams in the Pacific Northwest produce energy but disrupt salmon spawning, which damages the fishing industry (Keohane & Olmstead 2007). Negative transportation-related externalities include additional roadway development (which may decrease usable farmland), roadway congestion and marine debris (e.g. goods inadvertently dumped mid-ocean from container ships (Wikipedia 2011b)). Extracting raw materials from one region and transporting them to another region or importing components for durable goods manufacture, creates negative externalities. A major goal of the 'local food movement' is to reduce the cost of transporting foods from farm to consumer (Sustainable Table 2011).

The research and design process concomitant with this stage may create negative externalities (e.g. energy expended in office buildings, paper disposal) and positive externalities (e.g. inventing a new eco-friendly technology that lowers production costs; substituting a rare input critical to producing other products). Because 'more than 90% of a product's cost is determined in preproduction phases' (Chapman, Hopwood & Shields 2007, p. 743), the preproduction stage is critical to all subsequently incurred positive and negative externalities.

Production

Production-related negative externalities include the various types of pollution (e.g. noise, air, visual, land and water) and the consumption of nonrenewable resources. To illustrate, Figure 3.2 shows the stages in the manufacture of plastic products during which pollution (e.g. contaminated wastewater, toxic chemicals) and solid waste are created (U.S. EPA 2005).

Figure 3.1 Product life cycle

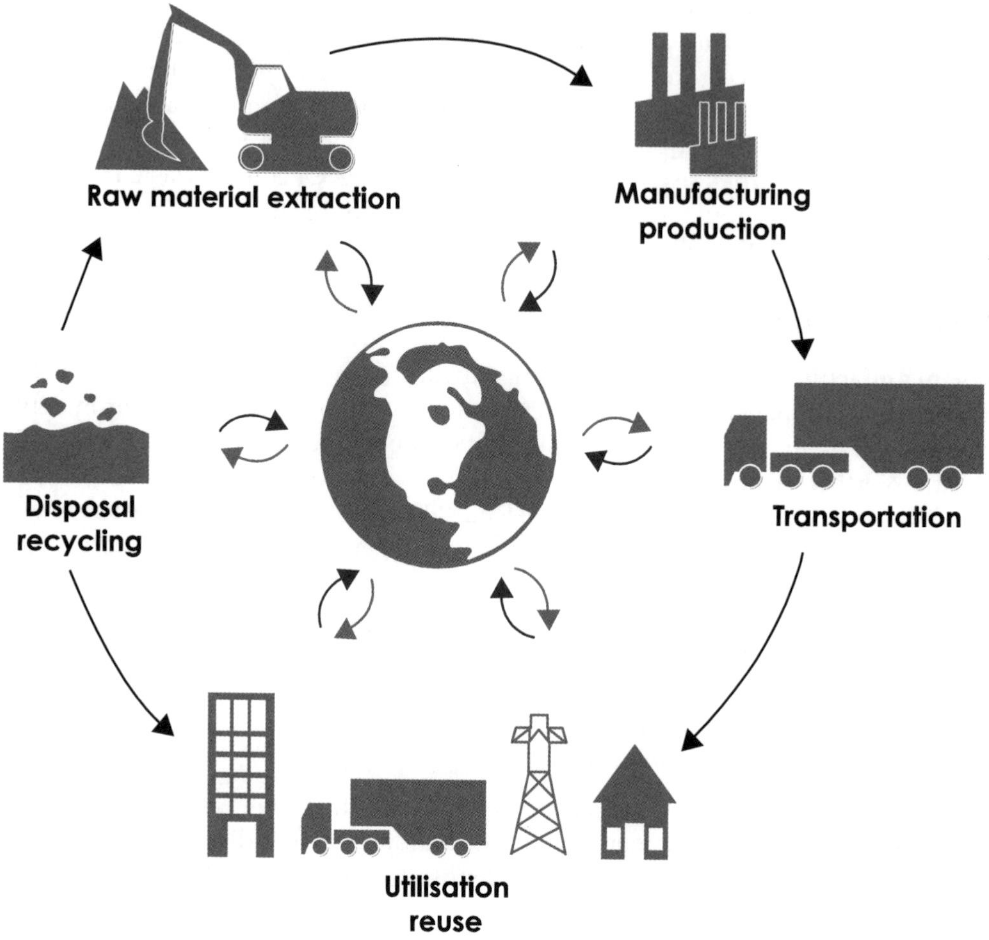

Source: Engineering 2008.

For manufacturers, negative externalities in this stage include energy production and consumption, natural resource extraction and depletion, and environmental

This stage may yield other negative externalities. For example, firms with lax safety standards pose higher risks to workers specifically and society in general as BP's Deepwater Horizon oil rig disaster illustrates. This incident squandered natural resources, financially crippled the Gulf Coast recreation and tourism industry, decimated the Gulf fishing industry and harmed consumers by depressing local housing prices.

The production phase also may create positive externalities. A firm that refurbishes an abandoned warehouse transforms a public eyesore into an aesthetically pleasing asset for the community. Companies can adapt manufacturing processes to use the waste by-products of other manufacturing processes as inputs; an extreme example is closed loop eco-parks. For example, sawmills produce large quantities of sawdust. Normally considered an environmental hazard, sawdust can be used to smoke meat, as an abrasive in soaps and polishes, as a packing material, as a soil nutrient and water retainer and as roughage for feedstocks (Harkin 1969).

Figure 3.2 Production stages for plastic products

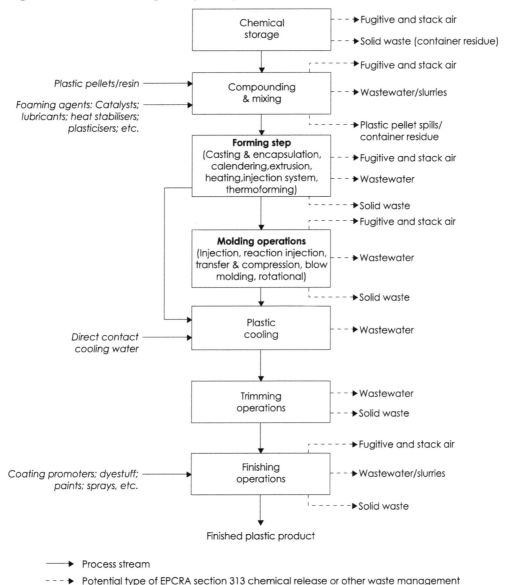

Source: U.S. EPA 2005, p. 16.

Regardless, input prices may not reflect externalities unincorporated in the cost of subcontracted components, in particular, components manufactured in less eco-conscious countries. Companies in developed countries often outsource component manufacturing to countries with lower labour costs, which are partially a by-product of laxer eco-controls. Externality-inclusive pricing requires eco-accounting of those components.

Distribution/usage/consumption

The many negative externalities created during product usage/consumption are difficult to identify and quantify; not only the total transportation costs within the channel of distribution, but also the costs associated with consumers' product search, acquisition and use. Consumption-related costs include packaging disposal, productivity losses related to product search time, and usage incompatibility. For example, one neighbour buys a new stereo system and is using it to entertain friends outdoors on a Saturday afternoon. This enjoyment precludes another neighbour from enjoying a peaceful meditation exercise. In addition, consumption can create positive externalities. For example, homeowners who install landscaping that enhances a neighbourhood's beauty will benefit their neighbours aesthetically and economically (i.e. increased home value).

However, consumers may use products in multiple and sometime unpredictable ways (e.g. toothpaste as a polish). As a result, accessing all consumption-related externality costs and benefits may be complex.

Disposal

Product disposal also creates negative externalities. Consumers expend time and energy resources, as well as causing air pollution and traffic congestion, when transporting a used product to a thrift store. Energy is consumed and pollution is generated when delivering paper or plastics from the consumption site to a recycling plant. In some cases, the lack of appropriate disposal systems can create stockpiles of spent products that are then discarded in an unacceptable fashion, such as e-waste exported from developed to developing countries.

Question 3: What are the environmental impacts of each externality?

The answer to this question requires answering a subset of questions.

Is the resource renewable? Renewable resources, such as forests, fisheries and clean air, can regenerate over time; whereas, non-renewable resources, such as fossil fuels, are finite. The eco-cost of a renewable resource depends on the time and expense required to replenish it.

If the resource is non-renewable, when will current production methods cause its exhaustion? Unless it is recyclable (e.g. aluminium), a non-renewable resource is depleted as it is used. While the resource remains critical to production, ever-dwindling stockpiles and reserves will drive prices upwards. Higher prices should encourage conservation of non-renewable resources via reduced usage or substitution.

How likely, and in what timeframe, are new production methods to emerge with different materials requirements and waste by-products? Consider the now ubiquitous microprocessor. The substrate for most current chips derives from a silicon wafer sliced from a cylindrical ingot of highly purified silicon. The fabrication process is wasteful, as only 43% of an ingot is used; the remainder is recycled or discarded. One unwanted by-product of the process is a large quantity of wastewater infused with toxic compounds. The process is energy intensive as well; for example, the chemicals used in fabrication must be distilled and expensive air filtration systems must be run (Environmental Literacy Council 2008; Williams, Ayres & Heller 2002). However, quantum (rather than digital), DNA-based and light-based microprocessors – with their unknowable arrival dates – may rely on vastly different fabrication technologies that are less polluting and energy intensive.

How will society value changes from 'au natural'? Can human-made objects exceed the aesthetics of the natural environment? For example, future consumers may prefer holograms of wilderness areas and unfettered economic growth to the expense of maintaining such areas. Does it matter now that the windmill farms in western Texas are ugly and noisy if no one lives nearby?

Does the cost of a negative externality equal the cost of returning the environment to its original form? The huge Fresh Kills landfill on Staten Island (a borough of New York City) is being reclaimed as a public park (Wikipedia 2011c). Many people would argue that a public park is an improvement over the land's original state; thus, one could argue that the park is a positive externality of the landfill.

At each stage of the product lifecycle, multiple negative externalities are created. Some of these are more obvious initially; for example, loss of green space (loss of beauty); loss of recreational areas (due to manufacturing facilities, waste disposal areas, pollution); decreased air, water and soil quality; noise pollution; and loss of species. Some resources, such as fish, may regenerate if the species has not become extinct. However, other resources, such as petroleum, are in finite supply (Keohane & Olmstead 2007). Such factors may affect the value placed on a resource and its use.

Question 4: What costing approach is best for determining externalities? How should net present value of all future costs be calculated?

Once externalities and their costs have been determined, how should costs be allocated? As a fixed cost per unit manufactured and sold? As the harm to society of adding another unit – such as one more car produced or one more tree felled – to equalise marginal cost with marginal benefit? If fixed-cost-per-unit-manufactured-and-sold is used, then the buyer of every unit will share the eco-burden equally. If marginal cost is used, then only some buyers may incur the burden because payments only would be assessed on output exceeding a predetermined level.

Externality-inclusive pricing should consider the entire cost/benefit domain across the lifecycle. Are externalities confined to a single consumer group, or are they local, state wide, nationwide or even global? Is the effect short- or long-lived (i.e. benefit/harm to future generations)? For example, pollution can be a local problem, as with chemical runoff that degrades the local water supply, or global problem, as with transnational air pollution (Ono 1998).

An 'efficient [environmental] policy maximises the present value of net benefits to society' (Keohane & Olmstead 2007, p. 28). Because environmental degradation can affect current and future generations, the discount rate represents a key assumption. 'Discounting comes into play only when there is a temporal lag between costs and benefits' (Heinzerling 1999, p. 1912). To what extent should the preferences of future generations be discounted, assuming such preferences can be predicted? Politicians resisting the rapidly growing US budget deficit berate economic-stimulus-focused politicians for saddling future generations with the cost of current consumption. Is the future so uncertain that future generations should be required to fend for themselves, or is the current generation obligated to serve as economic and environmental steward for future generations?

Should the current generation sacrifice some economic growth or material quality of life to preserve the environmental for future generations, which in effect redistributes income from the current generation to future generations, or should the free market activity determine eco-preservation efforts (Baumol 1968)? Uncertainty about future technological innovations complicates a discount-rate assumption. Perhaps some future technology will eliminate all negative externalities associated with personal transportation.

Economies of scale and the increasing marginal cost for each unit of pollution abatement may dictate that environmental quality first be allowed to decline and then periodically improved (Keohane & Olmstead 2007). Depending on the pollutant, the number of polluters, the quantity expelled into the environment by each polluter and the cost of redundant scrubbing technology for each polluter, it may be more efficient to slowly contaminate the environment and then periodically repair any damage. In essence, it may be more cost effective to assign clean-up specialists to environmental repair rather than mandate each polluter purchase and install expensive anti-pollution devices. Of course, each polluter would pay the clean-up specialist in proportion to the eco-damage caused.

Question 5: How effectively can pricing capture the costs/benefits of externalities?

Unless mandated by a government or other agency, market forces dictate the externality costs factored into a product's price. For example, the cost of some car-related externalities, such as air pollution and roadway maintenance, can be determined and allocated readily through gasoline taxes. However, costs such as noise pollution and loss of land to roadways are more subjective and hence more difficult to determine and allocate.

Another problem is posed by the non-global nature of pricing mechanisms. Sans a global mechanism, polluting firms merely can relocate to a country that does not impose pollution surcharges. Of course, polluting firms in such countries already enjoy this cost benefit. Agreements such as multilateral environmental and trade agreements are critical to ensuring fairness and externality-adjusted prices. The UN Environmental Programme realises the need for mutually supportive trade and environmental policies (U.N. Environment Programme 2007).

Question 6: What externalities are being ignored in a lifecycle analysis?

In a lifecycle analysis, only 'material and energy flows are assessed, thus ignoring some externalities (such as supply security) and technology reliability and flexibility' (Owen 2004, p. 131). Of course, other externalities like reduced biodiversity are almost impossible to calculate. These externalities apply across activities; relative to transportation, for example, are the costs of road development, but maintenance of those roads, as well as the costs associated with oil dependency, are not included (Parry, Walls & Harrington 2007). The US alone spends between '$39 billion and $89.5 billion annually to secure the production and transport of foreign oil' (International Center for Technology Assessment 2005, p. 3). When waterways are dammed to generate hydroelectricity, fisheries are destroyed (Perkins 1998). Externalities with an unclear effect on the environment may be overlooked. For example, the effects of global warming on increased natural disasters, such as major floods and hurricanes, cannot be estimated with certainty (Bickel *et al.* 2006).

Sometimes overlooked are social welfare costs, such as increased illness, lower quality of life and livelihood loses. Assigning monetary values to health damage may entail three domains: (1) medical costs, (2) opportunity costs, such as productivity losses, and (3) disutility costs, such as pain and suffering, decreased ability to enjoy leisure activities, concern about the future, and trickle-down effects on the family members of the injured person (Bickel *et al.* 2006). Over-harvesting a fishing area harms the lifestyles of an entire region as well as the eco-balance of the waters. As a result, a local fishing industry may disappear, leaving communities worse off and altering income-generating opportunities.

Conclusion

Externalities are an important aspect of sustainability discussions and considerations. In this chapter, we explored various options to account for positive and negative externalities, ranging from voluntary payments by consumers to legal fines and penalties. Each option discussed has advantages and disadvantages. We focused on internalising externalities by adjusting pricing accordingly, which would avoid much of the political gaming inherent to the other options. Our cradle-to-grave question-set provides a preliminary step toward a more robust framework for setting societally fair prices that include most, if not all, externalities.

References

Alsmadi, S. (2007), "Green Marketing and the Concern over the Environment: Measuring Environmental Consciousness of Jordanian Consumers," *Journal of Promotion Management* 13 (3/4), 339-361.

Baker, D. R. (2010), "Cap and Trade: Details on Emissions Up in the Air," *San Francisco Chronicle,* http://www.sfgate.com/cgi-bin/article.cgi?file=/chronicle/archive/ 2010/12/18/ BUKO1GRUPP.DTL&type=news (accessed 19 December 2010).

Baumol, W. J. (1968), "On the Social Rate of Discount," *The American Economic Review*, 58 (4), 788-802.

Bickel, P., R. Friedrich, H. Link, L. Stewart, L, and C. Nash (2006), "Introducing Environmental Externalities into Transport Pricing: Measurement and Implications," *Transport Reviews*, 26 (4), 389-415.

Blackman, A. and W. Harrington (2000), "The Use of Economic Incentives in Developing Countries: Lessons from International Experience with Industrial Air Pollution," *The Journal of Environment & Development*, 9 (1), 5-44.

Blankenship, K. (2002), "MD Port Administration Seeks 'Green' Options for Dredge Materials," *Chesapeake Bay Journal*, 12 (5), http://www.bayjournal.com/article.cfm?article=702 (accessed 9 January 2011).

Boje, D. M. (1999), "Green Life Cycle and Accounting Praxis," http://web.nmsu.edu/~dboje/TDgreenlifecycle.html (accessed 21 December 2010).

Carbonfund (2010), "How Carbon Offsets Work," http://www.carbonfund.org/site/pages/how_it_works/?gclid= CKmuobmSnKYCFQTrKgodx0Q_mw (accessed 2 January 2011).

Cave, D. (2010), "In Recession, Americans Doing More, Buying Less," *The New York Times*, http://www.nytimes.com/2010/01/03/business/economy/03experience.html?pagewanted=1&_r=1&sq=experienceconsumption&st=cse&scp=1 (accessed 8 January 2011).

Center for Responsive Politics (2011), "Influence & Lobbying: Environment," http://www.opensecrets.org/lobby/indusclient.php?lname=Q11&year=2009 (accessed 4 April 2011).

Chapman, C. S., A. G. Hopwood, and M. D. Shields (2007), *Handbook of Management Accounting Research, Volume 2*, Oxford, UK: Elsevier.

Curvy Road (2010), "About Fractional Ownership," http://www.curvyroad.com/AboutFractionalOwnership.html (accessed 6 January 2011).

Department of Environmental Conservation (2010), "The Electronic Equipment Recycling and Reuse Act," http://www.dec.ny.gov/chemical/65583.html (accessed 31 December 2010).

do Paco, A. M. F. and M. L. B. Raposo (2010), "Green Consumer Market Segmentation: Empirical Findings from Portugal," *Journal of Consumer Studies*, 34 (4), 429-436.

Engel, S., S. Pagiola, and S. Wunder (2008), "Designing Payments for Environmental Services in Theory and Practice: An Overview of the Issues," *Ecological Economics*, 65 (4), 663-674.

Engineering, NIoSaTsM (2008), "Product's Lifecycle," *Wikimedia Commons*, http://commons.wikimedia.org/wiki/File:Product_lifecycle.svg (accessed 3 October 2010).

Enterprise Holdings, Inc. (2010), "Empowering our Customers: Carbon Offset Program," http://www.keystogreen.com/carbon_offset.html (accessed 19 December 2010).

Environmental Literacy Council (2008), "Computer Chip Life Cycle," http://www.enviroliteracy.org/article.php/1275.html (accessed 8 January 2011).

European Commission (2010), "Environment Directorate-General," http://ec.europa.eu/dgs/environment/index_en.htm (accessed 1 January 2011).

Forester, T. (1988), *The Materials Revolution: Superconductors, New Materials, and the Japanese Challenge*, Cambridge, MA: The MIT Press.

Frischknecht, R., H. J. Althaus, C. Bauer, G. Doka, T. Heck, N. Jungbluth, D. Kellenberger, and T. Nemecek (2007), "The Environmental Relevance of Capital Goods in Life Cycle Assessments of Products and Services," *Journal of Life Cycle Assessment,* http://www.esu-services.ch/fileadmin/download/Frischknecht-2007-CapitalGoods_IntJLCA.pdf (accessed 5 January 2011).

Fullerton, D. and G.E. Metcalf (2001), "Environmental Controls, Scarcity Rents, and Pre-existing Conditions," *Journal of Public Economics*, 80 (2), 249-267.

Galbraith, J. K. (1956), *American Capitalism: The Concept of Countervailing Power, rev. ed.,* Cambridge, MA: Houghton Mifflin Company.

Garigliano, J. (2007), "Own a Lamborghini—Part Time," *Fortune Small Business,* http://money.cnn.com/magazines/fsb/fsb_archive/2007/02/01/8399941/index.htm (accessed 5 January 2011).

Goldman, M. I. (1972), "Externalities and the Race for Economic Growth in the USSR: Will the Environment Ever Win?" *Journal of Political Economy,* 80 (2), 314-327.

Goodstein, E. (2003), "The Death of the Pigovian Tax? Policy Implications from the Double-Dividend Debate," *Land Economics,* 79 (3), 402-414.

Green Car Congress (2008), "French Government Declares Car Feebates System a Success," http://www.greencarcongress.com/2008/08/french-governme.html (accessed 13 April 2011).

Greene, D. L., P. D. Patterson, M. Singh, and J. Li (2005), "Feebates, Rebates and Gas-guzzler Taxes: A Study of Incentives for Increased Fuel Economy," *Energy Policy,* 33 (6), 757-775.

Gupta, S. and D. T. Ogden (2009), "To Buy or Not To Buy? A Social Dilemma Perspective on Green Buying," *Journal of Consumer Marketing,* 26 (6), 376-391.

Hardin, G. (1998), "Extensions of 'The Tragedy of the Commons'," *Science* 280, No. 5364, 682-683.

Hardin, G. (2009), "The Tragedy of the Commons," *Journal of Natural Resources Policy Research,* 1 (3), 243-253.

Hardin, G. J. (1969), "The Tragedy of the Commons," *Ekistics* 27, No. 160, 168-170.

Harkin, J. M. (1969), "Uses for Sawdust, Shavings, and Waste Chips," *U.S. Department of Agriculture,* http://www.fpl.fs.fed.us/documnts/fplrn/fplrn208.pdf (accessed 8 January 2011).

Hawken, P., A. Lovins, and L. H. Lovins (1999), *Natural Capitalism,* New York: NY: Little, Brown and Company.

Heidkamp, P, D. Hanink, and R. Cromley (2008), "A Land Use Model of the Effects of Eco-labeling in Coffee Markets," *Annals of Regional Science,* 42 (3), 725-746.

Herbig, P. A. and D. D. Butler (1993), "The Greening of International Marketing," in *Environmental Issues in the Curricula of International Business, The Green Imperative,* A. T. Mintu, H. R. Lozada, and M. J. Polonsky, eds., New York, NY: International Business Press.

Hendrickson, C., A. Horvath, S. Joshi, and L. Lave (1998), "Economic Input-Output Models for Environmental Life-Cycle Assessment," *Policy Analysis,* 32 (7), 184-191.

Heinzerling, L. (1999), "Discounting Life," *Yale Law Journal*, 108. 1911-1915.

Hong, B. D. and E. R. Slatick (1994), "Carbon Dioxide Emission Factors for Coal," *Quarterly Coal Report, January-April 1994,* http://www.eia.doe.gov/cneaf/coal/quarterly/co2_article/co2.html (accessed 12 April 2011).

Hopper, J. R. and J. McCarl Nielsen (1991), "Recycling as Altruistic Behavior: Normative and Behavioral Strategies to Expand Participation in a Community Recycling Program," *Environment and Behavior,* 23 (2), 195-220.

Howell, K. (2009), "Is Algae the Biofuel of the Future?" *Scientific American*, http://www.scientificamerican.com/article.cfm?id=algae-biofuel-of-future (accessed 10 January 2011).

Hybrid Center (2011), "State and Federal Hybrid Incentives," http://go.ucsusa.org/hybridcenter/incentives.cfm (accessed 1 January 2011).

Hydroponic Farming (2010), "Hydroponic Farming," http://hydroponicfarming.net/ (accessed 5 January 2011).

International Center for Technology Assessment (2005), "Gasoline Cost Externalities: Security and Protection Services," http://www.icta.org/doc/ RPG%20security%20update.pdf (accessed 11 January 2011).

John, A. and R. Pecchenino (1994), "An Overlapping Generations Model of Growth and the Environment," *The Economic Journal,* 104 (427), 1393-1410.

Joshi, S. (2000),"Product Environmental Life-Cycle Assessment Using Input-Output Techniques," *Journal of Industrial Ecology,* 3 (2 & 3), 95-120.

Keohane, N. and O. Olmstead (2007), *Markets and the Environment, Foundations of Contemporary Environmental Studies Series,* Washington, DC: Island Press.

Kim, O. and M. Walker (1984), "The Free Rider Problem: Experimental Evidence," *Public Choice,* 43 (1), 3-24.

Laroche, M., J. Bergeron, and G. Barbaro-Forleo (2001), "Targeting Consumers Who are Willing to Pay More for Environmentally Friendly Products," *Journal of Consumer Marketing,* 18 (6), 503-520.

Meadows, D., J. Randers, and D. Meadows (2004), *Limits to Growth: The 30-Year Update,* White River Junction, VT: Chelsea Green Publishing Company.

McGuire, M. C. (1982), "Regulation, Factor Rewards, and International Trade," *Journal of Public Economics,* 17 (3), 335-354.

McKitrick, R. and R. A. Collinge (2000), "Linear Pigovian Taxes and the Optimal Size of a Polluting Industry," *Canadian Journal of Economics,* 33 (4), 1106-1119.

Minnesota GreenStep Cities (2010), "Solid Waste Reduction," http://greenstep.pca.state.mn.us/bestPracticesDetail.cfm?bpid=22 (accessed on 13 April 2011).

Motavalli, J. (2009), "4 Energy Technologies That Could Replace Oil and Coal," http://www.thedailygreen.com/environmental-news/latest/renewable-energy-460510 (accessed 10 January 2011).

NaturalGas.org (2010), "Natural Gas and the Environment," http://www.naturalgas.org/environment/naturalgas.asp (accessed 12 April 2011).

News of Future (2011), "Oil Price to Reach US $350 in Near Future," http://www.newsoffuture.com/oil_price_in_near_future_peak_oil.html (accessed 9 January 2011).

Oil Price (2011), "Crude Oil and Commodity Prices," http://www.oil-price.net/ (accessed 9 January 2011).

Ono, T. (1998), "Consumption Externalities and the Effects of International Income Transfers on the Global Environment," *Journal of Economics,* 68 (3), 255-269.

Owen, A. D. (2004), "Environmental Externalities, Market Distortions and the Economics of Renewable Energy Technologies," *Energy Journal,* 25 (3), 127-156.

Parry, I. W. H., M. Walls, and W. Harrington (2007), "Automobile Externalities and Policies," *Journal of Economic Literature,* 45 (2), 373-399.

Pearson, N. O. (2010), "India to Raise $535 Million from Carbon Tax on Coal," *Bloomberg Businessweek,* http://www.businessweek.com/news/2010-07-01/ india-to-raise-535-million-from-carbon-tax-on-coal.html (accessed 31 December 2010).

Perkins, R. (1998), "Electricity Deregulation, Environmental Externalities and the Limitations of Price," *Boston College Law Review,* 39 (4/5), 993-1059.

Porat, A. (2009), "Private Production of Public Goods: Liability for Unrequested Benefits," *Michigan Law Review,* 108 (2), 189-227.

Pretty, J., C. Brett, D. Gee, R. Hine, C. Mason, J. Morison, M. Rayment, G. Van Der Bijl, and T. Dobbs (2001), "Policy Challenges and Priorities for Internalizing the Externalities of Modern Agriculture," *Journal of Environmental Planning and Management,* 44 (2), 263-283.

Rajah, N. and S. Smith (1994), "Using Taxes to Price Externalities: Experiences in Western Europe," *Annual Review of Energy and Environment,* 19, 475-504.

Randall, A. (2007), "A Consistent Valuation and Pricing Framework for Non-commodity Outputs: Progress and Prospects," *Journal of Agriculture, Ecosystems, and Environment,* 120 (1), 21-30.

Recyclebank (2010), http://www.recyclebank.com/ (accessed 19 December 2010).

Sagan, D. (2007), *Notes from the Holocene: A Brief History of the Future,* White River Junction, VT: Chelsea Green Publishing Company.

Shrum, L.J., J. A. McCarty, and T. M. Lowrey (1995), "Buyer Characteristics of the Green Consumer and Their Implications for Advertising Strategy," *Journal of Advertising,* 24 (2), 71-82.

Söderholm, P. and T. Sundqvist (2003), "Pricing Environmental Externalities in the Power Sector: Ethical Limits and Implications for Social Choice," *Ecological Economics,* 46 (3), 333-350.

Steinacker, A. (2006), "Externalities, Prospect Theory, and Social Construction: When Will Government Act, What Will Government Do?" *Social Science Quarterly,* 87 (3), 459-476.

Stevens, T. H., J. Echeverria, R. J. Glass, T. Hager, and T. A. More (1991), "Measuring the Existence Value of Wildlife: What do CVM Estimates Really Show?" *Land Economics,* 67 (4), 390-400.

Sustainable Table (2011), "Eat Local, Buy Local, Be Local," http://www.sustainabletable.org/issues/eatlocal/ (accessed 9 April 2011).

Tanner, C. and S. Wölfing Kast (2003), "Promoting Sustainable Consumption: Determinants of Green Purchases by Swiss Consumers," *Psychology & Marketing,* 20 (10), 883-902.

TerraPass (2011), "Wedding Carbon Footprint Calculator," http://www.terrapass.com/wedding/, (accessed 4 April 2011).

The Nature Conservancy (2011), "About Us, Vision and Mission," http://www.nature.org/aboutus/visionmission/index.htm (accessed 4 April 2011).

U, N. Environment Programme (2007), "Trade-related Measures and Multilateral Environmental Agreements," http://www.unep.ch/etb/areas/pdf/ MEA% 20Papers/TradeRelated_ MeasuresPaper.pdf (accessed 6 January 2011).

U. S. Department of Energy (2011), "Consumer Energy Tax Incentives," http://www.energy.gov/taxbreaks.htm (accessed 1 January 2011).

U. S. Environmental Protection Agency (2005), "Profile of the Rubber and Plastics Industry, 2nd ed.," Washington, D.C., http://www.epa.gov/compliance/resources/publications/assistance/sectors/notebooks/rubplasn.pdf (accessed 21 December 2010).

U. S. Environmental Protection Agency (2010a), "National Emission Standards for Hazardous Air Pollutants," http://www.epa.gov/ttn/atw/mactfnlalph.html (accessed 1 January 2011).

U. S. Environmental Protection Agency (2010b), "Summary of the Clean Water Act," http://www.epa.gov/lawsregs/laws/cwa.html (accessed 1 January 2011).

USC Energy Institute (2010), "Hydrocarbon Processing," http://energy.usc.edu/research/conventional_energy/hydrocarbon.html (accessed 9 January 2011).

Wikipedia (2011a), "Vertical Farming," http://en.wikipedia.org/wiki/Vertical_farming (accessed 10 January 2011).

Wikipedia (2011b), "Marine Debris," http://en.wikipedia.org/wiki/Marine_debris (accessed 9 April 2011).

Wikipedia (2011c), "Fresh Kills Landfill," http://en.wikipedia.org/wiki/ Fresh_Kills_Landfill (accessed 9 January 2011).

Williams, E. D., R. U. Ayres, and M. Heller (2002), "The 1.7 Kilogram Microchip: Energy and Material Use in the Production of Semiconductor Devices," *Environmental Science & Technology,* 36 (24), 5504-5510.

Zilberman, D. (2002), "Negative Externalities and Policy," http://are.berkeley.edu/courses/ARE253/2004/handouts/negativeexternalities.pdf (accessed 1 January 2011).

Zipcar (2011), "Is Zipcar for Me?" http://www.zipcar.com/is-it/ (accessed 5 January 2011).

Urban water: Accounting for behavioural differences

BETHANY COOPER

ABSTRACT

An extended and severe drought in southern Australia accompanied by policy failures in the allocation of water resources has created a difficult environment for urban water managers and users. Mandated restrictions over the use of water have been a common response to shortages and substantial attention is focussed on the efficacy of different approaches to deal with water shortages (see, for example, ABC News 2009). Essentially, this paper discusses the welfare costs associated with implementing urban water restrictions. This study also recognises the importance of policy makers considering preference heterogeneity across the population when developing urban water policy.

This paper aims to increase our understanding of the urban water context in Australia and to recognise issues that should be considered during the development of urban water policy. More specifically, it focuses on addressing the efficacy of water restrictions as a means of rationing urban water. Water restrictions have been applied in almost every major urban city in Australia. Invariably water restrictions invoke discussion around the trade-offs between different forms of rationing (see, for example, Barrett 2004). Thus, these matters are also contemplated in this analysis by reflecting on the supply and demand management strategies available to urban water utilities.

The role of water utilities includes providing a degree of supply security to manage the risk of running out of water at some identified (or notional) future point in time. This is achieved by water utilities making judgements around supply risks and trade-offs with managing present and future demands. For instance, trade-offs are made when choosing between harvesting and distributing alternative water sources (e.g. recycled water), augmenting current supplies (e.g. desalination plants) and implementing demand-side measures such as those involved in the enforcement of explicit restrictions on consumption (e.g. urban outdoor water restrictions). In addition, state-owned water utilities are often required to balance a range of broader 'social' obligations, such as sending conservation messages and ensuring that the poor are not disadvantaged (see, for instance, ESC 2009). In balancing these considerations, there is little evidence that water authorities have explicitly considered water consumers' preferences (Hensher, Shore & Train 2006); rather, the emphasis of attention has been given to the political costs of severe water shortage and the political risks associated with 'running dry', with less emphasis on real changes to consumer lifestyles and preferences (although some social marketing is often used to encourage more responsible usage).

In contrast to shoring up supplies by tapping new water sources (including harvesting existing untapped rainwater), urban water can be managed through two broad approaches to demand. One approach involves rationing by either limiting the quantity of water available to customers or invoking some constraints over water-using behaviour (which includes pricing mechanisms). Extensive controversy surrounds the notion of restricting indoor water consumption through urban allocations with some describing this as being 'socio-politically distaste(ful)' (Brennan, Tapsuwan & Ingram 2007). In addition, blanket restrictions based on indoor water use face other problems, given the extreme level of heterogeneity associated with indoor water consumption, infrastructure and the difficulty of monitoring and enforcing indoor water usage. Conversely, the regulation of outdoor water consumption is more socially acceptable and more plausible. Regulations can be implemented by means of restricting usage to particular days of the week, the time of day and particular forms of watering devices (e.g. hoses instead of sprinklers). However, such restrictions still require a user voluntarily complying as monitoring is impractical. Outdoor water use can be classified as 'conspicuous consumption' and thus restrictions can also potentially be enforced through other community members reporting their neighbours for recalcitrant behaviour. Regardless of the practicality of this approach, it is not without its costs.

Neo-classical economics has much to say about the mechanics of rationing scarce resources and how to minimise related costs. Much of this contribution is based on the axiom of rationality and is encapsulated in the notion of homo economicus (Andreoni 2001). This notion considers humans as rational and self-interested actors. Economic theory suggests that an increase in the price of a good is likely to lead to a decrease in customer demand for that product, either by altering consumption levels or by promoting switching to alternative products. Thus, theoretically at least, price can be used to as a mechanism to ration (i.e. curtail use) of urban water in preference to the imposition of quantitative (i.e. quotas) or behavioural constraints (i.e. mandatory restrictions). In most cases, using price to ration a scarce resource will also induce lower costs than rationing determined on some other basis, as market forces manage behaviour rather than extensive monitoring and enforcement mechanisms.

In general, the effectiveness of prices in determining the allocation of water has been widely researched (see, for instance, ABARE 1993; Barrett 2004; Dalhuisen *et al.* 2003; DEST 1996; Productivity Commission 2005; Sibly 2006). Grafton and Ward (2008) suggest that mandatory water restrictions in urban Australia should be removed and the volumetric price of water increased to regulate water demand when required, for as such water prices are possibly too low. Sibly (2006) also advocates the importance of using efficient pricing increases to address water shortages in Australian metropolitan areas. Regardless of these findings, the standard approach to urban water demand management is to set water prices independent of the water in storage or available supply, and to restrict consumption via water restrictions (Grafton & Kompas 2007), that is, to ignore supply and focus on demand.

Grafton and Ward (2008) identify three main notions that underpin the justification for rationing water as opposed to charging a higher volumetric price. First, if water is perceived as a basic need then using price to allocate it may be considered inequitable. Second, where household water consumption is not metered, increasing the water price in the form of a fixed charge provides no financial incentive to consumers to reduce their demand. Third, it may be more effective to implement a rationing scheme rather than raise the price if an immediate and temporary reduction in demand is required (Grafton & Ward 2008).

Additionally, Barrett (1996) shows that prices alone are not always effective in reducing water consumption. That is, the financial benefits gained by consumers through pricing do not act as a sufficient incentive to fully engage in conservation, which could possibly be associated with the relatively low price charged in many developed markets. Connelly *et al.* (1992) also suggest that consumers perceive user-pays pricing as an unfavourable water conservation option. They argue against price structures based solely on the need to restrict consumption due to the essential nature of the resource. Moreover, it has been claimed that there is a risk that experts can overestimate the effectiveness of tariffs to solely manage water demand (De Young & Robinson 1984), that is, pricing will not have the desired demand effects. Thus, whilst economic theory would generally favour water rationing based on price, there is some evidence in the literature at least that this approach is potentially attended by other limitations. Subsequently, compliance with quantitative forms of rationing is likely to be required for some time yet.

Economic efficiency is often not paramount in the urban water setting (Edwards 2006), with social and political objectives dominating regulators' decision making. Voluntary water restrictions constrain (or at least impose prohibitions on) particular uses of water, but do not require households to reduce their water use *per se*. Therefore, water restrictions do not directly address the fundamental issue of 'total use of water' and furthermore householders' freedoms regarding water use are substantially limited. Understandably, there is conjecture about the positive and negative consequences of restrictions of this form.

Politicians favouring water restrictions commonly play the 'moral suasion' card (Brennan, Tapsuwan & Ingram 2007), as residents are asked to do the 'right thing'. There are also appeals made on the basis of intergenerational equity, that is, use less water to ensure water for your children (see, for instance, Goulburn Valley Water 2010; Water Corporation 2010). It has become common for proponents of restrictions to claim that the public supports water restrictions in general and, by implication, the punitive measures that attend them.

The apparent enthusiasm for urban water restrictions in some political spheres raises important questions about how water consumers view the attenuation of their rights to readily use water. Being able to identify the alternative segments within the population and identifying those who are most enthusiastic about paying to avoid water restrictions is an important element to developing effective policy, of course one needs to also target those that do not comply with voluntary restrictions.

Cooper, Burton and Crase (in press) investigated householders' willingness to pay to avoid urban water restrictions in cities across New South Wales and Victoria. Their study identified estimates of individuals' willingness to pay to entirely avoid water restrictions, which builds on the idea that water may have a very inelastic demand. Cooper, Burton and Crase (in press) found that people's sensitivity to water restrictions across a number of dimensions appears to differ between groups within the population. On the one hand, a portion of the sample strongly supported restrictions to the point that they cannot countenance the use of markets to alleviate any of the attendant costs (i.e. they opposed higher costs). However, on the other hand the extreme level of heterogeneity associated with outdoor water consumption implies that uniformly rationing the volume of water allocation per household is far from an adequate policy response and does not cater to the unique characteristics and demand patterns of households.

Contrary to the implied value of 'saving water' that dominates popular thinking, Cooper, Burton and Crase (in press) suggested that particular segments within society actually value not being subject to water restrictions and thus would pay more for access to water. The research also showed that attitudinal variables (e.g. attitudes toward water restrictions) and particular value sets (e.g. environmental values) play some part in influencing an individual's willingness to pay to avoid water restrictions (see Cooper, Burton & Crase in press). Similarly, it also showed that respondents that differ across socio-demographic variables such as income and education appear to receive differing levels of utility from avoiding water restrictions. In addition, exogenous factors such as the severity and duration of water restrictions and whether the respondent had a lawn were shown to have an influence on the willingness to pay to avoid water restrictions (see Cooper, Burton & Crase in press).

In general, the majority of urban water consumers appear to have accepted the bureaucratic regulation on their water usage as evidenced by their general compliance with restriction regimes. However, from a policy perspective, the compliance of urban water users should not be taken to imply that there is no motivation for reform or that it is appropriate to apply a bureaucratic approach to water management in preference to markets. Accordingly, the research by Cooper, Burton and Crase (in press) reveals that a substantial portion of the sample supported being able to buy their way out of water restrictions. Respondents' willingness to pay to avoid water restrictions indicates that they are having an impact on human welfare. Alternatively, there is a group of respondents who do not prima facie gain utility from avoiding water restrictions.

In summary, the drought that has dominated southern Australia for the first decade of this century has led to a number of challenges for policy makers in this context. This discussion has increased our understanding of the demand management mechanisms applied in response to the drought. There seems little doubt that the current policy setting could be improved, and acting on the preference heterogeneity across the population would be a useful starting point. For instance, acknowledging the existence of different preferences amongst segments might lower the transition costs associated with a different policy setting. This matter is worthy of greater consideration in a policy context and provides useful insight for developing further research.

References

ABARE (1993) Australian Bureau of Agricultural and Resource Economics. Use of economic instruments in integrated coastal zone management. Canberra: Resource Assessment Commission.

ABC News Online (2009) Australian Broadcasting Corporation. Water price hike 'too much' for low-income families? [online] Available: http://www.abc.net.au/news/stories/2009/09/04/2676246.htm [Accessed 6 October 2009].

Andreoni, J. (2001) Economics of philanthropy. In International Encyclopedia of the Social and Behavioural Sciences, eds. N. Smelser and P. Baltes. United States: Elsevier Ltd.

Barrett, G. (1996) The impact of pricing and household income on urban water demand: explaining the variations. Proceedings of the 25th Annual Conference of Economists. Canberra, Australia.

Barrett, G. (2004) Water conservation: the role of price and regulation in residential water consumption. Economic Papers. 23(3): 271-285.

Brennan, D., Tapusuwan, S. and Ingram, G. (2007) The welfare costs of urban outdoor water restrictions. Australian Journal of Agriculture and Resource Economics. 51(3): 243-261.

Connelly, K., Buchanan, K., Forster, C. and Gow, H. (1992) Melbourne water resources review interim report: water for our future. Melbourne: Melbourne Water.

Cooper, B., Burton, M. and Crase, L. (in press) Urban Water Restrictions: Attitudes and Avoidance. Water Resources Research.

Dalhuisen, J., Florax, R., de Groot, H. and Nijkamp, P. (2003) Price and income elasticities of residential water demand: a meta-analysis. Land Economics. 79(2):292-308.

De Young, R. and Robinson, J. (1984) Some perspectives on managing water demand: public and expert views. Canadian Water Resources Journal. 9: 9-18.

DEST (1996) Department of Environment, Sport and Territories. More with less: initiatives to promote sustainable consumption. Environmental Economics Research Paper No.3. Canberra, Australia.

Edwards, G. (2006) Whose values count? Demand management for Melbourne's water. Economic Record. 82(1): 54-63.

ESC (2009) Essential Services Commission. Water [online] Available: http://www.esc.vic.gov.au/public/Water/Our+Role.htm [Accessed 10 February 2009].

Goulburn Valley Water (2010) Saving Water [online] Available: http://www.gvwater.vic.gov.au/Saving_Water/save_water.asp [Accessed 10 January 2009].

Grafton, Q. and Kompas, T. (2007) Pricing Sydney Water. Australian Journal of Agricultural and Resource Economics. 51(3): 227-241.

Grafton, Q. and Ward, M. (2008) Prices versus rationing: Marshallian surplus and mandatory water restrictions. The Economic Record. 84: S57-65.

Hensher, D., Shore, N. and Train, K. (2006) Water supply security and willingness to pay to avoid drought restrictions. Economics Record. 256(82): 56-66.

Productivity Commission (2005) Regulation and its review 2005-2006, Annual Report Series [online] Available: http://www.pc.gov/annualreports/regulation_and-its_review/regulationreview0506 [Accessed 14 December 2007].

Silby, J. (2006) Urban water pricing. Agenda. 13: 17-30.

Water Corporation (2010) Water mark: water for all, forever [online] Available: http://www.watercorporation.com.au/_files/PublicationsRegister/8/Watermark_Summer_2010.pdf [Accessed 8 January 2010].

Chapter 4

Marketing communication

Marketing communication in and for sustainable society

RICHARD J VAREY

ABSTRACT

It is no use saying, "We are doing our best". You have to succeed in doing what is necessary.

Winston Churchill

In Ecotopia, the modern-day assumption that people are born to produce has been abandoned in favour of a more modest place for each person and their collective society in a stable-state living web, in balance with nature. Energy, knowledge, skills and materials are resources for the necessities of life and sustainable wellbeing. Technologies that are harmful to the ecosystems are deliberately rejected, and many consumer goods are considered ecologically offensive and are not available. Industrial proliferation is restricted; basic necessities are standardised and of the highest quality – sturdy, durable and self-repairable. Electronic devices are compact, light, low energy-users and simply recycled when no longer functional.

Business is conducted online. Some television channels are actually parts of the government structure – citizens watch and expect to participate. News isn't merely provided by this apparatus: the apparatus *is* the news. The entertainment channels present advertisements in a block between shows, and these are limited to announcements without simulations and adjectives; many are directly comparative, providing sane information among the viewpoints, personalities and imagery of so-called normal content. Since productivity and output growth are not goals, the types and amounts of advertising are regulated, and augmentation is required with public service broadcasting. Corporate media monopolies are no longer tolerated, and decentralised responsibility and personalisation is prolific and craft-based. (See Callenbach 1975 for the full story of those who chose a different life pathway.)

Introduction

In such a scenario, we might imagine what 'marketing communications' would be for and what the form of such activity would be. This chapter is a conceptual discussion leading to implications and anticipations for marketing managers of an emerging radically different commercial space.

The discussion addresses the purpose and form of marketing interaction and communication that is consistent with 'strong sustainability' and thus with the principles of ecology. A mechanistic, transactional communication system, which is not always very communicative, is not capable of supporting the interactional, ecologically minded form of value-realising enterprise. The transcendence of transactional marketing interactions will be illustrated in 'strong' relationship marketing, and this will be shown to be a transition towards marketing in and for sustainability, explained in terms of ecological principles. In this form of marketing, relationships are taken into account, and that they are a fundamentally changing phenomenon is acknowledged. The term 'relationship' is used to represent a process of human interaction, including conversations-in-context with awareness of history and anticipations of a desirable future.

Strong sustainability can be defined as the prerequisite and foundation of any human development. It requires preservation of the integrity of all ecosystems, and the ability of ecosystems to recover from disturbance and re-establish stability, diversity and resilience. It results in a human society that lives and develops as an integral part of an environment that has ecological integrity – a society that is directly supported by ethics, values and worldview, in which people know that they are integral with the ecological systems of the biosphere. People desire the integrity of those systems (summarised from SANZ 2009). Thus, the core condition is societal ethics and values. Citizens value highly the non-material sources of happiness, and they don't assume economic growth necessarily creates prosperity. They affirm the deep interdependence of all people and the value of local community, and they operate with smaller environmental footprints and greater cooperation. Nature is valued and revered intrinsically; citizens assume responsibility for their impact on the integrity of all the ecosystems in which they are engaged. For marketing, this implies 'market mechanisms that work to maximise community well-being and the happiness of individuals within the limits of ecological principles' (SANZ 2009, p. 4).

In a strongly sustainable society, in place of an attitude of exploitation, is an attitude of respect and the obligation of stewardship. Instead of the widely held belief that human welfare depends on consumption (broadly defined), the belief is that human welfare depends on our relationship to the natural world and to each other, and on inner attitudes, as well as on consumption. Humans are not defined as consumers and producers, but as constituency members and citizens who consume and produce. The market has less dominance in worldly affairs, so rather than accepting that decisions (of efficiency) are best made in markets, decisions are made in the political arena and local communities as well as in markets. Strong sustainability is a transcendent holistic perspective on the relationship of individuals, society and nature.

It is noted that the core concepts of ecology, sustainability and wellbeing (and happiness) are consistent with the 'relationship economics' of relational marketing in its fullest extent. Further, the common fundamentals are central to the macro-marketing perspective: interaction, relationship, engagement, valuation, service and social/societal learning, all understood from a holistic system perspective. There is an 'eco logic' for marketing communication in sustainable society; rather, provisioning interaction to satisfy needs in which marketing activities play a part.

There will be a different, higher-order enterprise logic within which marketing communication will be purposed and enacted. What might be termed 'welfare marketing' (Varey 2010) provides regionally/locally sourceable, durable products of high quality, for service through shared use. Production is local and small scale, with environment management inherent in relational clusters and networks. A rethink of the private-public divide in service provision is necessary, recognising the already growing significance of social enterprise and community-based business. The internet (Web 2.0 and 3.0, and beyond) supports the evolution and application of distributed intelligence, including eco-consciousness, in social media and other platforms for communicative interaction (Varey & Ballantyne 2006; Varey 2008). This fosters the requisite social capital – the degree of associativeness and trust - for healthy democratic concurrence to complex problems. Connections come to the fore, and the image of an industrial 'mass' of atomised individuals with few bonds for common missions is overtaken by constructive and increasingly integrated social movements.

Marketing itself is understood at the macro level as constructive engagement (Schultz 2007) consistent with the strong sustainability transcendence of the 'sell more "green" stuff' of the weak sustainability reformist worldview: 'Connection is the overarching condition required for sustainability' (SANZ 2009, p. 1). Ecological, needs-based 'holistic marketing' (Wasik 1996) is deeply associative, mutual, collaborative and capable of supporting eco-consciousness and restorative sustainable consumption. In the long view, marketing communication is evolving from persuasive sales messaging to interaction management in support of sustainability marketing and mindful eco-conscious consumption.

Sustainable society

The future sustainable society is the context for future marketing. From the shallow understanding of 'taking goods to market', the growing acknowledgment of 'marketing in society' is a stepping stone towards fully acknowledging a form and purpose of marketing for society or social business (Varey 2011). This in turn identifies the societal conditions for deliberate strategic communicating and from this the form, function and purpose of marketing communication.

It is already plainly evident that society is undergoing profound change, and that this is changing marketing and communication for marketing. It is not an overstatement to say that 'the future is what we are changing in to'. We can understand this by realising that society is not a fixed entity but rather a process made up of a mixture of what is now, what has been and what is coming to be: dead, living and to be born in invention. It is also helpful to think in terms of distinct abstractions or emphases – spatial and temporal. In the spatial emphasis, an entity is conceived as an organisation or distribution; whereas in the temporal emphasis, it is a process. A change is, of course, fundamentally implied! The concept of marketing began in an age of expansion. For the future, the process nature of marketing comes to the fore.

To act for what we want society to become, some foresight and judgement is required. Raskin and colleagues have developed a set of plausible future pathway definitions to address the sustainability of nature and society in terms of resource use, environmental impacts and social conditions (Raskin, Banuri, Gallopin *et al.* 2002; Raskin, Electris & Rosen 2010). Thus the quality of development is understood in terms of degree of wellbeing in human lives, the strength of communities and the resilience of the biosphere. The social dimensions of sustainability are expressed as enhancement of social stability and resilience, reduction of poverty and hunger, and de-materialisation of lifestyles. The environment and resources dimensions of sustainability are the mitigation of greenhouse gas emissions, protection of natural resources and preservation of habitats.

Market forces and policy reform pathways emerge gradually from dominant governing forces of development and are a weak response to the crisis of industry-ecosystem imbalance. Fortress world and great transition are fundamental restructurings of world order; one is a nightmare scenario, whilst the alternative promises truly enriched lives.

Conventional world perspectives on the future assume the persistence of dominant forces driving development and globalisation, and that these strategies have the resilience to tolerate and recover from socio-ecological crises to succeed in maintaining rapid economic expansion:

- Market forces – free market optimism remains dominant so the mainstream view is market-centred, growth-oriented globalisation (development). There is uncertainty about sufficiency of resources and the maintenance of ecological resilience. The challenge is to maintain bio-physical and economic sustainability in conditions of profound inequalities of rich and poor.

- Policy reform – a corrective substitute for the failings of market forces in government-led redirection of growth toward sustainability goals. It requires massive government-led sustainability efforts to redirect the economy and promote technological innovation to meet wide-ranging sustainability targets. Also required is continued growth in developing countries and redistribution of wealth based on deep widespread commitment to economic equity. This necessitates unprecedented political will for the necessary regulation and economic, social technological and legal mechanisms.

Alternative visions of the future recognise on the one hand the failure to respond effectively and efficiently to the challenge of resource depletion, habitat degradation, diminishing quality of life, and social unrest, and on the other a radical cultural transformation that transcends and ecologically revitalises:

- Fortress world – an authoritarian path in response to mounting crises as instability and conflict triggers descent into chaos as market adaptations and policy reform are insufficient to avoid destabilisation. Powerful elites impose authoritarian order in an attempt to control a damaged environment and intolerant and resistant people. Sustainable development is abandoned to emergency measures and fragmented initiatives in response to habitat degradation and social conflict crises.

- Great transition – a fundamental transformation to sustainable society brought about in values-led change in the paradigm of global development. This is driven by deepening crises and the desire for a global, just sustainable civilization. The good life is redefined in terms of creativity, leisure, relationships and community engagement. A steady-state economy is reached with egalitarian income distributions resulting in most people's lives being better, with greater social cohesion. Remaining crises of sustainability are confronted for reconciliation and cooperation with more effective pluralistic governance arrangements.

Strong sustainability – beyond reformation

It is now commonplace to distinguish *weak sustainability* and *strong sustainability* (SANZ 2009). Ecologism is a radical critique of social, economic and political practices that takes seriously propositions about the finitude of the planet (Pugh 1996). Thus,

> ... the advocates of ecologism believe in extensive interference in economic, social and political institutions. In this context, sustainability requires a new (environmental) political ideology because it cannot, according to the advocates of ecologism, be accommodated within the inherited ideologies of capitalist liberalism, state socialism or their compromised variants. The new political ideology would have biocentrism as its significant stance, in contrast to a damaging anthropomorphism (Pugh 1996, pp. 1–2).

Environmentalism, on the other hand,

> can be set within existing political ideologies. It is reformist in a pragmatic way, centring upon concerns of institutionalising environmentally relevant adaptations. Some examples of application would include conservation, pollution control, waste recycling and improvements to squatter settlements in developing countries. (Pugh 1996, p. 2)

There are many and growing efforts to redress environmental damage, reduce waste and improve the living conditions of the poor (Cunningham 2008; Holdgate 1996; Steffen 2006). Yet, at best this achieves a somewhat less unsustainable way of life, but not a sustainable society. The underlying assumption that wealth is the basis of wellbeing and that it derives only from consumption is not challenged, and indeed is reinforced. Strong sustainability moves beyond – transcends – the necessary-but-not-sufficient eco-efficiency that is displayed in green products (Bosselmann 1995; Kassiola 2003; Speth 2008).

Sustainability is simply about not using a source[1] faster than it can regenerate (Cunningham 2008, p. 23); thus, sustainability is not enough, since there is a 'pathological disconnect between wealth creation and its effect on the world' (p. 71). Further,

> ... the primary problem with sustainable development (as currently practiced) is that it attempts to make sustainable all three modes of the development lifecycle: de-wealth (industrial consumption), pre-wealth (conservation), and re-wealth (restoration). All three are in need of greening, no doubt, but only the latter two modes are inherently sustainable (p. 350).

Environmental problems are results of failures of coordination among people in their use of natural resources; we are both dependent on our habitat and capable of changing it (Wills 1997). Our culture, out of tune with nature, has needed and produced consumers (Bosselman 1995; Hamilton 2003, 2008; Hamilton & Denniss 2005). For an overview from the marketing perspective, see Varey (2010), and on consumer society see Smart (2010). In affluent society, the marketing system extends the definition of wealth to keep the productive system profitable, and since the late 20th century, the threshold of over-consumption, critical imbalance and inequitable distribution has been breached.

Alan Watts said that we are not actually materialists at all – we carelessly use materials promiscuously and often with contempt (wastefully creating trash). We don't sufficiently respect our scarce material habitat in a 'consumption society' that is heedlessly hoarding matter and burning energy (cited in Benett & O'Reilly 2010).

So, can the business of business merely be business in the form of an inhuman money-making machine? Or, must it be enterprise in harmony with humans and nature, creating sustainable wealth (quality of life, wellbeing) and intelligent consumption (benefits that exceed the costs)? And all this in accord with the ecological imperative of use within carrying capacity and resilience, continuous improvement and responsible enrichment, gauged by Green GDP and happiness? A choice has to be made. Biological, social, ecological, spiritual and cognitive needs are not well satisfied by the economic development that treats humans as machines and defines needs as only material and technological, that is, those that can be satisfied by economic development (Goldsmith 1992).

Marketing that supports sustainable society is needed:

> Our enormously destructive economy demands that we make sustainable consumption our way of life, that we transform the buying and use of goods into rituals for a better world, that we seek our spiritual satisfaction, our inspirational status, in ethical, low-carbon, ever smarter consumption. We

---

[1] Note that a re-source is a renewable source. Strictly, a source cannot regenerate.

need things conserved, shared, reused, recycled, slowed down and treasured at an ever deeper level. (Porritt, in Grant 2007, p. xii)

Ecological principles

The modernist (industrial) worldview is getting us deeper into trouble as the biosphere is disrupted – an ecological mindset is necessary for an alternative way forward. Capra and Pauli (1995) define ecological principles for business that highlight the significance of informative and communicative interaction:

- Interdependence – all (social) ecosystem members are interconnected in a web of relationships.

- Ecological cycles – continual cycles of energy and resources-exchanges are enacted in their interaction and there is energy flow in the communicative interaction in the cognitive 'space' or 'place' (relationscape) that interests us in this discussion.

- Partnership – there is interplay of competition and cooperation.

- Coevolution – interdependent fluctuations (flexibility) in the interplay of creation and mutual adaptation.

- Diversity – the stability of the social ecosystem depends on the degree of complexity.

- Sustainability – the ecosystem organises according to these principles to maximise sustainability in a limited resource base.

Alternative value systems are evident and a choice has to be made and courses of action selected for determined goals (Table 4.1):

Table 4.1 Fundamental values

Materialistic values	Alternative 'ecologistic' values
Egoistic individualism (competition)	Cooperation
Hostility to nature (resources for use)	Living in nature
Material growth to satisfy needs and wants	Material modesty with psycho-spiritual growth to sustain life
'Think-big' technology to conquer	Decentralised ecologically-suitable technologies
Hierarchical structures for command and control	Easily comprehensible relationships on the human scale
Specialisation and division of labour	Interconnected systems
Oppression and control	Harmony and balance
Anthropocentric (white, male) [Left brain]	Ecocentric [Right brain]

Recently, there has been an outgrowth of interest in service-dominant logic (Vargo & Lusch 2004) for marketing as an inclusive holistic explanation of marketing's function in society. Is a commercial manifestation of the transition towards the ecological worldview, and has highlighted the significance of interaction, communication and relationship. Service is understood as the basis of commerce and as fundamentally relational and thus ethical.

Marketing in and for sustainable society and wellbeing

We are living through a wave of fundamental transformative change, the early stages of which was noticed in the marketing discipline by Fisk (1974). This raises the fundamental question of marketing's relationship to the environment, survival and quality of life and the ecological crisis (see an overview in Varey 2010, and a critique in Varey & McKie 2010).

The industrialisation or 'massification' of the market has advanced the separation of production and consumption so that producers and consumers are distanced – spatially, temporally and mindfully – and don't meet. Consumers who don't produce have difficulty in judging 'true' value – the meaning and worth – of goods and services, and are reliant on the biased signalling of price and enticing advertising images.

Production produces objects for consumption, but also the motive for, and the manner of, consumption (see Smart's analysis 2010). Marketing is an intermediary that manages the market between production and use; in the managerialistic way of thinking, marketing is solely the deliberate, strategic seller's action of demand management. Although consumers are said to have choice, the intention is that the producer does the choosing so that buyers and users select 'under the influence' from what is offered – the influence is exerted primarily through sales messaging.

The goal of sustainability comes to the fore when we recognise the contradiction of modern society's provisioning system. There is a common purpose in population growth and higher material standard of living. This assumes infinite resources and that only more is good (not less). That ignores the truth of a finite habitat. The capacity of the environment to renew and restore resources that are used up and degraded (consumed, damaged, taken out of circulation, i.e. the natural and the public become private and for sale) and to repair the damage caused by the exploitation of those resources is limited and declining under the weight of a growing population of increasingly aspirant citizens who pursue material wealth through consumption.

Marketing, almost all of which is now the tool of capitalist corporatism and market fundamentalism which assume the power and capacity of corporate control of markets to provide for society's needs, is in distress. Modern capitalism itself is in distress because it does not deliver on the promise of limitless happiness. Witness the current financial crisis and the attendant insecurity in our societies.

This is not merely an economic problem and is absolutely not to be resolved through further growth. It is resolutely a political problem, specifically a problem of governance – about how we decide what use to make of limited resources and finite sinks for waste and pollution; how we co-negotiate valuations of people, nature, community, and intellectual and cultural accomplishment. Our consumer society has already passed the point of affluence, bringing the purpose of modern marketing into question. For most of us, our basic material needs are satisfied, so we seek in ever-growing consumption the satisfaction of wants that consumption cannot possibly deliver, or only to a tiny minority of us. Growth-driven consuming may even undermine all of this pursuit of contentment. Not only are the costs of consumption much greater than orthodox economics recognises, as is now widely acknowledged, but the benefits are also much less than we expect. More is not always better, it is often worse. Excess is pathological, and we see the evidence in social breakdown— loneliness, depression, stress, crime, fragmented communities, suicide and 'busyness'. Whereas the still dominant model of society promises limitless opportunities for a better life it cannot deliver and is already creating degenerations of life; an alternative is needed through a great transformation. This will centre regeneration and sustenance.

Ubiquitous ecological consciousness is needed. Wrong thinking about life entrusts neo-liberal economics and capitalism to find the solution to how to live a better life. Wrong thinking in economics assumes humans are rational, selfish maximisers. Wrong thinking in marketing uncritically takes the neoclassical market model and its neoliberal purpose. Transformative change is needed to combat and repair the degradation. For that we need to change our thinking about the problem and the means to the solution.

In examining the idea of post-industrial marketing, Kadirov and Varey (2010a) argue that marketing evolution goes through three general phases – impairment, enrichment and transcendence – to manifest the future. These phases match Immanuel Kant's thesis, anti-thesis and synthesis (Kant, 1934). The authors envision that the post-industrial era will be marked by qualitative leaps along several dimensions, leaving behind the limiting discourses of marketing impairment versus its gradual enrichment. We envision that marketing transcendence beyond thesis-antithesis dialectics will occur within four domains: marketing identity, value creation, interactivity and environmental impact.

The orthodox (competitive, transactional) marketing principles are the thesis that has been put forward by marketing practitioners to solve immediate and proximate problems of micro-level demand management. Recent developments in re-discovering the centrality of the customer – such as total quality, business process re-engineering, mass customisation and relationship marketing – are temporary antithetical fixes that do not take full account of society as a whole. We see evidence of the transcendence in the emergence of the discipline of macro-marketing, which takes as the unit of analysis the creation of value for all, including future generations, and focuses on the relationships of people, society, and nature.

Kadirov and Varey (2010b) see 'marketplace wisdom' as a characteristic of the progress towards a post-industrial marketing system. Marketplace wisdom is manifested in the development and application of oppositional values, beliefs and differing cultures pertaining to the marketing system in its long-term development.

The phenomenon of marketplace wisdom is a cognitive construct guiding market behaviour that may derive from two broad perspectives, namely survival and wisdom.

Capitalism has evolved from a shareholder form that emphasises growth and extraction and the force of the 'market' in determining resource use to a corrective for the distribution and welfare failures of the market. More recently, an 'intentional inclusive ecosystem economy' has begun emerging, which is fundamentally transformative, regenerative and focused on ecosystem renewal (Scharmer 2010). This is significant in understanding marketing communication and other domains of public communication, since a stakeholder focus rests on negotiation and dialogue, and an ecological mindset emphasises collective action from common attention, awareness and will. In a collective action problem, everyone in a group has a choice between two alternative courses of action. If everyone defects, that is, chooses the individualistically rational option, the outcome (in their own estimation) for everyone involved would be inferior to that of cooperation.

Purposeful public conversation and participatory public planning is an aspect of deepening (direct) democracy, in which a core purpose is the enhanced capacity for collaboration and innovation. The value-realising web of relationships is envisioned by Scharmer (2010) as open-minded (transparent, reflective), open-hearted (empathic, inclusive) and open-willed (action oriented, cooperative, co-creative). The web supports communities of knowledge creation in a 'learning system' that intelligently coordinates the economy. Whereas in the industrial/managerial mindset, marketing is an abstract entity comprising a set of tools and techniques, in the evolving ecosystem economy, marketing is the conversations of collective action.

Society needs to engage the values that are drawn upon for deciding courses of action as citizens, voters and consumers; yet mainstream approaches to tackling environmental crises do not question the dominance of individualistic and materialistic values. Marketers with the short-term, micro-level foci are not concerned with motivations for consumerism (ever more consumption)! In motivating pro-environmental behaviour change, it is necessary to engage with values – and to distinguish attitudes and values. The tool for this is not marketing strategy, but political strategy with a radical change agenda (Crompton 2008; Kassiola 1990). The strategic, green marketing approach to behavioural change has been to circulate appeals to an individual's self-interest and social status to be derived from buying less wasteful eco-products. The analogy with product marketing strategies is obvious – in the weak form of sustainability, marketers take for granted the consumer choice of consumer sovereignty and the preservation of lifestyles. But, this is not capable of generating the widespread systemic changes urgently needed. Environmental changes will not be met with a narrow focus on economic self-interest and environmental prudence. Action is needed beyond the 'business case for sustainable development'. We clearly need to distinguish between authenticity of people's needs and inadequacies of what is offered to meet them (Roszak 1978).

An alternative enterprise logic

The sustainability crisis has widely been understood as an environmental problem, as something business needs to account for, a risk to be avoided or mitigated, or a tax borne. The business community has been going along with this to some extent, but there is apparent tension and restraint, even satisficing. Now, in a dysfunctional global economy and damagingly competitive environment, sustainability is being pushed aside as a luxury while business focuses on efficiencies and the bolder ones look to innovate their way out of recession (itself a tortured technical assessment of slowed growth).

But it's not an and/or choice to be faced. The solution is and/and. The reformist, weak sustainability of compliance, corporate social responsibility, cost reduction and limits, is faltering. A corrective strong sustainability is the only sensible way forward. Strong sustainability is an outcome-focused all-encompassing response to the crisis of crises. It is a process that builds prosperous businesses creating innovative products and services; businesses founded on financial rewards earned in responsible use of resources for community wellbeing.

Zuboff and Maxmin's analysis (2002) reveals the demise of the dominant 20th century business model (managerial capitalism) and the grassroots emergence of an alternative enterprise logic that locates value in the citizen-customer (the emergent Service-Dominant Logic for marketing recognises this) and highlights the shift to consumer advocacy (more on this crucial idea later). Combined psychological individuation of processes of consumption as a means to self-determination and distributed capitalism redefines the purpose for commercial activity – from the adversarial relations of producer and consumer to positioning the corporation as supporting participant, not driver, of society's provisioning. Citizens are trying to make sense of their lives in unique and private ways with their own meanings. They want support in living as they choose – they want to be served and supported.

Zuboff and Maxmin (2002) identify the 'transaction crisis' in which the latent relationship value is unrecognised in the standard enterprise logic – the set of assumptions, attitudes and practices – that was invented to manage the production of things. Yet, transaction value and relationship value are quite distinct in their source. The standard enterprise logic creates adversarial relationships for the transactional extraction of value. Relationship value is latent in a person's subjective experience, so inherently dispersed in constituencies and communities not under central corporate ownership and control. Whereas exchange implies dependency, relationship is interdependency.

In modern corporations, commercial technologies have been used to simplify, allowing expansion and cost reduction. The main assumption is that producers create value and consumers are distant, an abstraction. The partial-person consumer is locked out, and the partial-person employee is locked in! In century-old business logic, people are treated as objects/things to be manipulated – transactions are revenue units. Relationships with customers are mediated by marketing, public relations, etc. whose relationships with customers are, in turn, mediated by advertising agencies, market researchers, etc. – all in the name of customer focus. Yet:

> *Advertising and public relations firms extol the primacy of the end consumer precisely because just the opposite is true. The relationship between producers and end consumers has more typically been characterized by disdain and conflict. If the current wave of platitudes about customer service and satisfaction were true, then the frustration, stress, and anxiety that is the transaction crisis would have long ago disappeared. Instead, they are growing with each passing year (Zuboff & Maxmin 2002, p. 184).*

So is there really power shifting to the consumer? Yes, we have access to more information, but this accelerates commoditisation towards lowest price, often at the expense of quality. Yes, we seem to have more choice among products, channels, formats and prices. We can choose to withdraw purchasing power from one seller and invest it in another, and we have freedom to buy or not buy. But, once the decision to buy is made, most of us must conform to sellers' rules. Further, the shift to electronic media is evidence of the frustration, to be seen in the effort to depersonalise, to avoid wasted time, and the degrading inconveniences and insults.

The value maximised to produce shareholder wealth is *transaction value* – the consumer is a means or troublesome obstacle in this, and consequences for others in the system are ignored. Profit is assumed to be good, even if at the expense of others in the system or even the long-term wealth of the corporation; thus, transactions are managed to maximise profit yield. What may be in the interests of customers and contributes to building long-term relationships is interpreted as 'value destruction' when seen to be reducing immediate profits.

Increasingly now commercial technologies are being used to manage complexity at the level of the individual, opening up the possibility of previously unavailable value realisation. For a vision of the emerging future, we need to adopt relationship economics. This perspective recognises that in the shift from mass consumption to the individuation of consumption, there is potential for interdependence, and thus, a different form of value - *relationship value*. It is understood that firms don't create value – they can only help realise latent value. Relationship value does not depend on goods, or customised services – it is realised in activities of deep support. Products are subordinated to new forms of advocacy and assistance that enable people to pursue their goals of psychological self-determination.

In this way of thinking, marketing communication is not only promotional messaging but also a transcendent higher-order system of coordinated collaboration conversations in a web of dynamic enterprise partnerships and alliances.

Marketing communication in transition

We are interested here in the purpose and form of communication-for-marketing-for-society that is compatible with the great transition to a healthy enduring society and indeed may support it coming about. And it is helpful to notice, as discussed in the next section, the forms that fit in the alternative pathways. Thus we can speak of the orthodox market forces form of marketing communication (perhaps seen in relationship marketing), as well as the policy reform form (social Marketing) and a fortress world that would seem to deny the apparently democratic marketing process.

In the modern world, social and environmental problems are largely treated as scientific-technical problems rather than as values-based, normative-moral problems (Kassiola 1990). The examination of underlying values regarding a social problem and a prescription of appropriate value changes is a political philosophical process, toward a new social order:

> ... the basic social problems constituting the contemporary industrial crisis have no technical solutions but instead require scientific and value political analysis as well as political creativity regarding the nature of a sustainable, desirable society and how to construct it (Kassiola 1990, p. 24).

Tools emerge from underlying values, in their purpose and their use. Thus, marketing communication is a technology or set of tools in this sense, and we are interested here in the viability of such deliberate corporate communication practices in a changing society.

Marketing communication, initially in its advertising form and now in its highly proliferated media and channels, came to the fore in the shifting emphasis from manufacturing to marketing-as-brand-building. The purpose was to ensure the market demand for produced goods and services, and so markets have not been free under the effects of effective marketing. Goods are translated into sources of pleasure and ways to avoid losing status and prestige, thus propagating the consumerist lifestyle (Smart 2010). Marketing communication, then, is an organised system of commercial information and persuasion (Williams 1980). An early assumption has endured – that people need to be persuaded to consume, and then attracted to the seller. Advertising has been at the heart of cultivated desire (Smart 2010), with the purpose of conditioning, stimulating and shaping consumption behaviour. Advertising is deemed successful when desire is stimulated and people are motivated to purchase. Further reflection reveals that the desirable effect is, then, discontent and dissatisfaction, and this requires that consumers are not allowed to be autonomous but must be treated as persuadable, suggestible, influence-able and entice-able.

We want to understand what is driving the adoption of new technologies for interaction and communication, as well as what are the effects of their use. Information and communication technologies (commercially applied media) bring producers and consumers closer, so there is heightened influence of one on the other. In addition, these technologies have supported the transformation of production into informational goods and services in a so-called information economy with fundamental intelligence value. So it's not the Internet that changes our patterns of consumption but the other way around. Desire for a different quality of life through psychological self-determination (to experience in reality the pleasures of the imagination), according to Zuboff and Maxmin (2002), leads to demand for particular goods and services, then inspiring changes in tools and techniques of production and distribution.

Informing and persuading – but is that communicating?

Marketing communication can be traced back to the birth of advertising in the 18th century, and has been evolving on the back of technology developments. For some decades, marketing communication resources were essentially reproductive and distributive. The marketing communication objective was to inform the (mass) market in order to establish and consummate market exchanges, that is, to bring citizens into the role of consumer by persuading them that product purchase was a preferable option, and then into the role of customer by influencing their product/brand preferences.

The human race has developed communication as an adaptive mechanism that we can use to recognise and respond to threats to our wellbeing by cooperating. Conflict, competition and cooperation are three modes of human interaction that are mediated, in differing degrees, by communication. However, in an age of mediating technologies, we have become deluded into thinking that communication is merely about sending 'messages' and moving 'information'. We have almost universally succumbed to a simplistic ideology that is convenient for the technological handling of information for control and decision processes. Often when we talk about communication, it is not the wider and subtle communication that we talk of, but the transmission of signals along wires.

The western culture psychological perspective has been dominant and misleading in management thinking. The prevailing model or metaphor for marketing communication has been the conduit or messaging channel (Varey 2000, 2002). Consistent with the ecological, cyclical rather than linear, models are more helpful in understanding human communication and what is required for responsive and responsible management of communication for productive business enterprises. Causal assumptions can be discarded in taking a view of communication in and of corporations (i.e. corporative communication) as both stimulator and stabiliser. However, social, political and cultural phenomena can be more richly understood if their linguistic and discursive (interactive) nature is addressed with a constructionist perspective on social reality. Communication cannot be understood without reference to knowledge, understanding, information, meaning and sense. A social constructionist theory of communication is a widened framework for the analysis of communication in a complex and holistic fashion.

Marketing communication-as-advertising has transactional objectives: to inform, remind, persuade, assure/reassure, motivate and reward. To accomplish connection and co-creation objectives requires a different 'technology' – inter-action.

Marketing inter-action

The market to which marketing is understood to be applied today and tomorrow, as market maker, has come to be understood as a conversation (Locke *et al.* 2000), rather than a message board. The World Wide Web (as it has been made through interaction, from 1.0 content posting, to 2.0 interaction, to 3.0 development and application of distributed intelligence), with its interactivity and collaborativity and resulting creativity and applications for social networking, has brought dynamic changes from informing to participating. Indeed, we can think of ourselves as now living in an 'interaction society' (Ballantyne & Varey 2006; Varey 2005, 2006, 2008). User-generated content is now commonplace. Social media is essentially a category of online media where people are talking, participating, sharing, networking and bookmarking online. Most social media services encourage discussion, feedback, voting, comments and sharing of information; consequently, most of the information and other content on these sites is generated by users and not provided to them. It's more of a conversation than the one-way broadcast of corporate media. It encourages users to stay connected or linked to other sites, resources and people, thereby growing the community and the interaction that constitutes it. Once upon a time, citizens were treated as spectators (referred to as 'audience') of corporate sales presentations; now they are participating 'media prosumers'. Jenkins (2006) calls this the 'convergence culture' or 'participatory culture'.

The marketing process can be explained as a complex, dynamic, adaptive interaction system, revealing a conversational nature (Varey 2008). Such interaction directs and coordinates, but also co-creates since such interactional work has innovative capacity in that a problem is collaboratively appreciated (Cooperrider & Whitney 2005) and courses of action to resolve emerge in the interaction. We can discern two forms of interaction: informative and communicative (Varey & Ballantyne 2006). This cognitive construction all occurs in socially interacting minds – resources are constructed to make sense of the world using pooled resources and cooperative application of skills. This is the service logic – resource integrators co-creating 'somethings' of value: there is collective meaning-making in interaction. This is quite different in effect from much so-called 'communication' that isn't very communicative. (Dervin, Foreman-Wernet & Launterbach 2003).

Our language reproduces assumptions and ideologies. On the one hand the industrial mechanism (extract, design/make, market/distribute, use/consume, discard) is a control logic. It's linear, transactional, monological, distributional, man-made, reductive, mechanistic, anthropocentric. The alternative interactive logic focuses on the cyclical, relational, dialogical, connected, engaged. It is constructive, ecological, natural, humanistic, organic, integrated and ecocentric.

In the linear mindset, marketing has been considered to be productive for the seller in its sales communication reproductive form when grabbing attention and forming attachment, that is, in taking control of purchase decisions (Galbraith 1969). In managing demand, a commercial culture is fostered in which life is understood as a sequence of problems for which solutions can be purchased. Brand management focuses on competitive differentiation in stimulating and appealing imagery, associations, trademarks and brand names, and product and packaging design. In the 'value realisation' mindset, marketing is productive for both buyer and seller (partners) in the productive effect of service in interaction.

The progressive industrialisation (i.e. massification) of higher education in recent decades is illustrative. The typical and still commonplace university lecture is just a messaging form of communication. A single teacher presents information to many learners at the same rate; they are afforded little opportunity for response (affordance) and while this is expediently convenient for the talker, the effect is nothing like as certain as they would want. There is way less discipline than is assumed; it is a matter of arranging the context for salience, significance, important, etc. (Leonard 1968). Contrast this with the tutorial or project supervision relationship.

Relationship marketing as relational practice

Manifestations of the transition from managerial to distributed enterprise logic can be observed in the emergence and evolution of relationship marketing in regard to attitude towards people: the relationship treated as an object or the relationship treated as an affiliation and 'we-ness'.

The weak form of marketing reform re-discovers customer centrality to provide more communication in 'touchpoints', but the data-driven relationship is simulated, with only pseudo intimacy, absent of cooperative reciprocity and authentic commitment and trust.

The strong radicalist form of relationship marketing – advocacy – generates 'communicative communication', is more ethical and is the mode for committed change-making in interaction. Effective relational marketing avoids passive listening on both parts and conversational engagement progressively spells the death of advertising in its mass broadcast form as the primary way to sell. Instead personalised 'conversation snippets' that truly inform, that is, generate knowledge, are connection outcomes.

I see considerable scope in Zuboff and Maxmin's concept of 'deep support' (2002) as the next phase of evolved relationship marketing and the re-purposing of marketing that is consistent with the sustainability and wellbeing imperative. In this view, citizens are members of constituencies (publics) in the various spheres of their lives (as partners, workers, parents, relatives and so on), and engage in interdependent relationships with advocates, based on dialogue, inquiry, empathy, integrity, authenticity, trust, creativity and collaboration. There is collaborative coordination of action and decisions to realise relationship value (resource integration in the language of SDL – asset inputs in the form of intellectual, emotional, behavioural, digital and physical resources) in a federation of support network enterprises.

There is inherent accountability and responsibility for the entire consumption experience in the advocacy relationship, and this distinguishes 'deep support' from goods and services that may be a part of the 'service'. Advocacy and engagement replace promotional messaging as the core work of marketing. Marketing communication ceases to be a distinct tool or means to marketing ends, since communication is the mode in which marketing is truly a relationship value realisation process. Maybe it won't even be called 'marketing' in the future when it focuses on work done to help individuals (I prefer the term 'service').

The distributed enterprise logic brings together people, markets and digital/online technologies (e.g. social media) in a new configuration. Relationship marketing may then be truly realised in its relational 'connecting' form. Thus relational marketing is the form of marketing that realises relational value through advocacy. Two scenarios can illustrate the distinctions being made in the form of social organisation. An exchange situation is contrasted with an interaction situation. The clear distinction is the engagement of people in supporting those in need through value-realising conversations – the re-humanisation of the marketing-service process.

The *touting products* scenario is commonplace in a consumer society, as citizens are treated as profit sources and might feel under competitive siege, with pervasive pressure to buy value-bearing goods and services (Figure 4.1).

In response to the latest in a series of advertisements soliciting custom, Mrs P sent a small order for some low-cost printed address labels. Since receiving her labels, she has also received a number of direct mail offers, including the latest 68-page and 20-page glossy brochures displaying a cornucopia of product offerings. Mrs P has had no other contact from the supplier and has never been asked to provide any information about her circumstances and needs. This is a very occasional low-value purchase, so she feels no need for a commitment and has received little recognition beyond the obvious follow-up on a sales record.

Perhaps somewhat ironically (unintentionally), the supplier is called IdentityDirect, specialising in personalised items, which are commodity labels, ornaments and novelty items over-printed with the customer's name. For example, a $20 soccer ball can have your son's name printed on it for only $70! Yet, the latest mailing does not have a letter included, only an order form with a name and address, and addressed to 'Dear customer' (hardly personalised). The mailing package includes a prize draw enticement to buy more, presumably motivated by a 'sell more' intention. The goods are offered as personalised, but the service is not.

The *supportive service* scenario is recognisable in the advocacy perspective, as citizens are seen as living in a web of constituencies and reaching out to the wider web of adjunct federated resource integrators (Figure 4.2). Value is realised in committed relationships, and the producer-consumer distinction loses its significance.

The Patient Advocate Foundation mediates and arbitrates for patients to remove obstacles to healthcare including medical debt crisis, insurance access issues and employment issues for patients with chronic, debilitating and life-threatening illnesses. The service is provided as an employment benefit, with a patient advocate who helps their clients' employees to navigate through the insurance system. For instance, rather than the employee having to deal with a hospital's billing department and the appeal process when a claim is denied, the advocate will do that.

Figure 4.1 Competitive exchange encounters

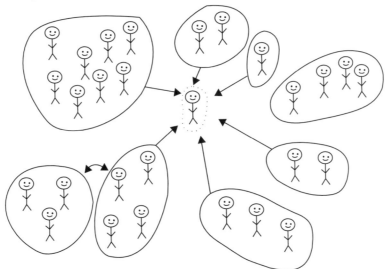

One employee underwent treatment for a lymphoma. The insurance company rejected the claim for the cost of the radiation treatment because they said it was 'elective', and they also refused to pay for the interpretation of a PET scan. Thus, whilst willing to pay for a test to detect cancer, they didn't want to pay for the doctor to interpret the test(!), even though the insurance policy states it pays 100 per cent of costs.

The head of the employer's Human Resources Department contacted the patient advocate, and that person contacted the hospital and insurance company and they were able to negotiate with the insurance company to secure the payment. In the end, the advocate got the insurance company to pay 100 per cent of the radiation treatments and the employee also received a rebate for the PET scan reading fee. When people are sick they reach out for help and support. Advocates ensure that they are not mistreated as rationale consumer choice makers in having to deal with multiple often competing producers.

Insights and Implications: Marketing communication in and for sustainable wellbeing

> *We're all texting each other and saying nothing - lobotomized sheep farmed by the corporations, bleating, lifetime consumers shorn of our money, kept fat on a diet of mediocrity and distracted by any noisy, colourful, empty promise. (Almond 2005, p. 20)*

What will marketing communication be in a sustainable society? To foresee this requires an ecological perspective.

Figure 4.2 Coordinated collaborative service interaction network

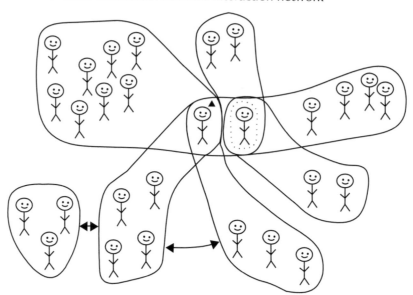

Marketing communication is orthodoxically thought of as a sub-discipline of marketing that focuses on deploying communication tools. Also, marketing communication is strategic communication and therefore has to be managed. I prefer to take the view that communication is the value-realising mode of marketing, that is,

> ... the managerial system that ensures timely and comprehensive input to the corporate information and decision-making processes, and the consequent production and expression of credible, persuasive representations of beneficial exchange opportunities with actual and prospective customers and other stakeholders (Varey 2002, p. 128).

Progressively, exchange will give way to collaborative realisation.

We have considered the forthcoming transformation to a service value economy to support a sustainably healthy society and how the transition is manifest in shifting emphasis on service, relationship and subjective experience and socially-constructed meaning, knowledge and identity. The transformation to a sustainable society implies increasingly organised society, so there is a need for more communicative communication, both informative interaction and communicative interaction, and a shifting emphasis from speaking, to listening, to conversing – from passive action to active participation.

This can be observed in the rise of social media, brand communities and other peer-to-peer value realisation. We are experiencing the transition from limited means under corporate control to a participatory creative mode capable of enabling us to learn our way out of the crisis (Milbrath 1989) by supporting good decisions and choices. Thus we are observing the emergence of the participatory mode of policy-making for and with stakeholders (see Vickers 1965, 1983, for a human system explanation of the general idea of policy making and action). Connection and participation are core enactments of a distributed capitalism (Zuboff & Maxmin 2002). Ultimately, in a fully marketised world with full connectivity, advertising will wane and relationality will assume far greater significance and effect.

The sustainability imperative heralds a higher-order purpose and form for marketing communication that contributes to solving the problem of survival and prosperity. This instead of driving the cause (overconsumption and consumption dependence, and the resulting social and cultural dis-ease) by promoting individualism, materialism and private property, and selling the promise of happiness through accumulation, that takes us to 'the edge of the apocalypse' (Speth 2008).

Nowadays we can't sensibly separate marketing and service, as marketing now largely means service management (Grönroos 1990, 2000, 2007; Vargo & Lusch 2004, 2008). This insight is coming to the fore – increasingly this means organising to realise relationship value. In the beginning was the trading concept, then industrialisation caused conditions that required a marketing concept, now in the context of a sustainability imperative, the marketing concept is once again prominent and valid. Peter Drucker long ago saw the purpose of business as to serve the customer (1973).

As a macro-level phenomenon, marketing is a social coordination mechanism; whereas seen only from the micro-level, it is a profit-making tool. The issue of 'what is the future of marketing in a sustainable society?' has arisen from the over-managerialisation of the marketing concept – in pursuit of firm profit, marketing has been over-successful in promoting consumption.

The market is commonly understood in orthodox economics as an efficient means of making collective choices through the automatic mediation of individual preferences. This 'market' is a linear abstraction – the separation of the individual (but standardised) consumer with appetite (them, who can't make) and the profit-seeking originator (us, who don't consume what is made) – thus a transmission (distribution) mentality is inevitable in both persuasion (communication) and logistics (re-assignment of ownership). Marketing's purpose then is to cross the divide to the distant (separate and unequal) consumer, to promote preferential consumption and provide/deliver value through 'buy more now' consumer messaging. A few citizens took the lead as producers, and everyone else followed as consumers. Transaction economics assumes value is produced in corporate space, incorporated in to products, and distributed to the mass of consumers. The service logic shows that this model has outlived its relevance and is increasingly dysfunctional. The mechanistic, instrumental way is not suitable for the actual need of society precisely because it dehumanises and treats the problem as technical when it is really political.

A mass (market) mindset cannot discern people as individuals, nor as self-determiners; whereas the alternative relationship economics recognises value realisation in the individual space, which does not revolve around goods acquisition. 'Deep support' is the accompanying business purpose if relationship value is to be realised, requiring accountable, responsible support in the consumption experience – what has been called advocacy' (Zuboff & Maxmin 2002). This focuses on collaboration, requiring mutual respect and trust (commitment) and acute alignment of interests (stakeholding and gain-sharing), all enabled by and operating on the basis of an enduring relationship for the convergence/integration of resources to realise latent value, and perfectly consistent with ecological principles (Capra & Pauli 1995).

The whole idea of sustainability marketing (a term coined by Belz and Peattie 2009) raises concerns over the consequences of commercial promotional marketing communication and its corporate controlled 'one-way push' pressures on society, which treats citizens as targets for magic-bullet-messages. Negative consequences include raised expectations and unfulfilled promises, promotion of conspicuous consumption, adversarial exchange in the face of the desire for truth and authenticity, resource use in terms of both scale and opportunity costs, waste and excess. Promotional marketing creates dissatisfaction – it's an irritant; whereas contentment reduces the insatiable urge to consume. Product advertisements tend to obscure social costs generated by the patterns of consumption they stimulate. It is vital that information from stakeholders is equally supported and that there are legal restrictions on the advertising of resource-intensive, wasteful and unhealthy products. Social theorist Geoffrey Vickers observed that 'In the market, as in politics, advocates of rival values appeal to individuals for their support and do all they can to mould these individuals' valuations to support them' (reprinted in Adams, Forester & Catron 1987, p. 53). He thought this well before the advent of the Internet and proposed a societal descriptive and informative central information bank that is not image-making. Vickers foresaw the need for independent information rather than persuasion. Such a public information system in place of advertising would be far more efficient – less wasteful – since so much marketing is wasteful because much so-called value (i.e. value-in-exchange) is inauthentic puffery designed to competitively win-over hearts and minds and encourage consumption. Capra (1983) has also concluded that following ecological principles would require the restructuring of information, thus curtailing and reorganising mechanisms of advertising and establishing the importance of independent monitors – the press, NGOs, activists and social movements and other constituencies.

In the alternative distributed enterprise logic, an 'action space' (Zuboff & Maxmin 2002, p. 293) is where higher-order relationship value is realised in interaction (collective action) through advocacy (see also Urban 2005). In an 'infinite game', the purpose is to keep playing to create value – this requires engaging with others in a relationship that is rewarding for all. A finite game, on the other hand, begins with an end in mind – winning. This is always a zero-sum outcome (Carse 1986; Collins & Murphy 2010).

Despite current trends, it is not simply a matter of selling a managed experience, but fundamentally of supporting the realisation of psychological self-determination (Zuboff & Maxmin 2002) for the co-realisation of value in harmonious life. With the evident value shift among a growing portion of the population, consumption is not so central to life experience, as more of us look towards ecologically harmonious ways of living. Instead of hunting for customers (lawful prey) for products, advocates collaboratively coordinate service with customers.

When marketing is understood as the means to profit, it is reduced to a set of tools and techniques of persuasion and motivation. When the transcendent understanding of marketing as a mode of relationship value realisation is to the fore, then not only content, but also the form (activities, media, channels) of the communicative action platform is made important. When selling values is important and not only informing, then substance, moderation and responsibility gain greater significance for citizens in pursuit of purposeful pleasure (Benett & O'Reilly 2010).

How will we get from here to there? Significantly, interaction management is transcendent – both extending and including – not substitutive (*there* includes here). Social historian Raymond Williams explains how a culture always comprises a mix of values: residual, dominant and emergent (1965). The strong form of relationship marketing that seeks advocacy relationships is part of the transition from a goods-based value economy, to a service-based value economy, and from a transactional to contractual to participational social organisation. Whereas marketing has long been operated as an imposition of order, it is increasingly adopted for the co-construction of order.

So, evidently, the marketing discipline has a substantial role to play in socially learning the pathway to a sustainable society and a key responsibility in leading the sustainability strategy and guiding the corporation to the establishment, implementation and maintenance of the strategy – either as a business opportunity or in recognition of corporate complicity in driving the ecological crisis. It may be adopted only weakly as a tactical product focus (green marketing) or strongly as a strategic rethink on the purpose of commercial enterprise. Such responsible marketing requires that action be authentically taken toward the expressed or supposed wishes or interests of the others who it affects.

Ballantyne *et al.* (2011) address the concept of value 'pro-positioning', arguing that reciprocal value propositions reveal opportunities for focal firm engagement with suppliers, customers and other beneficiaries beyond sale/purchase transactions, as part of a platform for communicative interaction. In summary, we position reciprocal value propositions as a communication practice that brings exchange activities, relationship development and knowledge renewal closer together. Marketing communication isn't simply a means to exchange, it is the mode of value co-creation.

We've begun our journey to Ecotopia, in the transition from a predominantly goods-oriented commerce to a service economy, from a production and selling focus to organising for the realisation of relationship value. So, what will marketing communication be like in the society of the future? Here are some anticipations:

Some goods are distributed in simple exchange, and everything else necessary to sustained wellbeing is accomplished through solution-making interaction.

Ecological disturbances (unacceptable effects) originating in the market (production, consumption) are regulated to harness the market to solve the problems it causes and restrain by legal prohibitions. The market is operated as an instrument of public policy and supplemented by publicly-controlled 'organs'.

Marketing is mostly concerned with provision of 'interaction resources' – some are public/grass-roots/bottom-up and some corporate/top-down/command-and-control/central planning. Interaction resource management is a corporate capability that is highly valued in society.

Tools (means) and values (ends) – and means and mode – are clearly recognised. Interdependence implies relational form and that implies interactional systems, since form follows from purpose.

Value-realisation conversation and sustainable society are not optional add-on accessories in the search for the holy grail of competitive advantage.

Post-branding, product image and corporate image, in terms of visibility and character, are no longer issues of getting noticed and being accepted, and are no longer acceptable as impersonal substitutes for knowing real people. Decisions and choices are supported with reliable knowledge, comprising authentic social meanings capable of transforming lifestyles and attitudes.

Online connection supports 'smart shopping' that is re-personalised and unmediated: strong sustainability necessitates that marketing communication be for connecting and co-creating.

The way of doing business has been redesigned – marketing is an interaction system comprising conversation and participation for support and recognises when people need people, and products are only means to an end.

The prosperous and popular enterprise federations are celebrated as adjuncts to communities. They invest in strong service connection commitments and don't need to scatter dollars to find new customers to replace disillusioned defectors; they choose to play the infinite game.

Many people choose to work as firm-based advocates – and increasingly as network-based advocates for federations of partners, in 'extended enterprises'.

Enterprise is inherently responsibly responsive, and is rewarded for good service.

Service interaction has come of age.

References

Adams, Guy B., John Forester, and Bayard L Catron Eds. (1987), Policymaking, Communication, and Social Learning: Essays of Sir Geoffrey Vickers. New Brunswick, NJ.: Transaction Books.

Almond, Marc (2005) In Search of the Pleasure Palace: Disreputable Travels, London: Pan Books.

Ballantyne, David and Richard J Varey (2006), "Creating value-in-use through marketing interaction: The exchange logic of relating, communicating and knowing," Marketing Theory, 6 (3), 335-48.

Ballantyne, D., P. Frow, R J. Varey, and A. Payne (2011), "Value propositions as communication practice: Taking a wider view," Industrial Marketing Management, 40.

Belz, Frank-Martin and Ken Peattie (2009), Sustainability Marketing: A Global Perspective. Chichester: John Wiley & Sons.

Benett, Andrew and Ann O'Reilly (2010), Consumed: Rethinking Business in the Era of Mindful Spending. New York: Palgrave Macmillan.

Bosselmann, Klaus (1995), When Two Worlds Collide: Society and Ecology. Auckland, New Zealand: RSVP Publishing.

Callenbach, Ernest (1975/1990), Ecotopia: A Novel About Ecology, People and Politics - The Notebooks and Reports of William Weston. London: Bantam Books.

Capra, Fritjof (1983), The Turning Point - Science, Society and the Rising Culture. London: Flamingo.

Capra, Fritjof and Gunter Pauli Eds. (1995), Steering Business Toward Sustainability. Tokyo: The United Nations University.

Carse, James P. (1986), Finite and Infinite Games. New York: Random House.

Collins, Nathalie and Jamie Murphy (2010), "Playing the Infinite Game," Journal of Customer Behaviour, 9 (4), forthcoming

Cooperrider, David L and Diane Whitney (2005), Appreciative Inquiry: A Positive Revolution in Change. San Francisco, CA.: Berrett-Koehler.

Crompton, Tom (2008), "Weathercocks & Signposts: The environment movement at a crossroads." London: WWF-UK.

Cunningham, Storm (2008), reWealth! New York: McGraw-Hill.

Dervin, B., L. Foreman-Wernet, and E. Launterbach Eds. (2003), Sense-Making Methodology Reader: Selected Writings of Brenda Dervin. Cresskill, NJ.: Hampton Press.

Drucker, P F. (1973), Management: Tasks, Responsibilities, Practices. London: Heinemann.

Fisk, G (1974), Marketing and the Ecological Crisis. New York: Harper & Row.

Galbraith, J K (1969), The New Industrial State. Harmondsworth UK: Penguin Books.

Goldsmith, Edward (1992), The Way: An Ecological World View. London: Rider/Random Century.

Grant, John (2007), The Green Marketing Manifesto. Chichester: John Wiley & Sons.

Grönroos, C. (1990), Service Management and Marketing: Managing the Moments of Truth in Service Competition. Lexington, MA.: Lexington Books.

Grönroos, C. (2000), Service Management and Marketing: A Customer Relationship Management Approach (2nd ed.). Chichester: John Wiley & Sons.

Grönroos, Christian (2007), In Search of a New Logic for Marketing: Foundations of Contemporary Theory. Chichester: John Wiley & Sons.

Hamilton, Clive (2003), Growth Fetish. Crows Nest, NSW: Allen & Unwin.

Hamilton, Clive and Richard Denniss (2005), Affluenza: When Too Much is Never Enough. Sydney: Allen & Unwin (Australia).

Hamilton, Clive (2008), Freedom Paradox: Towards a Post-secular Ethics: Allen & Unwin.

Holdgate, Martin (1996), From Care to Action: Making a Sustainable World. London: Earthscan Publications.

Jenkins, Henry (2006), Convergence Culture: Where Old and New Media Collide. New York: New York University Press.

Kadirov, Djavlonbek and Richard J Varey (2010a), "Future marketing: dialectics of post-industrial development," Journal of Customer Behaviour, 9 (4), 357-77.

Kadirov, Djavlonbek and Richard J Varey (2010b), "Towards post-industrial marketing: marketplace wisdom," Journal of Customer Behaviour, 9 (4), 379-98.

Kant, I. (1934). *The Critique of Pure Reason* (J. M. D. Meiklejohn, Trans.). London: Dent.

Kassiola, Joel Jay (1990), The Death of Industrial Civilization: The Limits to Economic Growth and the Repoliticization of Advanced Industrial Society Albany, NY.: State University of New York Press.

Kassiola, Joel Jay (2003), Explorations in Environmental Political Theory: Thinking About What We Value. Armonk, NY.: M E Sharpe.

Leonard, George B (1968), Education and Ecstasy: New York: Delacorte Press.

Locke, C., R. Levine, D. Searls, and D. Weinberger (2000), The Cluetrain Manifesto: The End of Business as Usual. Cambridge, MA.: Perseus Books.

Milbrath, Lester W (1989), Envisioning a Sustainable Society: Learning Our Way Out. Albany, NY.: State University of New York Press.

Pugh, Cedric Ed. (1996), Sustainability, the Environment and Urbanization. London: Earthscan Publications.

Raskin, Paul, Tariq Banuri, Gilberto Gallopin, Pablo Gutman, Al Hammond, Robert Kates, and Rob Swart (2002), "The Great Transition: The Promise and the Lure of the Times Ahead." Boston, MA.: Tellus Institute/Stockholm Environment Institute.

Raskin, Paul D, Christi Electris, and Richard A Rosen (2010), "The Century Ahead: Searching for Sustainability," Sustainability, 2 (1).

Roszak, Theodore (1978), Person/Planet: The Creative Disintegration of Industrial Society. London: Gollancz.

SANZ (2009), "Strong Sustainability for New Zealand: Principles and Scenarios ". Auckland: Sustainable Aotearoa New Zealand (SANZ).

Scharmer, Otto (2010), "Seven Acupuncture Points for Shifting Capitalism to Create a Regenerative Ecosystem Economy," Oxford Leadership Journal, 1 (3).

Schultz, Clifford J (2007), "Marketing as Constructive Engagement," Journal of Public Policy & Marketing, 26 (2), 293-301.

Smart, Barry (2010), Consumer Society: Critical Issues and Environmental Consequences. London: Sage Publications.

Speth, James Gustave (2008), The Bridge at the Edge of the World: Capitalism, the Environment, and Crossing from Crisis to Sustainability. New Haven, CT.: Yale University Press.

Steffen, Alex Ed. (2006), Worldchanging: A User's Guide for the 21st Century. New York: Harry N Abrams.

Urban, Glen (2005), Don't Just Relate - Advocate: A Road Map to Profit in an Era of Customer Power. Upper Saddle River, NJ.: Prentice Hall.

Varey, Richard J (2000), "A Critical Review of Conceptions of Communication Evident in Contemporary Business & Management Literature," Journal of Communication Management, 4 (4), 328-40.

Varey, Richard J (2002), Marketing Communication: Principles and Practice. London: Routledge.

Varey, Richard J (2005), "Informational and Communicational Explanations of Corporations as Interaction Systems," in The Interaction Society: Practice, Theories and Supportive Technologies, Mikael Wiberg, Ed. Hershey, PA.: Information Science Publishing.

Varey, Richard J (2006), "Accounts in Interactions: Implications of accounting practices for managing," in Communication as Organizing: Empirical and Theoretical Explorations in the Dynamic of Text and Conversation,, Francois Cooren and James E Taylor and Elizabeth Van Every, Eds. Mahwah, NJ.: Lawrence Erlbaum Associates, 181-196.

Varey, Richard J (2008), "Marketing as an Interaction System," Australasian Marketing Journal, 16 (1), 78-93.

Varey, Richard J (2010), "Marketing Means and Ends for a Sustainable Society: A Welfare Agenda for Transformative Change " Journal of Macromarketing, 30 (2), 112-26.

Varey, Richard J. (2011), "A sustainable society logic for marketing," Social Business, 1 (1), 1-15.

Varey, Richard J and David Ballantyne (2006), "Relationship Marketing and the Challenge of Dialogical Interaction," Journal of Relationship Marketing, 4 (3), 11-28.

Varey, Richard J and David McKie (2010), "Staging consciousness: Marketing 3.0, post-consumerism and future pathways," Journal of Customer Behaviour, 9 (4), 321-34.

Vargo, Stephen L and Robert F Lusch (2004), "Evolving to a New Dominant Logic for Marketing," Journal of Marketing, 68 (1), 1-17.

Vargo, Stephen L and Robert F Lusch (2008), "Why "service"?," Journal of the Academy of Marketing Science, 36 (1), 25-38.

Vickers, Geoffrey (1965), The Art of Judgment: A Study of Policy Making. London: Chapman & Hall.

Vickers, Geoffrey (1983), Human Systems are Different. London: Harper & Row.

Wasik, John F (1996), Green Marketing and Management: A Global Perspective. Cambridge, MA.: Blackwell Publishers.

Williams, Raymond (1965), The Long Revolution. London: Pelican Books.

Williams, Raymond (1980), Problems in Materialism and Culture. London: Verso.

Wills, Ian (1997), Economics and the Environment: A Signalling and Incentives Approach. St Leonards NSW: Allen & Unwin.

Zuboff, Shoshana and James Maxmin (2002), The Support Economy: Why Corporations are Failing Individuals and the Next Episode of Capitalism. New York: Viking Books/Penguin Books.

Introduction

With growing consumer concerns about the environment, 'green marketing' strategies have become increasingly common in the marketplace. A Google search of news articles which contain the words 'green' and 'marketing' from 1980 to 2010 reveals approximately 393 thousand documents. The number of news articles published each year shows a fairly steady growth over time, as well as spikes in the early 90s, and again around 2007–2008. Researchers interested in green marketing have investigated what green actually means (Kilbourne 1995), issues associated with green advertising (Scammon & Major 1995) and profiles of green consumers (Roberts 1996). One area that, while important, has received relatively little attention is the concept of sustainability in green marketing.

Webster's dictionary defines the word sustain as 'To keep in existence; maintain or prolong'. When applied to the ability of humans to live on the earth, this idea is often referred to as 'sustainability'. Sustainability became a more widely used term after the publication of the United Nations Brundtland Report (Nations 1987), which proposed the need for sustainable development. According to the Brundtland Report, sustainable development is development which 'meets the needs of the present without compromising the ability of future generations to meet their own needs'. This definition was proposed to have two key parts: a focus on the 'essential needs' of the world's population, in particular the poor or underprivileged, and the 'limitations' placed on the environment by current technological and social structures which influence its ability to meet needs in the future. Sustainability as a whole has broadly been described as containing three main areas; environmental, social and economic (Adams 2006). From an environmental perspective, practices such as greenhouse gas emissions, fossil fuel consumption, ground water pollution and toxic waste production are often seen as not sustainable. Despite its importance, environmental sustainability is only one aspect of overall sustainability that is seen to also include aspects of social and economic sustainability. From a macro-marketing perspective, it is important to assess the systemic effects of the different aspects of sustainability. These three categories are conceptualised as being inherently linked to each other (i.e. economic acts aspects may affect the environment, the environment may affect social aspects and social aspects may affect economic aspects).

While the concept of sustainability is not a new one, it is arguable that all environmental advertisements have, at some level, an implied aspect of sustainability. For example, advertising that touts reduced pollution outputs at an energy plant implies that the company is making an effort to behave in a more sustainable manner; however, it is important to note that behaving more sustainably does not equate to sustainability. In order to properly comprehend the concept of sustainability in environmental advertising, this investigation will review pertinent literature on green advertising and sustainability and then present the results of a content analysis of environmental advertisements in the United States. This study seeks to illuminate how consumers perceive environmental advertisements, if consumers can distinguish between sustainable and unsustainable advertising messages and if consumers perceive differences between sustainable and unsustainable messages in terms of subject and clarity. Finally, we assess the overall implications of sustainability in environmental advertising on the economic and social components of sustainability.

Environmental advertising

Environmental advertising began to find footing in the US in the early 1970s. Over the next two decades scrutiny of this advertising and criticisms for its lacking understandability, uniformity and credibility culminated in US state and federal governments forming taskforces to monitor environmental claims and curtail inaccurate 'green washing' by businesses (Attorneys-General 1990; Commission 1992). Compliance with these efforts, however, was largely voluntary and after a short retreat from environmental advertising (Aho 1992; Dagnoli 1992; Schlossberg 1991), green marketing and consumer complaints about it have increased (Pfanner 2008).

In response to the growing usage of environmental advertising and the importance of environmental advertising to consumers, scholars have studied many facets of environmental advertising. In the consumer literature authors have investigated divergent topics including opinions about public policy options to reduce air pollution (Aaker & Bagozzi 1982), perceptions of environmental advertising claims (Carlson, Grove & Kangun 1993; Kangun, Carlson & Grove 1991), investigations of individual variables in an effort to predict environmentally responsible consumption (Balderjahn 1988) and antecedents of recycling behaviour (McCarty & Shrum 1994). Marketing strategy topics include measurements of the effect of environmental marketing strategies on firm performance (Baker & Sinkula 2005), firm compliance with FTC/EPA packaging guidelines (Mayer, Scammon & Zick 1992; Scammon & Mayer 1991), concepts such as 'enviropreneurial' marketing strategy (Menon & Menon 1997) and 'eco-centric' management (Shrivastava 1995).

Firm-relevant consumer outcomes of environmental advertising have also been explored. Examples include green advertisements aiding in communication of a firm's pro-environmental image (Iyer & Banerjee 1992), increasing demand for environmentally friendly products (Wong, Turner, & Stoneman 1996), and enhancing the communication effectiveness of services advertisements (Chan, Leung & Wong 2006). Yet, consumers' scepticism about the truthfulness of environmental advertising claims continues to mount (Pfanner 2008).

One frequent explanation for this growing consumer doubt about the value in green advertisements is the lack of depth or meaning in environmental messages, yet the majority of environmental advertising research does not include a measure of the depth of the environmental message. One exception is a content analysis of environmental advertising by Banerjee, Gulas and Iyer (1995). These authors differentiate advertisements based upon the 'ad greenness', referring to the extent of the environmental focus in the advertisement. Ads that were vague in their environmental contribution, often using key words such as 'earth-friendly' without additional description, were coded as *shallow*. Advertisements which included specific environmental issues such as recycling or re-use, but lacked details specific to the firm or product, were coded as *moderately green*. The greenest advertisements, which focused on specific environmental measures with definite environmental outcomes, were classified as *deep green*. This evaluation of the degree, or depth, of environmental focus is to our knowledge, the only one in the field. While most environmental advertising studies evaluate ads as either green or not green, environmentalists allow for a continuum of environmental orientation and action (Naess 1973). It is our opinion that sustainability advertising messages may have a 'deep green' component. It is the purpose of this study to expand upon the current environmental advertising literature by introducing a definition of sustainable advertising, investigating consumer perceptions and ability to use this definition, and to examine sustainable ads within current environmental typologies.

Sustainability

'No witchcraft, no enemy action had silenced the rebirth of new life in this stricken world. The people had done it themselves' (Carson 1962).

The current conception of environmental sustainability has grown out of the modern environmental movement, whose start has often been at least partially attributed to Rachel Carson's book *Silent Spring* in 1962. Carson's book is thought to have affected perceptions of the environment in two ways: first, by pointing out the significant negative effect of human activities on the environment, and second, by assigning a large portion of the responsibility to economic factors (Kilbourne & Beckmann 1998).

Despite the large amount of research conducted on environmental aspects of marketing, relatively few articles have specifically investigated environmental sustainability in isolation. Of the articles that have investigated sustainability, some have focused on micromarketing aspects of the sustainability dilemma (O'Hara 1995; Van Dam & Apeldoorn 1996) as well as micromarketing perspectives on the relationship between sustainability and quality of life (Kilbourne, McDonagh & Prothero 1997). Other articles include theories about communicating sustainability messages (McDonagh 1998; Signitzer & Prexl 2008) and the way consumers access information when buying sustainable products (Oates *et al.* 2008). Notably absent from this literature is an investigation of how consumers perceive claims about environmental sustainability and if they can identify green advertising claims that make assertions about sustainability. In other words, we have yet to understand the impact claims of environmental sustainability have on consumers or if they are aware of advertising content related to environmental sustainability. As previous work has revealed levels of green in advertising (Banerjee, Gulas & Iyer 1995), it is important to investigate how sustainability messages might contribute to this effect.

Definition of environmental sustainability

As environmental advertising becomes more commonplace and relevant in the eyes of consumers, it is important to investigate both the prevalence and perception of environmental sustainability claims. In order to assess advertising messages about environmental sustainability we conceptualise environmental sustainability as environmentally relevant practices which ensure the continued ability of humans to inhabit the earth indefinitely. This definition matches the one suggested in the previous discussion. A sustainable message should include the following aspects: (1) it should be future oriented (i.e. it must speak about how actions will impact the future), and either (2) have some statement about how resources are being used or will be used at a level that allows for a continued use of that resource or to live in harmony with the earth, or (3) may include a statement about a sustainable relationship or natural balance with the environment. This conceptualisation draws on the key portions of sustainability suggested by the Bruntland Report which are that it must be forward looking (part 1) and that it must focus on the ability to meet needs in the future (parts 2 and 3). In this case, the future needs are conceptualised from an environmental standpoint as the ability to use natural resources or to maintain a natural balance. It also fits with the general conception of the word 'sustain' by emphasising the ability to maintain natural resources and interact with the environment in perpetuity.

Extending existing environmental advertising typologies to include sustainability

As a goal of this study is to expand existing work on environmental advertising claims by including sustainability, it is important to utilise previous work on environmental advertising claims. As such, this paper extends the environmental advertising typologies proposed by Carlson *et al.* (1993) in their content analysis of environmental advertising claims. In their article, the authors utilise two claim typologies, one which analysed the misleading or deceptive nature of the advertising claim, and the other which analysed the focus of the claim. This paper will add an additional level of analysis by including a measure of the advertisements' sustainability to the existing typologies.

Utilising the developed definition of sustainable, this study will ask consumers to identify sustainability messages in environmental advertising in order to determine if they are capable of recognising sustainability related messages in advertising copy. Second, consumers will be asked to utilise the previously established typologies to classify the advertising copy. This will advance knowledge about environmental advertising by expanding the continuum on which environmental advertising has been assessed by consumers. As sustainability is the focus of most environmental movements and many business ventures today, it is imperative that advertisers know if consumers can differentiate between sustainable and non-sustainable environmental statements. If a differentiation can be made: are sustainable claims more environmentally meaningful to consumers than less environmentally impactful 'green-washing' claims? If consumers are unable to identify sustainable claims, should firms focus on creating and communicating such complex messages to consumers? In addition to investigating consumers' perceptions of the depth of environmental advertising messages, this study also investigates the interaction between sustainability claims and the other environmental advertising typologies in order to determine if consumers perceive sustainable messages to differ in terms of their focus or clarity as compared to non-sustainable messages. Importantly, the primary unit of analysis in this study is the entire advertising message copy. As the definition of sustainability includes multiple parts and any message attempting to communicate sustainable practices or products would most likely require multiple sentences and claims, this study utilises the entire advertising message copy in order to evaluate the sustainability of the advertisement. This differs from previous work that utilises specific environmental claims within advertisements as the unit of analysis.

Method

This study employs a content analysis to expand previous research into the nature of environmental advertising claims. Content analysis is a useful technique for providing an understanding of patterns that can be used in the creation of new theory or the testing of existing theory (Kolbe & Burnett 1991). Foundations of conducting a high quality content analysis include objectivity, systematisation, sampling procedures, and reliability (Kassarjian 1977). Each of these issues received special attention in this study. Objectivity was addressed by training content evaluators and providing examples as to the rules and procedures established for ad evaluation. Independence of the evaluators was maintained throughout the process by isolating them from other judges during the rating process. Data collection based upon clearly identifiable characteristics (i.e. message type) aids in the systematisation of the analysis (Holsti 1969). The evaluated stimulus materials were systematically sampled advertisements from a wide range of source possibilities including magazines and newspapers. Additionally, previous environmental advertising content analyses, upon which this study builds, have used a similar sample (c.f. Carlson *et al.* 1993). Reliability of the results is calculated as inter-rater reliabilities and is reported. The division and categorisation of the advertisements reviewed is based upon a four-stage process as described below, each with independent consumer judges (see Table 4.1 in the Appendix for demographic information on the judges within each stage). The first stage involved identifying environmental advertisements. The second stage identified which message components were claims and which were environmental claims. The third stage identified the sustainability of environmental advertisements. Finally, the fourth stage evaluated these messages on the environmental claim typology and presence of misleading and/or deceptive content categorisations used by Carlson *et al.* (1993). We will now describe each stage of the process in detail.

Stage 1: Stimulus materials

The sample of environmental advertisements used in the analyses was identified using the same procedure as put forth by Carlson *et al.* (1993). First, 16 magazine titles from the popular press were selected from the various categories of magazines regularly delineated in *Advertising Age* at the time (1992) (e.g. 'Science/Electronic/Mechanical' and 'Weeklies/Biweeklies'), for example, *Scientific American, Popular Mechanics* and *Time*. In addition, two national newspapers were reviewed" *The Wall Street Journal* and *USA Today*. A cross section of categories was used to systematically vary the sources of the environmental ads. Within each magazine title, all issues for two years (2007 and 2008) were obtained. A random selection of daily newspaper editions from this same time period were selected for review. Environmental advertisements within each issue were identified by an independent judge previously briefed on environmental advertising. Following this selection, the ads selected as environmental were reviewed by two researchers. In total, 85 advertisements were included representing various categories (as identified by *Advertising Age*) across the magazine and newspaper titles (see Table 4.2 in the Appendix for a breakdown of advertisements from each source).

Stage 2: Identification of environmental claims

Three new judges were then asked to evaluate the entire copy from each of the 85 environmental advertisements and identify: 1) each claim made in the copy and 2) whether or not each claim was an environmentally oriented claim. The authors reconciled the results of the three raters by eliminating all advertisements where all three raters did not agree on at least one claim as environmental. This conservative approach to insure that only advertisements with clearly agreed-upon environmental claims progressed to the next round resulted in the elimination of 28 advertisements. The remaining 57 advertisements, which all three raters agreed on the identification and classification of at least one environmental claim, progressed to the next group of raters to evaluate the sustainability of the message. As a check to the identification of environmental advertisement selection in stage 1, only two of the 85 advertisements were classified as having no specific environmental claims by all three stage 2 judges.

Stage 3: Evaluation of sustainability

Stage three sought to ascertain if consumers could differentiate between environmental and sustainability claims in environmental advertising. To this end, three new judges were enlisted to evaluate the entire copy from each of the 57 environmental advertisements identified in stage 2. These judges were versed on the definition of sustainability and were provided with an instruction sheet and examples (see Appendix) regarding how to evaluate environmental messages according to the definition. Each judge was asked to evaluate each of the 57 advertisements as either sustainable or not sustainable. In order to continue to the next round of ratings, all three judges had to agree that an advertisement was either sustainable or not sustainable. All three judges agreed on the classification of 43 of the 57 advertisements giving an inter-rater reliability of .88 based on the proportional reduction in loss approach (Rust & Cooil 1994). In addition to providing dichotomous 'yes or no' responses to whether or not advertising messages were sustainable, we allowed raters to explain their decisions in writing. These qualitative results were compiled verbatim and analysed by the authors.

Stage 4: Typology evaluations

The final stage involved three judges[2] categorising the 43 environmental advertisements identified in stage 3 based upon the environmental advertising typologies developed by Carlson *et al.* (1993) (see Appendix). The environmental claim typology speaks of the nature of the claim, and specifically if the advertising claim is related to the product advertised, a production process undergone by the firm advertising, a claim oriented toward the overall image of the firm, or if the claim was actually an environmental fact. The misleading and/or deceptive advertising claim typology addresses the level of perceived deception in the claim and can fall into the categories of outright lie, omission, vague/ambiguous or acceptable. Each judge was given an instruction sheet detailing the typologies and provided examples of environmental advertising categorised using the typologies (see Appendix). The judges were asked to classify the entire ad copy based upon the typologies. If the judge believed the advertisement included multiple categories (i.e. spoke about both a product and a process), they were asked to code the message as per the dominant category. Based upon the Rust and Cooil (1994) method for evaluating inter-rater reliability for multiple categories and multiple raters, the environmental claim typology yielded an inter-rater reliability of .86. The misleading and/or deceptive typology yielded an inter-rater reliability of .96. Similarly to stage 3, stage 4 raters were encouraged to detail their categorisation experience in writing at the end of the document.

Results

In evaluating the difference between the number of environmental advertisements in stage 1 and stage 2, where raters first choose entire environmental advertisements and then choose environmental claims from ad copy, we find a decrease from 85 to 57 advertisements. This drop is mostly accounted for by our conservative inclusion protocol, which required all three raters to agree that some specific portion of the ad was an environmental claim. We felt this was important because subsequent analyses assume that all messages are environmental in nature.

While the majority of this differential is due to our conservative inclusion of ads only if all three raters agreed on some portion of the environmental claims included, there were two ads that all three raters agreed contained no environmental claim. This, along with statements by our raters describing how some of the copy seemed 'odd' or 'almost didn't make sense' until they thought of the ads as environmental suggests there is some environmental aspect of the advertisements that does not come across in the ad copy alone. This missing cue that allows raters to identify these advertisements as environmental and make sense of the corresponding copy may be visual, as a majority of the advertisements selected by raters in stage 1 included environmental visual elements such as grass,

---

[2] Four judges were enlisted for this process, but the fourth judge did not categorise a number of the messages and thus was excluded from analysis.

streams, trees, wildlife and sky. However, a discussion of the visual environmental components of ads is outside the scope of this paper.

The results from stage 3, where raters evaluated the sustainability of messages, shows that consumers are generally capable of evaluating whether or not an ad contains a sustainability message as based upon this paper's definition. Of the 43 advertisements agreed upon by all raters as either being sustainable or non-sustainable in message type (agreement inter-rater reliability score of .88 (Rust & Cooil 1994)), 14 were rated as sustainable in nature while 29 were identified as not related to sustainability; resulting in a ratio of approximately 1/3 of environmental ads being classified by consumers as sustainable in nature and 2/3 of environmental ads identified as not sustainably oriented. Of particular interest in this phase were the qualitative responses of our judges. Utilising the sustainability definition provided, the raters noted individual guidelines for evaluating a long-term orientation in the messages. For example, the energy message below was judged sustainable by all raters.

> *Chevron Steps Taken: Investing over $15 billion a year to bring energy to market; developing energy through partnerships in 26 countries, committing hundreds of millions annually to alternative and renewable energies to diversity supply; since 1992, have make our own energy go further by increasing our efficiency by 24%.*

One judge noted that the message qualified as sustainable due to the long-term nature of the renewable partnership: '1992 was a while ago (when the partnership began), so they are obviously investing in longer-term solutions'.

Similarly, specific actions such as reforestation and programs including environmental education were noted by the consumers as speaking toward a long-term solution and qualifying the message as sustainable. Environmental messages that consumers questioned the sustainability of were noted as not having 'concrete plans to keep it going', or consumers stated they were unsure if the firms' sustainable actions 'will actually last'. In related comments, consumer judges rebuked messages that had 'no mention of the future beyond the next 5 years', and those that only gave 'lip service' to the future: 'despite saying "future" and "tomorrow", they don't really say anything about the future'.

The functions of advertising are broadly broken into informative and persuasive aspects (Leffler 1981; White 1959). From the responses of consumers in this study, we can derive that environmental claims within advertising act as a source of information but vary on the degree to which they are persuasive. Some sustainability claims are viewed as more persuasive by consumers. The information included in the advertisement may be partially responsible for this finding. Interestingly, we find that consumers often evaluated sustainability claims that pointed out firm environmental shortcomings as more credible and persuasive than claims that ostensibly provided more information.

Clearly, consumers are capable of evaluating claims based upon the very complex definition of sustainability. Yet, based on the qualitative responses listed during the evaluation process, it also appears that consumers are willing to accept advertising messages that approach sustainable or admit their shortcomings. One respondent noted that a message describing its actions as only a start qualified as sustainable because 'a start implies there will be a continuing effort'. While the authors feared that very few of the messages would be classified as sustainable based upon the stringent definition, consumers appeared to be willing to give firms credit for actions if the firms were upfront and 'honest in what they are doing and what they're not'. While many of the firm messages probably did not actually meet the requirement of allowing indefinite future use of resources, contributions in this direction that were judged as meaningful by consumers were rewarded with a sustainable rating.

In stage 4, the raters evaluated the two environmental advertising typologies created by Carlson *et al.* (1993), the environmental claim typology and the misleading/deceptive typology for the 43 ads agreed on as being either sustainably or not sustainably related. The results for each typology can be found in Table 4.3 below. Notably, of the sustainably related claims, approximately 43% were identified as being image based claims. While for the non-sustainability related claims, 47% were identified as product claims. These were respectively the largest percentage categories for the environmental claim typology.

The results of the misleading/deceptive typology showed that the dominant category for both sustainable and non-sustainable messages was the acceptable category, with 57% (24) of evaluations for sustainable messages and 49% (43) for non-sustainable messages rated as acceptable. The next highest category was vague/ambiguous, as 31% (13) of sustainable ads and 43% (37) of non-sustainable ads were rated as vague or ambiguous by the consumers. Interestingly, none of the raters deemed any of the messages to be outright lies, and the omission category was sparsely used with approximately 12% (5) of sustainable claims resulting in this rating and 8% (7) of non-sustainable claims being classified as omissions.

It is important to note that these results differ from Carlson *et al.* (1993) as we instructed all raters to evaluate the entire message and did not ask them to evaluate specific claims in stages 3 and 4. As noted earlier, sustainability messages must be evaluated based upon the entirety of the ad copy as sustainability entails multiple aspects that are typically unable to be communicated in a single sentence or claim. As such, we choose to investigate whether or not consumers can use existing claim typologies to evaluate entire advertising messages. As described previously, we asked consumers to identify the dominant aspect of the advertisement as applied to each typology. As our reliability statistics show, consumers were able to perform this task very well.

It is interesting to note that the qualitative results from stage 4 focused on a perceived inability by consumers to classify messages according to the misleading/deceptive typology. Specifically, raters complained that they possessed 'insufficient knowledge to assess the message claim typology' or had 'insufficient knowledge to assess the believability' of the environmental message. These responses suggest that consumers are aware of the often highly technical claims being made in environmental messages. It also suggests that consumers recognise that they neither 1) possess the knowledge needed to determine if a message includes a lie or omission, nor do they 2) have the ability or intent to access such knowledge from external sources. In essence, consumers feel many environmental advertisements include credence claims that are unable to be assessed.

Discussion

Consumers, as demonstrated by the results of the content analysis, are capable of identifying if a message is sustainability related, the general type of message being made (environmental message typology) and the relative worth and clarity of the information being presented (misleading/deceptive typology). From a marketing strategy point of view, it is clear that messages related to sustainability are seen as having an impact on the organisation's image (43% of sustainability messages were evaluated as image related vs. 25% for non-sustainability messages), while non-sustainability related messages tended to be product specific (47% of non-sustainability messages were evaluated as product messages vs. 26% for sustainability messages). We suggest a potential explanation for this trend may relate to the attributions being made by consumers after viewing a given message. If consumers view a sustainability related message, they may make attributions about the social responsibility of the organisation as a whole. Conversely, if consumers view a non-sustainability related message, they may make no attributions about the organisation as a whole and instead focus on the message specifics leading to fewer image classifications.

From a managerial perspective, this provides the opportunity for marketers to align advertising goals with the demonstrated perceptual trends of consumers. An organisation seeking to promote its overall environmental image may want to focus on aspects of sustainability in their advertisements, while an organisation primarily seeking to raise awareness of a single product may want to avoid messages of sustainability. In addition, the results suggest that managers need to be mindful of the presentation of advertising messages. While the majority of sustainability advertisements were deemed acceptable as per the misleading/deceptive typology (57%), many were also identified as being vague (31%) or omitting information (12%).

From a systems view, it is important to measure the instance of messages perceived as sustainable. If changes in the frequency of such messages can be measured, it may suggest that social paradigms of consumption are changing to reflect sustainability congruent values. The presence of sustainability related messages suggests that social views may already be affecting companies' beliefs of how to operate in an environmentally conscious manner. Companies are clearly utilising environmental sustainability as an important aspect of organisation image, if not yet as a competitive advantage. Unfortunately, neither of these changing aspects are significantly impacting the economic aspect of sustainability in the US as, from an economic perspective, the US cannot continue its current economic and consumption policies without creating a permanent deficit for other parts of the world.

Future research

Future research on environmentally sustainable advertising, consumer perceptions of such messages and the impact of sustainable messages on consumer actions is needed. Researchers should investigate if sustainable messages and other forms of 'deep green' advertising impact consumers more than more superficial or 'green washing' types of environmental advertising. While this study shows that consumers are able to evaluate the complex notion of sustainability in environmental advertisements, it is not known if sustainable claims lead to improved commitment from consumers, increased believability of claims or spur consumers to perceive the firm as more trustworthy. This paper is one step toward illuminating how consumers perceive environmentally sustainable claims, but much work remains in this area.

References

Aaker, David A. & Richard P. Bagozzi. 1982. Attitudes Toward Public Policy Alternatives to Reduce Air Pollution. *Journal of Marketing & Public Policy* 1:85-94.

Adams, William M. 2006. The Future of Sustainability: Re-thinking Environment and Development in the Twenty-first Century, edited by R. o. t. I. R. T. Meeting. Geneva, Switzerland.

Aho, Debra. 1992. Be Precise; Don't Overstate Claims. *Advertising Age* 62:8–10.

Attorneys-General, National Association of. 1990. The Green Report: Findings and Preliminary Recommendations For Responsible

Environmental Advertising. November.

Baker, William E. & James M. Sinkula. 2005. Environmental Marketing Strategy and Firm Performance: Effects on New Product Performance and Market Share. *Journal of the Academy of Marketing Science* 33 (4):461-475.

Balderjahn, Ingo. 1988. Personality Variables and Environmental Attitudes as Predictors of Ecologically Responsible Consumption Patterns. *Journal of Business Research* 17 (1):51-56.

Banerjee, Subhabrata, Charles S. Gulas & Easwar Iyer. 1995. Shades of Green: A Multidimensional Analysis of Environmental Advertising. *Journal of Advertising* 24 (2):21-31.

Carlson, Les, Stephen J. Grove & Norman Kangun. 1993. A Content Analysis of Environmental Advertising Claims: A Matrix Method Approach. *Journal of Advertising* 22 (3):27-39.

Carson, Rachel. 1962. *Silent Spring: The Sea Around Us*. New York: Houghton Mifflin.

Chan, Ricky Y.K., T.K.P. Leung & Y.H. Wong. 2006. The Effectiveness of Environmental Claims for Services Advertising. *Journal of Services Marketing* 20 (4):233-250.

Commission, Federal Trade. 1992. Guides for the Use of Environmental Marketing Claims. Washington, D.C.

Dagnoli, Judann. 1992. Green ads wilt: NAD chief. *Advertising Age* 63 (4).

Holsti, Ole R. 1969. *Content Analysis for the Social Sciences and Humanities*. Reading, MA: Addison-Wesley.

Iyer, Easwar, and Bobby Banerjee. 1992. Anatomy of Green Advertising. Paper read at Advances in Consumer Research, at Provo, UT.

Kangun, Norman, Les Carlson, and Stephen J. Grove. 1991. Environmental Advertising Claims: A Preliminary Investigation. *Journal of Public Policy & Marketing* 10 (2):47-58.

Kassarjian, Harold H. 1977. Content Analysis in Consumer Research. *Journal of Consumer Research* 4 (1):8.

Kilbourne, William E. 1995. Green Advertising: Salvation or Oxymoron? *Journal of Advertising* 24 (2):7-19.

Kilbourne, William E., and Suzanne C. Beckmann. 1998. Review and Critical Assessment of Research on Marketing and the Environment. *Journal of Marketing Management* 14 (6):513-532.

Kilbourne, William, Pierre McDonagh, and Andrea Prothero. 1997. Sustainable Consumption and the Quality of Life: A Macromarketing Challenge to the Dominant Social Paradigm. *Journal of Macromarketing* 17:4-24.

Kolbe, Richard H., and Melissa S. Burnett. 1991. Content-Analysis Research: An Examination of Applications with Directives for Improving Research Reliability and Objectivity. *The Journal of Consumer Research* 18 (2):243-250.

Leffler, Keith B., 1981. Persuasion or Information: The Economics of Prescription Drug Advertising.

Journal of Law and Economics. 24: 45-74.

Mayer, Robert N., Debra L. Scammon, and Cathleen D. Zick. 1992. Turning the Competition Green. Paper read at Proceedings of the 1992 Marketing and Public Policy Conference, at Chicago.

McCarty, John A., and L. J. Shrum. 1994. The recycling of solid wastes: Personal values, value orientations, and attitudes about recycling as antecedents of recycling behavior. *Journal of Business Research* 30 (1):53-62.

McDonagh, Pierre. 1998. Towards a Theory of Sustainable Communication in Risk Society: Relating Issues of Sustainability to Marketing Communications. *Journal of Marketing Management* 14 (6):591-622.

Menon, Ajay, and Anil Menon. 1997. Enviropreneurial Marketing Strategy: The Emergence of Corporate Environmentalism as Market Strategy. *The Journal of Marketing* 61 (1):51-67.

Naess, Arne. 1973. The Shallow and the Deep, Long-Range Ecology Movement. *Inquiry* 16 (May):95-100.

Nations, United. 1987. Our Common Future. In *Brundtland Report*. Oxford: Oxford University Press.

O'Hara, Sabine U. 1995. Sustainability: Social and Ecological Dimensions. *Review of Social Economy* 54 (4).

Oates, Caroline, Seonaidh McDonald, Panayiota Alevizou, Kumju Hwang, William Young, and Leigh-Ann McMorland. 2008. Marketing Sustainability: Use of Information Sources and Degrees of Voluntary Simplicity. *Journal of Marketing Communications* 14 (5):351-365.

Pfanner, Eric. 2008. Cooling Off on Dubious Eco-Friendly Claims. *The New York Times*.

Roberts, James A. 1996. Green Consumers in the 1990s: Profile and Implications for Advertising. *Journal of Business Research* 36 (3):217-231.

Rust, Roland T., and Bruce Cooil. 1994. Reliability Measures for Qualitative Data: Theory and Implications. *Journal of Marketing Research* 31 (1):1-14.

Scammon, Debra L. , and Robert N. Mayer. 1991. Environmental Labeling and Advertising Claims: International Action and Policy Issues. In *Association for Consumer Research Summer Conference*. Amsterdam.

Scammon, Debra L., and Robert N. Mayer. 1995. Agency Review of Environmental Marketing Claims: Case-by-Case Decomposition of the Issues. *Journal of Advertising* 24 (2):33-43.

Schlossberg, Howard. 1991. Marketers Say State Laws Hurt Their Green Efforts. *Marketing News*, 8.

Shrivastava, Paul. 1995. Ecocentric Management for a Risk Society. *The Academy of Management Review* 20 (1):118-137.

Signitzer, Benno, and Anja Prexl. 2008. Corporate Sustainability Communications: Aspects of Theory and Professionalization. *Journal of Public Relations Research* 20 (1):1-19.

Van Dam, Ynte K., and Paul A. C. Apeldoorn. 1996. Sustainable Marketing. *Journal of Macromarketing* 16:45-56.

White, Irving S. 1959. The Functions of Advertising in Our Culture. *Journal of Marketing* 24 (1): 8-14.

Willer, David. 1967. *Scientific Sociology*. Englewood Cliffs, NJ: Prentice-Hall.

Wong, Veronica, William Turner, and Paul Stoneman. 1996. Marketing Strategies and Market Prospects for Environmentally-friendly Consumer Products. *British Journal of Management* 7 (3):263– 81.

Appendix

Table 4.1 Judge demographics

Stage 1	1 Professional previously briefed on environmental advertising
Stage 2	2 PhD students and 1 undergraduate student previously briefed on environmental advertising claims
Stage 3	2 Professionals and 1 PhD student previously briefed on the authors' definition of sustainability
Stage 4	2 Professionals and 1 PhD student previously briefed on the two typologies utilised

Table 4.2 Sources of environmental advertisements

Category	Total environmental advertisements	Category	Total environmental advertisements
Business/ National* *Business Week Fortune*	15	Weeklies/Biweeklies *New Yorker Newsweek Time U.S. News and World Report*	10
Newspapers *USA Today Wall Street Journal*	18	Science/Electronic/ Mechanical* *Discover Omni Popular Science Scientific American*	13
General* *Atlantic Utne Reader*	3	Music/Entertainment* *Rolling Stone*	5
Men's* *Esquire Popular Mechanics*	18	Home* *Better Homes and Gardens*	4
			86 Ads

* Categories as used by *Advertising Age*

Table 4.3 Message type and misleading/deceptive cell frequencies

Sustainable messages (14 advertisements x 3 judges)					
Claim type	**Product**	**Process**	**Image**	**Environmental fact**	
Vague/ambiguous	(23) 3 (27)	(15) 2 (20)	(32) 8 (44)	(0) 0 (0)	13 (31)
Omission	(20) 1 (9)	(0) 0 (0)	(40) 2 (11)	(40) 2 (67)	5 (12)
False/outright lie	(0) 0 (0)	(0) 0 (0)	(0) 0 (0)	(0) 0 (0)	(0)
Acceptable	(29) 7 (64)	(33) 8 (80)	(33) 8 (44)	(4) 1 (33)	24 (57)
	11 (26)	10 (24)	18 (43)	3 (7)	42 (100)

Non-sustainable messages (29 advertisements x 3 raters)					
Claim type	**Product**	**Process**	**Image**	**Environmental fact**	
Vague/ambiguous	(46) 17 (41)	(22) 8 (44)	(27) 10 (45)	(5) 2 (33)	37 (43)
Omission	(29) 2 (5)	(43) 3 (17)	(14) 1 (5)	(14) 1 (17)	7 (8)
False/outright lie	(0) 0 (0)	(0) 0 (0)	(0) 0 (0)	(0) 0 (0)	(0)
Acceptable	(51) 22 (54)	(16) 7 (39)	(26) 11 (50)	(7) 3 (50)	43 (49)
	41 (47)	18 (21)	22 (25)	6 (7)	87 (100)

Phase 3: Advertising message evaluation instruction sheet

We are interested in what people consider to be sustainability messages in environmental advertisements. In order to assess this we would like you to evaluate the following advertisements.

Sustainability is defined as practices which ensure the continued ability of humans to inhabit the earth indefinitely.

Sustainability messages should include the following aspects:

1. it should be future oriented (i.e. it must speak about how actions will impact the future)

And either

2. have some statement about how resources are being used or will be used at a level which allows for a continued use of that resource or to live in harmony with the earth.

or

3. may include a statement about a sustainable relationship or natural balance with the environment.

Examples of Sustainable and non-sustainable messages:

Sustainable message

>   *We've cut our dependence on fossil fuels to the point where we can run our factories with renewable energy for generations to come. It's our way of helping humanity maintain a balance with the world.*

Not a sustainable message (as there is no reference to being able to sustain the consumption or the production practices)

>   *We're cutting emissions by 3% per year with our new hybrid technologies. If every American drove a hybrid vehicle we would cut 30 million pounds of ozone destroying emissions each year. Together we can make a difference.*

Please classify each message as being sustainable or not sustainable. If you have a difficult time making a decision, please provide a brief explanation for your final decision for that advertisement at the end of the document.

For example: Message number (5) Because this had the word sustainable, I rated it as yes, but it wasn't very long.

Phase 4: Advertising message evaluation instruction sheet

We are investigating how consumers perceive environmental advertising messages. Below, are two typologies we would like you to evaluate the following messaged based on. The first typology regards the focus of the environmental message while the second typology discusses the believability or deceptiveness of the message. Please read each message and then mark the category which you feel the overall message fits within for each of the two typologies. Please see below for an example. If, for any message, you feel none of the categories 'fits', do not mark any of the boxes for that typology; instead, briefly note your reasoning in the space.

Misleading/deceptive message claim typology (Vague or ambiguous, omission, lie, or okay)

Vague or ambiguous – The message contains a phrase or a statement that is too broad to have a clear meaning. For example,

> *We are an environmentally friendly company. (What is an environmentally friendly company?)*

Omission – The message omits important information to evaluate its truthfulness. For example,

> *We are spending 100 million on clean energy research. (When? Over how many years? What is clean energy?) OR This product contains no CFCs. (When in fact it contains other harmful chemicals.)*

Lie – The message is inaccurate or a fabrication. For example,

> *This product is made from recycled materials. (When in fact it is not.)*

Okay–The message is accurate and not misleading or deceptive.

Type of message claim typology (Process, product, image, or environmental fact)

Product orientation – The message focuses on the environmentally friendly attributes that a product possesses. For example,

> *This product is biodegradable.*

Process orientation – The message deals with an organization's internal technology, production technique, and or disposal method that yields environmental benefits. For example,

> *Twenty percent of the raw materials used in producing this good are recycled.*

Image orientation – The message associates an organization with an environmental cause or activity for which there is broad-based public support. For example,

We are committed to preserving our forests.

We urge that you support the movement to preserve our wetlands.

Environmental fact – The message involves an independent statement that is ostensibly factual in nature from an organization about the environment at large, or its condition. For example,

The world's rain forests are being destroyed at a rate of 2 acres per second.

Chapter 5

Distribution

Sustainable distribution

Sivakumar Alur

Abstract

Sustainable distribution is a key component of sustainable marketing. Sustainability as a concept in distribution is applicable across all the sectors, products and services and at national and international levels. Logistics involving warehousing and transportation can greatly contribute to sustainable distribution. Food distribution is one of the well-researched areas of sustainable distribution. Several factors influence sustainability in goods distribution that includes packaging, lead-time, postponement as a strategy and information & communication technology. In sustainable services distribution, capacity utilisation is a key element. Transportation management is an important aspect that can help foster sustainable distribution. Managing transportation has now extended to reverse logistics too at the end of the product lifecycle. Several countries have noted the negative externalities of unsustainable distribution and have devised legislation to foster sustainable distribution. Thus, many factors have increasingly forced marketers across the world to make sustainable distribution as part of their sustainable marketing agenda.

Introduction

Distribution in marketing consists of two broad elements, namely channel management and physical distribution management. In the case of retailers, distribution also involves the sourcing of goods from producers. Channel management refers to management of channel partners (individuals/organisations) in distribution process. It deals with relationships and rewards/incentives for various functions of distribution. Physical distribution management or Logistics relates to inventory and transportation management. Marketer's interactions during the management of these two activities are increasingly viewed from a lens of sustainability. Sustainability has gained prominence in marketing due to the efforts of Non Government organisations (NGOs) and the concern of governments for the environment. Sustainable marketing has also become important with the increasing environmental consciousness of consumers and the corporate world. Sustainability is a broader concept than environmental concerns as it encompasses economy, environment and societal dimensions. Integrating sustainability in distribution management therefore means sustainable channel, inventory and transportation management.

Sustainable distribution (Kleindorfer *et al.* 2005; McKinnon 2003) is an important component of sustainable marketing. A prominent feature of sustainable distribution is Green Logistics. Green Logistics relates to less energy-intensive options for warehousing and transportation. Recent change has been the inclusion of logistics of used products at the end of their lifecycle

Sustainable distribution is relevant at both national and international levels. It is relevant in emerging markets because social, economic and environmental constraints are dominant in these markets. In developed markets, the availability of several options makes sustainable distribution one of many options – but not necessarily the preferred option. This chapter aims to present sustainable distribution as a holistic alternative to existing distribution philosophies. It highlights the crucial role of environmental sustainability in distribution.

The sections of this chapter are organised as follows. The chapter firstly discusses food distribution. Food is a fast moving consumer good and distributed widely. Its implication on sustainable distribution is important. The next section deals with the factors that affect physical goods distribution. It details the major factors that affect the sustainable distribution of physical goods. Subsequently, sections deal with reverse logistics, sustainable services distribution, social sustainability, negative externalities and government regulation and marketers. The chapter ends with a conclusion covering an overview of the concept of sustainable distribution.

Food distribution

Food distribution (Husti 2006; Powell 1995) has received particular attention in relation to sustainable distribution due to its impact on transportation and therefore its effect on environment. 'Food miles' (Pretty *et al.* 2005) is a concept used in relation to sustainable food distribution. It argues for limiting food transportation where possible and, therefore, encouraging local food production and consumption. The concept also has repercussions for the economy and society. The more local production and consumption that takes place, the greater the local economy will benefit. In addition, the medical community encourages the consumption of native fruit and vegetables as a healthy alternative to fast food.

Sustainable food distribution affects the supply chain from production to consumption (MacGregor & Vorley 2007). The growing of fruit and vegetables with physical characteristics that help in efficient distribution is one example – like cubic watermelons (i.e. watermelons that are grown to be square). These watermelons increase the efficiency of transport space utilisation ensuring effective distribution. Another factor in food distribution that affects sustainable distribution is understanding consumption. Effective food demand forecasting ensures efficiency of effort and cost in relation to inventory and transportation management.

An emerging issue related to sustainable distribution is water, which is a scarce resource. The amount of water used in food processing is quite high (Chapagain *et al.* 2006). Severe competition exists for water used for drinking, industrial and agricultural purposes (Ridoutt *et al.* 2009). The exploitation of ground water and a lack of rainwater harvesting or water conservation and management activities have exacerbated the problem. Water distribution with minimal losses has now increasingly become a concern of even corporate entities. Ground water table lowering due to excess exploitation in an Indian state resulted in banning of multinational soft drink brand across several countries. Marketers can encourage sustainable distribution by sourcing food products from suppliers who use minimal water in production. However, this is effective only if it is done in the same number of food miles. Embedded water content in foods has an impact on distribution as it can lead to faster product deterioration. In addition, it could also indirectly support inefficient water usage.

Factors affecting sustainable physical goods distribution

Several factors play an important role in attaining success in sustainable physical goods distribution. The subsequent sections of this chapter detail the role of each of these factors and its impact on sustainability.

Packaging

Packaging is a key component of distribution. Product packaging can be reduced using effective product design (Peattie 2001). Additionally, flexible packaging design can enable volume reduction during transport by vehicle space efficiently. Packaging that can facilitate the seamless transfer of goods from one transport mode to another will increase the overall efficiency of the transportation. Containerisation is one useful way of reducing the environmental effects of distribution; multimodal transport using containers eliminates energy being spent repackaging, loading and unloading. Bulk products without packaging can also be effectively transported using containers. Reduction in packaging weight and packaging layers also ensures waste reduction. Biodegradable (Leaversuch 2002) and recyclable packaging is another way of helping sustainable distribution. Reusable packaging that helps the consumers to use containers for future storage is another sustainable method of promoting packaging. This method reduces future packaging needs and thus the transport burden.

Multi-layered packaging serves several purposes like product protection and transport safety, but packaging weight reduction is a major step through which manufacturing and marketing firms can support distribution (Kassaye & Verma 1992; Lan & Mei 2008). Weight reduction efforts could include cardboard sleeve reduction, change from glass to plastic and use of lightweight glass. Weight reduction results in less waste post product-use and fuel savings in transportation. Thus, it contributes to sustainable distribution and reducing the carbon footprint of the firms involved.

Effect of lead-time

Lead-times in input and output production and consumption have an impact on sustainability across product categories. For many food products, while consumption occurs almost daily, inputs are seasonal and output needs to keep pace with changes in consumption. Manufacturers and marketers can minimise warehousing by matching production and consumption, but this is a difficult task. In such situations, where warehousing is necessary, sustainable distribution needs to strive to reduce environmental impacts and costs. Good warehouse design (Ballis 2006) can minimise energy costs and therefore contribute to sustainable distribution. A picking-and-packing operations study can also reduce energy use by optimising operations (Hsieh & Tsai 2006). Within a large warehouse, staff and machines expend energy picking goods and packing them for transport in the shortest possible time. These two operations when aggregated for various goods and locations and vehicle sizes become complex. A picking-and-packing operations study provides a practical view of the constraints and helps to facilitate a smooth functioning of the warehouse with minimal effort and energy.

Another avenue for reducing environmental impact and cost reduction is warehouse consolidation. Having several small warehouses closer to retail stores increases servicing efficiency; however, it also increases the cost of inventory and warehouse maintenance. Warehouse consolidation aids inventory cost optimisation and warehousing cost reduction. The key to effective warehouse consolidation is better routing and scheduling. The route taken from the supply warehouse to the centralised distribution warehouse of the retailer to the store can be mapped for optimising the trips required. Understanding of the goods flow in time sequence and vehicle capacity utilisation can help better scheduling. These activities require data analysis with the help of information technology tools to optimise routing and scheduling and achieve warehouse consolidation. A dramatic way to facilitate sustainable distribution is to minimise warehousing. The transfer of goods from one transport vehicle to another at a hub eliminates the need for large storage spaces. It also reduces redundant unloading and reloading. Minimising warehouse storage and promoting cross docking thus ensures energy, time and wastage reduction.

Postponement of production

Distributed or delayed finished-goods production (Alderson 2006; Pagh & Cooper 1998; Van Hoek 2001), or postponement until the point of supply to the consumer, is another example of sustainable distribution. The decorative paints industry is a classic case in this sustainable distribution initiative. Before the introduction of tinting machines, a single production site produced several SKUs (stock keeping units) of decorative paints in large volumes and shipped them to many parts of a country. Increased production, storage and transportation costs used to be the norm as the consumption patterns of individual SKUs differed across different locations. The advent of tinting machines made a difference in the entire value chain. Large quantities of the base chemical liquid and small quantities of dye colours are now available at the paint retail outlet. The retailer can prepare and sell varying paint quantities and colours as per consumer requirements instead of looking for available SKUs on the shelf. Storage space requirements for decorative paint retailers have also reduced as a result. Shifting final goods production to the consumer end (Ernst & Kamrad 2000) has enabled the producer to contribute to sustainable distribution (Yang *et al.* 2005)

The role of information and communication technology

Information and communication technology (ICT) is a major contributor towards sustainable distribution (Janelle & Gillespie 2004). Channel partners can manage demand-side volatility and supply-side constraints effectively with greater information transparency across the value chain. Demand-side volatility and supply-side constraints have the largest effect on inventory management and transportation. Excess inventory and inefficient transport the results of an absence of information (Chouinard *et al.* 2005; Daugherty *et al.* 2005). The whiplash effect is a common phenomenon observed in many supply chains. In this phenomenon, small changes in consumer demand create effects of larger magnitude at different supply chain levels. The whiplash effect (Lee *et al.* 1997) magnifies with further increases in the number of supply chain levels. Shorter distribution chains and greater information sharing prevents the whiplash effect by promoting better coordination and efficient functioning of the distribution chain.

A lack of information can occur due to communication links being unavailable, especially in rural areas of emerging economies. In these emerging economies, information on supply and demand of goods is minimal. Distribution channel partners can maximise profits on goods in such contexts using information that they possess. Such situations deter information sharing across the distribution channel. They can thus hinder information flow. Mobile communication and its rapid spread in rural areas recently, however, have made information transfer faster and easier. Thus, ICT development has greatly enhanced the prospects of sustainable distribution in rural areas.

Tracking distribution vehicles through GPS (geographical positioning systems) is another way of using ICT to improve vehicle movements and fleet management.

GPS helps in optimising routing and scheduling (Gebresenbet 1999) and assists with coordinating reverse logistics.

Capacity utilisation

A key dimension of services distribution is capacity utilisation. When firms do not utilise resources to their maximum, capacity at that moment is lost. Conversely, better service-capacity utilisation (Kimes 1989; Oliva & Kallenberg 2003) results in sustainable services distribution when demand exists. A good example of this phenomenon is mobile phone towers. A tower's capacity can be outsourced, and different phone services providers can thus avoid setting up multiple towers. In this example there is also a benefit to community health as additional towers result in greater radiation. Thus, tower sharing is a great example of sustainable distribution of services with environmental, economic and social benefits.

Another example of excess capacity utilisation is educational infrastructure. In emerging economies like India, the government's capacity to invest in educational infrastructure is lower. Using existing school, college or university educational infrastructure effectively for a larger reach of service provision is an example of sustainable distribution. Users can utilise infrastructure in two or three shifts. Public-private partnerships for sharing or maintaining the infrastructure can help in reducing unnecessary capacity development. This option is economical as increased existing capacity utilisation reduces costs. It reduces the stigma of having studied in evening or night schools instead of a regular day school. Moreover, income-earning opportunities for teachers and students increase due to this arrangement. In addition, the availability of services in more shifts provides flexibility for both teachers and students. Thus, this arrangement also serves social sustainability.

Transportation management

Transport management (Vanek & Morlok 2000) is an important element of sustainable distribution. Several modes of transport have different impacts on distribution (Murphy & Poist 2000). In the case of road transport, which is the more common form of goods distribution, the nature of vehicles bought, the way vehicles are driven and how transporters use vehicles, greatly determine sustainable distribution (Piecyk & McKinnon 2008; Rodrigue, J. P., Slack, B. & Comtois, C. 2001). Hybrid or electric vehicles (Macharis, C., Van Mierlo, J. & Van Den Bossche, P. 2007) help reduce air and noise pollution and reduce the use of fossil fuels. Larger multi-axle vehicles help in carrying larger quantities of goods at the same time compared to several smaller vehicles and thus increase efficiency (Simons, D., Mason, R. & Gardner, B. 2004). Governments play an important role in both passenger and goods transport. Governments can promote sustainable distribution with incentives for modal shift (Dinwoodie 2006), for example, shifting from road to rail transport. They can also have disincentives like congestion charging and speed limits to reduce impacts of unsustainable transportation. Several governments across the world have helped in shaping sustainable distribution by spatial planning, communication efforts with the transport industry and development of new infrastructure for smooth movement of goods.

Shipping and waterways are an important component of global trade logistics. 'Greening' the shipping industry (Michaelowa & Krause 2000) has implications for greening world trade generally. In this industry, sustainable distribution starts with energy efficient ships that have lesser weight, using light and composite materials, efficient hull design etc. In addition, the use of renewable energy sources namely electric power, solar and wind power in combination with cleaner fuel forms for powering ships can significantly reduce the effect of burning fossil fuels. The shift from the presently common bunker fuel to less polluting fuel in itself can have a big impact on reducing ocean pollution levels. Another target area for sustainable shipping is port operations (Bateman 1996). Reduction in turnaround time and the utilisation of machinery to speed up operations can control energy wastage. Increased lifts per hour, per crane, double container lifting and an increase in container ship size will all facilitate greater efficiency. Greater efficiency with the current energy consumption results in more sustainable distribution.

Distribution of gas and liquids through pipelines is an economically and environmentally efficient means of delivery. Pipelines can connect the points of exploration, production, storage and final consumption of these products (Bersani 2008). One of the main advantages of the pipelines is that they eliminate the usage of fuel in transportation. In many cases, companies use pressure and gravity in pipelines as methods to effect product delivery. Pipeline transport is largely reliable and especially helpful in the transportation of hazardous gases and liquids. They reduce injuries and deaths that plague other modes of transport and are thus, helpful as a safe method of transport (James 1980). Pipelines are available all through the year and anytime of the day and therefore represent a ready mode of transport. Backhaul is absent in pipeline transportation and this further reduces the pollution impact compared to other modes of transport. Another crucial advantage of pipeline delivery is the lower (almost zero) product damage.

Reverse logistics

Reverse logistics (Dowlatshahi 2000) has gained prominence as part of green logistics especially in the context of e-waste generation. Effective reverse logistics helps in the sustainable functioning of the consumer electronics supply chain (Chouinard, M., D'Amours, S. & A t-Kadi, D. 2005). Consumers's enhanced consumption of durables and Businesses's faster rates of new technology introduction and obsolescence have accentuated the key environment mantras – reduce, reuse and recycle. While anti-consumption philosophy and regulatory mandates for longer technology lifecycles may work, in a free market economy, managing this consumption and disposal cycle becomes crucial. Biodegradability of materials on disposal is a crucial determinant of the environmental sustainability of products. For consumer durables, reuse and recycling are methods for effecting sustainable distribution. Reuse would represent, for example, the use of refurbished consumer durables like mobile phones. Underdeveloped country consumers can use usable mobile phones disposed of by developed country consumers. This could also happen within emerging economies between urban to rural areas. However, reverse logistics must facilitate the reprocessing or refurbishing of products that are sold as pre-owned products for low-income consumers (Chan 2007). When marketers assure consumers of product longevity, then possession of such goods, economically and socially, is a sustainable proposition. However, a key issue is the passing off pre-owned products as new products. Unsuspecting consumers who are illiterate or not informed enough to make the distinction can fall prey to marketers who exploit them.

Hazardous e-waste collection is sustainable distribution through reverse logistics. If left alone in a landfill, e-waste may cause enormous damage to land water and air and thus affect the health of those who live nearby. Companies involved in reverse logistics collect this e-waste and extract usable materials. Thus they improve waste disposal and contribute to sustainable distribution. Recovering, for example, copper from motherboards of disposed computers/laptops and reselling it for (re)use by computer manufacturers requires the back-up of a strong reverse logistics system. In many developed countries, reverse logistics is mandated for manufacturers and marketers of such electronic products (Mutha & Pokharel 2009). They need to set up a system to ensure that product disposal is environmentally friendly. In many developing countries, laws are either absent or lax in implementation. In such cases, entrepreneurs involved in reverse logistics facilitate sustainable e-waste disposal. They not only help in protecting the environment but also benefit economically. Moreover, they help the society through employment opportunities in the reverse logistics business.

Sustainable services distribution

Sustainable services distribution (Halme *et al.* 2004; Van Der Zwan & Bhamra 2003) is a marketing concept to be considered in relation to holistic sustainability. Offering online services is an important way to contribute to sustainability – economically and environmentally. Serving consumers online reduces several repetitive manual processes in the banking and mutual fund services industries and increases the speed of consumer responses. Online consumer services (Vandermerwe & Oliff 1990) reduce paperwork, contributing to paper usage reduction and the use of less cash in services industries. The reduction of cash transactions has a social benefit too. In several developing countries, the black economy thrives as most transactions are only in cash. The recording of online monetary transactions provides the government with a trail that could be useful in tracing illegal activities. Thus, paperless electronic monetary transactions help governments by facilitating the move from the unorganised to the organised formal sector.

Provision of traditional banking services for rural populations is difficult due to remoteness, low transaction value and infrequent transactions. A sustainable banking services distribution method for financial inclusion is through the business correspondent model. This is a financial services expansion model, where large banks outsource retail-banking activities to local organised entities like rural non-government organisations (NGOs). The retail bank benefits as it can cater to a larger target population at a lesser cost instead of providing a fully operating branch that is uneconomical for low transaction levels. Simultaneously, it also provides local employment. The business correspondent model provides a safe way of lowering non-performing assets, as the correspondents are local entities. ICT facilitates this form of sustainable banking services distribution through low-cost, mobile, automated teller machines (ATMs) and other technologies that facilitate paperless transactions. In addition, in countries like India, biometric cards can help hasten the pace of technology adoption in financial transactions.

Another major outcome of ICT is the development of business process outsourcing (BPO) for efficient services distribution. In large countries like India, when several consumers start purchasing or using new services, multiple service providers replicate similar processes as for example complaint handling in the same industry. This makes services distribution unsustainable. Business process outsourcers specialise in several business processes and serve multiple clients, making the industries more economically and environmentally sustainable. Many business process outsourcers specialise in service industries like insurance. They provide specialised and skilled training in the processes they supply. This specialisation and outsourcing leads to greater societal benefits. Staff are skilled-up, making them more employable and giving them a greater opportunity of higher income earning.

Negative externalities

Current unsustainable forms of distribution have several negative externalities (Delucchi 2000). Various forms of pollution, namely land, air, water and noise, severely affect public health. Road transport development is particularly responsible for crop/forest destruction, as new wider road building requires greater and greater land acquisition. It also leads to reduction of open spaces especially in densely populated countries where the land area is minimal. The movement of heavy and other vehicles at faster speeds to increase efficient freight transport has also resulted in the increased number of accidents and injuries. Other negative effects have been damage to buildings due to construction of transportation highways and traffic. The building of several complex bridges and other transport structures has also resulted in visual pollution. Researchers have documented negative impacts on marine life substantially due to increased marine logistics. Poor fuel quality, inefficient and old ships and dumping of ship waste in ocean waters have polluted the ocean floor. Pollutants ingested by marine life enter the human system through the seafood consumed. Thus, not only offshore drilling for extracting fossil fuels but international trade is a contributor to unsustainable living. Sustainable and ethical sourcing and impacts on community health and nutrition are becoming serious issues to counter negative externalities of unsustainable distribution.

Government regulation and marketers

In some developed countries like the UK, governments have been working towards sustainable distribution. These sustainable distribution efforts have mainly targeted transportation management (Lampe & Gazda 1995), and they relate primarily to road transport as in many countries road transport is the most frequent mode for freight transport. Regulation on load factor requirements (McKinnon 2000), weight regulations, zonal designations, temporal restrictions and taxation are methods used to minimise the negative externalities of distribution through transport. Marketers have attempted sustainable distribution by eliminating small orders, reducing delivery frequency and increasing their average order size. While sustainable distribution is just a component of the sustainable supply chain, efforts of the government (Aibin, L. I., Min, Z. & Lili, B. 2009; Prakash 2002) and the marketers are likely to succeed if all supply chain participants were to encourage and support a sustainable supply chain.

Conclusion

The manufacturer, marketer, wholesaler and retailer are typical entities that are involved in distribution. However, other entities like warehouse owners, logistics companies, transport firms and ICT entities provide key support functions in product distribution. All these entities need to cooperate in the efforts towards a sustainable distribution system. A commitment to a sustainable supply chain and the attitude of promoting a green marketing environment are crucial for the success of efforts at promoting sustainability. While green logistics can contribute significantly to sustainable distribution, economic and social dimensions are equally important for the holistic implementation of the concept. Partnership across the distribution value chain is a key ingredient for the success of these efforts. Green alternatives for every step of the distribution process simultaneously considering the social and economic dimensions are important. In services distribution, the consumer also plays a role in adopting sustainable alternatives of service consumption.

Sustainable distribution is not only a country-level initiative but also a global requirement for a better planet for the future. International trade can contribute to sustainable distribution through exchange of expertise and trade information. Global transportation requires careful consideration in a global supply chain. Companies need to add environmental and social costs to the economic costs of operating a global supply chain. Marketing decision making in goods distribution internationally must exhibit consideration of sustainability criteria. In addition, government and marketers need to collaborate to make sustainable distribution a reality for attaining the ideals of societal marketing.

References

Aibin, L. I., Min, Z. & Lili, B. 2009. 'An Analysis of Incentive and Monitoring Mechanisms to Describing How Government Encourage Enterprises to Develop Green Logistics [J].' *Ecological Economy*, 3.

Alderson, W. 2006. 'Marketing efficiency and the principle of postponement.' *A Twenty-First Century Guide to Aldersonian Marketing Thought*, 109-13.

Ballis, A. 2006. 'Freight Villages: Warehouse design and rail link aspects.' *Transportation Research Record: Journal of the Transportation Research Board*, 1966:-1, 27-33.

Bateman, S. 1996. 'Environmental issues with Australian ports.' *Ocean & Coastal Management,* 33:1-3, 229-47.

Bersani, C. 2008. 'Sustainable Distribution of Petrol Products to Service Stations Based on Demand Forecast, Inventory and Transportation Costs.' *Advanced Technologies and Methodologies for Risk Management in the Global Transport of Dangerous Goods,* 194.

Chan, H. K. 2007. 'A pro-active and collaborative approach to reverse logistics - a case study.' *Production Planning & Control,* 18:4, 350-60.

Chapagain, A. K., Hoekstra, A. Y., Savenije, H. H. G. & Gautam, R. 2006. 'The water footprint of cotton consumption: An assessment of the impact of worldwide consumption of cotton products on the water resources in the cotton producing countries.' *Ecological economics,* 60:1, 186-203.

Chouinard, M., D'Amours, S. & A t-Kadi, D. 2005. 'Integration of reverse logistics activities within a supply chain information system.' *Computers in Industry,* 56:1, 105-24.

Ciliberti, F., Pontrandolfo, P. & Scozzi, B. 2008. 'Logistics social responsibility: Standard adoption and practices in Italian companies.' *International Journal of Production Economics,* 113:1, 88-106.

Daugherty, P. J., Richey, R. G., Genchev, S. E. & Chen, H. 2005. 'Reverse logistics: superior performance through focused resource commitments to information technology.' *Transportation Research Part E: Logistics and Transportation Review,* 41:2, 77-92.

Delucchi, M. A. 2000. 'Environmental externalities of motor-vehicle use in the US.' *Journal of Transport Economics and Policy,* 34:2, 135-68.

Dinwoodie, J. 2006. 'Rail freight and sustainable urban distribution: potential and practice.' *Journal of Transport Geography,* 14:4, 309-20.

Dowlatshahi, S. 2000. 'Developing a theory of reverse logistics.' *Interfaces,* 30:3, 143-55.

Ernst, R. & Kamrad, B. 2000. 'Evaluation of supply chain structures through modularization and postponement.' *European Journal of Operational Research,* 124:3, 495-510.

Gebresenbet, G. 1999. 'Promoting effective goods distribution through route optimization and coordination to attenuate environmental impact–the case of Uppsala.' *Uppsala: University of Agricultural Sciences, Department of Agricultural Engineering.*

Halme, M., Jasch, C. & Scharp, M. 2004. 'Sustainable homeservices? Toward household services that enhance ecological, social and economic sustainability.' *Ecological economics,* 51:1-2, 125-38.

Hsieh, L. & Tsai, L. 2006. 'The optimum design of a warehouse system on order picking efficiency.' *The International Journal of Advanced Manufacturing Technology,* 28:5, 626-37.

Husti, I. 2006. 'The main elements of sustainable food chain management.' *Cereal Research Communications,* 34:1, 793-96.

James, J. G. 1980. 'Pipelines considered as a mode of freight transport a review of current and possible future uses.' *Environmental Geochemistry and Health,* 2:1, 1-25.

Janelle, D. G. & Gillespie, A. 2004. 'Space–time constructs for linking information and communication technologies with issues in sustainable transportation.' *Transport Reviews*, 24:6, 665-77.

Kassaye, W. W. & Verma, D. 1992. 'Balancing Traditional Packaging Functions with the New" Green" Packaging Concerns.' *SAM Advanced Management Journal*, 57:4.

Kimes, S. E. 1989. 'Yield management: a tool for capacity-considered service firms.' *Journal of Operations Management*, 8:4, 348-63.

Kirchgeorg, M. & Winn, M. I. 2006. 'Sustainability marketing for the poorest of the poor.' *Business Strategy and the Environment*, 15:3, 171-84.

Kleindorfer, P. R., Singhal, K. & Wassenhove, L. N. 2005. 'Sustainable operations management.' *Production and Operations Management*, 14:4, 482-92.

Lampe, M. & Gazda, G. M. 1995. 'Green marketing in Europe and the United States: an evolving business and society interface.' *International Business Review*, 4:3, 295-312.

Lan, W. & Mei, Y. 2008. 'Green Packaging Design on the Principle of 3R.' *Packaging Engineering*, 2.

Leaversuch, R. 2002. 'Biodegradable polyesters: Packaging goes'green'.' *Plastics Technology*, 48:9.

Lee, H. L., Padmanabhan, V. & Whang, S. 1997. 'The Bullwhip Effect In Supply Chains1.' *Sloan management review*, 38:3, 93-102.

Lijuan, H. 2008. 'Discussion on the Necesity of Developing Green Logistics.' *Science*, 11.

MacGregor, J. & Vorley, B. 2007. " *Fair Miles*": *The Concept of" food Miles" Through a Sustainable Development Lens.* International institute for environment and development (IIED).

Macharis, C., Van Mierlo, J. & Van Den Bossche, P. 2007. 'Combining intermodal transport with electric vehicles: Towards more sustainable solutions.' *Transportation Planning and Technology*, 30:2-3, 311-23.

McKinnon, A. 2000. 'Sustainable distribution: opportunities to improve vehicle loading.' *Industry and environment*, 23:4, 26-27.

McKinnon, A. 2003. 'Sustainable freight distribution.' *Integrated futures and transport choices: UK transport policy beyond the 1998 white paper and transport acts*, 132.

Michaelowa, A. & Krause, K. 2000. 'International maritime transport and climate policy.' *Intereconomics*, 35:3, 127-36.

Murphy, P. R. & Poist, R. F. 2000. 'Green logistics strategies: An analysis of usage patterns.' *Transportation Journal*, 40:2, 5-16.

Mutha, A. & Pokharel, S. 2009. 'Strategic network design for reverse logistics and remanufacturing using new and old product modules.' *Computers & Industrial Engineering*, 56:1, 334-46.

Oliva, R. & Kallenberg, R. 2003. 'Managing the transition from products to services.' *International Journal of Service Industry Management*, 14:2, 160-72.

Pagh, J. D. & Cooper, M. C. 1998. 'Supply chain postponement and speculation strategies: how to choose the right strategy.' *Journal of business logistics*, 19, 13-34.

Peattie, K. 2001. 'Towards sustainability: the third age of green marketing.' *The Marketing Review*, 2:2, 129-46.

Piecyk, M. & McKinnon, A. 2008. 'A survey of expert opinion on the environmental impact of road freight transport in the UK in 2020.'

Pitta, D. A., Guesalaga, R. & Marshall, P. 2008. 'The quest for the fortune at the bottom of the pyramid: potential and challenges.' *Journal of Consumer Marketing*, 25:7, 393-401.

Powell, J. 1995. 'Direct distribution of organic produce: sustainable food production in industrialized countries.' *Outlook on Agriculture (United Kingdom)*.

Prakash, A. 2002. 'Green marketing, public policy and managerial strategies.' *Business Strategy and the Environment*, 11:5, 285-97.

Pretty, J. N., Ball, A. S., Lang, T. & Morison, J. I. L. 2005. 'Farm costs and food miles: An assessment of the full cost of the UK weekly food basket.' *Food Policy*, 30:1, 1-19.

Ridoutt, B. G., Eady, S. J., Sellahewa, J., Simons, L. & Bektash, R. 2009. 'Water footprinting at the product brand level: case study and future challenges.' *Journal of Cleaner Production*, 17:13, 1228-35.

Rodrigue, J. P., Slack, B. & Comtois, C. 2001. 'Green logistics.' *Handbook of Logistics and Supply-Chain Management*, 2, 339-50.

Simons, D., Mason, R. & Gardner, B. 2004. 'Overall vehicle effectiveness.' *International Journal of Logistics Research and Applications*, 7:2, 119-35.

Stern, L. W. & Weitz, B. A. 1997. 'The revolution in distribution: challenges and opportunities.' *Long Range Planning*, 30:6, 823-29.

Van Der Zwan, F. & Bhamra, T. 2003. 'Services marketing: taking up the sustainable development challenge.' *Journal of Services Marketing*, 17:4, 341-56.

Van Hoek, R. I. 2001. 'The rediscovery of postponement a literature review and directions for research.' *Journal of Operations Management*, 19:2, 161-84.

Vandermerwe, S. & Oliff, M. D. 1990. 'Customers drive corporations green.' *Long Range Planning*, 23:6, 10-16.

Vanek, F. M. & Morlok, E. K. 2000. 'Improving the energy efficiency of freight in the United States through commodity-based analysis: justification and implementation.' *Transportation Research Part D-Transport and Environment*, 5:1, 11-29.

Yang, B., Yang, Y. & Wijngaard, J. 2005. 'Impact of postponement on transport: an environmental perspective.' *International Journal of Logistics Management, The*, 16:2, 192-204.

Sustainable consumption and the retailer: Will fashion ethics follow food?

ELAINE RITCH, MONIKA SCHRÖDER, CAROL BRENNAN AND MIKE PRETIOUS

ABSTRACT

Consumers are said to be increasingly applying sustainable concerns within the decision-making process when choosing food products, however the fashion industry has been slower to respond to the sustainability agenda. Food producers and UK supermarkets offer consumers alternative sustainable options which are both easily accessed and comparable in price. This research explores consumers' efforts to transfer sustainable consumption interest to fashion, using garment labels found within mass-market retailers. The findings include a number of barriers which prohibited the participants from consuming fashion ethically, for example, sustainable product availability in mass-market fashion retailers. The participants compared their increased knowledge of food production and access to alternative food options, as this had resulted in increased confidence. The chapter concludes that fashion retailers could potentially offer consumers similar alternative products, and that by offering information and actively addressing concern for sustainability, this could result in a competitive advantage.

Introduction

To address the ever increasing consumer concern regarding the ethics of production, retailers are providing alternative solutions to standard products, and this responsiveness is resulting in enhanced profitability (The Co-operative 2009). The supermarket sector is a prominent example. The retailers in this sector are competing to be the 'greenest', and they are being judged on the availability of ethical alternatives as well as encouraging consumers to behave ethically, for example by providing recycling facilities and reducing packaging (Yates 2009). In view of the popularity of organic, locally produced and fair trade food, it is worth considering that such consumer attitudes and behaviours in relation to food could also influence the marketing of fashion.

Fashion is described as 'a style that is popular at a particular time, especially in clothes, hair, make-up' (Cambridge Dictionary 2011). Fashion styles or trends change continuously (Christopher, Lowson & Peck 2004) and are validated by consumers (Piamphongsant & Mandhacitara 2008) through accepting or rejecting the prevailing styles (Damhorst 2005). Therefore, consumers' appearances reflect their level of involvement with fashion (Solomon & Rabolt 2009). Due to consumer demand for new fashion, a decrease in garment price and the use of developing economies to reduce production costs (Allwood *et al.* 2006; Aspers 2008), the impact of the industry on the environment is growing (O'Cass 2004).

There is a body of evidence suggesting current consumption levels in the fashion industry are unsustainable (Centre for Sustainable Fashion 2009) and that consumer behaviour requires a change in order to be ethical. However, consumer behaviour is habitual and change will need to be facilitated using additional consumer benefits (Memery, Megicks & Williams 2005; Schaefer & Crane 2005). Academic and media reports have indicated that consumers are increasingly concerned about the ethics of production and the environmental impact of the manufacturing process and products purchased; although, there is lower awareness among consumers of fashion industry ethics (Solomon & Rabolt 2009). Consumers may be reluctant to change their habits or engage with practices ordinary consumers cannot comprehend and from which they are physically removed (Carrigan & Attalla 2001; Lyon 2006; Sayer 2000). Prothero and Fitchett (2000) propose a move towards consumption for the benefit of the environment, to improve working environments and the planet's resources. Moreover, they advocate that the mass adoption (mass market) of ethical consumption is necessary to achieve 'long-term and wide-ranging environmental change' (p. 52).

This research is concerned with current consumer behaviour regarding fashion perception and whether consumers would respond positively to the application of sustainable principles within the mass market production of fashion garments, for example, fair trade fashion where the workers' conditions and salaries are not exploitative and organic cotton where the environment is protected from pesticides. This chapter discusses the context and theoretical frameworks for sustainable marketing in the retail sector, with a specific focus on fashion but also addressing the opportunities to learn from other retailers, particularly those selling food.

Ethical consumer behaviour and awareness will be discussed in relation to both food and fashion. The data collection is then discussed and this is followed by the findings including consumer perceptions of the ethical alternative products which are available within both food and fashion sectors, as well as how ethical behaviours have been adopted when known and understood. While the study was conducted in the UK, its findings will be of international interest for the marketing of food and fashion.

Context

Consumers have become engaged with sustainability issues as they affect food – including fair trade, organic produce and local sourcing – much more quickly than they have engaged with similar issues as they affect the fashion clothing sector. This point will be addressed elsewhere in the chapter. For most supermarkets and other general merchandise retailers, there is little evidence that product development is geared to consumer concerns regarding sustainability in a non-food context. A notable exception to this rule is Marks and Spencer, whose 'Plan A' initiative covers a large array of merchandise categories (Marks and Spencer 2011). Tesco take a broad view of corporate social responsibility (CSR) (Tesco 2011) and recently introduced a line of clothing in collaboration with the sustainable fashion label 'From Somewhere' (Carter 2010). The major UK multiple clothing retailers have until recently been less engaged than food retailers with the sustainability agenda, and tend to focus their corporate social responsibility activity more on the ethics of the supply chain than on other areas. Examples of this approach include Next's 'Corporate Responsibility' web page (Next 2011), which covers the retailer's responsibilities towards suppliers, customers, people (employees), community and the environment and Arcadia's 'Fashion Footprint' (Arcadia 2011), which similarly encompasses social responsibility, community and the environment. Notable in terms of the approach to sustainability of all these retailers is that much of their activity is not heavily used as a marketing tool, except through their websites, and occasionally as part of in-store merchandising. Engagement with consumers has thus been largely passive rather than active; however, Marks and Spencer (see above) and the co-operative movement have promoted their sustainability agendas to consumers, with some success.

Sustainable consumption encompasses ethical concerns regarding scarce resources and methods of production alongside the profitability of the business (Defra 2009; Moisander, Markkula & Eraranta 2010; Schaefer & Crane 2005). This focuses the attention of companies on planning their strategies so that neither people nor the planet are exploited to generate profits (Lee & Sevier 2008). The equal application of these aspects resulting in sustainability is reflected in Figure 5.1 below. For this to be successful, current barriers to sustainable consumption require investigation in order for a solution to be provided (Hiller Connell 2010). Therefore it is imperative to understand how consumers apply ethics to consumption. Moisander, Markkula and Eraranta (2010) suggest that in response to consumer demand for sustainable products, retailers will provide alternative products. However, without information, consumers will struggle to apply ethical concerns.

Figure 5.1 The application of factors to ensure sustainability

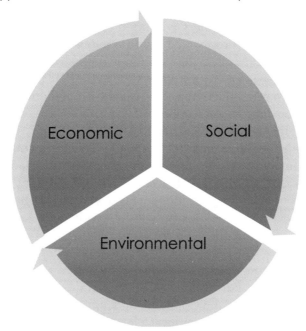

There has been extensive research regarding consumer behaviour in general, incorporating attitudes, behaviours and ethical intentions. The following section outlines consumer awareness and introduces the need for consumers to have information in order to apply ethical concerns to their consumption.

Ethical consumer behaviour

Previous research has found consumers are concerned about the way goods are produced and the resulting impact upon the environment. They are informed about unethical practices by the media (Carrigan & de Pelsmacker 2009), and those with a particular interest will search for information regarding the production of the goods they wish to purchase. Responsive behaviours include opting for toiletries and cosmetics that have not been tested on animals (Cowe & Williams 2001) or being concerned for animal welfare (Schröder & McEachern 2004) or chemical free food production. Producers and retailers have started to recognise growing concern for food production, for example the use of pesticides and genetically modified food, and the result has been the availability of alternative products (Low & Davenport 2006; Schaefer & Crane 2005). There is also a strong argument from consumer advocacy bodies in the UK, such as Consumer Focus, that retailers should 'choice edit' unsustainable products so that sustainable consumption becomes more mainstream and it is not left to 'green consumers' to lead the way (Yates 2009).

Consumer awareness

Information is integral to ethical consumption (McDonald *et al*. 2009) and consumer awareness has increased through the media (O'Cass 2004). Improved knowledge encourages consumers to support ethical retailers (Dickson 2000) and to reduce consumption through voluntary simplicity (Shaw & Moraes 2009). To simplify the decision-making process, consumers will often apply heuristics, recalling what is already known about the product or brand (Solomon & Rabolt 2009). This is especially true when the required information is not listed on the product (Aspers 2008). Retailers are increasingly developing CSR initiatives and codes of conduct to appease consumer concerns over ethical issues and align themselves to consumers' values; however consumers are sceptical of such marketing claims and this has earned the term 'greenwash' (Yates 2009). Although retailers could make use of current social codes of conduct, for example Social Accountability 8000 or International Labour Organisation minimum requirements (Made By 2007), many retailers adopt internal auditing which is either not independent (Harrison 2009) or carried out by accountancy organisations who have not had the relevant training (Lee 2003). Further, both complexity within production (e.g. cotton growth, finishing processes, construction) and transient relationships with factories do not provide a platform for consistent implementation of codes of practice. Therefore retailers rely upon self-regulation and struggle to offer assurance of responsible production to consumers. Furthermore, CSR and codes of conduct are voluntary (McCallum 2008), and their development and application are inconsistent. For consumers to gain confidence in ethical claims, transparency and independent labelling will be required (Schröder & McEachern 2004).

Availability of ethical food in the retail sector

Appropriate labelling has been most prominent in the food sector, where fair trade and organic produce are widely available in supermarkets. The Fairtrade logo is said to be recognised by over half of the UK population (Black 2008) and Fairtrade UK sales in 2009 were over £800 million, despite the global financial crisis during this period (The Ecologist 2010). The availability of Fairtrade merchandise in mainstream supermarkets has contributed to this growth (do Paço & Raposo 2010) and some supermarkets have narrowed consumer choice by only offering Fairtrade-labelled bananas or Fairtrade tea and coffee (Carrigan & de Pelsmacker 2009). This enables consumers to recognise the brand when shopping, saving time and offering an assurance that the consumers' values are shared by the retailer.

In contrast, the fashion industry is failing to provide opportunities for consumers to purchase fair trade or ethically sourced clothing (Connelly & Shaw 2006). Despite the involvement of many UK fashion retailers with the Ethical Trade Initiative (Barrientois & Smith 2006), little progress has been made in this sector for either implementing a 'living wage' or addressing environmental concerns. Similarly, Made By (ND) and Fair Wear Foundation (2009), who offer international verification and transparency, have the potential to offer consumers assurance of acceptable workers' conditions and salary, yet only one UK fashion retailer has opted to take up this opportunity.

The Soil Association (ND) certifies cotton using the same logo as organic food, taking up the opportunity to link with a logo which is already familiar to consumers. Organic produce allows consumers to purchase food which has not been subject to chemicals and pesticide use (Ethical Company Organisation 2008); this is considered preferable because the application of pesticides depletes the soil and discourages ecosystems, and it is also thought to contribute to ill health and compromise taste. Organic cotton is cultivated without pesticides and it typically requires less energy (Hamer & Anslow 2008), however cultivation is water intensive (Allwood et al. 2006). The application of pesticides contributes to an estimated 20,000 deaths of cotton farmers annually, as well as impacting the environment (Allwood *et al.* 2006). The Aral Sea in Uzbekistan has reduced dramatically in size because of the amount of water used in local cotton production and this has resulted in environmental damage, impacting the health of the local population (Allwood *et al.* 2006; Black 2008). But the use of man-made fibres is not the solution. Two thirds of clothing purchased in the UK is made from man-made materials, polymers derived from oil (a scarce resource) using an energy-intensive process that contributes to global warming (Fletcher 2008). Further, polymers take over 200 years to decompose despite their potential for recycling (Defra 2007). Current developments include synthetic fibres derived from renewable resources and compostable materials (Fletcher 2008).

The fashion retail sector

The fashion industry is important globally because it provides employment for around 26.5 million people (Allwood *et al.* 2006; Black 2008; Defra 2007). Within the UK, £38 billion is spent annually on clothing, with women's wear accounting for £24 billion (Defra 2007; Easey 2009). The cyclical nature of fashion, where styles and trends are continually changing (O'Cass 2004), drives consumers who are fashion conscious to update their wardrobes (Hayes & Jones 2006). This is in direct contrast to sustainability (Black 2008), whereby scarce resources are protected, re-used and recycled. Fashion garments can be acquired from other sources, like charity shops, passing through informal networks, swapping (known also as swishing) and online auctions (Winakor 1969), but the consumer's drive to be fashionable results in a competitive retail environment (Easey 2009). Within the UK, this market is dominated by national and international fashion chains, where clothes are produced on a large scale and styles are largely similar (Easey 2009; Solomon & Rabolt 2009). These retailers are typically found in prominent city-centre shopping locations and in malls (Lee 2003) and mass production has ensured accessibility and affordability for consumers, where once fashion was a luxury only the wealthy could afford (Solomon & Rabolt 2009).

Although previous research has explored the concept of ethical consumption (Carrigan & Szmigin 2004; Devinney, Eckhardt & Belk 2007), it has been limited in regard to fashion. Studies exploring consumer perceptions of ethical fashion indicate the entrance of ethical fashion within mainstream retailers (Fisher *et al.* 2008; Joergens 2006; Shaw *et al.* 2007; Shaw & Tomolillo 2004); however, this is still very limited. Both Hiller Connell (2010) and Shaw and Tomolillo (2004) identify barriers for ethically committed consumers who, while not claiming to be particularly fashion conscious, still struggle to purchase suitable clothing to create a professional appearance. Shaw and Tomolillo (2004) conclude that multinational retailers have the potential to introduce sustainable, organic and fair trade clothing within the mass market. In contrast Joergens (2006) sought to explore the opinion of younger consumers, who are more interested in following fashion and who purchase fashion-orientated products more frequently. Small focus groups of around ten participants found a distinct lack of knowledge, awareness and concern, with blame apportioned to limited information, alternatives and affordability. Morgan and Birtwistle (2009) carried out research into young fashion-orientated consumers' disposal of fashion garments and found that the purchase of new clothing occurred weekly and included two to three garments. These consumers preferred lower prices allowing for the purchase of more items. Further, the participants were influenced by celebrity and made frequent purchases to mimic certain celebrities; in contrast, knowledge of the ethical issues surrounding the fashion industry was low.

Technology is currently being developed to provide solutions through innovation (Kilbourne, McDonagh & Prothero 1997), for example, self-cleaning fabrics. Additionally, many fabrics could potentially be recycled for re-use. Few consumers currently recycle textiles (Black 2008; Morgan & Birtwistle 2009); although fibres can be reclaimed and re-used for the manufacture of new fabrics and garments (Waste Watch 2005). 'Upcycling' involves restructuring clothes or waste fabric into a new garment (Defra 2008), and Junky Styling are at the fore of this, deconstructing second hand men's suits into restyled bespoke tailored, twisted garments and using vintage garments and fabrics (Fletcher 2008). Consumer adoption of the solutions was seen as pivotal to a successful response being obtained, and retailers would benefit from understanding consumer concerns and ensuring that purchase criteria were met, therefore gaining competitive advantage. Rogers (2003, p. 119) believes 'how a social problem is defined is an important determinant of how we go about solving it, and ultimately of the effectiveness of the attempted solution'.

Research methods

The aim of this research is to understand consumer behaviour with regard to purchasing fashion apparel and to explore the ethics of fashion production with which consumers engage and the options consumers would adopt to consume sustainably. The research method seeks to clarify real life consumer experiences as reflected through the current consumer market (Moisander, Markkula & Eraranta 2010; Thomson, Locander & Pollio 1989). Therefore the data were collected through unstructured phenomenological interviews to explore a holistic understanding of the application of ethical concerns within real life experiences 'as lived' (Easterby-Smith, Thorpe & Jackson 2008; Thomson, Locander & Pollio 1989, p. 135). As qualitative research is concerned with a particular perspective rather than generalisation, the findings are not representative of the population (Creswell 2009). Therefore the research does not confirm or dispute the existence of phenomena; rather it reiterates an individual experience (Schwandt 2003). To ensure the focus of the research is maintained, primers (labels and pictures) were introduced to explore consumer perception of the relevant topics (Thompson &

Haytko 1997); for example, the 'Global Girlfriend' label, stressing the ethical values of the brand (Figure 5.2) and Marks and Spencer's 'Plan A' label, which highlights that the garment attached was produced in an 'Eco factory' (Figure 5.3). The interviews were taped and transcribed and the interpretation process included individual and collective analysis of emerging themes and developing the meaning behind the narratives (Easterby-Smith, Thorpe & Jackson 2008; Thomson, Locander & Pollio 1989).

Figure 5.2 Global Girlfriend label (front and back)

Global Girlfriend specializes in style and *human rights* with our fairly traded line of apparel and accessories hand-made by women and communities in need. We work with over 20 women's non-profit organizations globally to design products that not only fit your unique style but really make a difference!

This *Global Girlfriend* item was made for you by:

A fair trade organization in Nepal which aims to improve the lives of Nepal garment makers as well as improve the environment. The fun Giggle Organics line is made from 100% organic cotton and dyed using pure vegetable dyes. Hand embroidery is added by women working from their homes in the Kathmandu Valley and its surrounding villages.

Figure 5.3 Marks and Spencer's Plan A label (front and back)

Sample selection

To gain a richer perspective on the experience of consuming fashion, the sample focused on women. Through greater involvement in fashion than men (Goldsmith & Clark 2008; Gutman & Mills 1982), women tend to purchase fashion items more frequently (Workman & Studak 2006), and they do so for reasons other than utilitarian. The use of clothing as self-expression can be subtle and consumers with a high level of interest in fashion will prioritise fashion-related consumption (O'Cass 2004). Ming Law, Zhang and Leung (2004) describe the needs of fashion consumers as shown in Figure 5.4:

Figure 5.4 Consumers' fashion needs according to Ming Law, Zhang and Leung (2004)

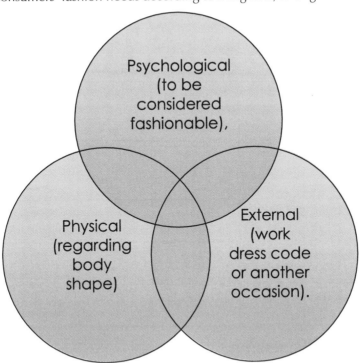

Further, to add to the complexity of fashion consumption, women were sought who work professionally and are thus required to adhere to expected norms in terms of appearance (Miller-Spillman 2005). Women are increasingly employed outside the home; currently sixty per cent earn their own income, and this also facilitates fashion consumption (Lee & Bhargava 2004). In fact Shaw and Tomolillo (2004) identified this as a specific barrier to consuming ethical fashion. Finally, the sample concentrated on mothers of pre-school or primary school children. Previous research has identified mothers as primary care givers (Carrigan & Szmigin 2006) and the gatekeepers to the consumption behaviours of their families (Dickson 2001). Children introduce further complexity through developing needs and wants, and they require clothes more frequently due to physical growth. This impacts fashion sales. Previous research (Boden 2006) has found children are increasingly influenced by popular cultural icons and the use of imagery in expressing identity, pressurising parents for fashion to conform amongst their peers. And the purchase patterns of mothers are more likely to be driven by a greater engagement with environmental issues or concerns over health; thus they might buy, for example, organic food (Szmigin, Carrigan & O'Louchlin 2007; Tsakiridou *et al.* 2008) or practise recycling (Diamantopoulos *et al.* 2003; Dickson 2001). The participants for this pilot study were purposively selected to satisfy the criteria, and interviews were held at their convenience in Edinburgh, UK. The sample characteristics can be found in the Table 5.1.

Table 5.1 Sample characteristics

Sample characteristics	Age	Number of children	Occupation	Number of hours worked weekly	Size of the household	Marital status
Participant 1	41	4	Befriending service co-coordinator	32	6	Married/co habiting
Participant 2	28	1	Primary school teacher	FT	3	Single
Participant 3	43	2	Lecturer	FT	4	Married/co habiting
Participant 4	43	2	Manager	25	4	Married/co habiting
Participant 5	42	2	Lecturer	PT	4	Married/co habiting

Findings and discussion

All but one of the participants were in their early forties and either married or cohabitating, with one who was aged 28 years and single. All had children who attended primary school, ranging from one child to four. Two participants worked full time, the other three worked part time and although no specific uniform was required for work, all had occasions when smarter clothing was expected. This smarter clothing was obtained from mass market fashion retailers and supermarkets where it was recognised that choice was limited by what was available that season. Two of the participants indicated a greater interest and involvement with fashion, purchasing fashion garments more frequently, while the remaining three participants were less engaged in this activity. From the interviews, five main themes emerged and these will be discussed in relation to the points raised within the literature.

Barriers to consuming fashion ethically

Hiller Connell (2010) suggests that understanding the barriers that prevent consumers from consuming sustainably will lead to a potential solution. This research identifies the main barriers as lack of information, perception of ethical fashion as not being mainstream fashion, accessibility and price. All of the participants purchased fashion in national and international fashion retailers (Easey 2009; Solomon & Rabolt 2009) which were easily accessible (Lee 2003). Further, two participants browsed charity shops on occasion preferring the ethical alternative of purchasing second-hand clothing to buying from mass market fashion retailers. Although the participants were not purchasing fashion to maintain the increasingly rapid changes in style (Hayes & Jones 2006; Morgan & Birtwistle 2009; O'Cass 2004), it was recognised that their children needed clothes regularly to meet demands of growth. Furthermore, it was recognised that all of the children had opinions on the style of clothing desired and were influenced by cultural imagery to express an identity that they felt reflected how they wanted to be perceived. This is consistent with previous research, where consumers who were not actively involved in fashion struggled to purchase ethical clothing (Fisher *et al.* 2008; Jeorgens 2006; Shaw *et al.* 2007; Shaw & Tomolillo 2004). The participants made efforts to behave sustainably. All passed children's clothing on to other families who could use them, or to charity shops (reducing the usage of scarce resources (Black 2008)), as well as purchasing or accepting second hand clothing for their own children.

> *School clothes, it's probably all hand-me-downs, all from the second hand uniform sale. (5)*

> *Because everybody benefits from that, that's a second generation ethical purchase in that you are not creating the need for new products. (4)*

Behaving sustainably

The participants were all engaged with known environmental concerns and had incorporated appropriate behaviours into their lifestyles. Further, campaigns informing and encouraging consumers to re-use plastic bags and use cloth bags were acknowledged by the participants (Ritch, Brennan & MacLeod 2009) and all re-used bags. This behaviour was extended by two participants who took bags when shopping for products other than food, for example fashion shopping. These participants also commented that fashion retailers did not encourage re-use of bags.

> *That's a massive change, the fact that we all take bags now... I would have to say that's been a really positive change... and you do really feel annoyed with yourself if you don't have bags with you, which you know does happen, because you don't always plan to go shopping... but I do generally have a bag stuffed inside my handbag now. (5)*

> *Even if I was going clothes shopping…if I bought my first thing I would just use that bag for the rest of the day. (2)*

Therefore the participants all responded to sustainable behaviours which were known, but did not actively seek additional information. All of the participants recycled household waste, re-used shopping bags and had adapted food consumption to include fair trade and organic produce as well as considering animal welfare. Further, the participants discussed reducing car trips, voluntary simplicity and repairing products rather than buying new; thus it could be assumed they had responded to campaigns to behave sustainably. This is consistent with previous research showing behaviours are habitual and that change is dependent upon ease of contributing (Memery, Megicks & Williams 2005; Schaefer & Crane 2005). Participants had obtained information about sustainable practices through the media (Carrigan & de Pelsmacker 2009; O'Cass 2004), and although they reacted to information which was known and, despite an interest in ethical issues, the participants did not actively seek additional information.

> *It's really hard, because you buy the same products over and over again, so you actually stop checking, don't you, whereas if I see a new product, I am then, perhaps reading the label or... then I am probably looking to see what's actually in it. (5)*

> *I don't read, I don't put myself ... In the place of information, about all these things, because if I think if I knew more, I would change my habits, again. Because I think I can't, if I know, I can't do wrong, really,... I think it's also that I'm just, I'm tired, of, of kind of, campaigning, em, and making my life hard..., I just sort of made myself suffer, and em, and I think I can't do that anymore... (4)*

Although all of the participants recycled glass, paper and cardboard, damaged or worn garments were disposed of as refuse, as described by previous research (Black 2008; Morgan & Birtwistle 2009). Only one participant had knowledge that clothing past its best could be recycled as 'rags' and therefore was accepted by charity shops.

Available information

The lack of available information on ethical orientation was noted by all participants and this is consistent with previous literature. Consumers required information on the production process, from the material used and the journey to the retailer.

> *I would love to know, you know we know, food miles is something that is incorporated into what we buy in food, but I would like to have a history of the garments that are on offer. I would like to know. I mean they do say where they come from but you never really know what it entails'.(1)*

This is consistent with other research where mass adoption by both retailers and consumers is required to promote sustainability (Prothero & Fitchett 2000). All of the major supermarkets in the UK contribute to encouraging consumers to make ethical choices, through offering bags for life and recycling facilities as well as including fair trade and organic alternatives available for purchase, and this contributes to altruistic feelings.

> *If it is the mainstream ones that took it on then that would be even better. I think that is how the general mass of population is changed (1)*

In the place of information, participants applied heuristics based upon what was known or once heard (Solomon & Rabolt 2009), so the validity or current status of the information was not updated.

> *I haven't gone to the extent to check any of the places where I shop, what their stance actually is, you know, because I have just assumed that because I am paying more... that there are less ethical issues with that, and that's just an assumption that I have made because of the price that I am paying. (5)*

But I probably do twang [meaning twig], if you buy a pair of jeans for £6, you can't help but think about where, you know, whose blood am I wearing those over. So I think that probably, when you are only doing it, like once in a blue moon, you know, I probably assuaged my guilt that way, but I can't imagine, being a, …. a regular shopper. (Participant 5)

You trust the reputation of these bigger stores. (4)

The participants were unaware of the impact the fashion industry had on the environment, for example, the energy used in production (Hamer & Anslow 2008; Morgan & Birtwistle 2009), deaths of farmers who employed chemicals to increase cotton production (Allwood *et al.* 2006) and the negative impact upon the environment (Allwood *et al.* 2006; Black 2008). In contrast, the participants had responded to media campaigns highlighting animal welfare which had changed their perception and opted for purchasing local produce to reduce carbon emissions through transportation.

… I was thinking more about the people who make the clothes and… like doing better for them rather than thinking about it in terms of like the environment. (3)

Definitely I have bought organic cotton products and probably, if I had to choose between the two and the price was similar, I would probably choose organic … (5)

Availability of ethical fashion garments within the mass market

Although two of the participants recognised that purchasing second hand clothing was ethical through not requiring new production and material, it was mainly assumed that purchasing ethical fashion would reflect concern for the workers involved in production (Solomon & Rabolt 2009). Further, there was confusion over what impact the fashion industry had on the environment.

Because it would be very easy to just, eh, you know, get something from a sweatshop… you hear terrible things about… people working such long hours and you know, they have to work really long hours and get paid so little, and they work every day. They don't have weekends, and holidays, and things… we are quite happy to sit here with our £2 shirts and … (4)

Do you want the blood of them on your hands? (5)

Ethical fashion was not perceived as 'fashionable' through following current fashion trends or structured styles but rather baggy and 'ethnic', therefore, it was considered that ethical fashion attracted a 'certain' kind of person.

But you would find that in a certain kind of shop, would you… you'd have to shop in a certain kind of retailer then, if you were going to seek it, wouldn't you, because it's not available on the high street. (5)

To gain acceptance, ethical products have to be comparable, with ethical status as a competitive advantage, something with Shaw and Tomolillo (2004) believe could be achieved. Consistency and transparency within the supply chain could potentially be communicated through labelling.

> As a general rule, I think clothes shopping is the one area where I feel least able to make choices, which are ethical in terms of knowing the origins of something. I think with food shopping now, I've got it down to quite a fine art, and I always try to buy fair trade products and there are companies that you know that aren't good to use and you don't use them and you can make that choice and I feel that with clothes, I don't really know. (1)

> I bet you would feel quite pleased if you found something like that (referring to the Global Girlfriend label). (5)

> The retailer should be forced to be more upfront and there should be some credibility in that, you know. You should be proud, to say, you know, ... no animal, or child, or, person in another country has, has suffered through manufacture of this product. (4)

Alignment with the availability of ethical food products

The availability of ethical food products in mainstream supermarkets was appreciated by the participants, especially as it was 'much larger than many years ago' and this is consistent with previous research recognising ease of accessibility (do Paço & Raposo 2010; Memery, Megicks & Williams 2005; Schaefer & Crane 2005) and this has potentially raised consumer awareness of ethical issues through the provision of alternatives (Carrigan & de Pelsmacker 2009; Low & Davenport 2006; Schaefer & Crane 2005). Further, this had not only increased access to ethical food products, but the price was considered less prohibitive. When considering the price of organic and fair trade options, the participants indicated that this enabled the criteria to be evaluated:

> I would look at the price, you know, if organic was...pretty similar, I would then choose to buy the organic. (5)

> No that's the thing, you wouldn't necessarily know where to buy it and also ... It needs to be made clearer just how important it is, to be buying it if you can. And yeah, just to make sure that you know where you can buy it. And, because I don't know if they have got big signs like this in the shops or not (Marks and Spencer Plan A). But if you knew, kind of where you could go, to buy affordable stuff. (Part 2)

> It's more in my case to do with food just because that is where I have been most aware but for clothing and everything that we buy it is also an issue, but I think that with food production there has been a very high profile awareness for years and years and years about the conditions of production and what you are actually contributing to when you buy this product... (1)

All of the participants reported purchasing fair trade products, facilitated by the recognisable 'Fairtrade' mark (Black 2008). However, despite recognising supermarkets had increased ethical food products, supermarket fashion was not considered ethical and this is an area where mainstream fashion retailers are not providing alternatives for consumers (Connolly & Shaw 2006).

> *Well I think it's more obvious with food, but then. I think, because it's right there. If you look then you can see the Fairtrade sign, or whatever right …. in front of you . And if … all the organic stuff is altogether, … as well. So you know that you are not checking things individually. (2)*

> *I can remember buying some school shirts for [my son] and they were two pounds, for two shirts and I just, almost couldn't buy them because they were too cheap, because [] I thought how could someone have actually grown the cotton and harvested the cotton, and then woven it into material and somebody else cuts it up, makes it into a shirt, and then it has to be packaged, and then it has to be shipped, and it, it still costs one pound and everybody's taken their cut on the way. And I'm not sure. (4)*

Similarly, organic produce allows consumers to purchase food products which have not been subject to chemicals and pesticides (Ethical Company Organisation 2008) and this has not transferred to fashion. Participant 4 was concerned with the chemical application of Teflon to school clothing and struggled to find information and clothing which was affordable and accessible which did not contain Teflon.

> *But I can remember reading an article about how it wasn't good for the children's' skin and that [if it was] worn next to the skin, it was a chemical that could be taken into [] and I've almost got to the point that [] I am out of kilter with everyone in the rest of the world. (4)*

The participants had greater awareness of the impact food production had upon the environment and what processes were involved within production. This could be a result of information obtained from the media as well as available information on corporate websites.

> *Well, I suppose because they have seen the same stuff that I have seen, or you know like, because people are coming more aware about, like…. big Hugh Fearnley Whittingstall campaign, wasn't there. I think that a lot of people woke up to it a little bit more after that. Em, … just like free range eggs, you know, people now know that battery farming, for eggs, is cruel so, people don't buy a battery egg. (5)*

Similar information regarding fashion ethics is more complex and has been subject to claims of greenwash (Yates 2009). This coupled with other media stories discrediting claimed ethical commitments from mass market fashion retailers results in consumers' feelings of helplessness, scepticism and distrust, especially when claims are ambiguous or misleading.

> *A bit like food products, you know, no additives, but it didn't have any additives in the first place, you know, it's that kind of issue. (5)*

As concluded by Schröder and McEachern (2004), transparency and status, independently endorsed, would enable consumer confidence in ethical claims.

Conclusion

Sustainable consumption is increasingly recognised by consumers (Carrigan & de Pelsmacker 2009) and this research identified that consumers are keen to reward retailers who address ethical issues when the products are affordable, accessible and of the same style/quality – with ethical production as an additional perceived attribute. The participants had all changed their behaviour when they had the knowledge and it was convenient, accessible and affordable. Sustainability in relation to clothing was not considered as important because clothes are purchased less frequently than other products and longevity is expected. Furthermore, due to a lack of point-of-purchase information, ethical issues are not considered during the shopping experience.

The participants felt informed and aware of food ethics, recognised through logos, which made ethical choices easier. It was noted that the media plays a role in providing the participants with information about the advantages of ethical food and, in contrast, the lack of information regarding the ethical impact of the fashion industry inhibits informed choice and discourages positive consumption. Furthermore, the consumer requires guidance, though labelling, to understand the production process and the ethical benefits. This should encourage retailers to consider consumers' distaste for unethical production where there is a negative impact on the planet and the people involved in production (Lee & Sevier 2008). In addition, fashion retailers should also be encouraged by the recognition that consumers appreciate the availability of alternative products in mainstream fashion outlets and harness this consumer demand to provide alternative fashion garments (Moisander, Markkula & Eraranta 2010). This would enable the adoption by mainstream consumers of garments/labels produced using ethical production (Prothero & Fitchett 2000).

The methodology was considered appropriate to understanding ethical fashion consumption within a 'real life' context. Although the participants discussed the purchase of other products as well as fashion consumption, due to the unstructured interviews, the discussions centred around consumption expectations and sustainable behaviours incorporated into lifestyles. For example, Participant 4 discussed the ambiguity of the varying price of sofas; however, this reflected confusion about the true value of the products. This confusion was also present in relation to the price of supermarket clothing – when school polo shirts could be purchased for £2 and this price did not reflect the full cost of the material, construction and transportation to the UK, as well as the retailer maintaining profit. The participants were able to describe how their ethical values and beliefs were frequently compromised by lifestyle restrictions, for example, time and finance. Further, the participants also described the areas in which they felt able to behave sustainably and how this contributed to feelings of satisfaction. This included the application of ethical values when they were in a position to do so (McDonald et al. 2009).

The consumers discussed their experience of purchasing fashion along with the lack of knowledge and available information, making natural comparisons to what is known about food. The findings also indicate consumers' willingness to adopt ethical behaviour when it is known and understood, and this could be linked to the media in influencing behaviour. An example of this is the effect of television programme like one on UK Channel Four where Hugh Fearnley-Whittingstall explored the battery farming of chickens and eggs and how this has impacted consumer behaviour (O'Cass 2004). Trust of a retailer was also discussed and values are matched as the consumer seeks to apply their own moral and ethical values to those of the retailer, and when negative information from the media is obtained, consumers adapt their behaviour accordingly. As the participants access fashion through mass market fashion retailers who reflect their sense of identity and self, it would be pertinent if this trust also aligned with consumers' morals and values. Consumers apply heuristics to the decision-making process to simplify the available choices (Solomon & Rabolt 2009), particularly when the consumer has to juxtapose consumption along with competing demands, for example working mothers who are restricted by time and financial budgets.

Therefore, it can be suggested that ethical fashion consumption will follow the trend in food, if consumers are offered a viable alternative which aligns with their morals and values; however there are a number of obstacles which exist currently. For example, consumers require further information from retailers regarding the production processes in order to make an informed decision. Additionally, the ethical attributes of a fashion product need to be made desirable, following fashion trends and be equivalent or marginally more expensive to compete with mainstream fashion. Finally, mass market fashion clothing was primarily purchased by the participants and convenience is an important aspect of the shopping experience. Taken overall, these changes offer an opportunity for retailers to realign with consumers' expectations and to maintain a competitive advantage.

References

Allwood, J. M., Laursen, S. E., de Rodriguez C. M. and Bocken, N. M. 2006. *Well Dressed? The present and future sustainability of clothing and textiles in the United Kingdom*. University of Cambridge Institute for Manufacturing.

Arcadia (2011) http://www.arcadiagroup.co.uk/assets/pdfs/responsibility_report_2009.pdf (Accessed 8 April 2011).

Aspers, P. 2008. Labelling fashion markets. *International Journal of Consumer Studies*. 32 (6) pp 633 – 638.

Barrientos S and Smith S. 2006. Report on the ETI Impact Assessment 2006. The ETI labour practice: Do workers really benefit? *Institute of Development Studies*. [Online] Available from: http://www.ethicaltrade.org/sites/default/files/resources/Impact%20assessment%20Part%203,%20implementing%20codes.pdf [Accessed 8 April 2011].

Black, S. 2008. *Eco–chic: The Fashion Paradox*. London. Black Dog.

Boden S. 2006. Dedicated followers of fashion? The influence of popular culture on children's social identities. *Media Culture Society*. 23. Pp 289 – 298.

Cambridge Dictionary. 2011. Fashion Cambridge University Press. [Online] Available from: http://dictionary.cambridge.org/dictionary/british/fashion_1 [Accessed 8 April 2011].

Carrigan, M. and Attalla A. 2001. The myth of the ethical consumer – do ethics matter in consumer behaviour? *Journal of Consumer Marketing*. 18 (7) pp 560 – 578.

Carrigan, M. and de Pelsmacker, P. 2009. Will ethical consumers sustain their values in the global credit crunch? *International Marketing Review*. 26 (6) pp 674 – 687.

Carrigan, M. and Szmigin, I. 2006. "Mothers of invention": maternal empowerment and convenience consumption. *European Journal of Marketing*. 40 (9/10) pp 1122 – 1142.

Carrigan, M, Szmigin, I. and Wright, J. 2004. Shopping for a better world? An interpretive study of the potential for ethical consumption within the older market. Journal of Consumer Marketing. 2. Nu6. Pp 401 – 417.

Carter K. 2010. Tesco launches recycled clothing collection. Guardian [Online] Available from: http://www.guardian.co.uk/lifeandstyle/green-living-blog/2010/mar/02/tesco-ethical-fashion-range [Accessed 8 April 2011].

Centre For Sustainable Fashion. 2009. Tactics for Change. London College of Fashion [Online] Available from: http://www.sustainable-fashion.com/wp-content/uploads/2009/09/CSF%20Volume%203_Tactics%20for%20Change.pdf [Accessed 8 April 2011].

Christopher M, Lowson R and Peck H. 2004. Creating agile supply chains in the fashion industry. *International Journal of Retail & Distribution*. 32 (8) Pp 367 – 376.

Connolly J and Shaw D. 2006. Identifying fair trade in consumption choice. Journal of Strategic Marketing. 14. December 2006. Pp 353 – 368.

Cowe R and Williams S. 2001. *Who are the ethical consumers*? The Co-Operative Bank.

Creswell J W. 2009. *Research Design. Qualitative, Quantitative and Mixed Methods Approaches*. 3rd Edition. California: Sage.

Damhorst M L. 2005. Fashion as a social process. In Damhorst M L, Miller-Spillman K A and Michelman S O of the collected work *The Meaning of Dress*. Fairchild Publication. Inc: New York. Pp 403 – 447.

Defra 2009. Product roadmaps: Clothing. Department for Environment, Food and Rural Affairs. [Online] Available from: http://www.defra.gov.uk/environment/business/products/roadmaps/clothing.htm [Accessed 8 April 2011].

Defra 2008. *Summary report: second sustainable clothing roadmap stakeholder meeting (March 2008)*. Department for Environment, Food and Rural Affairs. May 2008.

Defra. 2007. *Sustainable clothing roadmap briefing note December. 2007: Sustainability impacts of clothing and current interventions*. Department for Environment, Food and Rural Affairs.

Devinney T, Eckhardt G and Belk R. 2007. Why don't consumers behave ethically? The social construction of consumption. Available from http://www2.agsm.edu.au/agsm/web.nsf/AttachmentsByTitle/TD_Paper_SocialConstruction/$FILE/Social+Construction.pdf [Accessed 8 April 2011].

Diamantopoulos, A., Schlegelmilch B B, Sinkovics R R and Bohlen G M. 2003. Can socio-demographics still play a role in profiling green consumers? A review of the evidence and an empirical investigation. *Journal of Business Research*. 56. Pp 465 – 480.

Dickson, M A. 2001. Utility of No Sweat Labels for Apparel Consumer: Profiling Label Users and Predicting Their Purchases. *The Journal of Consumer Affairs*. 35 (1) pp 96 – 119.

Dickson, M. A. 2000. Personal Values, Beliefs, Knowledge, and Attitudes Relating to Intentions to Purchase Apparel from Socially Responsible Businesses. *Clothing and Textiles Research Journal*. (18) pp 19 – 30.

do Paço, A. M. F. and Raposo, M. L. B. 2010. Green consumer market segmentation: empirical findings from Portugal. *International Journal of Consumer Studies*, 34. (4) pp 429-436.

Easey, M. 2009. *Fashion Marketing*. (3rd Edition). Oxford: Wiley-Blackwell.

Easterby-Smith, M. , Thorpe, R. and Jackson, P R. 2008. *Management Research*. 3rd Edition. London: Sage.

Ethical Company Organisation. 2008. *The Good Shopping Guide*. 7th Edition. London: Ethical Marketing Group.

Fair Wear Foundation. 2009. About. Fair Wear Foundation [Online] Available from: http://fairwear.org/about [Accessed 8 April 2011].

Fisher, T., Cooper, T., Woodward, S, Hiller, A. and Goworek H. 2008. *Public Understanding of Sustainable Clothing: A report to the Department for Environment, Food and Rural Affairs*. Defra: London.

Fletcher K. 2008. *Sustainable Fashion and Textiles: Design Journeys*. London: Earthscan Publications Ltd.

Goldsmith, R. E. and Clark, R. A. 2008. An analysis of factors affecting fashion leadership and fashion opinion seeking. *Journal of Fashion Marketing and Management*. 12 (3) pp 308 – 322.

Gutman, J. and Mills, M. K. 1982. Fashion Life Style, Self-Concept, Shopping Orientation and Store Patronage: An Integrative Analysis. *Journal of Retailing*. 58. (2) Summer 1982. pp 64 -86.

Hamer E and Anslow M. 2008. 10 reasons why organic can feed the world. The Ecologist [Online] Available from:

http://www.theecologist.org/trial_investigations/268287/10_reasons_why_organic_can_feed_the_world.html [Accessed 8 April 2011].

Harrison R. 2009. Clothes shops undressed. Ethical Consumer Research Report. *Ethical Consumer* [Online] Available from: www.ethicalconsumer.org [Accessed 8 April 2011].

Hayes , S. G. and Jones, N. 2006. Fast fashion: a financial snapshot. *Journal of Fashion Marketing and Management*. 10 (3) pp 282 – 300.

Hiller Connell, K. Y. 2010. Internal and external barriers to eco-conscious apparel acquisition. *International Journal of Consumer Studies*. 34 (3) pp 279 – 286.

Joergens, C. 2006. Ethical fashion: myth or future trend? *Journal of Fashion Marketing and Management*. 10 (3) pp 360 – 371.

Kilbourne, W., McDonagh, P. and Prothero, A. 1997. Sustainable Consumption and the Quality of Life: Macromarketing Challenge to the Dominant Social Paradigm. *Journal of Macromarketing.* 17 (1) pp 4 – 24.

Lee, M. 2003. *Fashion Victim.* New York: Broadway Books.

Lee, M. and Sevier, L. 2008. The A –Z of Eco Fashion. The Ecologist [Online] Available from: http://www.theecologist.org/green_green_living/clothing/269326/the_a_z_of_e co_fashion.html [Accessed 8 April 2011].

Lee, Y. G .and Bhargava, V. 2004. Leisure Time: Do Married and Single Individuals Spend it Differently. *Family and Consumer Sciences Research Journal.* 32. pp 254 – 274.

Low, W. and Davenport, E. 2006. Mainstreaming fair trade: adoption, assimilation, appropriation. *Journal of Strategic Marketing.* 14. pp 315 – 327.

Lyon, S. 2006. Evaluating fair trade consumption: politics, defetishisation and producer participation. *International Journal of Consumer Studies.* 30. (5) pp 452 – 464.

Made-By. 2007. Made-By in a nutshell. What does Made-By wish to achieve? *Made-By* [Online] Available from: http://www.made-by.nl/downloads/madebynutshell.pdf [Accessed 8 April 2011].

Made By (ND) Fashion with respect for people and the planet. Made By [Online] Available from: http://www.made-by.org/partner-brand [Accessed 8 April 2011].

Marks and Spencer (2011). http://plana.marksandspencer.com/ [Accessed 8 April 2011].

McCallum, H. 2008. Consumers and the environment. *Consumer Policy Review.* 18 (3) pp 61-62.

McDonald, S., Oates, C., Thyne, M., Alevizou P and McMorland L A. 2009. Comparing sustainable consumption patterns across product sectors. *International Journal of Consumer studies.* 33. pp 137 – 145.

Memery J., Megicks, P. and Williams, J. 2005. Ethical and social responsibility issues in grocery shopping: a preliminary typology. *Qualitative Market Research: An International Journal.* 8 (4) pp 399 – 412.

Ming Law K, Zhang Z M and Leung C S. 2004. Fashion change and fashion consumption: the chaotic perspective. Journal of Fashion Marketing and Management. Volume 8. Number 4. Pp 362 – 374.

Miller-Spillman, K. A. 2005. Dress in the Workplace. In Damhorst M L, Miller-Spillman K A and Michelman S O of the collected work *The Meaning of Dress.* Fairchild Publications Inc: New York. pp 217 – 259.

Moisander, J., Markkula, A. and Eraranta, K. 2010. Construction of consumer choice in the market: challenges for environmental policy. *International Journal of Consumer Studies.* 34. pp 73 - 79.

Morgan, L. R. and Birtwistle. G. 2009. An investigation of young fashion consumers' disposal habits. *International Journal of Consumer Studies.* Volume 33. Pp 180 – 198.

Next plc 2011 http://www.nextplc.co.uk/nextplc/corporateresponsibility/ [Accessed 8 April 2011].

Morgan, L. R. and Birtwistle, G. 2009. An investigation of young fashion consumers' disposal habits. *International Journal of Consumer Studies*. 33. pp 180 – 198.

O'Cass, 2004. Fashion clothing consumption: antecedents and consequences of fashion clothing involvement. *European Journal of Marketing*. 38. (7) pp 869-882.

Piamphongsant T and Mandhachitara R. 2008. Psychological antecedents of career women's fashion clothing conformity. *Journal of Fashion Marketing and Management*. 12 (4) Pp 438 – 455.

Prothero, A. and Fitchett, J. A. 2000. Greening Capitalism: Opportunities for a Green Commodity. *Journal of Macromarketing*. 20 (1) pp 46 – 55.

Ritch, E. L., Brennan, C. and MacLeod, C. 2009. Plastic bags politics: modifying consumer behaviour for sustainable development. International Journal of Consumer Studies. 33 (2) pp 168 – 174.

Rogers, E.M. 2003. Diffusion of Innovation 5th Edition. New York: Free Press.

Sayer, A. 2000. Moral economy and political economy, published by the Department of Sociology, Lancaster University, Lancaster LA1 4YL, UK. Available from: http://www.comp.lancs.ac.uk/sociology/papers/sayer-moral-economy-political-ecomony.pdf. [Accessed 8 April 2011]

Schaefer, A. and Crane, A. 2005. Addressing Sustainability and Consumption. *Journal of Macromarketing*. 25. pp 76 – 92.

Schröder, M. J. A. and McEachern, M. G. 2004. Consumer value conflicts surrounding ethical food purchase decisions: a focus on animal welfare. *International Journal of Consumer Studies*. 28 (2) pp 168 – 177.

Schwandt T A. 2003. Three Epistemological Stances for Qualitative Enquiry. In Denzin N K and Lincoln Y S (Eds) *The Landscape of Qualitative Research: Theories and Issues*. 2nd Edition. London: Sage.

Shaw D and Moraes C. 2009. Voluntary simplicity: an exploration of market interactions. *International Journal of Consumer Studies*. Volume 33. pp 215 -223.

Shaw, D. and Tomolillo, A. C. 2004. Undressing the ethical issues in fashion: a consumer perspective. In; Bruce M, Moore C and Birtwistle G. *International Retail Marketing*. Oxford. Butterworth-Heinemann. pp 141 – 152.

Shaw, D., Shiu, E., Hassan, L., Bekin, C. and Hogg G. 2007. Intending To Be Ethical: An Examination of Consumer Choice in Sweatshop Avoidance. *Advances in Consumer Research*. 34. pp 31 – 38.

Soil Association (ND) Our Symbols and Standards. Soil Association [Online] Avaialbale from: http://www.soilassociation.org/Whyorganic/Whatisorganic/Oursymbolandstandards/tabid/213/Default.aspx [Accessed 8 April 2011].

Solomon, M. R. and Rabolt, N. J. 2009. *Consumer Behaviour in Fashion*. 2nd Edition. New Jersey: Pearson Prentice Hall.

Szmigin, I., Carrigan, M. and O'Lochlin, D. 2007. Integrating ethical brands into our consumption lives. Brand Management. 14 (5) pp 396 – 409.

Tesco (2011) Corporate Social Responsibility Report 2000 [Online] http://cr2010.tescoplc.com/~/media/Files/T/Tesco-Corporate-Responsibility-Report-2009/Tesco_CSR_2010.pdf [Accessed 8 April 2011].

The Co-operative. 2009. Ethical Consumerism Report 2009. The Co-operative Bank. Good with money [Online] Available from: http://www.goodwithmoney.co.uk/ethical-consumerism-report-09/ [Accessed 8 April 2011].

The Ecologist. 2010. Consumers lose interest in organic food. [Online] Available from: http://www.theecologist.org/News/news_round_up/461441/consumers_lose_interest_in_organic_food.html [Accessed 8 April 2011] .

Thomson, C. J. and Haytko, D. L. 1997. Speaking of Fashion: Consumers' Uses of Fashion Discourses and the Appropriation of Countervailing Cultural Meanings. *Journal of Consumer Research*. 24 (4) pp 343-353.

Thomson, C. J., Locander, W. B. and Pollio, H. R. 1989. Putting Consumer Experience Back into Consumer Research: The Philosophy of Existential-Phenomenology. *Journal of Consumer Research* 16 (2) pp 133-46.

Tsakiridou, E., Boutsouki, C., Zotos, Y .and Mattas, K. 2008. Attitudes and behaviour towards organic products: an exploratory study. *International Journal of Retail and Distribution Management*. 36 (2) pp 158 – 175.

Waste Watch. 2005. Teachers Resource Instant Expert. A whirlwind of issues relating to textile waste. *Waste Watch* [Online] Available from: http://www.recyclezone.org.uk/library/docs/Waste_Watch_TEXTILES.pdf.pdf [Accessed 8 April 2011].

Winakor G. 1969. The Process of Clothing Consumption. *Journal of Home Economics*. 61 (8) Pp 629 – 634.

Workman J E amd Studak C M. 2006. Fashion consumers and fashion problem recognition style. *International Journal of Consumer Studies*. 30 (1) pp 75 – 84.

Yates L. 2009. Green Expectations. Consumer Focus [Online] Available from: www.consumerfocus.org.uk/en/content/cms/Publications___Repor/Publications___Repor.aspx [Accessed 8 April 2011].

Chapter 6

Stakeholder influence

A multi-stakeholder perspective on creating and managing strategies for sustainable marketing

José-Carlos García-Rosell, Johanna Moisander and Kathryn Fahy

ABSTRACT

Ever since the introduction of sustainable development by the Brundtland Commission in 1987, both business and public organisations have been expressing their interest in and commitment to environmental and social causes – issues usually thought to be counter to profit maximisation – in new ways. In organisational practice, however, the very notion of sustainable development has remained ambiguous. As a strategic goal and set of values, sustainable development seems to take varied meanings in different political, socioeconomic and moral contexts. In this paper, we take a multi-stakeholder perspective on sustainable development and propose an action-research-based process model for developing dynamic, proactive strategies for managing the business-natural environment interface in the context of marketing and service development. We offer this model as a *strategic tool* for engaging stakeholders in the development and deployment of the organisational practices and capabilities needed for building dynamic and proactive environmental strategies. Using an empirical case, we illustrate the use of this tool in the context of sustainable tourism service design, in which a network of female, rural, small entrepreneurs were engaged in service development to clarify the notion of sustainability in business practice. Overall, it is argued that the development of marketing and business activity towards more sustainable policies and practices requires the deployment of bottom-up, multi-stakeholder approaches to strategising, which helps the organisation to integrate the perspectives and concerns of its key stakeholders into its strategy and day-to-day business practices.

Introduction

The introduction of sustainable development by the Brundtland Commission in 1987 brought a new perspective to the role of business in society (World Commission on Environment and Development 1987). Since then, business and public organisations have been expressing their interest in and commitment to environmental and social causes – issues usually thought to be counter to the idea of profit maximisation – in new ways. In organisational practice, however, the very notion of sustainable development has remained ambiguous (Doane 2005; Gladwin, Kennelly & Krause 1995; Greenfield 2004). As a strategic goal and set of values, sustainable development seems to take varied meanings in different political, socioeconomic and moral contexts. In this chapter, our aim is to propose a process model for clarifying the notion of sustainability in business practice. We offer this model as a tool for developing dynamic, proactive strategies for managing the business-natural environment interface in the context of marketing and service development.

In the existing literature, a myriad of concepts have been used to theorise and discuss sustainable development in relation to organisational practice (Carroll 1998, 1999; Collier & Esteban 1999; Collier & Wanderley 2005; Doane 2005; Maignan & Ferrell 2004; Matten & Crane 2005; Matten, Crane, & Chapple 2003; Rondinelli & Berry 2000). Much of the discussion is framed around marketing concepts such as green marketing (Mintu & Lozada 1993), environmental marketing (Coddington 1993) and sustainable marketing (Fuller 1999), which are portrayed somewhat unreflectively as simple management tools. The starting point of this chapter, however, is that these marketing concepts represent strategic goals and values that can be achieved only through complex socio-cultural processes and collaborative practices by which marketers, consumers and other stakeholders, as different 'knowledge communities', make sense of, negotiate and transform the meaning of sustainable development in business practice. The ambiguous and potentially contested nature of sustainability and sustainable development arises mainly from the idea that different knowledge communities, or stakeholders, will each enter the fray with their own specialised and lay knowledge and potentially divergent objectives. This variation in objectives presents challenges in interpreting, sharing and integrating knowledge from other communities (Bechky 2003; Boland & Tenkasi 1995; Brown & Duguid 1991; Carlile 2004; Dougherty 1992; Lervik *et al.* 2007; Lervik, Fahy & Easterby-Smith 2010). Therefore, the development of marketing and business activity towards more sustainable policies and practices requires the deployment of bottom-up multi-stakeholder approaches to strategising, which helps the organisation integrate the perspectives and concerns of its key stakeholders into marketing strategy and day-to-day business practice.

In this chapter, we discuss a multi-stakeholder perspective on sustainable marketing (Fry & Polonsky 2004; Hemmati 2001; Maignan, Ferrell & Ferrell 2005; Polonsky 1995; Polonsky & Ottman 1998) and propose an action-research-based process model for creating and managing environmental strategies in interaction with the internal and external stakeholders of the organisation. We offer this model as a strategic tool (Clark 1997; Moisander & Stenfors 2009) for engaging stakeholders in the development and deployment of the organisational practices and capabilities needed for building dynamic and proactive environmental marketing strategies. Using an empirical case, we illustrate the use of this model in the context of sustainable service design and development.

A multi-stakeholder perspective on sustainable marketing

In building the process model for creating and managing proactive strategies for sustainable marketing proposed in this chapter, we start with an extended concept of marketing as 'the activity, set of institutions, and processes for creating, communicating, delivering, and exchanging offerings that have value for customers, clients, partners, and society at large' (American Marketing Association 2007). From this perspective, marketing is understood not so much as a function but as a process that expands beyond the boundaries of the firm to include different stakeholders (Fry & Polonsky 2004; Maignan, Ferrell & Ferrell 2005; Polonsky 1995). Theoretically, we draw primarily from the literature on multi-stakeholder perspectives on sustainable development (Hemmati 2001), resource-based views of proactive environmental strategies (Rueda-Manzanares, Aragón-Correa & Sharma 2007; Sharma & Vredenburg 1998) and action research (Zuber-Skerritt 1996).

Multi-stakeholder thinking

The term 'multi-stakeholder' is used here in reference to the equitable representation of three or more stakeholder groups and their views in processes that encompass dynamic relationships and social interactions. According to Hemmati (2001), multi-stakeholder processes are based on the democratic principles of transparency and participation and aim to develop partnerships and strengthened networks among stakeholders. In relation to sustainability, multi-stakeholder processes offer a wealth of subjective perspectives and experiences that allow stakeholders to construct the knowledge and capabilities needed to deal with environmental and social challenges.

In the context of sustainable marketing, the multi-stakeholder perspective draws attention to the limitations of simply expanding the marketing mix beyond the customer and extends the analytical scope to broader networks of secondary stakeholders that take part in the marketing process. Multi-stakeholder thinking problematises the assumption that stakeholders are isolatable, clearly identifiable, individual entities that are independent from each other (Buchholz & Rosenthal 2005). Instead, it views stakeholders as social actors, embedded in webs of relationships, who actively engage with each other and with the organisation in culturally and politically complex marketplace environments. The complex and contested nature of environmental and social sustainability issues also means that conceptualisation of issues and appropriate solutions are far from straightforward (Howard-Grenville 2007; Purvis et al. 2000). Thus, multi-stakeholder thinking opens up an analytical perspective that helps organisations to clarify the many different and often-conflicting interests and expectations they face in the market and to develop proactive environmental strategies in terms that are relevant to the diverse stakeholders.

Resource-based view of proactive environmental strategy

The resource-based view emphasises the strategic importance of particular resources, capabilities and competences in enabling organisations to conceive of, choose and implement their competitive strategies (Barney & Zajac 1994, p. 6). It is assumed that an organisation's competitive advantage, performance and survival in the market depend significantly upon its ability to develop and deploy particular organisational resources and capabilities that help the organisation function more efficiently than its competitors. Organisational resources include both the tangible and intangible assets of the firm. In contrast to resources, capabilities have been defined as 'a firm's capacity to deploy *[r]esources*, usually in combination, using organisational processes, to effect a desired end' (Amit & Schoemaker 1993, p. 35) and in terms of 'the socially complex routines that determine the efficiency with which firms physically transform inputs into outputs' (Collis 1994, p. 145).

Previous empirical research has suggested that proactive environmental strategies are associated with a number of organisational capabilities, including those of organisational learning, continuous innovation and stakeholder integration (Rueda-Manzanares, Aragón-Correa & Sharma2007; Sharma & Vredenburg 1998). This literature also tells us that the development of these organisational capabilities is enhanced through engaging with a broad range of external stakeholders. From this perspective, sustainable marketing may be viewed as a proactive environmental and societal strategy, which is based on continuous organisational learning and innovation through cross-stakeholder management (Rueda-Manzanares, Aragón-Correa & Sharma 2007; Sharma & Vredenburg 1998). Through the processes and practices embedded in these capabilities, an organisation is able to integrate, reconfigure, gain and release resources that may help promote environmental and social objectives (Eisenhardt & Martin 2000, p. 107).

In the strategy field, organisational learning is often understood in terms of the successful alignment of the organisation with a changing external environment (Easterby-Smith 1997; Fiol & Lyles 1985). This literature distinguishes between adaptations made by organisations in response to a changing business environment, which should not assume that much reflection and learning has taken place, and that of organisational learning, defined as 'the development of insights, knowledge, and associations between past actions, the effectiveness of those actions, and future actions' (Fiol & Lyles 1985, p. 811).

In this line of research, organisational learning has also been understood as operating at different levels characterised in terms of lower- or higher-order learning (Fiol & Lyles 1985) or as single- or double-loop learning (Argyris & Schön 1978). These different levels of learning denote a distinction between incremental and transformational change in organisational practices or between routine versus more radical organisational learning respectively (Easterby-Smith, Crossan & Nicolini 2000). Lower-order learning is assumed to take place within established organisational rules and routines and seeks to maintain current orders; whereas higher-order learning aims to change organisational rules and norms and often occurs in contexts characterised by ambiguity and complexity (Fiol & Lyles 1985), such as those presented by environmental and social sustainability pressures (Sharma & Vredenburg 1998).

Research suggests that a capability for such higher-order learning may be developed through engaging in proactive relationships with a wide variety of stakeholders in ways that facilitate experimentation with new ideas (Sharma & Vredenburg 1998). More social constructivist approaches to learning in organisations also point to the importance of the social aspects of learning, which moves away from an information processing view of learning in favour of a view of learning and knowledge construction as a collective endeavour, where learning takes place as people do things together (Blackler 1995; Brown & Duguid 1991; Engeström 1989; Lave & Wenger 1991; Orr 1996; Star 1992; Wenger 1999). Research suggests that through the 'socially complex' (Sharma & Vredenburg 1998, p. 740) practices of engaging directly with stakeholders (employees, customers, local community members, NGOs, legislators, suppliers and other members of society) in joint negotiation and problem solving activities around sustainability issues, organisations can develop novel perspectives and new knowledge in relation to environmental and socially responsible practices (Rueda-Manzanares, Aragón-Correa & Sharma 2007; Sharma & Vredenburg 1998).

Action research methodology

In this chapter, action research refers to a systematic mode of inquiry that is based on a reflective process of progressive problem solving and action in collaboration with the participants of the study. In building our model, we use the principles of action research primarily as a methodological tool for developing professional practice, based on the diagnosis of a particular real-life situation (Levin 1948). From this perspective, the aim is thus to generate practical knowledge (Reason & Torbert 2001) and build theory from practice (Schultz & Hatch 2005) by studying attempts of the practitioner-participants to improve the quality of their own practice (Whitehead 1994).

Our model, which is illustrated in Figure 6.1, is based specifically on the action research cycle proposed by Zuber-Skerritt (1996) and the stakeholder-marketing model introduced by Maignan, Ferrell and Ferrell (2005). We propose this process model as a tool for business practitioners to use when engaging with stakeholders to develop and manage proactive strategies for sustainable marketing.

Figure 6.1 A process model for integrating stakeholder perspectives into sustainable business strategy

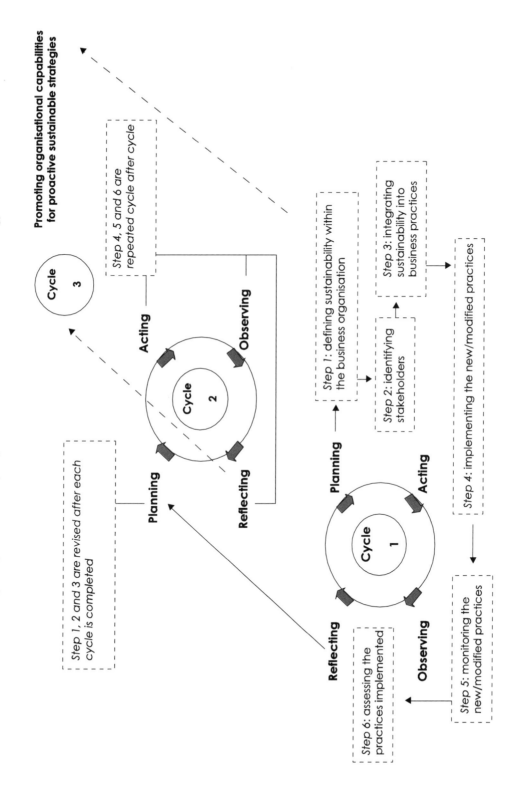

The model depicts a systematic and cyclical process of simultaneous inquiry and action, which is geared to creating practical knowledge and shared understandings of sustainability in collaboration with the multiple stakeholders of the organisation.

In Cycle 1, the process is made up of four phases: planning, acting, observing and reflecting. The planning phase consists of three steps: definition of sustainability, identification of stakeholders and integration of sustainability. Whereas the first two steps help define a more comprehensive path for building environmentally enlightened marketing strategies, the third step involves incorporating sustainability within business practices. The modified practices are then implemented in the acting phase and are monitored during the observing phase. Steps four and five open up an opportunity to explore stakeholder interactions in relation to the organisation. In the reflecting phase, step six invites members of the organisation and stakeholders to assess critically their business processes and practices in relation to sustainability. After these four phases, a new cycle begins (Cycle 2), and the process is repeated until a satisfactory solution is achieved

Next, we will illustrate how the model can be used for launching multi-stakeholder processes and for engaging stakeholders in the development and deployment of the organisational practices and capabilities needed to build dynamic and proactive strategies for sustainable marketing.

Empirical case: Sustainable service design in tourism

To elaborate on the multi-stakeholder perspective on sustainable marketing proposed in this chapter, we discuss an empirical case of sustainable tourism service design. In this design, a network of female, rural, small entrepreneurs from the northern Finnish province of Lapland were engaged in service development to clarify the notion of sustainability in business practice.

The case discussed here is drawn from a development project carried out by the Regional Development and Innovation Services (RDIS) unit of the University of Lapland, which is committed to promoting sustainable development, wellbeing and equality among its local stakeholders and in society more generally. The aim of the development project was to engage a network of entrepreneurs in the development of proactive strategies for sustainable marketing and service t development in the field of tourism. A small team from the RDIS unit conducted the development project. José-Carlos García-Rosell worked as the principal researcher in the team.

The network consisted of eight female craft entrepreneurs operating in different service areas such as catering, hospitality, pottery, natural health care, tourist tours, gastronomy, artistic photography, twig crafting and interior decoration. Despite the variety of services that they offered, all the network participants represented themselves as small business owners in the tourism sector who maintained close relationships with their local communities. As their main motivations for joining the network, the participants articulated a desire to learn techniques of sustainable service design and an opportunity to network with the other entrepreneurs of the region who were interested in conducting their business in sustainable ways. The ages of the network participants ranged from 35 to 65, and the number of employees they employed ranged from one to six, depending on the season.

The development project consisted of two action research cycles that took place over a period of 14 months. The empirical materials used in the project were fieldwork data obtained by means of participant and non-participant observation, convergent interviews, focus groups and documentary materials. Participant observation of the meetings and workshops of the network and non-participant observation of the service encounters between entrepreneurs and their customers constitute the main source of data for the project. In addition, eight convergent interviews (Dick 1990) with the network participants and two customer focus groups (Moisander & Valtonen 2006) were conducted. The objective of the interviews and focus groups was to map out and clarify the multiple meanings of sustainability among the network participants as well as to identify the patterns of convergence and divergence in these meanings. The topics discussed in the interviews and focus groups revolved around sustainable development in relation to tourism and the services that the network members offered. Finally, documentary materials (brochures, newspaper articles, and websites) were collected and used as supplementary, secondary data.

Service development in the context of the tourism business was the chosen research setting because it offers a good opportunity for exploring multi-stakeholder processes. It also illustrates the ways in which particular capabilities such as organisational learning, continuous innovation and cross-stakeholder management can be collaboratively developed and deployed in interactions with the stakeholders of an organisation. People who participate in the service development process are in continuous interaction with the internal and external stakeholders of the organisation. Thus, it may be argued that they would, therefore, have enhanced possibilities for understanding the multiplicity and complexity of the stakeholder views, needs and expectations that may be involved in the implementation of sustainable marketing strategies (Polonsky & Ottman 1998). These individuals are the first to detect changes in the environment and help the organisation adapt its services to emerging market trends and developments. Moreover, tourism offers a particularly good empirical context for exploring the practices and processes of multi-stakeholder service development. In the everyday practice of the tourism business, the activities of service design, production and consumption characteristically overlap to a considerable degree, and the interaction between the organisation and its stakeholders – particularly the customers – is remarkably intense (Valtonen 2010).

Sustainable service development: Developing capabilities for organisational learning and innovation through cross-stakeholder management

In this section, we illustrate how the approach and the model that we propose can be used for creating and managing sustainable strategies for marketing and service design. We describe how the model was employed in the development project in our empirical case, discussing how particular organisational capabilities associated with organisational learning and innovation were developed and deployed during the two cycles of the process.

Cycle 1: Planning – definition of sustainability, identification of stakeholders and integrating sustainability into business practices

In the *planning phase* (steps 1 to 3) of the development project, the two first steps – the definition of sustainability and the identification of key stakeholders – were intertwined. To start off the planning phase, eight convergent interviews (Dick 1990) were conducted to map out the network members' views and ideas on sustainability and to identify emerging areas of convergence and divergence to be discussed and further elaborated on in subsequent network meetings. The interviews were open-ended and revolved around participants' views and conceptions of sustainable development in business practice. Secondary sources (e.g. brochures, newspaper articles and websites) were also collected and analysed to supplement the interview data.

After the convergent interviews, a memo of the emerging themes and ideas was given to the members of the network. The memo was later used in a meeting where the network members were instructed to work on a shared understanding of sustainability and the project task, based on the themes and topics that had emerged in the interviews. The meeting was held in a bed-and-breakfast establishment owned by one of the entrepreneurs; it lasted four hours.

Interviews and the secondary data were instrumental in sparking a collaborative learning process within the network. The meeting in which these data were discussed oriented the members of the network to their task and helped them to focus on the concerns and expectations of different stakeholder groups. By collaborating on analysing the data, the network members were able to create a tentative template for a shared vision of sustainability and set preliminary goals for the service design task at hand.

Discussions in the meeting led the entrepreneurs automatically to step 3, which was to establish a set of collectively agreed-upon sustainability objectives for the service design process and to identify the means of achieving these objectives. These discussions also enabled them to map out the key issues in integrating sustainability into everyday business practice. The process proceeded through brainstorming and design sessions in which members of the network collaborated to design a two-day program of tourist activities based on the services that they offered. In these sessions, the scope of the program and the sustainability attributes to be accentuated were defined in a dialogue with the local community. The establishment and consolidation of trust-based relationships within the network and the local community was viewed as important for building up the knowledge base and capabilities that were necessary for the development of sustainable services in the tourism sector. Particularly, the engagement of local community members in the process helped the network members identify aspects and dimensions of environmental concern that were not explicit in the initial understandings of sustainability and how to integrate these into service development.

Cycle 1: Acting – implementation of the modified business processes

In the *acting phase* (step 4), the two-day program of tourist activities designed in step 3, was delivered to a group of tourists by the network members under the supervision of José-Carlos García-Rosell and two other members of the project team. The program included a range of activities, such as a pottery workshop, snowshoeing tour, twig crafting, Vedic Art workshop and a visit to a local gallery. The aim of this implementation initiative was to test the service design developed by the network members in a controlled and monitored environment.

For the participants of the network, the initiative offered an opportunity to systematically analyse and improve their capabilities to establish trust-based collaborative relationships with their stakeholders and to learn about their customers' and other stakeholders' views of sustainability. Above all, participation in the program test provided the network members with a creative environment for identifying and experimenting with new opportunities for service design development at the interface of firm–customer interactions.

Cycle 1: Observing – observing stakeholder interaction and monitoring the delivery of the modified service

The *observing phase* (step 5), which in this case overlaps with the implementation phase, was conducted by monitoring the delivery of the services included in the program of tourist activities, and by observing the interaction between the network members and their stakeholders during the program.

Observation was based on techniques of participant and non-participant observation. While the observation was made mainly by the RDSI project team, the participating network members were also encouraged to observe and take notes about their interactions with their customers and other stakeholders.

The resulting data were documented in 15 pages of field notes, 150 photographs and a 60-minute video recording of the implementation activity, including interactions of the participating entrepreneurs with their employees, customers and the local community. The data were analysed and summarised according to emergent themes and were subsequently used as a basis for discussions in the meetings in the following phase.

Cycle 1: Reflecting – assessing the modified business practices

The *reflecting phase* (step 6) of the development project was conducted using a customer focus group, which was moderated by the principal researcher of the project, and a network workshop, which subjected the sustainable service design developed for the tourism program to internal and external assessment.

The focus group was organised immediately after the implementation of the two-day tourist program. Focus groups were considered appropriate for this type of evaluation task because they help to generate cultural talk (Moisander & Valtonen 2006) and elicit multiple perspectives on a particular social issue. The focus group session included a visual exercise (Heisley & Levy 1991) in which the customers were asked to respond to five photographs, which featured the customers themselves participating in the different activities of the program.

Parallel to the focus group, the entrepreneurs of the network gathered in a workshop in which they reflected upon their experiences with the customers and the program of tourist activities as a whole. Notes taken during this particular session were later brought to a subsequent reflection meeting, which was held three weeks later for the purpose of refining and improving the program by considering the perspectives of their customers and other stakeholders.

A two-page summary of themes and perspectives that emerged in the customer focus group and data collected by the principal researcher in the different meetings and informal discussions that took place during the planning phase were also used in the reflection meeting. This particular data set included the views of local community members and representatives of the RDSI unit.

The entrepreneurs participating in the project saw the reflection process as useful for opening up the channels of communication with their stakeholders and identifying new aspects of sustainability in their services and the program as a whole. As representatives of small firms, they also emphasised the value of collaboration as an important resource for the development of sustainable service designs.

Cycle 2: Planning

The first cycle of planning, acting, observing and reflecting brought new insights and useful ideas for redesigning the program, but a number of issues emerged that called for further investigation. Most importantly, the members of the network learned that they needed to know more about the perspectives of potential new customers as well as the local community members and public organisations on sustainable development as a social issue. Therefore, a second cycle of action research was conducted.

The *planning phase* of the second action research cycle was based on three initiatives. First, another focus group was organised to learn about the perspectives of potential customers on sustainability and tourism. The group consisted of five Spanish citizens, who had booked but not yet experienced the tourism services of the network. The aim of this initiative was to grasp potential consumers' assumptions about the different elements, aspects and attributes that make tourism services sustainable. The focus group discussion, which was conducted in Spain by a local researcher, was transcribed, analysed and summarised in emergent themes.

Second, a group of vocational tourism students from a small village in the Finnish province of Lapland (aged 25–56), who were not involved in the development project, were asked to write short essays about their perceptions of sustainable development in relation to tourism. These essays provided important insights into the local interpretations of sustainable tourism and thus complemented the observational data obtained during the first cycle of the development project. Third, additional documentary materials (mainly policy documents and reports) were analysed for further insights into the ways in which regional development agencies address the idea of sustainable development.

Summaries of the insights gained through these three initiatives, combined with the reflections from the first cycle, were then discussed in several subsequent network meetings and workshops, which focused on redesigning the tourism program. By integrating the perspectives of additional stakeholders into the development project, the network was able to recognise important trends and business opportunities for the entrepreneurs participating in the development project.

Cycle 2: Acting, observing and reflecting

In the *acting phase* of the second cycle, the redesigned program of tourist activities was delivered to a Spanish delegation that was visiting the university involved in the development project. The delegation was accompanied by an interpreter, who was travelling with the group. Over a period of three days, the members of the delegation participated in a variety of leisure activities that the tourism program offered in a small northern town situated in Finnish Lapland, using the services of the network members. Again, this was a good opportunity for the entrepreneurs to learn and integrate stakeholder concerns into their service designs, this time in a new context with different, foreign customers.

The *observing phase* of cycle two was, again, based on participative and non-participative observation, which was made by one of the members of the research team. Altogether, 100 photographs were taken during this particular step. The participating entrepreneurs were also encouraged to make notes on the delivery of their services and to document their experiences of the program in general as the basis for discussion and reflection in subsequent meetings. On this occasion, they were better prepared and more experienced in deploying the implementation of observation techniques.

In the *reflecting phase*, the redesigned program was assessed by organising a stakeholder workshop on sustainable tourism. The aim of the workshop was to test the revised program of tourist activities, to further elaborate on the variability of perspectives among the multiple stakeholders of the network members and to confront the stakeholders' views with those of the network members. The stakeholder participants of this workshop included local activists and policy makers, customers and employees of the network members, as well as a Spanish delegation representing the potential customers of the network.

The workshop was facilitated by the project team, and simultaneous interpretation in Spanish was offered by the interpreter accompanying the Spanish delegation.

The workshop was audio recorded, transcribed, analysed and used as a basis for identifying themes and topics for further discussion and reflection. While the workshop was organised to collect empirical material for reflection by the participants of the development project, it became itself a reflective multi-stakeholder process.

Data collected in different stages of the second cycle were used as the basis for discussions in the meetings in the last step of the project. A total number of three reflection meetings were held with members of the network. A local expert on EU funds was invited to one of the meetings because the entrepreneurs realised that a better understanding of the sustainability rhetoric of development organisations could open up new opportunities for EU-funding.

Overall, the network members were satisfied with the process and expressed their willingness to continue cooperating with each other after the end of the project. By creating positive collaborative relationships with their business partners, local communities and local policy makers, and by integrating the perspectives of these stakeholders into their learning processes, the network members were able to develop and deploy the type of capabilities that are needed for building sustainable service designs and proactive environmental strategies. The following comment of one of the entrepreneurs in the workshop validates this point:

> *The opportunity to develop a tourism program in cooperation with these colleagues [network members] and in continuous interaction with members of the community, the university [RDSI] and our clients has opened up our minds to totally different ways of approaching sustainability [...] Now we are better able to address these concerns with our services.*

Conclusions

The need for organisations to engage with multiple stakeholders to develop knowledge about environmental practices is increasingly being acknowledged. The practice of engaging with multiple stakeholders, however, is a potentially challenging social endeavour. This chapter offers a strategic tool in the form of a process model for creating and managing, in collaboration with organisational stakeholders, proactive strategies for sustainable marketing and service development. We provide an illustration of the model in practice by way of an empirical case of a multi-stakeholder sustainability development project in the tourism sector.

We also draw attention to the nature of organisational learning that can be generated through engagement with multiple stakeholders on sustainable marketing and service development. We outlined the differences between adaption in response to changes in the organisational context and the kinds of learning that might be required for business practitioners to more fully make sense of, and incorporate issues of, environmental and social sustainability in their service development practices. Exposure to others' interpretations and experimentation with alternative practices can generate novel perspectives and initiatives that lead to the type of higher-order learning that characterises firms with proactive environmental strategies.

Our empirical illustration of the process model shows the kinds of active, collective learning in real-life problem-solving situations that can take place when business practitioners engage in reflective processes of inquiry and action in collaboration with multiple external stakeholders. The entrepreneurs participating in the project emphasised the valuable insight it allowed into dimensions of environmental and social concern that had not previously been explicitly articulated. Perhaps even more importantly for the entrepreneurs, the process also facilitated the integration of such dimensions into service development and the monitoring of stakeholders' engagement with modified service offerings. The development of capabilities for establishing trust-based collaborative relationships with key stakeholders was also important in the experience of project participants.

We admit that the scope of this chapter is limited to a description of the action research-based process model. The outcomes of this study are more complex than we are able to present in this section of the book. Indeed, our aim here is to suggest a model that provides a foundation for building and managing environmental strategies in collaboration with different stakeholders, rather than to present conclusive evidence. While our chapter has drawn attention to the potentialities of integrating multi-stakeholder thinking, a resource-based perspective and action research methodology, there is a need for future research that examines the implementation of the model under different circumstances and new variants. First, it would be worthwhile to apply the model to a different organisational and business context. Second, future studies could examine the implementation of the model with a larger number of stakeholder groups. Third, from the perspective of service development, it would be interesting to explore the model in relation to more commercial models of user-driven innovation and stakeholder involvement in service development.

References

American Marketing Association (2007) The American Marketing Association releases new definition for marketing. Available at: http://www.marketingpower.com/AboutAMA/Pages/DefinitionofMarketing.aspx, Accessed, October 30 2010.

Amit, Raphael and Paul J. H. Schoemaker (1993), "Strategic Assets and Organizational Rent," *Strategic Management Journal*, 14 (1), 33-46.

Argyris, C and D. A Schön (1978), *Organizational Learning: A Theory of Action Perspective*, London: Addison Wesley.

Barney, Jay B. and Edward J. Zajac (1994), "Competitive Organizational Behavior: Toward and Organizationally-Based Theory of Competitive Advantage," *Strategic Management Journal*, 15, 5-9.

Bechky, Beth A. (2003), "Sharing Meaning across Occupational Communities: The Transformation of Understanding on a Production Floor," *Organization Science*, 14 (3), 312-30.

Blackler, Frank (1995), "Knowledge, Knowledge Work and Organizations: An Overview and Interpretation," *Organization Studies*, 16 (6), 1021-46.

Boland, R J and R V Tenkasi (1995), "Perspective Making and Perspective Taking in Communities of Knowing," *Organization Science*, 6 (4), 350-72.

Brown, John S and P Duguid (1991), "Organizational Learning and Communities-of-Practice: Toward a Unified View of Working, Learning, and Innovation," *Organization Science*, 2 (1), 40-57.

Buchholz, Rogene A. and Sandra B. Rosenthal (2005), "Towards a Comtemporary Conceptual Framework for Stakeholder Theory," *Journal of Business Ethics*, 58, 137-48.

Carlile, Paul R (2004), "Transferring, Translating, and Transforming: An Integrative Framework for Managing Knowledge across Boundaries," *Organization Science*, 15 (5), 555-68.

Carroll, Archie B. (1998), "The Four Faces of Corporate Citizenship," *Business and Society Review,*, 100 (1), 1-7.

--- (1999), "Corporate Social Responsibility: Evolution of a Definitional Construct," *Business and Society*, 38 (3), 268-95.

Clark, Delwyn N. (1997), "Strategic Management Tool Usage: A Comparative Study," *Strategic Change*, 6 (7), 417-27.

Coddington, Walter (1993), *Environmental Marketing: Positive Strategies for Reaching the Green Consumer*, London: McGraw-Hill.

Collier, Jane and Rafael Esteban (1999), "Governance in the Participative Organization: Freedom, Creativity and Ethics," *Journal of Business Ethics*, 21 (2/3), 173-88.

Collier, Jane and Lilian Wanderley (2005), "Thinking for the Future: Global Corporate Responsibility in the Twenty-First Century," *Futures*, 37 (2/3), 169-82.

Collis, David J. (1994), "Research Note: How Valuable Are Organizational Capabilities?," *Strategic Management Journal*, 15, 143-52.

Dick, Bob (1990), *Convergent Interviewing*, Chapel Hill: Interchange.

Doane, Deborah (2005), "Beyond Corporate Social Responsibility: Minnows, Mammoths and Markets," *Futures*, 37, 215-29.

Dougherty, D. (1992), "Interpretive Barriers to Successful Product Innovation in Large Firms," *Organization Science*, 3 (2), 179-202.

Easterby-Smith, Mark (1997), "Disciplines of Organizational Learning: Contributions and Critiques," *Human Relations*, 50 (9), 1085-113.

Easterby-Smith, Mark, Mary Crossan, and Davide Nicolini (2000), "Organizational Learning: Debates Past, Present and Future," *Journal of Management Studies*, 37 (6), 783-96.

Eisenhardt, Kathleen and Jeffery A. Martin (2000), "Dynamic Capabilities: What Are They?," *Strategic Management Journal*, 21 (10-11), 1105-21.

Engeström, Y (1989), "Developing Thinking at the Workplace: Towards a Redefinition of Expertise," San Diego: University of California Center for Human Information Processing.

Fiol, C. Marlene and Marjorie A. Lyles (1985), "Organizational Learning," *Academy of Management Review*, 10 (4), 803-13.

Fry, Marie Louise and Michael Jay Polonsky (2004), "Examining the Unintended Consequences of Marketing," *Journal of Business Research*, 57 (11), 1303-06.

Fuller, Donald A. (1999), *Sustainable Marketing: Managerial-Ecological Issues*, Thousand Oaks: Sage.

Gladwin, Thomas N., James J. Kennelly, and Tara-Shelomith Krause (1995), "Shifting Paradigms for Sustainable Development Implications for Management Theory and Research," *Academy of Management Review*, 20 (4), 874-907.

Greenfield, W.M. (2004), "In the Name of Corporate Social Responsibility," *Business Horizons*, 47 (1), 19-28.

Heisley, Deborah D. and Sidney J Levy (1991), "Autodriving: A Photoelicitation Technique," *Journal of Consumer Research*, 18 (3), 257-72.

Hemmati, Minu (2001), *Multi-Stakeholder Processes for Governance and Sustainability - Beyond Deadlock and Conflict*, London: Earthscan.

Howard-Grenville, Jennifer A (2007), *Corporate Culture and Environmental Practice: Making Change at a High-Technology Manufacturer*, Cheltenham: Edward Elgar.

Lave, Jean and E Wenger (1991), *Situated Learning: Legitimate Peripheral Participation*, Cambridge: Cambridge University Press.

Lervik, Jon E. , Mark Easterby-Smith, Kathryn Fahy, and Carole Elliott (2007), "Limits to Information Transfer: The Boundary Problem," *Ariadne*, 50 (Jan.), 1-6.

Lervik, Jon Erland, Kathryn M. Fahy, and Mark Easterby-Smith (2010), "Temporal Dynamics of Situated Learning in Organizations," *Management Learning*, 41 (3), 285-301.

Levin, Kurt (1948), *Resolving Social Conflicts: Selected Papers on Group Dynamics*, New York: Harper and Row.

Maignan, Isabelle, O. C. Ferrell, and Linda Ferrell (2005), "A Stakeholder Model for Implementing Social Responsibility in Marketing.," *European Journal of Marketing*, 39 (9/10), 956-77.

Maignan, Isabelle and O.C. Ferrell (2004), "Corporate Social Responsibility and Marketing: An Integrative Framework," *Journal of the Academy of Marketing Science*, 32 (1), 3-19.

Matten, Dirk and Andrew Crane (2005), "Corporate Citizenship: Toward an Extended Theoretical Conceptualization," *Academy of Management Review*, 30 (1), 166-79.

Matten, Dirk, Andrew Crane, and Wendy Chapple (2003), "Behind the Mask: Revealing the True Face of Corporate Citizenship," *Journal of Business Ethics*, 45 (1), 109-20.

Mintu, Alma T. and Héctor R. Lozada (1993), "Green Marketing Education: A Call for Action," *Marketing Education Review*, 3 (Fall), 17-23.

Moisander, Johanna and Sari Stenfors (2009), "Exploring the Edges of Theory-Practice Gap: Epistemic Cultures in Strategy-Tool Development and Use," *Organization*, 16 (2), 227–47.

Moisander, Johanna and Anu Valtonen (2006), *Qualitative Marketing Research: A Cultural Approach*, London: Sage.

Orr, J. E (1996), *Talking About Machines: An Ethnography of a Modern Job*, Ithaca, NY and London, UK: IRL Press, an imprint of Cornell University Press.

Polonsky, Jay (1995), "A Stakeholder Theory Approach to Designing Environmental Marketing Strategy," *Journal of Business & Industrial Marketing*, 10 (3), 29–46.

Polonsky, Michael Jay and Jacquelyn Ottman (1998), "Stakeholders' Contribution to the Green New Product Development Process," *Journal of Marketing Management*, 14, 533-57.

Purvis, Martin, Frances Drake, Jane Hunt, and Deborah Millard (2000), "The Manager, the Business and the Big Wide World," in *The Business of Greening*, ed. Stephen Fineman, London: Routledge, 13-34.

Reason, Peter and William R. Torbert (2001), "Toward a Transformational Science: A Further Look at the Scientific Merits of Action Research," *Concepts and Transformations*, 6 (1), 1-37.

Rondinelli, Dennis A. and Michael A. Berry (2000), "Citizenship in Multinational Corporations: Social Responsibility and Sustainable Development," *European Management Journal* (18), 70-84.

Rueda-Manzanares, Antonio, J. Alberto Aragón-Correa, and Sanjay Sharma (2007), "The Influence of Stakeholders on the Environmental Strategy of Service Firms: The Moderating Effects of Complexity, Uncertainty and Munificence," *British Journal of Management*, 19, 185-203.

Schultz, Majken and Mary Jo Hatch (2005), "Building Theory from Practice," *Strategic Organization*, 3 (3), 337-48.

Sharma, Sanjay and Harrie Vredenburg (1998), "Proactive Corporate Environmental Strategy and the Development of Competitively Valuable Organizational Capabilities," *Strategic Management Journal*, 19, 729–53.

Star, Susan Leigh (1992), "The Trojan Door: Organizations, Work, and the "Open Black Box"," *Systems Practice*, 5 (4), 395-410.

Valtonen, Anu (2010), "Small Tourism Firms as Agents of Critical Knowledge," *Tourist Studies*, 9 (2), 127–43.

Wenger, E (1999), *Communities of Practice: Learning, Meaning and Identity*, Cambridge: Cambridge University Press.

Whitehead, Jack (1994), "How Do I Improve the Quality of My Management?," *Management Learning*, 25, 137-53.

World Commission on Environment and Development, (WCED) (1987), *Our Common Future - the Brundtland Report*, New York: Oxford University Press.

Zuber-Skerritt, Ortrun (1996), *Introduction: New Directions in Action Research*, London: Falmer Press.

Stakeholder influence in organisational sustainability strategy

Jaime R Camino and Giuseppe E Adamo

ABSTRACT

The aim of the chapter is to look at the interaction between stakeholders and their collective influence on the organisation to adopt sustainable strategies. It describes and analyses the stakeholder's role in sustainable strategies, focusing on the marketing approach. First, stakeholder theory is reviewed in order to provide a reference framework. Second, stakeholders are described and analysed, and those relevant to environmental issues and sustainability are identified so that an understanding can be developed regarding which of the various classes of stakeholders are relevant to environmental issues and sustainability. Finally, an analysis of the links, interactions and bidirectional influences between stakeholder pressure and management choices within the marketing strategies is provided. Additionally, evidence from European organisations is presented.

Stakeholder theory

In recent times, stakeholder theory as a theory of the management of organisations and ethics has evolved and embraced different perspectives, including the contribution of philosophers, psychologists, economists and social scientists. The core of all approaches is the two-way strong relationship between organisations and groups as underlined by the earlier definition of the Stanford Research Institute (SRI), where stakeholders are 'those groups, without whose support the organisation would cease to exist' (SRI, 1963-cited in Freeman 1984, p. 31). Stakeholder theory can be used at least in three different ways (Donaldson & Preston 1995):

- descriptive theory, in order to describe and explain specific corporate characteristics and behaviours

- instrumental theory, in order to identify the connections, or lack of connections, between stakeholder management and the achievement of traditional corporate objectives

- normative theory, for interpreting the function of the corporation, including the identification of moral or philosophical guidelines for management.

Two main interrelated directions of investigation have emerged over time: 1) stakeholder identification, and 2) the study of the intensity and the goals of the relationship between organisations and stakeholders. According to the seminal definition of Freeman (1984, p. 46), 'a stakeholder in an organisation is any group or individual who can affect or is affected by the achievement of the organisation's objectives'. Donaldson and Preston (1995, p. 67) pointed out that stakeholders are 'persons or groups with legitimate interests in procedural and/or substantive aspects of corporate activity' and they are identified

> by their interests in the corporation, whether the corporation has any corresponding functional interest in them. The interests of all stakeholders are of intrinsic value. That is, each group of stakeholders merits consideration for its own sake and not merely because of its ability to further the interests of some other groups, such as the shareowners.

Evan and Freeman (1988) focused on the relationship between organisations and stakeholders in terms of benefits and rights that can be violated or respected by the firm. Considering also the time dimension of the relationship, Clarkson (1995) differentiates between primary and secondary stakeholders:

- Primary stakeholders are fundamental for an organisation's survival and include shareholders and investors, employees, customers and suppliers.

- Secondary stakeholders are the governments and communities that provide infrastructures and markets. Secondary stakeholders are not engaged in transactions with the corporation and are not essential for its survival such as the media and a wide range of special interest groups.

From a relationship point of view, stakeholder theory investigates how organisations and stakeholders collaborate (or not) in order to look after their own interests, such as value creation. Stakeholders belonging to the macro-environment are sometimes interested in social equity. Clients are looking for product quality and competitive prices, employees aim at good standards of life, while managers like power and autonomy. Banks ask for guarantees, major shareholders want to control organisations, while minor shareholders ask for high return on their investments. Two different approaches of shareholder value theory have emerged and are linked to the positions of Jensen (2001) and Freeman (1984).

The American approach is focused on shareholder value maximisation, since if all shareholders are satisfied it means that stakeholders have been satisfied too. The European approach embraces the social vision of the firm where all categories of stakeholder contribute to the value creation. At the beginning of 2000, both approaches converged, reinforcing that the organisation goal is the maximisation of shareholder values under the bond of all stakeholders' satisfaction. Post, Preston and Sachs (2002, p. 9) emphasise that

> the capacity of a firm to generate sustainable wealth over time, and hence its long-term value, is determined by its relationships with critical stakeholders

and

> any stakeholder relationship may be the most critical one at a particular time or on a particular issue'.

Nowadays, value creation includes human wellbeing as well as environmental protection, and these factors are becoming pillars of modern stakeholder theory. Stakeholders are important sources of information for firms and are also drivers of green strategies to promote sustainability, green product development and overall positive behaviour towards the environment, the population and the Earth. Several studies based on strategic management literature have been launched to determine the predictors of corporate environmental response (Aragon-Correa 1998; Bowen 2002; Sharma 1997), and previous research on organisations suggests that stakeholder pressures are critical drivers of corporate environmental response (Berry & Rondinelli 1998; Hoffman & Ventresca 2002). Marketing literature also recognises that stakeholders play a significant role in influencing organisations and markets (Davis 1992; McIntosh 1990; Polonsky 1994; Pujari, Wright & Peattie 2003; Varadarajan & Menon 1988), and past empirical research examines their influence on several aspects, for example, purchase of green products, environmental new product development and recycling programs. What marketing literature has not targeted, however, is a single integrated approach that examines the relationship between stakeholder management and green marketing strategies (GMSs). Various reasons have been advanced for this: (i) stakeholder theory is rarely applied to marketing practice (Polonsky 1995); (ii) there is no universally accepted definition of what constitutes a stakeholder (Polonsky, Schuppisser & Beldona 2003); (iii) there is little research into the relative attention that companies give to their stakeholders (Greenley & Foxall 1996); and (iv) the marketing literature is biased in its orientation to one specific stakeholder – the consumer (Fitchett 2004).

We should consider also that the concept of 'stakeholders' in the context of green marketing is quite different. A lot of stakeholders – the planet, various animal and plant species and future generations – are nebulous, and they cannot have a direct influence on marketing strategies. For example, all the iconic green marketing brands (Ben & Jerry's; Tom's of Maine; Bodyshop; Ecover; LL Bean; and Patagonia) were the result of the internally-orientated, value driven strategy and came usually from entrepreneurs with one vision and one idea – rather than being due to specific stakeholder pressure. Thus, although it is apparent that stakeholders influence corporate proactiveness, there is still little analysis of their impact. The following paragraphs will illustrate how stakeholders are identified, which are the main GMSs and how stakeholders influence GMS through influence on management. Finally, evidence from empirical studies is presented.

Identify and prioritise stakeholders

According to literature, stakeholder identification and salience can be based on stakeholders possessing one or more of three relationship attributes (Mitchell, Agle & Wood 1997):

- Power – the probability that one actor within a social relationship would be in a position to carry out his own will despite resistance.

- Legitimacy – a generalised perception or assumption that the actions of an entity are desirable, proper, or appropriate within some socially constructed system of norms, values and beliefs.

- Urgency – the degree to which stakeholder claims call for immediate attention.

The environmental and marketing literature recognises the need to address the interests of a wide diversity of relevant stakeholders (Garrod 1997). However, the theory is often unable to distinguish those who are stakeholders from those who are not (Phillips & Reichart 2000). Stakeholder identification, as well as its conceptualisation, is not univocal (see Agle, Mitchell & Sonnenfeld 1999; Carroll 1999; Clarkson 1995; Mitchell, Agle & Wood 1997).

There is little theoretical and empirical evidence on how managers prioritise the importance of stakeholders (Greenley & Foxall 1997), and this makes it difficult to determine how firms attribute importance to stakeholders. Business management literature provides two perspectives on stakeholder prioritisation. One is based on the idea that only the stakeholders with legitimate claims should be prioritised and identified, 'regardless of their power to influence the firm or the legitimacy of their relationship to the firm' (Mitchell, Agle & Wood 1997, p. 857). The underlying argument here is that firms are unable to satisfy the interests of all stakeholders because of natural restrictions inherent in all organisations regarding the use and availability of resources and capabilities. The second perspective, upheld by Clarkson (1995), suggests that all stakeholders related to the organisation should be prioritised and identified, because all stakeholder interests are legitimate and of intrinsic value, thus meriting consideration on their own terms (Donaldson & Preston 1995).

Marketing literature also offers two perspectives. Maignan and Ferrell (2004) maintain a restricted perspective of stakeholder prioritisation supported by evidence that marketing scholars focus on social responsibilities to two main groups of stakeholders: customers and channel members, and competitors (Day & Wensley 1988; Kotler 2002; Piercy & Cravens 1995; Webster 1992).

The second perspective underlines that all stakeholders' needs must be accounted for in the strategy process (Polansky 1996; Thomlison 1992). Barring a few discrepancies, the relationship marketing literature supports this perspective and the need to improve relations with customers and develop and enhance relations in supplier, recruitment, internal, referral and influence markets (Christopher, Payne & Ballantyne 1991). Gummesson (1999) argues that the bases for marketing are classic and special market relations (relationships with suppliers, customers, competitors and others who operate in the market), and that non-market relations (relationships to governments and the mass media and internal customers) have an indirect influence on the efficiency of firms.

According to this view, a firm's efficiency depends mainly on satisfying the classic and special market relationships, and a proactive attitude to its suppliers, customers and competitors will affect its orientation towards non-market relationships such as the one with the natural environment. According to Starik (1995), the natural environment has the status of stakeholder, providing constrains and opportunities to business life and human existence. The main problem is how to translate natural environmental claims in organisational strategy or, the other way around, how to give a voice to the natural environment, meditating between organisations and natural environment interests.

Green marketing strategies

The natural environment has only recently become an important issue in marketing literature (Fuller 1999; Polonsky 1994) and marketing strategy (Menon & Menon 1997; Ottman 1998). The concept of GMS is still not without critics, and several researchers' suggest it has weak conceptual and empirical development and limited applications to industry (Polonsky 1994). Studies tend to focus on business-to-consumer (B2C) markets (Crane & Peattie 1999) and ignore the fact that there is wide variation with respect to environmental awareness in business-to-business (B2B) markets, business-to-retailer (B2R) markets and business-to-government (B2G) markets (Charter, Elvins & Adams 2004).

Due to heterogeneity in the sizes of firms, technology, country of origin, income and structure, there is no generally accepted typology of GMS. A review of the different typologies of the GMSs of firms reveals that they were developed primarily with a strategic-management focus that emphasised operations functions within organisations, mostly linked to the production systems. Later on, several typologies including marketing functions were developed. Table 6.1 summarises the main strategies in both management and marketing literature.

Table 6.1 Different approaches to environmental strategies of firms

STRATEGIC MANAGEMENT LITERATURE	Author
Operations function focus	
From end-of-pipe strategies to cleaner technologies	OECD (1995)
From waste burden assessment to product design and production process	Sarkis (1995)
From environmentally responsible approaches towards product design to the design of industrial systems	Shrivastava (1995)
From end-of-pipe approach to sustainable development	Hart (1995)
From fundamental process changes to improvement systems	Klassen & Whybark (1999)
Operations & Marketing focus	
From beginners to proactivists	Hunt & Auster (1990)
From Why Me's, Smart Movers, to Enthusiasts	Simpson (1991)
From non-compliance to leading edge	Roome (1992)
From traditional management to environment-related management	Halme (1996)
From a compliance-based attitude to an innovative attitude	Azzone, Bianchi, Mauri, & Noci (1997)
From traditional firms, preventive firms, to 'cutting-edge firms'	Berry & Rondinelli (1998)
From deliberate reactive firm to deliberate proactive firm	Winn & Angell (2000)
From 'green business' to 'green-green business'	Isaak (2002)
MARKETING LITERATURE	**Author**
General business environment focus	
Independent, cooperative, and strategic manoeuvring	Zeithaml & Zeithaml (1984)
Defender-analyser-prospector	Walker & Ruekertl (1987); McDaniel & Kolari (1987)
Green marketing focus	
From defensive or reactionary to assertive or aggressive strategy.	McDaniel & Rylander (1993)
From consumption marketing to sustainable marketing	Sheth & Parvatiyar (1995)
From functional, business strategy level to strategic level	Menon & Menon (1997)
From passive greening to collaborative greening	Crane (2000)

In the marketing literature, the forerunners of environmental typologies (Zeithaml & Zeithaml 1984) focused on the general business environment, rather than on a distinctively green marketing perspective.

Similarly, McDaniel and Kolari (1987) and Walker, Orville and Ruekert (1987) adapted the Miles and Snow (1978) 'reactor-defender-analyser-prospector' classification to present their typologies. According to these authors, this classification is a useful theoretical framework for analysing the interaction between organisations and their environment and the marketing strategies they adopt. Miles and Snow (1978) had classified organisations according to adaptive decision patterns (including 'reactors', 'defenders' and 'analysers') and a more adaptive category ('prospectors'). However, the reactor group should be excluded from the continuum because it refers to organisations that have not actually identified any specific strategy. Defenders have narrow product-market domains, focus on maintaining their positions and tend not to search outside these domains for new opportunities. Analysers focus on maintaining their positions in core markets, but they also want to innovate at the margins by selective searching for new product opportunities. Prospectors make consistent efforts to innovate and produce changes in their industries, experimenting with potential responses to emerging environmental trends.

From a specifically green marketing focus, the typologies also present several evolutionary steps in proactive corporate environmental policies (see Crane 2000; McDaniel & Rylander 1993; Sheth & Parvatiyar 1995). In this respect, Menon and Menon (1997) have identified a progression in so-called 'enviro-preneurial' marketing strategies – including: (i) functional or tactical level; (ii) quasi-strategic (or business-strategic level); and (iii) strategic level. The first, the tactical level, is characterised by functional decisions oriented to achieve specific objectives, and by strategies guided by economic adaptation. The second, the quasi-strategic level, is characterised by a lack of uniform organisation-wide strategic effort to integrate environmental issues with the marketing strategy, and by managerial decisions oriented to achieving competitive advantage in their markets. The third, the strategic level, reflects top management decisions in integrating environmental issues and goals in a firm's micro-organisational and macro-organisational systems. However, in general, these green marketing typologies reflect a normative approach without an empirical basis (Pecotich, Purdie & Hattie 2003), or they are pertinent only to a particular industry (Clemens 2001).

From a firm-consumer relations point of view, GMSs tend to address to the following points: (i) analysis of the potential of green markets; (ii) actions oriented towards satisfying green market needs; (iii) analysis of competitors' green behaviour; and (iv) analysis of green consumer behaviour (Giuliettia *et al.* 2001). The analysis of market potential and competitor behaviour, as well as the satisfaction of market needs, are key steps in the process of developing and implementing green marketing strategy (Hooley, Saunders & Piercy 2004).

Charter, Elvins and Adams (2004) have suggested that green marketing should be broadened from its preoccupation with B2C markets to become a general management process that enables firms to satisfy *all* their target markets (B2B, B2R and B2G) with the right product (or service), at the right price, in the right place, in the right way.

The suggested approach is based on the following fundamental actions at the strategic level of marketing management: (i) an analysis of the potential of green markets; (ii) actions oriented towards satisfying green market needs; and (iii) an analysis of competitors' green behaviour. In addition, (iv) analysis of green consumer behaviour is included because it is a crucial factor in industrial policy given that consumer demand for goods ultimately leads to environmental problems (Polonsky 1994).

The analysis of market potential and the behaviour of competitors, as well as the satisfaction of market needs, are key steps in the process of developing and implementing a marketing strategy (Hooley, Saunders & Piercy 2004).

At the operative level of marketing management, the following marketing-mix actions should be taken: (i) use of distribution according to green criteria; (ii) politics of green product design; (iii) pricing of green products; and (iv) use of green advertising and green sponsoring.

The study of the relationship between green products and industry from a marketing perspective is relatively new (Baumann, Boons & Bragd 2002). However, because of the significant impact of a product's environmental characteristics in all target markets, the present operationalisation includes a consideration of green product design. Managers should be aware that green marketing begins with green design (Vasanthakumar 1993), and that product design constitutes an active interface between demand (consumers) and supply (manufacturers) (Baumann Boons & Bragd 2002). For example, super-concentrated laundry detergents save energy, packaging, space and money (Ottman & Terry 1998).

Green product pricing should be included because green industrial differentiation works only when green products reduce clients' costs (Wohlgemuth, Getzner & Park 1999). Similarly, green advertising should be added because consumers and industrial buyers can be influenced by advertising that reflects a company's commitment to the environment (Polonsky 1994). Several studies on the electronics and furniture industries (SAT 2003; Shaw 2000) and the automobile industry (De Cicco & Thomas 1999) confirmed this approach. Green distribution has to be included because product distribution systems can constrain green design solutions (OTA 1992) since they must guarantee the tangible ecological nature of the products on the market. Additionally, distribution often increases the environmental impact of products and is constantly regulated for environmental compliance (Isherwood 2000). Green product pricing was included because green industrial differentiation works only when green products reduce clients' costs (Wohlgemuth, Getzner & Park 1999).

Green marketing strategies and stakeholders pressure

Stakeholder management is the process used to identify, conceptualise and prioritise stakeholders in order to address environmental demands (Lamberg, Savage & Pajunen 2003; Maignan & Ferrell 2004). Previous literature suggests that the degree to which a firm understands and addresses environmental stakeholder demands is associated with more proactive environmental strategies (Berry & Rondinelli 1998; Hart 1995).

Marketing literature shows that stakeholder orientation is superior to customer orientation (Berman *et al.* 1999) and market orientation (Armstrong 2001) because it implies that the ultimate objective of a business is to create value for all of its stakeholders beyond just value to customers (Murphy *et al.* 2004).

From a marketing perspective, the stakeholder orientation not only lies at the core of relationship marketing (Polonsky, Schuppisser & Beldona 2002), but it is more congruent with the re-conceptualisation of the marketing concept, and it provides a long-term perspective to market orientation (Kimery & Rinehart 1998).

From a conceptual perspective, stakeholder pressure influences managerial choices because the pressure is perceived as a set of restrictions and/or opportunities. When pressure is perceived as being restrictive, organisations bring about swift socialisation to obtain legitimacy from stakeholders, as well as measurable outcomes and accountability (Weick 1995). Thus, managers can be prompted to adopt environmental strategies because of pressure from industry associations, environmental NGOs, government regulators, competitor actions and other industry stakeholders (King & Lennox 2000). When stakeholder pressure is viewed as an opportunity, however, it creates an incentive structure that promotes instrumental corporate green responsiveness as a means of obtaining positive public attention and increased stakeholder support (Cordano 1993; Dillon & Fischer 1992). Thus, customers, local communities and environmental interest groups encourage firms to consider ecological impacts in their decision making (Lawrence & Morell 1995).

Meanwhile, the empirical standpoint on corporate environmental strategies and GMSs is unclear. Hoffman (1997) has shown that companies facing a common industry context tend to adopt similar strategies in response to the institutional forces they experience. Other researchers, however, have found variability in the environmental strategies of companies operating in similar sociopolitical regulatory contexts (Aragon-Correa 1998; Hart & Ahuja 1996), as well as within the same industry (Sharma & Vredenburg 1998).

Stakeholders in the context of green marketing are different from the mainstream in the consideration of (a) the planet and other species as having a stake in what business does, and (b) the consideration of future stakeholders regarding the contribution of such strategies for sustainable development. Both of these sets of stakeholders will find it difficult to influence strategy directly. In addition, it was found that not all stakeholders are equally important for corporations when environmental strategies are being crafted (Buysse & Verbeke 2003), since they are variable and socially constructed (Mitchell, Agle & Wood 1997). Thus, while much of the marketing literature agrees that stakeholders influence the green responsiveness of markets, there is still little evidence of their impact on green marketing strategies.

Conflicting results could be explained by varying managerial cognitive interpretations of environmental claims and stakeholder interests, which ultimately determine the organisation's choice of environmental strategies (Fineman & Clark 1996; Sharma 2000). This view is supported by cognitive approaches to the study of groups (Porac & Thomas 1990; Tallman & Atchison 1996), which have suggested that managerial cognitive frameworks shape the whole organisation's strategy. Perceptions of stakeholder pressures could vary – depending on management's commitment to environmental issues (Buyse & Verbeke 2003). It is therefore necessary to determine whether the level of managers' perceptions of stakeholder pressure is associated with a firm's level of GMSs.

Although there is very little previous literature that empirically validates the direction of this influence, several authors suggest that stakeholders do influence corporate strategy. For example, Freeman (1984) has indicated that the 'stakeholder approach' deals with managerial behaviour in order to reply to stakeholders. Similarly, Roberts and King (1989) have suggested that stakeholders influence the formulation and direction of corporate strategies. This direction also appears in the environmental-marketing literature (see, Polonsky 1996; Polonsky & Ottman 1998). Several studies of environmental marketing continue to focus on consumers' choices (Schaefer & Crane 2005; Tanner & Wolfing Kast 2003); whereas the motivations that prompt managers to promote environmentally friendly marketing policies are still relatively unknown (Maignan & Ferrell 2004; Megnuc & Ozanne 2005).

The literature offers virtually no definitions of corporate environmental responsiveness from a marketing perspective. Indeed, very few studies have even considered how marketing thinking and practice contribute to the development of environmentally responsible practices and GMSs in organisations (Kralj & Markic 2007; Maignan & Ferrell 2004).

Murray and Montanari (1986) define corporative environmental market responsiveness (CEMR) as a set of corporate marketing initiatives aimed at mitigating a firm's adverse impact on the natural environment. The choice of appropriate corporate marketing initiatives requires the identification of the environmental needs of markets in terms of the traditional '4Ps' of the marketing mix (product, place, price and promotion). The use of these 4Ps in finding solutions to corporative environmental challenges is supported by isolated propositions in the scant literature on GMSs (Banerjee *et al.* 2003; Kilbourne & Beckman 1998; Rivera-Camino 2007).

The main assessment is that managers (their perceptions and values) are the *trait d'Union* between stakeholder pressure, natural environmental claims and green marketing strategies. Focusing on their perceptions will help to understand organisations' green marketing strategies accounting also for context variables such as the organisations' structure and the industry. This suggests that managerial interpretations of environmental issues play a key role in shaping the organisational context and determining the choice of administrative tools to implement strategies (Jackson & Dutton 1988). This supposition is coherent with authors who argue that organisational action is not a strict reaction to the pressures from the environment, since environmental forces are filtered and interpreted by managers (Levy & Rothenberg 2002).

The literature indicates the influence of personal values on managerial interpretations of environmental issues (Sharma 2000), underlying how personal values may affect the strategic decisions of board members in dilemmas involving shareholders and stakeholders (Adams, Burritt & Frost 2008).

The perceived benefits derived from the strategy will influence managerial actions also. For example, managers' beliefs that environmental strategy can be a source of future benefits influence internal organisational adjustments for environmental improvement (Rothenberg Maxwell & Marcus 1992). These beliefs will also promote a new firm's relations with its buyers and suppliers (Elkington 1994), support the firm's accreditation to environmental management standards and influence proactive environmental responsiveness strategies (Sharma 1997).

Previous literature suggests that managerial values and cognitive interpretations of environment and stakeholders determine a firm's choice of environmental strategies (Jennings & Zandbergen 1995; Sharma 2000). This assumption is also supported by cognitive approaches to the study of groups (e.g. Porac, Thomas & Baden-Fuller 1989; Porac & Thomas 1990; Reger & Huff 1993; Tallman & Atchison 1996), which suggest that managerial values shape a firm's strategy. Furthermore, personal values could influence pro-environmental behaviour (Karp 1996) and environmental corporate strategy (Hemingway & Maclagan 2004). Likewise, personal values influence environmental leadership (Egri & Herman 2000; Shrivastava 1994) and affect the nature and scope of corporate social responsibility (Robin & Reidenbach 1987). Managers' perceptions and values may also condition the planning process for strategic marketing (Kwaka & Satyendra 2000), the evaluation of performance of the functional unit (Walker & Ruekert 1987) and the operationalisation of marketing planning systems (McDonald 1996). Managerial interpretations of environmental issues are themselves highly influenced by perceived visibility, or exposure of firms to important stakeholders (Dutton & Duncan 1987). Visibility captures the extent to which phenomena can be seen or noticed; thus, firms are visible when they can be easily seen by relevant stakeholders (Bowen 2000).

With respect to context variables, Delmas and Toffel (2004) and Levy and Rothenberg (2002) likewise propose that managers' perceptions are moderated by organisational characteristics, such as the competitive position, and the organisation's visibility and size. Managers of small organisations, unlike larger ones, are unlikely to consider environmental concerns important to their business strategy. They lack the information and expertise to deal with environmental issues (Hutchinson & Hutchinson 1997) and their emphasis is on economic rather than social or environmental issues (Tilley 2000). Larger firms are more visible to customers, the media, environmentalists and government agencies and they face more pressure to adopt GMSs. Firm size has also been used as the proxy for political visibility (Dasgupta *et al.* 1997; Watts & Zimmerman 1990) since size can make companies more sensitive to reputation damages (Waddock & Graves 1997). Likewise, corporate social responsibility researchers and supporters of the political visibility perspective have suggested that larger firms are more exposed to the scrutiny of environmental pressure groups (Hutchinson & Hutchinson 1995). Thus, stakeholder scrutiny forces large firms to adopt a leadership posture on environmental issues (Henriques & Sadorsky 1996; Sharma & Nguan 1999). Annual sales and the multinational character of a firm can create visibility and may strongly affect the importance attached to various stakeholders. Delmas and Toffel (2004) suggest that environmental groups could target firms because of their market share position (or annual incomes).

On the other hand, firms can also become visible in a negative way by generating industrial pollution that impacts the environment (Goodstein 1994; Greening & Gray 1994; King & Lennox 2000). Considering that industry sectors vary significantly in pollution intensity (Dasgupta *et al.* 1996; Hartman, Wheeler & Singh 1997), and that larger polluters are more detectable by surrounding communities (Dasgupta *et al.* 1997), it is evident that a manager's attention to stakeholders will vary according to the circumstances of the firm's industry (Fineman & Clarke 1996). Distinct levels of coercive pressures exerted upon different industries may also lead firms to different environmental strategies (Milstein, Hart & York 2002), and various industry sectors may respond differently to environmental action drivers (Porter & van der Linde 1995).

Several studies have suggested that visibility can explain the diverse levels of a firm's environmental responsiveness (Bowen 2002) because stakeholders target more visible firms for social pressure (Getz 1995), and these firms must respond to stakeholders' demands in order to maintain their social legitimacy (Bansal 1995). Likewise, firm size has often been associated with discretionary disclosure practices (see, Gray Kouhy & Lavers 1995). Empirical research reveals significant relationships between firm size and environmental responsiveness (see Murphy, Poist & Braunschweig 1995; Stanwick & Stanwick 1998) since larger firms have more resources to allocate to environmental issues (Bowen 2000), and this could explain the firm's proactiveness. Also, multinational corporations are more strongly oriented towards environmental responsibility than national firms because they are more exposed to pressures from international customers, suppliers and competitors (Buysse & Verbeke 2003; Rugman 1995; Zyglidopoulos 2002). Several authors signal a positive relationship between competitive position and stronger commitment to environmental practices (Molina-Azorín *et al.* 2009) because competitive position generates a corporate reputation and organisational visibility among the stakeholders. Concluding, managers, through their behaviours and values, adopt and implement GMSs mediating between stakeholder pressure and context variables.

Empirical evidence

Relationships among managers, GMSs, stakeholders and context variables were studied in the light of the theory of planned behaviour (Ajzen 1991; Ajzen & Madden 1986) and the studies of personal values by Kahle (1983) and Rokeach

(1973). The LOV (List of Value) scale, related to and/or predictive of consumer behaviours, has been used for the purposes of cross-cultural comparison and consumer behaviour research. The theory of planned behaviour (TPB) focuses on three independent variables (attitudes, subjective norms and perceived behavioural control) which determine behavioural intention, posited as the immediate antecedent of behaviour. Although the TPB has not been previously used specifically in the context of marketing management, the theory has been utilised to examine human behaviour in relation to various environmental issues, including: recycling (Boldero 1995; Taylor & Todd 1995), green consumerism (Kalafatis *et al.* 1999; Sparks & Shepherd 1992), environmental ethics (Flanery & May 2000), pollution reduction (Cordano & Frieze 2000) and composting (Taylor & Todd 1997).

Two potentially conflicting aspects of the TPB model are of particular interest in the present context of stakeholder influence: (i) the intention-behaviour relationship; and (ii) the influence of past behaviour on current/future behaviour.

An empirical study was conducted to test the relationships among managers, stakeholders, the GMSs and an organisation's context. The survey population consisted of managers who were responsible for the environmental activities of their firms. These firms were located in eleven European Union (EU) countries collaborating in the research network of the European Business Environmental Barometer (Austria, Belgium, France, Italy, Holland, Norway, Portugal, Spain, Sweden, Switzerland and Germany). These countries had launched environmental programs to implement Agenda 21, the EU 6th Environmental Action Programme, and the environmental objectives of the Treaty of Amsterdam. For each country, the population of potential respondents was derived with care to ensure heterogeneity with respect to industrial sectors, organisational contexts and external influences, such as the degree of environmental regulation in each country.

The stakeholders' or environmental pressures perceived were evaluated in relation to sixteen driving forces (banks, suppliers, distributors. scientific institutions, consumer organisations, insurance companies, competitors, labour unions, voluntary agreements, press/media, etc.) that influence firms' willingness to undertake green marketing initiatives. These stakeholders were selected from prior theoretical and empirical research and divided in two main groups: market stakeholders (suppliers, customers and competitors) and non-market stakeholders (Institutions, internal consumers, ONGs, mass media, legals) (Buysse & Verbeke 2003; De Young 1996; Freeman 1984; Henriques & Sadorsky 1996; Hill & Jones 1992; King & Lennox 2000; Lawrence & Morell 1995).

The questionnaires were mailed to 15,000 potential respondents who were directly responsible for their firms' environmental activities; screening questions ensured that responses from other corporate personnel were eliminated. The final sample was heterogeneous in terms of industry sector (18% chemical products; 24% basic metals; 17% textiles and wood products; 20% food; 21% others) and size of business (62% small; 20% medium; 18% large). The response rate was 23% (3,253 valid completed questionnaires).

The objectives of this study were to identify the psychological and organisational variables that influence GMSs and how managers account for stakeholder pressures, as Figure 6.2 shows.

Figure 6.2 Path diagram of psychological and organisational variables' influence on green marketing strategies

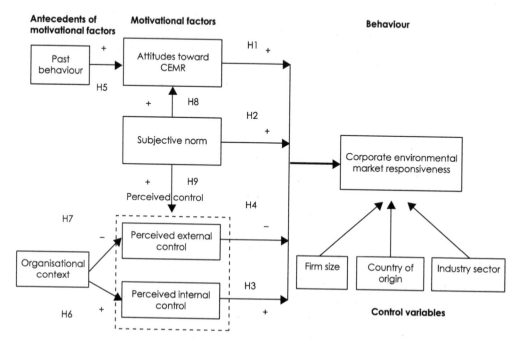

The data were analysed with LISREL structural equation modelling (SEM) software using Muthén's (1993) estimation methodology for models that measure categorical variables.

The research findings (Table 6.2) show that the behaviour of managers with respect to environmental policy is largely determined by social judgments and perceptions. In addition, the results show that organisational context restricts managers to a somewhat narrower range of strategic options than previous studies have suggested.

Stakeholders having a significant influence on managerial decision-making with regard to GMSs accords with the 'institutional' view of human behaviour (Zukin & DiMaggio 1990). Purposive managerial behaviour is guided, but not necessarily by economic factors and/or active agency (Di Maggio & Powell 1991; Oliver 1991). Thus there is evidence that the basic premise of institutional theory – that organisations tend to conform to the social influences that exist in their environments and that successful firms gain support and legitimacy by conforming to social pressures (Baum & Oliver 1991; DiMaggio & Powell 1983; Oliver 1991).

Table 6.2 Results of final model

Dependent variable	Loading	t-Student	Std. Dev.	R^2	Conclusions
Environmental Market Responsiveness-CEMR				0.67	
H1: Attitude influences CEMR	0.52	5.42	0.097		H1: supported
• Control: Firm size influences CEMR	0.51	4.63	0.12		Significant
• Control: Country effect influences CEMR	0.29	2.01	0.016		Significant
• Control: Industrial sector influences CEMR	0.11	0.07			Not significant
H2: The subjective norm influences CEMR	0.65	8.72	0.063		H2: supported
H3: Internal control perceived influences CEMR	0.58	5.76	0.011		H3: supported
H4: External control perceived influences CEMR	0.04	0.02			H4: not supported
Attitude				0.60	
H5: The past behaviour influences Attitude	0.81	6.15	0.021		H5: supported
H8: The subjective norm influences Attitude	0.69	4.02	0.14		H8: supported
Perceived External Control (PEC)				0.46	
H7: Organisational Context influences PEC	-0.77	-8.06	0.087		H7: supported
H9: The subjective norm influences PEC	0.25	3.09	0.060		H9: supported
Perceived Internal Control (PIC)				0.62	
H6: Organisational Context influences PIC	0.59	5.36	0.11		H6: supported

Antecedents both at manager and firm level play also a role in GMSs. In particular, past performance (in terms of environmental behaviour) was found to have a significant influence on managers' attitudes. This supports the view that past experience can have a significant impact on behaviour. It confirms that managers perceive and act upon environmental pressures in accordance with the history of their firms' environmental performance (Delmas & Toffel 2004), while challenging the opinion that habitual behaviour excludes deliberate decision making (Aarts, Verplanken & Van Knippenberg 1998). Rather, the decision-making process with regard to environmental issues appears to be conditioned by established norms, customs and behavioural dispositions (Schlicht 1993), which can prevent managers from recognising the potential economic benefits of defying established customs (Denzau & North 1994).

From the perspective of competitive advantage, the results show that managerial decisions do not stem from a choice among unlimited possibilities determined by purely internal arrangements, but rather from a narrowly defined set of legitimate options determined by a firm's organisational field (Scott 1991).

The study suggested also that the implementation GMSs is promoted most effectively when it addresses a range of psychological and organisational variables simultaneously. The psychological variables (perceptions and values) not only influence each other, but are also highly dependent upon the organisational context. The adequate organisational support increases the level of environmental behaviour and the perception of potential benefits.

The personal values of managers affect the perception and implementation of GMSs and moderate stakeholder pressure according to the different types of stakeholders. Managers with high 'sense of belonging' are more focused on the pressure deriving from legal and institutional stakeholders pertaining to the non-market group. Managers' senses of 'security' and 'warm relationship with others' affect positively the environmental proactiveness and the perception of non-market stakeholder pressure. Figure 6.3 shows and summarises all components that affect the organisations' GMSs.

Conclusion

Value creation remains the final objective of organisations in our economy. But organisations cannot ignore the context in which they operate and the network of relationships connecting organisations and their stakeholders.

Managers have the obligation to incorporate GMSs within their programs. As underlined by Post, Preston and Sachs (2002, p 9):

> the capacity of a firm to generate sustainable wealth over time, and hence its long-term value, is determined by its relationships with critical stakeholders'

and

> any stakeholder relationship may be the most critical one at a particular time or on a particular issue.

Moreover, GMSs should not be understood as a target, but as tools to improve company performance and create stable networks with both stakeholders and shareholders.

Figure 6.3 Drivers of green marketing strategies

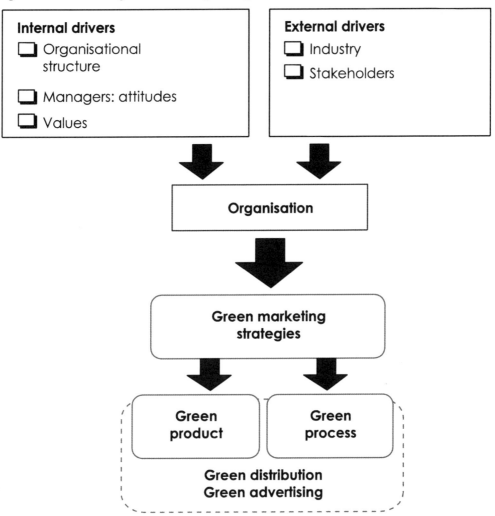

The firm's own economic sector, the organisational characteristics and the perceptions and values of managers all determine differences in GMSs. But what remains global and mandatory for all companies is the constant monitoring and the involvement within the decision-making processes of all the claims coming from relevant stakeholders. 'The key to solving the core strategic problem is to understand the firm's entire set of stakeholder relationships.' (Post, Preston & Sachs 2002, p. 8)

The simple dichotomy of firm-consumer is not valid today; more complex relationships are emerging and new stakeholders are soliciting more coherent and profitable approaches for each of the actors and actions involved in the production, distribution and consuming processes.

These relationships are the essential assets that managers must manage, and they are the ultimate sources of organisational wealth (Post, Preston & Sachs 2002).

References

Aarts, L., Verplanken, B., andVan Knippenberg, A. (1998). Predicting behavior from actions in the past: Repeated decision making or a matter of habit?. *Journal of Applied Social Psychology*, 28, 1355-1374.

Adams, C.A., Burritt, R. and Frost, G. (2008), "Integrating environmental management systems, environmental performance and stakeholder engagement", Association of Chartered Certified Accountants Research Monograph, ACCA, London

Agle, B., Mitchell, K., and Sonnenfeld, A. (1999). "Who matters to CEOs? An investigation of stakeholder attributes and salience, corporate performance, and CEO values". *Academy of Management Journal*, 42(5), pp. 507–525.

Ajzen, I. (1991). The theory of planned behavior. *Organization Behavior and Human Decision Processes*, 50, 179-211.

Ajzen, I., and Madden, T. (1986). Prediction of goal-directed behavior: Attitudes, intentions, and perceived behavioral control. *Journal of Experimental Social Psychology*, 22, 453-474.

Aragón-Correa, Juan A. (1998). "Strategic proactivity and firm approach to the natural environment." *Academy of Management Journal* 41 (5): 556-567.

Armstrong, J. (2001). Are there substitutes for market orientation?, ELMAR-Columbia University, July 2, 2001

Azzone, G., Bianchi, R., Mauri, R. and Noci, G. (1997). "Defining operating environmental strategies: programs and plans within Italian industries." *Environmental Management and Health* 8 (Part 1): 1-15.

Banerjee, S., Iyer, E., and Kashyap, R. (2003). Corporate Environmentalism: Antecedents and Influence of Industry Type, Journal of Marketing; 67 (2): pp.106-122.

Bansal, P. (1995). *Why do firms go green? The case for organizational legitimacy*. Templeton College/Faculty of Social Sciences. University of Oxford.

Baum, J. and Oliver, C. (1991). Institutional linkages and organizational mortality. *Administrative Science Quarterly*, 36, 187-218.

Baumann, H., Boons, F. and Bragd, A. (2002) "Mapping the green product development field: engineering, policy and business perspectives", Journal of Cleaner Production, Vol 10, pp. 409-425

Berman, S. , Wicks, A., Kotha, S., and Jones, T. (1999). "Does stakeholder orientation matter? The relationship between stakeholder management models and firm financial performance", Academy of Management Journal, Vol.42, 5, pp. 488-506.

Berry, M., and Rondinelli, D. (1998). Proactive corporate environmental management: A new industrial revolution. *Academy of Management Executive*, 2 (12), 1-13.

Boldero, J. (1995). The prediction of household recycling of newspapers: The role of attitudes, intentions, and situational factors. *Journal of Applied Social Psychology*, 25, 440-462.

Bowen, F. (2000). Environmental Visibility: A Trigger of Green Organisational Response?. *Business Strategy and the Environment*, 9 (2), 92-107.

Bowen, F. (2002). "Does Size Matter? Organizational Slack and Visibility as Alternative Explanations for Environmental Responsiveness", Business & Society, *(41) 1, pp. 118-124.*

Buchholz, R. (1998). *Principles of Environmental Management: The Greening of Business*, 2nd Ed., Upper Saddle River (N.J.): Prentice Hall.

Buysse, K., and Verbeke, A. (2003). "Proactive environmental strategies: a stakeholder management perspective." *Strategic Management Journal* 24 (5): 453-470.

Carroll, A. (1999). "Corporate Social Responsibility: Evolution of a Definitional Construct ", Business & Society, 38 (3), pp. 268-295.

Charter, M., Elvins, L. and Adams, G. (2004), Sustainable marketing: Understanding the obstacles to and opportunities for involvement of marketing professionals in sustainable consumption, Society of Non-Traditional Technology, Japan.

Christopher M, Payne, A., and Ballantyne, D. (1991) Relationship Marketing, Butterworth-Heinemann, Oxford.

Clarkson, M. (1995). "A stakeholder framework for analysing and evaluating corporate social performance", *Academy of Management Review*, 20 (1), pp. 92-117.

Clemens, B. (2001). "Changing environmental strategies over time: An empirical study of the steel industry in the United States", *Journal of Environmental Management*, 62 (2), pp. 221-231.

Cordano, M. (1993). "Making the natural connection: justifying investment in environmental innovation", Proceedings of the International Association for Business and Society, pp. 530-537.

Cordano, M., and Frieze, I. (2000). Pollution Reduction Preferences of U.S. Environmental Managers: Applying Ajzen's Theory of Planned Behavior. *Academy of Management Journal*, 4 (43), 627-641.

Crane, A. (2000). *Marketing, morality and the natural environment*, Routledge.

Crane, A., and Peattie, K. (1999), "Has Green Marketing Failed … Or Was It Never Really Tried?", *Proceedings of the 8th Business Strategy and the Environment Conference*, September 16th and 17th, University of Leeds, pp. 21-30.

Dasgupta, S., Hettige, H., and Wheeler, D. (1997) What Improves Environmental Performance? Evidence from Mexican Industry, *Development Research Group World Bank*, December.

Dasgupta, S., Huq, M., Wheeler, D., and Zhang, Z. (1996). Water Pollution in Chinese Industry: Abatement Costs and Policy Implications, *World Bank Policy Research Working Paper*, No. 1630.

Davis, J. (1992). "Ethics and Green Marketing", *Journal of Business Ethics*, 11 (2), pp. 81-87.

Day, G. and Wensley, R. (1988). "Assessing Advantage: A Framework for Diagnosing Competitive Superiority", Journal of Marketing, Vol.52, April, pp. 1-20.

De Cicco, J. and Thomas, M. (1999), "A Method for Green Rating of Automobiles", Journal of Industrial Ecology, Vol. 3 No. 1, pp. 55-76.

De Young, R. (1996). Some psychological aspects of reduced consumption behavior: The role of intrinsic satisfaction and competence motivation. *Environment and Behavior*, 28, 358-409.

Delmas, M., and Toffel, M. (2004). "Stakeholders and environmental management practices: An institutional framework", Business Strategy and the Environment, Vol.13, 4, pp. 209-222.

Denzau, A., and North, D. (1994). Shared mental models: Ideologies and institutions. *Kyklos*, 47 (1), 3-31.

Dillon, P., and Fischer, K. (1992). "Environmental management in corporations: Methods and motivations", *Center for Environmental Management*, Tufts University, Medford, MA.

DiMaggio, P. and Powell, W. (1983). The iron cage revisited: Institutional isomorphism and collective rationality in organizational fields. *American Sociological Review*, 48, 147-160.

DiMaggio, P., and Powell, W. (1991). *The new institutionalism in organizational analysis*, University of Chicago Press, Chicago

Donaldson, T., and Preston, L. (1995). "The stakeholder theory of the corporation: concepts, evidence, and implications", Academy of Management Review, Vol.20, 1, pp. 65-91.

Dutton, Jane., and Robert Duncan. (1987). "The creation of momentum for change through the process of strategic issue diagnosis." *Strategic Management Journal* 8: 279-295.

Egri P., and Herman S. (2000). "Leadership in the North American Environmental Sector: Values, Leadership Styles, and Contexts of Environmental Leaders and Their Organizations", Academy of Management Journal, Vol.43, 4, pp. 571-604.

Elkington, J. (1994). Towards the sustainable corporation: Win-win-win business strategies for sustainable development. *California Management Review*, 2 (36), 90-100.

Evan, W.M. and R.E. Freeman. (1988). A stakeholder theory of the modern corporation: Kantian capitalism. Eds. T. Beauchamp and N. Bowie. Ethical theory and business. Englewood Cliffs, NJ: Prentice Hall 75-93..

Fineman, S., and Clarke, K. (1996). Green Stakeholders: Industry interpretations and response. *Journal of Management Studies*, 33 (6), 715-730.

Fitchett, J. (2004), *Buyers be Wary: Marketing Stakeholder Values and the Consumer*, Research Paper Series, No. 19-2004 ICCSR, Nottingham University Business School.

Flannery, B., and May, D. (2000). Environmental Ethical Decision Making in the U.S. Metal-Finishing Industry. *Academy of Management Journal*, 4 (43), 642-662.

Freeman, R. (1984). *Strategic Management: A stakeholder approach*. Boston: Pitman.

Fuller, D. (1999). *Sustainable Marketing: Managerial-Ecological Issues*. Thousand Oaks, Ca: Sage.

Garrod, B. (1997). "Business strategies, globalization and environment." In Globalization and Environment. OECD: Paris; pp. 269-314

Getz, K. (1995). Implementing Multilateral Regulation-A Preliminary Theory and Illustration. *Business & Society*, 34 (3), 280-316.

Giuliettia, M., Price, C. and Waterson, M. (2001), *Consumer Choice and Industrial Policy: A Study of UK Energy Markets*, CSEM, WP 112, University of California Energy Institute, California University.

Goodstein, J. (1994). "Institutional pressures and strategic responsiveness: employer involvement in work-family issues", *Academy of Management Journal,* 37(2), pp. 350-382.

Gray, R., Kouhy, R. and Lavers, S. (1995). Corporate Social and Environmental Reporting: A Review of the Literature and a Longitudinal Study of UK Disclosure. *Accounting, Auditing and Accountability Journal,* 8 (2), 47-77.

Greening, D., and Gray, B. (1994). "Testing a model of organisational response to social and political issues", *Academy of Management Journal,* 37(3), pp. 467-498.

Greenley, G., and Foxall, G. (1996) "Consumer and Non-Consumer Stakeholder Orientations in UK Companies," Journal of Business Research, Vol.35, pp. 105-116.

Greenley, G., and Foxall, G. (1997). "Multiple Stakeholder Orientation in UK Companies and the Implications for Company Performance", Journal of Management Studies, Vol.34, 2, pp. 259-284.

Gummesson, E. (1999). Total Relationship Marketing; Rethinking Marketing Management From 4 Ps to 30Rs. Oxford: Butterworth Heinemann.

Halme, M. (1996). "Shifting Environmental Management Paradigms in Two Finnish Paper Facilities: A Broader View of Institutional Theory", Business Strategy and the Environment, Vol.5, pp. 94-105.

Hart, S. (1995). A natural-resource-based view of the firm. *Academy of Management Review,* 4 (20), 986-1014.

Hart, S., and Ahuja, G. (1996). "Does It Pay to Be Green? An Empirical Examination of the Relationship Between Emission Reduction And Firm Performance." Business Strategy and the Environment 5: 30-37.

Hartman, R., Wheeler, D., and Singh, M. (1997). The Cost of Air Pollution Abatement. Applied Economics, 29 (6), 759-774.

Hemingway, C.A., Maclagan, P.W., 2004. Managers' personal values as drivers of corporate social responsibility. Journal of Business Ethics 50 (1), 33–44. Henriques, I. and Sadorsky, P. (1999). The relationship between environmental commitment and managerial perceptions of stakeholder importance. *Academy of Management Journal,* 1, 42, 87-99.

Henriques, I., and Sadorsky, P. (1996). The determinants of an environmentally responsive firm: An empirical approach. *Journal of Environmental Economics and Management,* 30, 381-395.

Hill, C., and Jones, T. (1992). "Stakeholder–agency theory", *Journal of Management Studies,* 29(2), pp. 131–154.

Hoffman, A. (1997). *From heresy to dogma: An institutional history of corporate environmentalism.* San Francisco: New Lexington Press.

Hoffman, A., and Ventresca, M. (2002). *Organizations, Policy and the Natural Environment: Institutional and Strategic Perspectives,* (Eds.) Stanford, CA: Stanford University Press.

Hooley, G., Saunders, J. and Piercy, N. (2004), *Marketing Strategy and Competitive Positioning,* 3rd ed., Prentice Hall, London.

Hunt, C., and Auster, E. (1990). "Proactive environmental management: Avoiding the toxic trap." *Sloan Management Review* 31 (2): 7-18.

Hutchinson, A. and Hutchinson, F. (1997). *Environmental business management: Sustainable development in the new millennium.* London, McGraw Hill.

Hutchinson, A., and Hutchinson, F. (1995). Sustainable Regeneration of the UK's Small and Medium-Sized Enterprises Sector: Some Implications of S M E Response to BS 7750', Greener Management International, Vol.9, pp. 73-84.

Isaak, R. (2002). The Making of the Ecopreneur. *Greener Management International*, 38, 81-91.

Isherwood, K. (2000), *Mineral fertilizer distribution and the environment*, International Fertilizer Industry Association, UNEP, ISBN 2-9506299-4-6, March, Paris.

Italia Imballagio (2002), "Ecology and distribution", *The Magazine for Packaging*, March. available at: http://www.italiaimballaggio.it/italiaimballaggio/ 03_02/sezioni/ 04_envir/ art2_envir.html.

Jackson, S., and Dutton, J. (1988). "Discerning threats and opportunities." *Administrative Science Quarterly* 33:370-387.

Jennings, D., and Zandbergen, P. (1995). "Ecologically sustainable organizations: An institutional approach." *Academy of Management Review* 20: 1015-1052.

Jensen M C., (2001). Value Maximization, Stakeholder Theory, And The Corporate Objective Function," *Journal of Applied Corporate Finance*, Morgan Stanley, vol. 14(3), pages 8-21

Kahle, L. R. (1983). Social values and social change: Adaptation to life in America. New York: Praeger.

Kalafatis, S., Pollard, M., East, R., and Tsogas, M. (1999). Green marketing and Ajzen s theory of planned behavior: a cross-market examination. *Journal of Consumer Marketing*, 5 (16), 441-460.

Karp, D. (1996). "Values and their effects on proenvironmental behavior", Environment and Behavior, Vol.38, pp.111-133.

Kilbourne, W., and Beckman, S. (1998). Review and Critical Assessment of Research on Marketing and the Environment, Journal of Marketing Management, 14, 513-532.

Kimery, K. M., and Rinehart, S. M. (1998), "Markets and Constituencies: An Alternative View of the Marketing Concept," Journal of Business Research, Vol. 43, No. 3, pp. 117– 124).

King, A., and Lenox, M. (2000). Industry self-regulation without sanctions: The chemical industry s Responsible Care Program. *Academy of Management Journal*, 43, 698-716.

Klassen, R. and Whybark, D. (1999). The impact of environmental technologies on manufacturing performance. *Academy of Management Journal*, 42 (6), 599-615.

Kotler, P. (2002). Marketing Management, Prentice Hall; 11 edition.

Kralj, D., and Markic, M. (2007), M. Global Marketing and Environmental Excellence. International Journal of Energy and Environment 2007; 2 (1); 155-164

Kwaka, A., and Satyendra, S. (2000). "Marketing culture and performance in UK service firms." *The Service Industries Journal* 19 (2): 152-170.

Lamberg, J., Savage G. and Pajunen, K. (2003), "Strategic stakeholder perspective to ESOP negotiations: the case of United Airlines", *Management Decision*, Vol. 41 No.4, pp. 383-393.

Lawrence, A., and Morell, D. (1995). "Leading-Edge Environmental Management: Motivation, Opportunity, Resources and Processes." In *Research in Corporate Social Performance and Policy.* Ed. James Post. Greenwich, CT: JAI, 99-126.

Levy, D., and Rothenberg, S. (2002). "Heterogeneity and change in environmental strategy: technological and political responses to climate change in the global automobile industry." In *Organizations, policy, and the natural environment. Institutional and strategic perspectives.* Ed. Andrew J. Hoffman, and Marc J. Ventresca. Stanford University Press, 41-80.

Maignan, I., and Ferrell, O. (2004). Corporate Social Responsibility and Marketing: An Integrative Framework. *Journal of the Academy of Marketing Science*, 32(1), 3-19.

Mc Daniel, S., and Rylander, D. (1993). "Strategic Green Marketing." *Journal of Consumer Marketing* 10 (3): 4-10.

McDaniel, S., and Kolari, J. (1987). "Marketing strategy implications of the Miles and Snow strategic typology", *Journal of Marketing*, 51(Oct), pp. 19-30.

McDonald, M. (1996). "Strategic Marketing Planning: Theory and Practice and Research Agendas." *Journal of Marketing Management* 12: 5-27.

McIntosh, A. (1990. "The Impact of Environmental Issues on Marketing and Politics in the 1990s." Journal of the Marketing Research Society 33 (3): 205-217.

Megnuc, B., and Ozanne L. (2005), Challenges of the Green Imperative: A Natural Resource-based Approach to the Environmental Orientation-business Performance Relationship. Journal of Business Research; 58: 430-438.

Menon, A., and Menon, A. (1997). Enviropreneurial Marketing Strategy: The emergence of Corporate Environmentalism as Market Strategy. *Journal of Marketing*, 61 (1), 51-67.

Miles, R. and Snow, C. (1978). *Organizational strategy, structure and process.* New York: McGraw-Hill.

Milstein, M., Hart S., and York, A. (2002). Coercion breeds variation: the differential impact of isomorphic pressures on environmental strategies. In Hoffman, A., and Ventresca, (Eds), M Organizations, Policy, and the Natural Environment. Institutional and Strategic Perspectives, pp. 151-172, Stanford: Stanford University Press.

Mitchell, R., Agle, B., and Wood, D. (1997). "Toward a theory of stakeholder identification and salience: Defining the principle of who and what really counts", Academy of Management Review, Vol.22, pp. 853-886.

Molina-Azorín, J.F., Claver-Cortés, E., López-Gamero, M.D. and Tarí, J.J. (2009), "Green management and financial performance: a literature review", *Management Decision*, Vol. 47 No. 7, pp. 1080–100

Murphy, B., Maguiness, P., Pescott, C., Wislang, S., Ma, UJ., Wang, R. (2004). "Measuring Holistic Marketing Performance in a Stakeholder Relationship Marketing Model", Massey University at Albany, Working Paper, 04-26

Murphy, B., Poist, R., and Braunschweig, C. (1995). Role and relevance of logistics to corporate environmentalism: An empirical assessment. *International Journal of Physical Distribution and Logistics*, 25 (2), 5-19.

Murray, K, and Montanari, J. (1986). Strategic management of the socially responsible firm: Integrating management and marketing theory. *Academy of Management Review*, 11 (4), 815-827.

Muthén, B. (1993). Goodness of fit with categorical and other nonnormal variables. In K. A. Bollen & J. S. Long (Eds.), Testing structural equation models (pp. 205–234). Newbury Park, CA: Sage

OECD (Organisation for Economic Co-operation and Development) (1995) *Technologies for Cleaner Production and Products* (Paris: OECD).

Oliver, C. (1991). Strategic responses to institutional processes. *Academy of Management Review*, 16, 145-179.

OTA (1992), *Green Products by Design: Choices for a Cleaner Environment*, Office of Technology Assessment-E-541, NTIS order #PB93-101715, September.

Ottman, J. (1998). *Green marketing: opportunity for innovation*, (2nd Ed.), Lincolnwood (IL), NTC/Contemporary Books.

Ottman, J. and Terry, V. (1998), "Strategic marketing of greener products", *The Journal of Sustainable Product Design*, Vol. 5, April, pp. 53-57.

Pecotich, A., Purdie,F., and Hattie, J. (2003). "An evaluation of typologies of marketplace strategic actions", *European Journal of Marketing*, 37(3/4), pp. 498-529.

Phillips, R., and Reichart, J. (2000). "The environment as a stakeholder? A fairness-based approach", Journal of Business Ethics, Vol.23, 2, pp. 185–197.

Piercy, N., and Cravens, D. (1995). "The network paradigm and marketing organization", European Journal of Marketing, Vol.29, 3, pp. 7-34.

Polonsky, M. (1994). An Introduction to Green Marketing. *Electronic Green Journal*, 1(2), November.

Polonsky, M. (1995), "A stakeholder theory approach to designing environmental marketing strategy", *Journal of Business and Industrial Marketing*, Vol. 10 No. 3, pp.29-46.

Polonsky, M. (1996). "Stakeholder Management and the Stakeholder Matrix: Potential Strategic Marketing Tools", Journal of Market Focused Management, Vol.1, 3, pp. 209-229.

Polonsky, M. and Ottman, J. (1998). "Stakeholders contribution to the green new product development process", Journal of Marketing Management, Vol.14, pp. 533-557.

Polonsky, M. J., Schuppisser, D., and Beldona, S. (2002). "A Stakeholder Perspective for Analyzing Marketing Relatioçnships", Journal of Market-Focused Management, Vol.5, 2, pp. 109-126.

Polonsky, M., Carlson, L. and Fry, M. (2003), "The harm chain: a public policy development and stakeholder perspective", *Marketing Theory*, Vol. 3 No. 3, pp.345-364.

Porac, J., and Thomas, H. (1990). "Taxonomic Mental Models in Competitor Definition", *Academy of Management Review*, 15, pp. 224-240.

Porac, J., Thomas, H., and Baden-Fuller, C. (1989). "Competitive groups as cognitive communities: The case of the Scottish knitwear industry", *Journal of Management Studies*, 26, pp. 397-416.

Porter, M., and Van der Linde, C. (1995). Green and competitive. *Harvard Business Review*, 5 (73), 120-134.

Post, J., Preston, L., Sachs, S. (2002). Redefining the Corporation: Stakeholder Management and Organizational Wealth. Stanford University Press

Pujari, D., Wright, G., and Peattie, K. (2003). Green and competitive: Influences on environmental new product development performance, *Journal of Business Research*, 56 (8), 657-671.

Reger, R., and Huff, S. (1993). "Strategic groups: a cognitive perspective. Strategic", Management Journal, Vol.14, pp. 103-124.

Rivera Camino, J. (2007), Re-evaluating green marketing strategy: A stakeholder perspective, European Journal of Marketing, Vol. 41, Issue 11/12, pp. 1328 – 1358

Roberts, N. and King P. (1989). "The Stakeholder Audit Goes Public", Organizational Dynamics, Vol.17, 3, pp 63-79.

Robin, D., and Reidenbach, R. (1987). "Social Responsibility, Ethics, and Marketing Strategy: Closing the Gaps between Concept and Applications", Journal of Marketing, Vol.51, January, pp. 44-58

Rokeach, M. (1973). The nature of human values. New York: The Free Press.

Roome, N. (1992). Developing environmental management systems. *Business Strategy and the Environment,* 1, 11-24.

Rothenherg, S., Maxwell, J., and Marcus, A. (1992). Issues in the implementation of proactive environmental strategies. *Business Strategy and the Environment*, 1, 1-12.

Rugman, A. (1995). "Environmental regulations and international competitiveness: Strategies for Canada's West Coast forest products industry." *The International Executive* 37 (5): 451-65.

Sarkis, J. (1995). "Manufacturing Strategy and Environmental Consciousness", *Technovation,* 15(2), pp. 79-97.

SAT (2003), *State-of-the-Art Technology in the Electronics Industry Innovation System,* Summary Report, G1RT-CT-2002-05066, European Community Project-GROWTH programme, Austrian Society for Systems Engineering and Automation.

Schaefer, A. and Crane, A. (2005). Addressing Sustainability and Consumption. *Journal of Macromarketing*, 25(1), pp. 76-93.

Schlicht, E. (1993). On custom. *Journal of Institutional and Theoretical Economics*, 1, 178-203.

Scott, W. (1991). Unpacking institutional arguments. In W. Powell and P. DiMaggio (Eds.), *The New Institutionalism in Organizational Analysis* (pp. 164-182). University of Chicago Press, Chicago, IL.

Sharma, S. (1997). A longitudinal investigation of corporate environmental responsiveness: Antecedents and outcomes. *Academy of Management Best Paper Proceedings,* 460-464.

Sharma, S. (2000). Managerial Interpretations and Organizational Context as Predictors of Corporate Choice of Environmental Strategy. *Academy of Management Journal*, 4 (43), 681-697.

Sharma, S., and Nguan, O. (1999). The biotechnology industry and strategies of biodiversity conservation: the influence of managerial interpretations and risk propensity. *Business Strategy and the Environment*, 8, 46-61.

Sharma, S., and Vredenburg, H. (1998). "Proactive corporate environmental strategy and the development of competitively valuable organizational capabilities", *Strategic Management Journal*, 19(8), pp. 729-753.

Shaw, J. (2000), *Green marketing in industrial relationships - An investigation into the emerging green product strategy of an industrial equipment supplier for electricity utility companies*. IIIEE Master´s Theses, Serial number: 2000:28. Lund University.

Sheth, J., and Parvatiyar, A.(1995).Ecological Imperatives and the Role of Marketing. In: Polonsky, M. and Mintu-Wimsatt, A. (Eds.) Environmental Marketing - Strategies, Practice, Theory, and Research. The Haworth Press. New York-London.

Shrivastava, P. (1994). "Catastred Environment: Greening Organizational Studies." *Organization Studies* 15 (5): 705-726.

Shrivastava, P. (1995). "Environmental Technologies and Competitive Advantage." *Strategic Management Journal* 16 (Summer): 183-200.

Simpson, A. (1991). "The Greening of Global Investment: How the Environment, Ethics and Politics are Reshaping Strategies", The Economist Publications, January, London.

Sparks, P., and Shepherd, R. (1992). Self-identity and the theory of planned behavior: Assessing the role of identification with green consumerism. *Social Psychology Quarterly*, 55, 388-399.

Stanwick, P., and Stanwick, S. (1998). The relationship between corporate social performance, and organisation size, financial performance, and environmental performance: an empirical examination. *Journal of Business Ethics*, 17, 195-204.

Starik, M. (1995). Research on organisations and the natural environment: Some paths we have traveled, the field ahead. In D. Collins and M. Starik (Eds.), *Research in corporate social performance and policy, supplement*, Vol. 1 (pp. 1-41). Greenwich, CT: JAI Press.

Tallman, S., and Atchison, D. (1996). "Competence-Based Competition and the Evolution of Strategic Configurations", In *Dynamics of Competence-Based Competition*, Sánchez, R., Heene, A., and Thomas, H. (Eds.), Pergamon, pp. 349-375.

Tanner, C. and Wolfing Kast, S. (2003). Promoting Sustainable Consumption: Determinants of Green Purchases by Swiss Consumers. *Psychology and Marketing*, 20(10), pp. 883-902.

Taylor, S., and Todd, P. (1995). An integrated model of waste management. *Environment and Behavior*, 27 (5), 603-630.

Taylor, S., and Todd, P. (1997). Understanding the determinants of consumer composting behavior. *Journal of Applied Social Psychology*, 27 (7), 602-628.

Thomlison, B. (1992) "Environmental Consumerism Must Meet Needs of Corporate Stakeholders", Marketing News, Vol.26, 9, pp.12.

Tilley, F. (2000). Small firm environmental ethics: how deep do they go?. *Business Ethics: an European Review*, 9 (1), 31-41.

Varadarajan, R., and Menon, A. (1988). "Cause-Related Marketing: A Coalignment of Marketing Strategy", *Journal of Business Research*, 31 (2), pp. 93-105

Vasanthakumar, B. (1993), "Green Marketing Begins with Green Design", *Journal of Business & Industrial Marketing*, Vol. 8 No. 4, pp. 26-31.

Waddock, S., and Graves, S. (1997). "The corporate social performance-financial performance link", Strategic Management Journal, Vol.18, pp. 303-319.

Walker, O., and Ruekert, R. (1987). "Marketing's Role in the Implementation of Business Strategies: A critical Review and Conceptual Framework." *Journal of Marketing* 51 (July): 15-33.

Watts, R. and Zimmerman, J. (1990). "Positive Accounting Theory: A Ten year perspective", The Accounting Review, Vol.65, 1, January, pp.131-156.

Webster, F. (1992). "The Changing Role of Marketing in the Corporation." *Journal of Marketing* 56 (October): 1-17.

Weick, K. (1995). *Sensemaking in organizations*. Thousand Oaks, CA: Sage.

Winn, M., and Angell, L. (2000). Towards a Process Model of Corporate Greening, Organization Studies, 21(6), 1119-1147.

Wohlgemuth, N., Getzner, M. and Park, J. (1999), "Green power. Designing a green electricity marketing strategy", in Charter, M. and Polonsky, M.J. (Eds.), *Greener marketing. A global perspective on greening marketing practice*, Greenleaf Publishing Ltd., Sheffield, pp. 362-380.

Zeithaml, C., and Zeithaml, V. (1984). "Environmental Management: Revising the Marketing Perspective", Journal of Marketing, Vol.48, Spring, pp. 46-53.

Zukin, S. and DiMaggio, P. (1990). Introduction . In S. Zukin and P. DiMaggio (Eds.), *Structures of Capital: The Social Organization of the Economy*, pp. 1-56. Cambridge University Press, Cambridge, UK.

Zyglidopoulos, S. (2002). "The social and environmental responsibilities of multinationals: evidence from the Brent Spar case", Journal of Business Ethics, Vol.36,1/2, pp. 141-151.

Chapter 7

Future trends

Green marketing: What does the future hold?

Michael Polonsky

Abstract

The marketing of green goods is associated with a number of challenges that are related to consumer, business and regulatory processes and barriers. In focusing on consumers, this chapter identifies four critical issues that need to be addressed: 1) getting people to pay for the environment; 2) changing how people think about the environment; 3) communicating complex environmental information; and 4) bringing about changes in the behaviour of consumers. There are also a number of business issues that need to be considered and these too are also briefly addressed. In over-viewing these challenges a number of avenues for regulator action are identified, as well as opportunities for future research. Both can assist marketers in bringing about more responsible consumer and business behaviour.

Introduction

The chapters in this book show that green marketing is being explored from a multitude of perspectives. Many marketers and organisations are looking at green marketing as a mechanism for creating value; however, not all take the same view in regard to defining value or from whose perspective value is accrued. Increasingly, eminent scholars are calling for sustainability to be integrated into what most would define as traditional marketing (e.g. Kotler 2011; Hult 2011). Unfortunately, most of the research into green issues does not take a transformational perspective that examines how marketing can create value for consumers, the organisation and possibly most importantly the environment (Polonsky forthcoming). Rather many researchers focus on 'leveraging' environmental issues for corporate profit, often associated with positioning or targeting strategies (Crane 2000). In these approaches there is a desire to exploit the environmental interests of consumers, but not necessarily change the fundamental nature of consumption and exchange, which could be argued is at the root of the world's environmental problems (Varey 2010).

Future research into green marketing needs, therefore, to examine some very difficult issues, such as how can we satisfy the wants of 6.5 billion consumers in a sustainable way? This will require changes at the consumer, organisational and policy levels. One of the most fundamental questions is: how can we better integrate the true environmental costs into consumers and businesses decision making, while facilitating value?

In public debates over the environment there is frequent comment that assigning a dollar value to the environment will raise costs, which will risk economic growth, employment and quality of life. The arguments hardly ever focus on the fact that these measures almost completely exclude the impacts on the natural environment. This possibly arises because existing measures of economic wellbeing have no meaningful environmental value. This could be linked to the fact that some marketers promote improvements in society's quality of life based on material consumption. There are of course alternative measures of wellbeing that focus on broader human factors (life expectancy literacy, etc.); although even these tend to be short or medium term in nature and fail to take a systems approach whereby value is measured over hundreds of years and includes the natural environment.

Marketing is anthropocentric, where humans are seen as the centre of the system and the environment is a resource to be exploited – rather than where the environment is central and mankind is a guest on mother earth (Kilbourne, Beckmann & Thelen 2002). This means that consumers and marketers focus on human value to almost the exclusion of all else. For example, cigarettes don't get banned because of the economic flows they generate, even though some would argue that the health costs outweigh any economic benefits.

Given that we let other humans consume in a way that harms themselves rather than harming economic growth, is it any wonder that marketers cannot strive to protect the environment unless there are human defined financial incentives for doing so? Of course it is possible that consumers, firms and governments will realise that some environmental actions are illogical or even socially evil. For example, abhorrent practices such as slavery were outlawed; although this shift in behaviour took several hundred years and the practice is still an issue in some developing countries.

The question of where green marketing is going next revolves around a range of consumer, business and policy issues. Within the next sections the focus will be on four pressing consumer-focused issues for marketers dealing with environmental issues. One section will also outline some of the business issues, but unfortunately within the confines of this chapter it is not possible to extensively address all business issues. This chapter does not attempt to explicitly look at the policy issues, but some clear links to policy are identified within the consumer and business domain. Each section also identifies what are the green marketing research opportunities that can be pursued and thus assist marketing academics in contributing to positive transformational change.

Challenge 1: How do we get consumers to pay for the environment?

Researchers have extensively examined what can be done to change consumer behaviour. Authors have looked at issues of whether environmental orientation, awareness or knowledge makes consumers behave more responsibly (Diamantopoulos *et al.* 2003). The results are equivocal, with some finding that even when concern influences one environmentally-related behaviour, it does not impact other types of environmentally related behaviours (Thøgersen 2004).

Classic economics suggests that price is a good motivator for behavioural change. Around the world the increase in petrol (i.e. gas) prices has seen green and non-green consumers modify their behaviours, for instance, increasing their use of public transportation, utilising share car schemes or purchasing hybrids (Mills 2008). Thus, costs do trigger action and therefore a carbon tax that increases the prices to consumers should then trigger changes in behaviour. Unfortunately, governments frequently seek to minimise the impact of carbon on consumer prices and thus minimise any potential positive change associated with increased costs.

The increased costs of course also serve to stimulate investments, with consumers and businesses searching for new opportunities that limit the impact of new costs or create alternatives (Rosen 2001). For example, the advancements in hybrid car technology have been partly driven by the fact that there needs to be transportation alternatives as petrol prices rise. The increased consumer demand for these more responsible goods has a flow-on effect. Greater demand enables production economies of scale to arise, making newer technologies less expensive, which further triggers increases in demand. Yet all these changes are really dependent on the initial price triggers that result in the increase in demand for less harmful alternatives (i.e. less demand for harmful options). In the case of petrol, we are running out of oil, so there is a supply and demand driven price increase; whereas in other contexts, the impending shortages are further off in the future.

In regard to research directions there are, of course, opportunities to look at how consumers respond to alternative prices, rather than simply voluntary environmental options (MacKerron *et al.* 2009). However, I believe that the method by which prices are communicated to consumers requires examination. We tend to focus on acquisition price when in reality almost all goods have longer-term environmental costs associated with use and disposal, as well as lifecycle costs associated with good's production. Thus, understanding how consumers will respond to alternatives that capture environmental meaning is an important research opportunity.

Challenge 2: How do we make consumers care for or value the environment?

There is extensive research suggesting that some consumers are more environmentally oriented or concerned than others (Diamantopoulos *et al.* 2003). For example, there are consumer segments called 'voluntary simplifiers' who choose to limit their market-based consumption (McDonald *et al.* 2006). The question is, what are the underlying reasons that these differences arise? Some authors have argued that there may be cultural factors that explain the differences; others suggest it comes down to how consumers perceive the dominant social paradigm that they operate within (Kilbourne *et al.* 2009). I propose that these differences may unfortunately be hardwired into how consumers understand their role in the natural world. That is, consumers have an anthropocentric view that means they perceive the world and its resources as something to be exploited, rather than interacted with. The result is that consumers do not think about themselves as part of the natural system (Polonsky forthcoming).

The fact that the environmental impacts occur over the long term also means that marketers need to shift consumers away from focusing on short-term impacts or perspectives. This might explain why consumers respond to changing prices (i.e. a short-term shock resulting in them modifying their behaviour) rather than thinking about how their needs will have to be met in the future. The classic dictum 'penny wise and dollar foolish' suggests that consumers focus on the short-term acquisition costs rather than the longer-term ownership costs. As such, without some recognisable trigger of long-term effects (such as lifecycle pricing), consumers may be less likely to think about the longer-term outcomes of their consumption.

In terms of research, there are opportunities to better understand what it is that drives consumer understanding of environmental impacts of consumption and how this can be changed. If understanding and attitudes are based on the level of knowledge of consumers, are there ways to better inform them? This is discussed more below. Of course there are numerous examples of when consumers know purchases have negative consequences and still participate in these negative behaviours, for example, taking-up smoking or delaying giving it up (Walsh *et al.* 2010). Are inherent personality characteristics drivers of action and inaction? If this is the case, then regulatory policy actions might be required to bring about involuntary change. For example, governments outlawed the use of asbestos and there were no mass consumer complaints, even though in some instances this meant changing products. In another example, the Australian government set a date to phase out incandescent light bulbs because of their negative environmental impact; there was negligible consumer response, even though long-life alternatives were substantially more expensive at the time (Houri & El Khoury 2010). Thus, research could even explore consumer responses to regulatory change mandating behaviour modification as compared to voluntary action.

Challenge 3: How do we communicate complex environmental information?

Marketers have long been interested in the communication of information and how this impacts behaviour. Such research has been extensively explored in the environmental area in regard to alternative green advertising appeals and labelling (Leonidou *et al.* 2011). However, within the environmental area, there is the fundamental problem associated with identifying the agreed state of knowledge (i.e. what causes global warming, how bad is it and what do we need to do to prevent the negative consequences). As such, how do marketers and policy makers know exactly what environmental information should be communicated to consumers, let alone whether consumers will understand it or respond appropriately (Polonsky, Garma & Grau forthcoming)?

The issue of communicating information relates to whether we focus on the narrow specifics of how the information is disseminated or the broader issue of what types of information should be reported. Traditional advertising perspectives frequently focus on the framing of messages, rather than focusing on the complexity of the information delivered. Any environmental marketing communication needs to broaden the discussion beyond carbon issues to include environmental issues such as land salinity, ocean acidity, biodiversity and overpopulation (just to name a few). Thus, further research is needed to understand how to communicate this complex information in a way that consumers will understand and will influence behaviour. This will be made even more complicated if different countries or labelling schemes adopt different sets of communication standards, as already appears to be the case in regard to carbon offsets (Kollmuss, Zink & Polycaro 2008).

Within the communication area there is extensive opportunity for future research, ranging from evaluating alternative labelling approaches (D'Souza *et al.* 2007) to communicating the dimensionality of environmental issues (i.e. multi-dimensional environmental labels similar to nutritional labels). The issue of framing could also be examined, that is, how messages about the environmental are communicated and whether they are gain-focused or loss-focused (Obermiller

1995). The previous sections have identified other communication related issues, such as how does one better communicate the interconnection between man and the environment? That is, addressing the anthropocentric perspective that causes many of the environmental problems. Marketers could also promote alternative methods of 'want' satisfaction, shifting away from ownership which has already been explored to a lesser extent in research on de-marketing (Wall 2005). Of course all messages could also target different types of motivations, personality characteristics or demographics (D'Souza *et al.* 2007), thus enabling a range of meditating or moderating factors to be integrated in this area of research.

Challenge 4: What changes in behaviour will consumers accept?

The question of changing behaviour is difficult. Social marketing looks extensively at bringing about positive behaviour change and thus could be used to encourage consumers to modify behaviour to be less environmentally harmful. However, classical psychology theory suggests that consumers are sometimes reluctant to change behaviour, even when innovations are improvements on existing options (Bagozzi & Lee 1999). For example, in the early literature on recycling it was suggested that lowing costs of behaviour change makes change easier (Bagozzi & Dabholkar 1994). In marketing, we frequently talk about the role of switching costs as a way of locking-in a given behaviour. How do we reduce switching costs (Burnham, Frels & Mahajan 2003) to make behaviour change easier? In some of the examples discussed previously, these changes were mandated by governments, but the required changes to behaviours were minimal. For example, buying and installing one type of light bulb is an identical process to another, even though long-life bulbs cost more to acquire.

From a marketing perspective the question is: how do we bring about more substantial behaviour changes that involve greater costs, for example, getting consumers to switch from owning a car to joining a car sharing scheme? There is a loss of convenience and independence that might be too high for many consumers. However, there have been some attempts to de-market certain goods and behaviours (Wall 2005), like using less water or energy. Unfortunately, in some instances the goods that are presently available make behaviour change harder. For example, 'sleep modes' on electric goods are designed to make their use more convenient, but when the energy used to power this convenience is aggregated across all goods it has a substantial energy impact. Changing to alternatives is also harder simply because the infrastructure to support these alternative products is not yet readily available, such as recharge facilities for electric cars (Byrne & Polonsky 2001). Thus, some opposition to behaving responsibly arises because of a perceived loss of convenience.

Another issue associated with behaviour change is that we acquire goods for more than their functional abilities; they are an extension of one's self and one's identity (Belk 1988). This creates a huge environmental drain as we frequently purchase additional goods not because our old goods have lost functional abilities, but because they are out of date, out of fashion or don't conform to our evolving identity (or social norms). Think of all the clothing that gets produced simply to be consistent with the season's style or colours. In other instances we want the newest technology, even when we may or may not use the added functionality i.e. there are few 3D television shows, but some consumers still want 3D capable televisions. And of course there is limited discussion of what happens to the remaining functionally associated with discarded goods. In the case of some products, such as clothing, it has been suggested that capturing this value has massive environmental savings because less raw materials and clothing would be produced (Woolridge *et al.* 2006).

Rather than have goods reflect positive associations with one's image can we shift society to a state where ownership (or behaviour) for some goods is seen negatively? This is especially important when there is a significant link between a product and one's identity. For example, owing a car is seen as providing independence and success (i.e. people choose to use public transportation even though they do not have to). However, can we promote that leasing a car or simply having access to a car also carries positive identity associations.

Extensive opportunities exist to research drivers of consumer change, ways to overcome barriers to change and how self identify can better integrate positive environmental behaviour. Public policy might be significant (Wall 2005), for example within the smoking domain, restricting the places where one can smoke, increasing taxes raise the costs and reduces the convenience of consumption (Walsh *et al.* 2010). The warnings and graphic images on packages might be designed to make smoking be perceived as a negative product (i.e. negative identity), even to the smoker. There may environmental regulatory policies that can achieve similar outcomes? For example in Singapore there is a tax for driving into the city and the cost of a car's registration is linked to its age (as older cars are less fuel efficient), so that older cars are more expensive (Seik 2000). However, changing the role on identity might be harder, where there is not necessarily the same link to negative outcomes.

Challenge 5: The business context

Whist this paper has focused primarily on consumer marketing, it should be noted that environmental business marketing is potentially more important, especially when focusing on environmental impacts. The majority of marketing occurs through business markets and thus, based on sheer volume, it has a greater environmental impact than consumer consumption. There has already been some work on environmental purchasing in organisations (Drumwright 1994) and managerial orientation to environmental issues and how this impacts on organisational behaviour (Porter & Reinhardt 2007). Integrating environmental factors in this phase of the marketing process is essential as managers' planning decisions will affect the environmental impacts of goods as well as other product characteristics.

After all, marketers and organisational decision makers are individual consumers in their own right. As such, the individual problems identified above will influence how managers make business decisions (Duarte 2010). This, in turn, suggests that researchers could explore all the same individual issues in the context of organisation decision making. Some issues will potentially be less silent. For example, business decision making tends to take a longer-term perspective and thus might better integrate environmental costs into decision making because organisations frequently consider the payback period or return on investment of investments. One might ask why it is that consumers cannot do the same thing and take a longer-term perspective. Further research could look at whether managers make better consumer decisions simply because they are used to assessing purchases differently.

An examination of the broader decision-making processes within organisations is another possible research opportunity; this also has links to consumer issues. How do organisational units integrate environmental costs into decision-making models (Polonsky, Miles & Landreth Grau 2011)? If they rely solely on financial measures then they will overlook environmental impacts which cannot be easily translated into dollar values. Of course this means that businesses have a way of valuing the environment, and that this can be communicated across functional departments associated with operations and staff who may or may not have varying input into decision making.

Marketers promote a range of organisational strategies that might have negative environmental consequences, and these could be considered in research and strategy. For example, much of the research on bottom-of-the-pyramid marketing focuses on tapping the needs of poorer consumers. Yet do these strategies create increased environmental harm within the wider exchange system? Simply providing for the needs of the less advantaged is not necessarily less environmentally harmful. In fact, if these consumers have fewer opportunities to recycle or dispose of waste, targeting them with smaller quantities of goods be might increasing environmental harm. Of course innovations such as fair trade do ideally seek to positively impact the overall quality of life of disadvantaged producers, although in some instances even this is debated (Valkila 2009).

How do we get firms to reshape their business models to focus on value creation or value acquisition rather than goods acquisition (van der Zwan & Bhamra 2003)? This possibly requires new models where firms become more integrated and specialised. For example, logistics firms manage the process more efficiently and less environmentally harmfully than if each firm managed its own process. In some instances the changes are, however, more significant, and firms have to think about creating and transferring value in a less environmentally harmful way. One might argue that the shift in theoretical perspectives to service dominate logic will facilitate this, as it recognises the importance of co-creation, relying to service exchanges that are not necessarily grounded solely on goods manufacture and transfer (Maase & Dorst 2007). This will be a new challenge and will create opportunities for a range of innovative research into why some firms are better able to identify and address these new environmental realties than others.

Organisational performance and environmental issues is yet another avenue for research. However, rather than take the narrow financial perspective, studies need to look at environmental benefits and how these translates into performance (Hart & Ahuja 1996), rather than simply looking at 'purported' environmentalism (i.e. investments or promoted environmental activities) and financial performance. In this way broader measures of organisational performance are linked to actual environmental changes, but this does require new measures of performance that integrate the environment and financial success into a single metric, which does not exist at present.

Conclusions

Environmental marketing is here to stay and creates a range of strategic and research opportunities. One might anticipate that marketers who are usually considered to be more creative and innovative would be well positioned to address changes and be leaders in shaping consumer and business change. The difficulty is how to bring about these innovations so they will create value in a way that consumers and managers understand. Unfortunately, dollars have no environmental value, but are at present critical measures of organisational success and consumer value (Polonsky forthcoming). Thus, new ways of defining value that integrate the environment are needed.

No one likes change, especially changes that are discontinuous, that is, movement away from excising actions. However, marketers are well positioned to identify and provide solutions to business and consumer opportunities, of which addressing environmental issues will continue to be one of the most pressing. Marketers can make positive changes in regard to creating value that integrates environmental issues (Kotler 2011). We, the marketers, are actively involved in the value creation process and also critical facilitators of behaviour change. Thus we need to embed environmental issues as part of the fundamental structure of marketing and not simply consider it as an add-on feature or niche segment to be targeted. To do this we need to seek to integrate these macro-issues within traditional strategy decisions, broadening what we define as marketing to include restructuring consumption, value creation and how markets operate (Polonsky forthcoming).

This chapter and the book more generally, potentially raises more questions than it answers. What is clear from the material is that industry and academics are taking a range of approaches to consider environmental issues within marketing. Hopefully these will serve as stimulus for further innovations and investigations. We need to become part of the solution not drivers of the problem.

References

Bagozzi, R.P. and P.A. Dabholkar (1994) "Consumer Recycling Goals and Their Effect on Decisions to Recycle: A Means-End Chain Analysis," *Psychology and Marketing,* 11(4), 313–340.

Bagozzi, R.P. and K.H. Lee, (1999) "Consumers Resistance to, and Acceptance of Innovations," *Advances in Consumer Research* 26, 218-225.

Belk, R. W. (1988) "Possessions and the Extended Self," *Journal of Consumer Research,* 15(2), 139-168.

Burnham, T.A., J.K. Frels and V. Mahajan (2003) "Consumer Switching Costs: A Typology, Antecedents, and Consequences," *Journal of the Academy of Marketing Science,* 31(2), 109-126.

Byrne, M. and M.J. Polonsky (2001) " Impediments to Consumer Adoption of Sustainable Transportation: Alternative Fuel Vehicles," *International Journal of Operations and Production Management,* 21(12), 1521-1538.

Crane, A. (2000), "Facing the backlash: Green marketing and strategic reorientation in the 1990s," *Journal of Strategic Marketing,* 8(3), 277-296.

D'Souza, C., M. Taghian, P. Lamb and R. Peretiatko (2007) "Green decisions: demographics and consumer understanding of environmental labels," *International Journal of Consumer Studies,* 31(4), 371–376.

Diamantopoulos, A., B.B. Schlegelmilch, R.R. Sinkovics and G.B. Bohlen (2003) "Can socio-demographics still play a role in profiling green consumers? A review of the evidence and an empirical investigation," *Journal of Business Research, 56,* 465-480.

Drumwright, M. E. (1994) "Socially Responsible Organizational Buying: Environmental Concern as a Noneconomic Buying Criterion," *Journal of Marketing,* 58(3), 1-19

Duarte, F. (2010) "Working with Corporate Social Responsibility in Brazilian Companies: The Role of Managers' Values in the Maintenance of CSR Cultures," *Journal of Business Ethics,* 96(3), 355-368,

Hart, S.L. and G. Ahuja (1996) "Does it Pay to be Green? An Empirical Examination of the Relationship between Emission Reduction and Firm Performance," *Business Strategy and the Environment,* 5(1) 30–37.

Houri, A. and P. El Khoury (2010) "Financial and energy impacts of compact fluorescent light bulbs in a rural setting," *Energy and Buildings,* 42(5), 658-666.

Hult, G.T.M. (2011) "Market-focused sustainability: market orientation plus!" *Journal of the Academy of Marketing Science,* 39(1), 1-6.

Kilbourne, W.E., S.C. Beckmann and E. Thelen (2002) "The role of the dominant social paradigm in environmental attitudes: a multinational examination," *Journal of Business Research,* 55(3), 193-204.

Kilbourne, W. M. Dorsch, P. McDonagh, B Urien, A. Prothero, D. Marshell, J. Foley, A. Bradshaw, M.J. Polonsky and M. Gruhagen (2009) "The Institutional Foundations of Materialism in Western Societies: A Conceptualization and Empirical Test," *Journal of Macromarketing,* 28(4): 259-278.

Kollmuss, A., Zink, H., & Polycaro, C. (2008). *Making Sense of the Voluntary Carbon Marketing: A comparison of carbon offset standards.* Retrieved from World Wild Life Foundation http://tricorona.de/files/93ea78fc52f9fdaf0048dcf866d73004 wwf _standcomp_080305_web.pdf.

Kotler, P. (2011) "Reinventing marketing to manage the environmental imperative," *Journal of Marketing,* 75(4), 132-135.

Leonidou, L.C., C.N. Leonidou, D. Palihawadana and M. Hultman, (2011) "Evaluating the green advertising practices of international firms: a trend analysis," *International Marketing Review*, 28(1), 6 – 33.

McDonald, S., C.J. Oates, C.W. Young and K. Hwang (2006) "Toward sustainable consumption: Researching voluntary simplifiers," *Psychology and Marketing*, 23(6), 515–534.

MacKerron, G.J., C. Egerton, C. Gaskell, A. Parpia and S. Mourato (2009) "Willingness to pay for carbon offset certification and co-benefits among (high-) flying young adults in the U.K.," *Energy Policy*, 37, 1372-1381.

Maase, S.J.F.M. and K.H. Dorst (2007) "Exploring the (co-)creation of Sustainable Solutions," *The International Journal of Environmental, Cultural, Economic and Social Sustainability*, 2(6), 5-14.

Mills, M.K. (2008)" Environmentally-active consumers' preferences for zero-emission vehicles: public sector and marketing implications," *Journal of Nonprofit and Public Sector Marketing*, 19 (1), 1-33.

Obermiller, C. (1995) "The Baby is Sick/The Baby is Well: A Test of Environmental Communication Appeals," *Journal of Advertising*, 24(2), 55-

Polonsky, M.J., R. Garma and S. Grau (Forthcoming) "Western Consumers Understanding of Carbon Offset and it Relationship to Behavior," *Asia Pacific Journal of Marketing and Logistics*, Forthcoming.

Polonsky, M.J. (2011) "Transformative Green Marketing: Impediments and Opportunities," *Journal of Business Research*, Forthcoming.

Polonsky, M.J., M. Miles and S. Landreth Grau (2011) "The Four Questions of Climate Change Regulation: Implications for Business Executives," *European Business Review*, 23(4), 368-383.

Porter, M.D. and F.Reinhardt (2007) "A strategic approach to climate," *Harvard Business Review*, 85(10), 22-26.

Rosen, C.M. (2001), "Environmental Strategy and Comparative advantage: An introduction," *California Management Review,* Vol. 43 No. 93, pp. 8-15.

Seik, F.T. (2000) "Vehicle ownership restraints and car sharing in Singapore," *Habitat International*, 24(1) 75-90.

Thøgersen, J. (2004) "A Cognitive dissonance interpretation of consistencies and inconsistencies in environmentally-responsible behaviour," *Journal of Environmental Psychology, 24*, 93-103.

Varey, R.J. (2010), "Marketing Means and Ends for a Sustainable Society: A Welfare Agenda for Transformative Change," *Journal of Macromarketing* 30(2), 112-126.

Valkila, J. (2009) "Fair Trade organic coffee production in Nicaragua — Sustainable development or a poverty trap?" *Ecological Economics*, 68(12), 3018-3025.

van der Zwan, F. and T. Bhamra, (2003) "Services marketing: taking up the sustainable development challenge," *Journal of Services Marketing*, 17(4),.341 – 356.

Wall, A.P. (2005) Government demarketing: different approaches and mixed messages, *European Journal of Marketing* 39(5/6), 421-427.

Walsh, G., L. M. Hassan, E. Shiu, J.C. Andrews and G. Hastings, (2010) "Segmentation in social marketing: Insights from the European Union's multi-country, antismoking campaign", *European Journal of Marketing*, 44(7/8), 1140-1164

Woolridge, A.C., G.D. Ward, P.S. Phillips, M. Collins and S. Gandy (2006) "Life cycle assessment for reuse/recycling of donated waste textiles compared to use of virgin material: An UK energy saving perspective," *Resources, Conservation and Recycling*, 46(1), 94-103.

Encouraging consumer curtailment behaviours and eco-innovation adoption: Detailing the marketing challenge

JOHAN JANSSON, AGNETA MARELL AND ANNIKA NORDLUND

ABSTRACT

Much research on the environmentally significant behaviours of consumers has focused on behaviours that reduce environmental harm, such as saving energy and water. Although determinants of curtailment behaviours are important to understand, for environmental reasons it is also vital to understand the factors that drive or hinder consumers to adopt *innovations* that are less harmful for the environment, that is, eco-innovations. In this chapter we discuss two types of consumer behaviours as part of the solution to environmental sustainability issues and detail the marketing challenge in encouraging consumers to adopt such behaviours. We arrive at the marketing challenge matrix where determinants of adoption and non-adoption of curtailment behaviours and eco-innovations are illustrated. The matrix proposes different ways to encourage wider adoption of these behaviours. Since drivers are both similar and different for curtailment behaviours and eco-innovation adoption, but the overall goal is similar, an understanding of these factors and how to handle them in marketing efforts will contribute in the ongoing attempts at achieving environmental sustainability.

Introduction

Air pollution and dwindling fossil oil resources are two types of environmental problems stemming from current increases in personal mobility and energy usage. Such issues have therefore become concerns of international organisations, national governments and individual consumers. Pro-environmental behaviours are often viewed as one homogenous type of behaviours, but there are studies showing that consumers adopt different types of pro-environmental behaviours based on different motivational and contextual factors (Bratt 1999; Jansson, Marell & Nordlund 2010). As many types of organisations frequently use marketing and advertising campaigns in attempts to convince consumers and citizens to change attitudes and behaviours in a pro-environmental direction, a better understanding is needed of how consumers relate to different types of pro-environmental behaviours and what the motivating factors are for different types of behaviours.

Together with mounting pressure from environmental grass root movements and budding consumer environmental awareness, the growing concern for the environment has widely increased product development and the number of products marketed as environmentally friendly. This development has meant that many products and companies not previously thought of as pro-environmental have gone through a greening process (e.g. Bansal & Roth 2000; Rivera-Camino 2007). Together with the increase in the marketing of these green products, voices for less consumption as a solution to environmental problems are also being raised. Divisions of pro-environmental behaviours into categories go by several names. One type of behaviours are called 'curtailment behaviours' and involves behaviours that reduce energy and resource use. Another type has been called 'technology choices' (Stern 1992) or 'purchasing activities' (Barr, Gilg & Ford 2005) and involves the purchases of less environmentally harmful products and technologies such as eco-innovations.

The behaviours referred to as reduction or curtailment behaviours are perhaps the ones that are most often associated with an environmentally friendly lifestyle. From a marketing perspective, curtailment behaviours and changes in usage are related to establishing new habits of everyday routines; whereas the behaviour of adopting new technology is related to first time purchase situations. Theoretically, these two types of behaviours are addressed in different ways. We argue that there is a marketing challenge in bridging these two behaviours. Thus, in this chapter we discuss: (i) the theoretically different approaches connected to curtailment behaviours and eco-innovation adoption, and (ii) the marketing challenge in addressing adopters and non-adopters of curtailment behaviours and eco-innovation adoption. Finally, (iii) we present practical implications for influencing consumers, organisations and policy makers in an environmentally sustainable direction.

Sustainable consumer behaviours

Much of the early research assumed green consumer behaviours to be a unitary, undifferentiated group of behaviours (Bechtel & Churchman 2002; Stern 2000).

However, more recent research has shown that there are several different types of green behaviours that are carried out for different reasons and have different types of impacts on the environment. Of primary concern is what Stern (2000) refers to as private-sphere behaviours. Private-sphere behaviours are those with a direct impact on the environment and are set apart from, for example, activist behaviours and citizenly behaviours (such as voting for green parties). Using an impact-oriented perspective, environmental behaviours are defined as all types of behaviours that change the availability of materials or energy from the environment or alter the structure and dynamics of ecosystems or the biosphere (Stern 2000). An intent-oriented perspective on environmentally significant behaviours has, on the other hand, been defined as behaviours that are undertaken with the intention to change (normally, to benefit) the environment (Stern 2000, p. 408). With this definition, the intent of the individual actor comes into focus as a cause of green behaviour and hence distinguishes it from other types of behaviours. Together, both perspectives of environmentally significant behaviour are important for understanding consumer behaviour. The impact perspective is vital in order to identify and target behaviours that can make a large difference to the environment. On the other hand, it is also necessary to apply an intent-oriented definition of pro-environmental behaviour that focuses on people's underlying motives, as seen in their held values, beliefs, attitudes, etc., to understand and encourage different types of behaviours (Frey & Stutzer 2008; Stern 2000).

Based on the intent-oriented perspective, a common way of dividing and subdividing green consumer behaviours is into distinct categories based on the types of consumer decisions, such as 'curtailment behaviours' (Black *et al.* 1985; Stern & Gardner 1981) and 'technology choices' (Stern 1992) or 'purchasing activities' (Barr *et al.* 2005), involve. Behaviours of similar types tend to have similar patterns of social-psychological and socio-demographic predictors, and these predictors are not necessarily the same for different behavioural types. We use the term curtailment behaviours to denote pro-environmental behaviours that aim to reduce energy and resource consumption. We use the term eco-innovation adoption to denote behaviours where the individual consumer purchases more efficient innovations or products that are less harmful to the environment than the conventional alternatives on the market. As such, curtailment includes behaviours focused on conserving resources, and efficiency behaviours on the acquiring of more resource efficient products and technologies, which has also granted them the name technology choices. This categorisation is useful as a framework for understanding green consumer behaviours since it points to the differences in behaviours associated with the acquirement of products and, at the same time, the use of these products. Since much of the early research has focused on curtailment, we start by detailing this type of behaviour before moving into purchase behaviours such as eco-innovation adoption.

Curtailment behaviours

Curtailment behaviours are based on the notion that consuming less or decreasing the use of equipment and energy is beneficial for the environment. These behaviours include decreased car use, lowered indoor temperature, and water and energy conservation in the home. To have a substantial environmental effect these actions must be taken on an everyday basis and by many consumers. Because curtailment behaviours are associated with changing habits and often entail some discomfort on the individual level, they are hard to bring forth from policy and marketing perspectives (e.g. McKenzie-Mohr 2000). For example, numerous reports show why consumers prefer the environmentally damaging car and how difficult daily transportation habits are to break (Gardner & Abraham 2007; Nordlund & Garvill 2003).

The majority of research and theory development in pro-environmental consumer behaviours have used curtailment behaviours as the norm (Ölander & Thøgersen 1995). Recycling (Berger 1997; McCarty & Shrum 1994; Schultz, Oskamp & Mainieri 1995), reduction of car use (Bamberg, Hunecke & Blöbaum 2007; Nordlund & Garvill 2003) and energy conservation in the home (McMakin, Malone & Lundgren 2002; Ritchie, McDougall & Claxton 1981; Stern 1992) are therefore commonly used as operationalisations of pro-environmental behaviour. Although this research has contributed vital knowledge, the tendency to overlook purchase behaviours and technology choices might have hindered wider theoretical generalisations.

A possible explanation for the predominant focus on curtailment behaviours relates to the fact that these behaviours are relatively easy to study and design intervention programs for, compared with other types of behaviours (Lehman & Geller 2004). Another explanation might be that green consumer behaviour for a long time has been associated primarily with curtailment (expressed partly in the three-R mantra: Reduce, Reuse, Recycle). For example, Kempton *et al.* (1985) found that out of ten energy conservation actions mentioned by respondents, eight were curtailment behaviours. In a similar vein, when Europeans were asked what top three personal priorities citizens should have for protecting the environment, all three were curtailment behaviours: sort waste, reduce home energy consumption and use public transportation instead of the car (EC 2008). Ölander and Thøgersen (1995) argue for a third reason for the predominant focus on curtailment behaviours in that these behaviours involve a learning aspect. By continuously carrying out curtailment behaviour, it is hypothesized that the individual learns about environmental protection and thus the aggregated impact might be greater than in a situation where a one-time purchase of an eco-innovation is made.

Influences on curtailment behaviours

Since curtailment behaviours have been researched from many perspectives, a multitude of determinants have been found to influence these behaviours over time and across contexts. Among these are socio-demographic factors such as age, gender and education. However, socio-demographic factors generally explain little variance in the actual behaviour and thus there are many contradictory findings (e.g. Diamantopoulos *et al.* 2003).

Another set of factors that have been found to be influential are attitudinal factors such as values, beliefs, norms, abilities and opportunities (Stern, 2000; Ölander & Thøgersen 1995). It is generally seen that consumers with greener values, attitudes and preferences are performing or intend to perform curtailment behaviours to a higher degree. Environmental awareness and knowledge are also determinants generally found to have a positive influence on curtailment behaviours (Ellen 1994; Fraj-Andrés & Martinez-Salinas 2007). A fourth influential type of factor relates to routines and habits. Strong behavioural patterns can act as a barrier to switching to curtailment behaviours since these behavioural patterns are carried out with little or no deliberation on the actual behaviour (Eriksson, Garvill & Nordlund 2008).

Together with these micro-level or individual factors, several macro-level or contextual factors influence curtailment behaviours. Broadly, they can be categorised as political, economic, societal, interpersonal, and technological drivers and barriers facilitating or inhibiting different types of pro-environmental behaviours (Stern 2000). If significant external barriers exist, for example, if the behaviour is viewed as inconvenient or time consuming, the encouragement of curtailment behaviours will largely be unsuccessful no matter how well internal barriers are addressed (McKenzie-Mohr 2000).

A widely explored type of curtailment behaviour is private car usage. In the context of car use, curtailment behaviours include several possible actions such as drivers cutting down on the number and length of trips. Recently the term eco-driving has become popular, denoting car use that is more fuel-efficient and thus less environmentally harmful. Eco-driving includes driving at better-suited speeds, turning off the engine when immobile and coasting (instead of breaking) to reduce speed. Curtailment policy measures in a traffic context are often referred to as travel demand management (TDM) measures (Gärling & Schuitema 2007). These measures commonly include communication campaigns informing consumers of environmental effects and alternatives to car use for daily travel and thus target consumers' daily routines and already formed habits. However, since contextual, psychological, and affective factors tend to encourage private car use, there are many difficulties associated with TDM measures and changing travel behaviours. In addition, considering the continuous increase in traffic in most urban areas, TDM measures and associated campaigns seem to have a limited long-term effect. Partly, this is due to the habitual nature of curtailment behaviours where the implementation of TDM measures is often associated with breaking habitual behaviours. In fact, the use of the car on a daily basis is often referred to as a behaviour that rapidly develops into a habit (Eriksson *et al.* 2008). Encouraging the breaking of this habit requires more than non-coercive TDM measures, and the implementation of these is likely to impose severe constraints on individual consumer behaviours (Gärling & Schuitema 2007). Thus, in order to reduce the negative environmental impact of consumer behaviours in general and of car use in particular, there is also a need to focus on other types of solutions that do not impose the same types of discomfort or require the challenging changes of habitual behaviour to the same extent for the individual.

Eco-innovation adoption

The second category of environmentally significant behaviours is denoted eco-innovation adoption. This category includes pro-environmental behaviours where the consumer invests in more efficient innovations or products with the intent of reducing the impact on the environment. Examples of pro-environmental purchase behaviours include investing in extra (or new types of) insulation for the home, investing in energy-efficient light bulbs, and purchasing a more fuel-efficient or less polluting vehicle. Behaviourally, technology choices such as eco-innovation adoption involve one-time purchase decisions and there is an initial financial expense and a potential for future savings. In contrast to most curtailment behaviours, there is generally no perceived discomfort for the individual associated with these choices, making them easier to perform for most consumers. The carrying idea behind eco-innovation adoption and technology choices is to encourage consumers to switch from environmentally harmful product choices to more green, ethical and/or societally beneficial goods and services. Many of these products are viewed as innovations when introduced on the market and the term eco-innovation signifies that these types of innovations are supposedly better for the environment than ordinary products. As such, the technology purchase solution is more of an industry driven initiative, but public policy is also encouraging technological development for environmental reasons. In fact, one of the ten principles of the United Nation's global compact initiative is to 'encourage the development and diffusion of environmentally friendly technologies' (UN 2009).

Even though there is much literature on pro-environmental consumer behaviour there is a shortage of studies on consumer purchases with the intent of affecting the environment, and more research on purchases of specific products with environmental impact is necessary (i.e. Follows & Jobber 2000). In part, this lack of research can be attributed to the lack of available green products (and innovations) in the market in the past. However, during the last decade or so, this shortage has been replaced by everything from detergents and food, to vacations and cars marketed with environmental claims.

Influences on eco-innovation adoption

Since eco-innovation adoption is based more on general market principles where supply and demand of products are at the centre, both factors similar to and different from curtailment determinants have been found to influence eco-innovation adoption. As a starting point, innovation adoption research has focused on the relationship between adoption and socio-demographic factors as well. In general, it has been shown that early adopters have higher income and education than later adopters, especially in the category of high involvement products (Dickerson & Gentry 1983; Dupagne 1999; Martinez, Polo & Carlos 1998). The results can be explained by the fact that higher income indicates a greater financial ability to afford the latest products, and higher levels of education suggest a more open mindset (Wang *et al.* 2008). These results seem to be applicable to eco-innovations as well. In their study on solar heating, Guagnano *et al.* (1986), found that adopters had higher income and education than non-adopters. This was also the case for the study by Labay and Kinnear (1981) on solar energy systems. Concerning attitudinal factors and the influence on eco-innovation adoption there is a dearth of available research. In some cases it is assumed that since eco-innovations involve a substantial financial expense, attitudinal factors such as pro-environmental values and beliefs have little influence. The argument is that the lower the cost the easier it is for individuals to convert their attitudes into corresponding behaviour. However, there is evidence both for and against such a hypothesis (e.g. Best 2009; Derksen & Gartrell 1993; Diekmann & Preisendorfer 2003; Guagnano *et al.* 1995). Recent research has found that attitudinal factors such as values, beliefs, and norms (called the VBN-theory derived mostly from low-cost curtailment behaviours) has influence on the adoption of a high-cost high involvement eco-innovations such as the alternative fuel vehicle (Jansson *et al.* 2011).

An important distinction between curtailment behaviours and eco-innovation adoption concerns the tangible innovation itself. Promoting curtailment behaviours often means promoting behaviour changes that can be viewed as less tangible than an actual product; whereas factors influencing the adoption of an eco-innovation also include the characteristics of the product itself. Innovation adoption research has focused on factors such as perceived risk, relative advantage, complexity, compatibility, visibility and trialability (e.g. Rogers 2003). In an eco-innovation context, is has been found that risk, complexity and relative advantage explain the adoption of solar heating to a higher degree than demographic factors. Jansson (2011) also found that these six innovation-specific characteristics could differentiate between adopters and non-adopters of alternative fuel vehicles. In the same study it was found that adopters to a higher degree were novelty seekers, that is, they had a higher desire to seek out the new and different. Consumers high in novelty seeking tend to look positively on technology, have stronger intrinsic motivation to use such products and enjoy the stimulation of trying new ways to approach old problems (Hirschman 1980; Midgley & Dowling 1978). Thus, consumers might not only be motivated by environmental reasons when adopting an eco-innovation, but factors such as curiosity, image and status seems to play a vital role as well.

Given the similarities and differences between curtailment behaviours and eco-innovation adoption behaviours, a marketing challenge emerges in that efforts at encouraging these different types of behaviours require different approaches.

The marketing challenge

The diffusion of innovations and consumer adoption of new products, practices and ideas, have received considerable attention in the consumer and marketing literature. Marketing researchers have also made efforts to define consumer groups engaging in pro-environmental consumer behaviours, often in the form of segmentation and clustering studies (Diamantopoulos *et al.* 2003; Jansson *et al.* 2009; Roberts 1995).

As curtailment and eco-innovation adoption behaviours are different in nature, they call for different marketing approaches in order to engage consumers, organisations and policy makers. Even so, these types of behaviours share similar determinants, for instance values and attitudes such as caring for the environment (Jansson *et al.* 2010; Nordlund & Garvill 2003). Eco-innovation adoption leads to the acquiring of new products and perhaps also new technologies; whereas curtailment behaviours lead to reduction in the use of products (old and/or new). As awareness and need for action from many stakeholders to solve environmental problems increase, it becomes more and more important to encourage both curtailment of energy and resource use together with adoption of less environmentally harmful products such as eco-innovations. This calls for new thoughts in marketing. The challenge for marketers lies in bridging the knowledge gap between of what types of consumers are apt to react positively to curtailment focused efforts, and the types of consumers that are more green technology prone and how to encourage these types of different behaviours. Based on this distinction, the following sections focus on detailing this challenge for marketers and, based on current research in marketing and environmental psychology, suggest a pathway for marketers and organisations wishing to face this challenge with a successful outcome.

Introducing the marketing challenge matrix

Environmental sustainability is sometimes referred to as a moving target where there is no actual finish line. This is true for both technical development and for understanding consumer attitudes and behaviours, as well as for regulatory innovations. In line with other researchers, we argue that different consumers are likely to engage in different types of pro-environmental behaviours based on their individual ability frameworks (e.g. Ölander & Thøgersen 1995). It is at this point of intersection that the marketing challenge matrix is useful since it directs attention to possible ways forward in relation to curtailment behaviours and eco-innovation adoption jointly. As depicted in Figure 7.1, the two types of behaviours and adoption and non-adoption of these are graphed so that four areas emerge. Within each area, specific challenges to the encouragement of consumers towards increased environmental sustainability emerge. Below we detail the challenges in each box of the matrix.

Figure 7.1 The marketing challenge matrix

	Adoption of eco-innovations	Non-adoption of eco-innovations
Curtailment behaviour	• Encourage adoption of more eco-innovations (spill-over). • Use adopters as endorsers when communicating to non-adopters for example in blogs, advertising, showrooms, etc. • Use adopters to help firms in developing more/better eco-innovations. • Invite eco-innovation adopters and curtailers to inform policymakers of how efficient polices can be put in place to encourage wider adoption of both types of behaviours. • Assess attitudinal factors, eco-innovation adoption behaviour and curtailment behaviours in lead markets for different products and use this knowledge for developing other markets.	• Communicate social effects of adoption such as visibility. • Communicate the possible effects adoption might have personally, i.e. in saving money. • Promote high relative advantage and compatibility of eco-innovations. • Promote low risk and ease of use (low complexity) of the eco-innovation. • Make eco-innovation adoption more observable to influence visibility of both adoption and non-adoption. • Develop monetary incentive programs, together with other stakeholders, with a time limit for eco-innovation adoption (if price is found to be a barrier to adoption). • Develop incentives for improving curtailment behaviours in new behavioural domains. • Offer finance solutions for eco-innovations by integrating producers and financers (banks). • Develop strategic alliances among firms to communicate more attractive eco-innovations for consumers, for example, home owned wind turbines together with electric vehicles.
Non-curtailment behaviour	• Develop incentives for energy efficient use of eco-innovation/s. • Facilitate the development of curtailment behaviours by communicating the correct use of the adopted eco-innovation. • See box to the right for encouraging curtailment.	• Increase awareness of environmental problems for example by communicating the finite environmental resources. • Focus on stimulating either curtailment or eco-innovation adoption in the first step. • Communicate shared responsibility for the environment. • Build knowledge on how consumers can act within their action frames. • Communicate personal benefits of curtailing energy use, for example health and financial benefits. • Use personal channels such as social media campaigns to encourage curtailment. • Use social marketing tools in developing encouragement efforts. • Focus on breaking strong environmentally harmful habits. • Develop curtailment campaigns in cooperation with multiple stakeholders in order to remove contextual barriers. • See box on the top for encouraging eco-innovation adoption.

Curtailment and non-adoption

In the bottom right box we find consumers that neither perform curtailment behaviours nor adopt eco-innovations. Here consumers can be termed as unaware of environmental issues and unwilling or unable to curtail environmentally significant behaviours and adopt eco-innovations. In a previous study these consumers were labelled 'non-greens' (Jansson, Marell & Nordlund 2009). The challenge here is to communicate the importance of both curtailment behaviours and eco-innovation adoption. However, based on the notion that some consumers are more open to curtailment, and others to eco-innovation adoption, it is vital to first analyse these consumers in-depth to develop different communication strategies for different groups of these consumers. Specific strategies can then be designed to reach either curtailment prone consumers, eco-innovation adoption likely consumers, or both. Based on research in social marketing and integrated marketing communications, it is however wise to focus on one type of communication and encouragement at a time (Belch & Belch 2007; McKenzie-Mohr & Smith 2000).

To encourage curtailment behaviours, awareness building efforts are important at the early stages since awareness, environmental concern and values are related (Hansla *et al.* 2008). Research also shows that if consumers feel that their (individual) action can make a difference, they are more likely develop norms that in turn are likely to lead to curtailment behaviours (Stern 2000). In research terminology these motivations for pro-environmental behaviours are often termed 'ascription of personal responsibility' or 'perceived consumer effectiveness' (e.g. Thøgersen 1999). Once awareness is built and the consumer is looking for how to handle the problem, knowledge building efforts are important in order to inform what steps can be taken to reduce environmental harm of different behaviours (Ellen 1994). Since curtailment behaviours are usually less involving and costly, barriers to action are often perceived rather than related to infrastructure. Thus, saving energy in the home by turning off lights or changing indoor room temperature can be done by most people without major discomfort. An important part in curtailment encouraging efforts concerns so-called motive alliances where the several positive outcomes of a behaviour are emphasised simultaneously (e.g. Belz 2006). For example, by encouraging energy reduction for environmental, financial and personal wellbeing reasons both societal and personal goals can be met at the same time. In fact many curtailment behaviours share this combination of societal environmental and personal benefits upon performing the behaviour. Another example is eco-driving where a driver is educated in handling the car in a more fuel efficient manner. Saving fuel means saving money personally, but at the same time polluting less.

Research from a curtailment perspective has shown that in order to increase the likelihood of consumers to curtail for example energy use personal communication and also behavioural interventions are more effective than for example non-personal mass communication campaigns (e.g. Abrahamse *et al.* 2005; McKenzie-Mohr & Smith 2000). Since curtailment efforts are focused on changing everyday behaviours (as opposed to promoting a specific product or service) these campaigns can be informed by research and practise in the area of social marketing (Geller 1989; Maibach 1993). Within the social marketing toolbox are several measures to not only encourage curtailment behaviours but also to make them work for a longer time-period. By crafting commitments, prompts, incentive schemes and communicating convenience of curtailment, the likelihood of success increase (McKenzie-Mohr 2000).

Since many environmentally significant behaviours, such as using hot water and travelling to school/work, are carried out routinely without much prior deliberation, curtailment efforts should also focus on breaking environmentally damaging habits. Research has found that consumers who perform several curtailment behaviours, such as saving energy and water, also have weaker habits in terms of car usage than consumers who are less inclined towards curtailment (Jansson, Marell & Nordlund 2009). Encouraging the breaking of strong habits can be done by utilising intervention techniques. Research has found that when strong car habits are broken, the individual is likely to reflect more on related behaviours (Eriksson, Garvill & Nordlund 2008).

On a final note on encouraging curtailment behaviours, it has been said to be important to focus on social and personal norms (Biel & Thøgersen 2007; Griskevicius, Cialdini & Goldstein 2008). By making consumers aware of current norms and influencing them in a more pro-environmental manner, adoption of curtailment on a wider scale is likely to occur – since norms are a vital part of the individual's attitudinal makeup. This can be done for example by cooperating with other stakeholders in promoting particular curtailment behaviours (for example energy companies, environmental organisations and regulators). Cooperation between many stakeholders is likely to improve the speed at which societal norms can be steered in more pro-environmental directions.

Curtailment and non-adoption of eco-innovations

In the top right box we find consumers that do perform curtailment behaviours but have not adopted eco-innovations and we term them curtailers. The challenge here lies in both encouraging these consumers to maintain a high level of curtailment, but also in influencing the consumers to adopt eco-innovations. In contrast to performing curtailment behaviours, eco-innovation adoption requires a financial expenditure at the outset in order to gain personal or societal environmental benefits. However, by acquiring an eco-innovation, several advantages can also be achieved for the consumer. By understanding these factors in combination with targeting the consumers most likely to adopt, eco-innovation encouragement campaigns are likely more effective.

Since these consumers are already performing one type of pro-environmental behaviour, it is less necessary to focus on building awareness of environmental issues and feelings of responsibility. In fact, research has found that curtailers have a higher degree of environmental awareness and stronger environmental values than consumers that can be termed non-greens (Jansson, Marell & Nordlund 2009).

In this sense these consumers have adopted curtailment behaviours as their response to environmental problem awareness and are trying to avoid cognitive dissonance by acting on their beliefs and attitudes. It might be tempting to view these curtailers as 'finished' in terms of communication and encouragement efforts since they are performing the desired behaviours. However, it is important to realise that curtailment behaviours need continuous encouragement in order to be upheld when situational factors change over lifecycle stages. Continued encouragement of curtailment behaviours in relation to one type of behavioural category might possibly also lead to curtailment in other sectors (e.g. Thøgersen & Ölander 2003). Although research on these types of spill-over effects is scarce, intuitively, if the pro-environmental values and norms are in effect, curtailing household energy use might lead to curtailment of car fuel or travel in general. However, more research is needed in order to clarify these possible links. In any case, continued efforts in encouraging consumers in continuous curtailment by personal communications campaigns and social marketing efforts seem vital at this stage as well. It also becomes important to develop feedback systems that readily show (for the curtailer) the effectiveness of the curtailment efforts. Examples include energy displays in the home and fuel efficiency gauges in the car.

Since curtailers have been found to have a higher awareness of environmental problems and also show propensity to act to help solve these problems, it is highly likely that curtailers are among the first to consider adopting eco-innovations. From a marketing perspective it might therefore be wise to focus communication efforts regarding eco-innovations on these types of consumers. This builds on the notion that curtailment behaviours and adopting eco-innovations are two possible ways for consumers to help solve environmental problems.

Pro-environmental values, beliefs, and norms are important determinants for eco-innovation adoption. In fact, these attitudinal variables are consistently more effective in explaining adoption than socio-demographic data (Jansson 2011; Jansson, Marell & Nordlund 2010). For marketing segmentation purposes, the implication is that attitudinal factors are more reliable than socio-demographic factors. This is in general in line with findings both in consumer adoption of innovation research and in green consumer behaviour research (Diamantopoulos *et al.* 2003; Ostlund 1974). This does not mean that socio-demographics are unimportant dimensions, but that they are potentially more valuable used together with other factors. By using, for example, behavioural segmentation, a more precise targeting strategy that is more effective than primarily relying on socio-demographics can be developed.

The importance of norms in influencing eco-innovation adoption behaviour has been substantiated in several studies (Jansson 2011; Jansson, Marell & Nordlund 2010). This leads to several implications for marketers of eco-innovations. Firstly, by realising the importance of internalised norms, marketers of eco-innovations could develop influential strategies to encourage consumer eco-innovation adoption. For example, the results point to the importance of reinforcing the consumer attitude that adopting an innovation does have less negative environmental effect than purchasing an ordinary product. By emphasising the environmental difference that individuals' decisions make, there is a higher likelihood for adoption. In addition, by showing examples of other consumers having adopted, and their satisfaction with the decision, individual consumers will feel less alone in striving toward a less environmentally harmful transportation system. In this sense, using ordinary consumers as a reference group as opposed to, say, celebrities, might be more effective in building on the feeling of personal moral obligation to act.

Encouraging eco-innovation adoption is not only related to attitudinal factors as discussed above, but also to perceptions of the specific innovation. Although there are only a few studies on consumer adoption of eco-innovations results show that how innovation characteristics are perceived determines the level and speed of adoption. In this research it has been shown that the lower perceived risk and complexity of innovation is positively related to the adoption of solar heating (Guagnano *et al.* 1986). Complexity has also been found to have a negative influence on the adoption of load management for washing machines by energy managers of a utility company (Völlink, Meertens & Midden 2002). Furthermore, the higher the perceived relative advantage of the innovation in relation to other products, the more likely an individual is to adopt these innovations. Another important factor is trialability, that is, the degree to which an innovation may be experimented with, or tried on a limited basis, prior to adoption (Rogers 2003). However, in an eco-innovation context several studies have found no influence of trialability on adoption of innovations such as solar power, energy conservation intervention technologies and alternative fuel vehicles (Jansson 2011; Labay & Kinnear 1981; Völlink, Meertens & Midden 2002). On the other hand, Guagnano *et al.* (1986) found that adopters of solar heating technology perceived it to have a higher level of trialability than non-adopters did. Observability – the degree to which the innovation, or the results of adopting the innovation, is visible to others (Rogers 2003) – is also an important factor. Labay and Kinnear (1981) and Guagnano *et al.* (1986) found observability to have a positive impact in the eco-innovation context, as did Jansson (2011). According to some researchers, observability is one of the factors that have driven the adoption of alternative fuel vehicles such as electric hybrids in some consumer segments (cf. Kahn 2007). Based on this research, it might be wise for a firm marketing eco-innovations to focus on issues such as design and visibility of the product.

Eco-innovation adoption and non-curtailment

In the bottom left box we find consumers that have adopted eco-innovations but do not perform curtailment behaviours. Based on innovation adoption research, it can be assumed that these consumers to a higher degree than others have adopted the innovations for other reasons than primarily environmental (Jansson 2011). These consumers might view other benefits of these innovations as important such as financial or status value that they bring. For example it has been argued that the adoption of the Toyota Prius electric hybrid vehicle in several markets was driven by a combination of visibility/design factors and image/lifestyle determinants (cf. de Haan, Mueller & Peters 2006; Kahn 2007). By monitoring the attitudes and behaviours of these consumers, it might be possible to gain understanding on what type of communication strategies could be devised to encourage these consumers to use their eco-innovations in a (more) environmentally friendly way. These are likely similar to the ones discussed when trying to encourage non-adopters of both types of behaviours to increase their willingness for curtailment behaviours. Additionally manufacturers and marketers have a responsibility to inform adopters of eco-innovations of how to use them in the most energy efficient manner. For example, when adopting an alternative fuel vehicle, a course for the driver on eco-driving might be included with the purchase.

For marketing reasons it might also be wise to use adopters of eco-innovations as communicators in efforts to encourage other consumers to do the same by promoting the compatibility, low complexity and relative advantages in relation to other products on the market. As discussed above, adopters are likely to be effective communicators since they can be assumed to hold a social standing of relevance to other potential adopters (e.g. Rogers 2003). Finally it is obviously important to encourage eco-innovation adopters to maintain an interest in eco-innovations and by doing so also develop an interest in curtailment behaviours. Since new eco-innovations are continually being developed and marketed, there should be ample opportunity for reflecting on values and attitudes related to the environment when considering more eco-innovations. Our research has also shown that once a consumer has adopted an eco-innovation (an alternative fuel vehicle in this case), they express a higher willingness to adopt similar eco-innovations in the future (Jansson 2011; Jansson, Marell & Nordlund 2009). With this in mind we turn to the final box in the matrix in Figure 7.1.

Eco-innovation adoption and curtailment behaviours

Finally, in the top left box we find consumers that have adopted eco-innovations and perform curtailment behaviours. Here it might be tempting to work according to the strategy that no communication efforts are needed, but as with all types of behaviours, and considering the development in eco-innovation development, continuous efforts are needed. For example, the adoption of more types of eco-innovations might be encouraged. Although research on whether this spill-over might be effective is scarce (e.g. Bratt 1999; Thøgersen & Ölander 2003), it can be assumed that in order to fit with a green lifestyle, openness to eco-innovations in general as opposed to only specific innovation is highly likely. There might also be opportunities for organisations to use, for example, focus groups and user involved product development to rely on the experience of these adopters in the development and marketing of coming generations of eco-innovations. A similar case can be made in relation to policymaking so that policies can be devised that encourage rather than hinder eco-innovation adoption and development.

Furthermore it is important to use adopters as endorsers of eco-innovations and curtailment behaviours when communicating to non-adopters in blogs, advertising, showrooms, etc. By assessing attitudinal factors continually, eco-innovation adoption behaviour and curtailment behaviours in lead markets for different products can be analysed. This knowledge can then be used when developing other markets that are less advanced in terms of pro-environmental behaviours. Thus the spread of both curtailment behaviours and eco-innovation adoption to other markets is stimulated.

Limitations and suggestions for further research

The introduction of the conceptual marketing challenge matrix is a first step in detailing the challenges that lie ahead in promoting environmental sustainability. The conceptual reasoning builds mostly on the marketing perspective of encouraging consumers to work towards environmental sustainability. Nevertheless, any attempt at achieving change towards sustainability also needs to incorporate other stakeholders such as non-governmental organisations and policymakers. For the sake of clarity, we have made the conscious decision to exclude these (and other) stakeholders from the matrix. However, focusing on the marketing and consumer behaviour aspects of environmental sustainability does not preclude involving other stakeholders in encouraging curtailment and eco-innovation adoption. For example, teaming up with influential environmental organisations internationally, nationally or at the local level, might bring advantages such as wider recognition for firms wishing to encourage pro-environmental consumer behaviour.

Another limitation with the conceptual model detailing the marketing challenge is the apparent risk of trade-offs between stakeholders wishing to encourage consumers for environmental sustainability. For example, when certain eco-innovations become widely adopted in a society, unforeseen problems might develop in the form of not actually lessening the use of certain environmental resources, but in fact shifting them to other types. When an eco-innovation is adopted, it is not enough in itself; it also needs to be used in an environmentally sustainable manner otherwise re-bound effects might occur that offset the initial gain of the adoption decision (e.g. Berkhout, Muskens & W. Velthuijsen 2000). Research in this area would be useful given that the availability of eco-innovations seems to be increasing. However, from a marketing perspective, encouraging eco-innovation adoption does not have to be at odds with encouraging curtailment behaviours. By communicating that curtailment, on the other hand, might save money that in turn may be used for investing in eco-innovations, the two approaches can be viewed as being complementary instead of opposing. Using a longitudinal research approach, as opposed to most studies that rely on cross-sectional data, would be valuable in increasing the understanding of how curtailment and eco-innovation adoption encouragement influence consumer behaviour over time.

Conclusions

In this chapter we have proposed that environmental consumer behaviour can be categorised into curtailment behaviours and technology choices (eco-innovation adoption). Previous research reveals that these behaviours share similar determinants and that the determinants influence these behaviours differently. These findings lead to the conclusion that, when investigating green consumer behaviours, it is valuable to separate different types of behaviours in order to draw specific behaviour-relevant conclusions. This is in line with the view that determinants of green consumer behaviours are complicated to understand, and that understanding the level of specificity and multiplicity of motivations is important to further increase understanding and encouragement of green consumers. The introduction of the marketing challenge matrix enabled us to detail the challenges in four vital areas of consumer behaviour in relation to environmental sustainability. It shows the importance of viewing pro-environmental consumer behaviours as heterogeneous and being determined by multiple driving and hindering factors. Markets and policymakers can, based on their purposes and situational factors, use the model to gain insight into how efforts in encouraging different types of pro-environmental consumer behaviours might be more successful.

References

Abrahamse, W., Steg, L., Vlek, C., & Rothengatter, T. (2005). A review of intervention studies aimed at household energy conservation. *Journal of Environmental Psychology*, 25 (3), 273-91.

Bamberg, S., Hunecke, M., & Blöbaum, A. (2007). Social context, personal norms and the use of public transportation: Two field studies. *Journal of Environmental Psychology*, 27 (3), 190-203.

Bansal, P. & Roth, K. (2000). Why companies go green: A model of ecological responsiveness. *Academy of Management Journal*, 43 (4), 717-36.

Barr, S., Gilg, A. W., & Ford, N. (2005). The household energy gap: Examining the divide between habitual- and purchase-related conservation behaviours. *Energy Policy*, 33 (11), 1425-44.

Bechtel, R. B. & Churchman, A. (2002). *Handbook of environmental psychology*. New York; Chichester: Wiley.

Belch, G. E. & Belch, M. A. (2007). *Advertising and promotion: An integrated marketing communications perspective*. 7th ed. Boston: McGraw-Hill Irwin.

Belz, F.-M. (2006). Editorial: Marketing in the 21st Century. *Business Strategy and the Environment*, 15 (3), 139-44.

Berger, I. E. (1997). The demographics of recycling and the structure of environmental behavior. *Environment and Behavior*, 29 (4), 515-31.

Berkhout, P. H. G., Muskens, J. C., & W. Velthuijsen, J. (2000). Defining the rebound effect. *Energy Policy*, 28 (6-7), 425-32.

Best, H. (2009). Structural and ideological determinants of household waste recycling: Results from an empirical study in Cologne, Germany. *Nature and Culture*, 4 (2), 167-90.

Biel, A. & Thøgersen, J. (2007). Activation of social norms in social dilemmas: A review of the evidence and reflections on the implications for environmental behaviour. *Journal of Economic Psychology*, 28 (1), 93-112.

Black, J. S., Stern, P. C., & Elworth, J. T. (1985). Personal and contextual influences on household energy adaptations. *Journal of Applied Psychology*, 70 (1), 3-21.

Bratt, C. (1999). Consumers' environmental behavior: Generalized, sector-based, or compensatory? *Environment and Behavior*, 31 (1), 28-44.

de Haan, P., Mueller, M. G., & Peters, A. (2006). Does the hybrid Toyota Prius lead to rebound effects? Analysis of size and number of cars previously owned by Swiss Prius buyers. *Ecological Economics*, 58 (3), 592.

Derksen, L. & Gartrell, J. (1993). The social context of recycling. *American Sociological Review*, 58 (3), 434-42.

Diamantopoulos, A., Schlegelmilch, B. B., Sinkovics, R. R., & Bohlen, G. M. (2003). Can socio-demographics still play a role in profiling green consumers? A review of the evidence and an empirical investigation. *Journal of Business Research*, 56 (6), 465-80.

Dickerson, M. D. & Gentry, J. W. (1983). Characteristics of adopters and non-adopters of home computers. *Journal of Consumer Research*, 10 (2), 225-35.

Diekmann, A. & Preisendorfer, P. (2003). Green and greenback: The behavioral effects of environmental attitudes in low-cost and high-cost situations. *Rationality and Society*, 15 (4), 441-72.

Dupagne, M. (1999). Exploring the characteristics of potential high-definition television adopters. *Journal of Media Economics*, 12 (1), 35-50.

EC. (2008). Special Eurobarometer 295/ Wave 68.2: Attitudes of European citizens towards the environment: EC, European Commission, Brussels.

Ellen, P. S. (1994). Do we know what we need to know? Objective and subjective knowledge effects on pro-ecological behaviors. *Journal of Business Research*, 30 (1), 43-52.

Eriksson, L., Garvill, J., & Nordlund, A. M. (2008). Interrupting habitual car use: The importance of car habit strength and moral motivation for personal car use reduction. *Transportation Research Part F: Traffic Psychology and Behaviour*, 11 (1), 10-23.

Follows, S. B. & Jobber, D. (2000). Environmentally responsible purchase behaviour: A test of a consumer model. *European Journal of Marketing*, 34 (5/6), 723-47.

Fraj-Andrés, E. & Martinez-Salinas, E. (2007). Impact of environmental knowledge on ecological consumer behaviour: An empirical analysis. *Journal of International Consumer Marketing*, 19 (3), 73-102.

Frey, B. S. & Stutzer, A. (2008). Environmental morale and motivation.In Lewis, Alan, editor, *The Cambridge handbook of psychology and economic behaviour*. Cambridge: Cambridge University Press.

Gardner, B. & Abraham, C. (2007). What drives car use? A grounded theory analysis of commuters' reasons for driving. *Transportation Research Part F: Traffic Psychology and Behaviour*, 10 (3), 187-200.

Gärling, T. & Schuitema, G. (2007). Travel demand management targeting reduced private car use: Effectiveness, public acceptability and political feasibility. *Journal of Social Issues*, 63 (1), 139-53.

Geller, E. S. (1989). Applied behavior analysis and social marketing: An integration for environmental preservation. *Journal of Social Issues*, 45 (1), 17-36.

Griskevicius, V., Cialdini, R. B., & Goldstein, N. J. (2008). Social norms: An underestimated and underemployed lever for managing climate change. *International Journal of Sustainability Communication*, 3, 5-13.

Guagnano, G., Hawkes, G. R., Acredolo, C., & White, N. (1986). Innovation perception and adoption of solar heating technology. *Journal of Consumer Affairs*, 20 (1), 48-64.

Guagnano, G. A., Stern, P. C., & Dietz, T. (1995). Influences on attitude-behavior relationships: A natural experiment with curbside recycling. *Environment and Behavior*, 27 (5), 699-718.

Hansla, A., Gamble, A., Juliusson, A., & Gärling, T. (2008). The relationships between awareness of consequences, environmental concern, and value orientations. *Journal of Environmental Psychology*, 28 (1), 1-9.

Hirschman, E. C. (1980). Innovativeness, novelty seeking, and consumer creativity. *Journal of Consumer Research*, 7 (3), 283-95.

Jansson, J. (2011). Consumer eco-innovation adoption: Assessing attitudinal factors and perceived product characteristics. *Business Strategy and the Environment*, 20 (3), 192-210.

Jansson, J., Marell, A., & Nordlund, A. (2009). Elucidating green consumers: A cluster analytic approach on pro-environmental purchase and curtailment behaviors. *Journal of Euromarketing*, 18 (4), 245-67.

Jansson, J., Marell, A., & Nordlund, A. (2011). Exploring consumer adoption of a high involvement eco-innovation using value-belief-norm theory. *Journal of Consumer Behaviour, 10 (1), 51-60.*

Jansson, J., Marell, A., & Nordlund, A. (2010). Green consumer behavior: Determinants of curtailment and eco-innovation adoption. *Journal of Consumer Marketing*, 27 (4), 358-70.

Kahn, M. E. (2007). Do greens drive Hummers or hybrids? Environmental ideology as a determinant of consumer choice. *Journal of Environmental Economics and Management*, 54 (2), 129-45.

Kempton, W., Harris, C. K., Keith, J. G., & Weihl, J. S. (1985). Do consumers know "what works" in energy conservation? *Marriage & Family Review*, 9 (1), 115-33.

Labay, D. G. & Kinnear, T. C. (1981). Exploring the consumer decision process in the adoption of solar energy systems. *Journal of Consumer Research*, 8 (3), 271-78.

Lehman, P. K. & Geller, E. S. (2004). Behavior analysis and environmental protection: Accomplishments and potential for more. *Behavior and Social Issues*, 13 (1), 13-32.

Maibach, E. (1993). Social marketing for the environment: using information campaigns to promote environmental awareness and behavior change. *Health Promotion International*, 8 (3), 209-24.

Martinez, E., Polo, Y., & Carlos, F. (1998). The acceptance and diffusion of new consumer durables: Differences between first and last adopters. *Journal of Consumer Marketing*, 15 (4), 323-42.

McCarty, J. A. & Shrum, L. J. (1994). The recycling of solid wastes: Personal values, value orientations, and attitudes about recycling as antecedents of recycling behavior. *Journal of Business Research*, 30 (1), 53-62.

McKenzie-Mohr, D. (2000). Fostering sustainable behavior through community-based social marketing. *American Psychologist*, 55 (5), 531-54.

McKenzie-Mohr, D. (2000). Promoting sustainable behavior: An introduction to community-based social marketing. *Journal of Social Issues*, 56 (3), 543-54.

McKenzie-Mohr, D. & Smith, W. (2000). *Fostering sustainable behaviour: An introduction to community-based social marketing*. Philadelphia, Chipping Norton: New Society, Jon Carpenter.

McMakin, A. H., Malone, E. L., & Lundgren, R. E. (2002). Motivating residents to conserve energy without financial incentives. *Environment and Behavior*, 34 (6), 848-63.

Midgley, D. F. & Dowling, G. R. (1978). Innovativeness: The concept and its measurement. *Journal of Consumer Research*, 4 (4), 229-42.

Nordlund, A. M. & Garvill, J. (2003). Effects of values, problem awareness, and personal norm on willingness to reduce personal car use. *Journal of Environmental Psychology*, 23 (4), 339-47.

Ölander, F. & Thøgersen, J. (1995). Understanding of consumer behaviour as a prerequisite for environmental protection. *Journal of Consumer Policy*, 18 (4), 345-85.

Ostlund, L. E. (1974). Perceived innovation attributes as predictors of innovativeness. *Journal of Consumer Research*, 1 (September), 23-29.

Ritchie, J. R. B., McDougall, G. H. G., & Claxton, J. D. (1981). Complexities of household energy consumption and conservation. *Journal of Consumer Research*, 8 (3), 233-42.

Rivera-Camino, J. (2007). Re-evaluating green marketing strategy: A stakeholder perspective. *European Journal of Marketing*, 41 (11/12), 1328-58.

Roberts, J. A. (1995). Profiling levels of socially responsible consumer behavior: A cluster analytic approach and its implications for marketing. *Journal of Marketing Theory and Practice*, 3 (4), 97-117.

Rogers, E. M. (2003). *Diffusion of innovations*. 5. ed. New York: Free press.

Schultz, P. W., Oskamp, S., & Mainieri, T. (1995). Who recycles and when? A review of personal and situational factors. *Journal of Environmental Psychology*, 15 (2), 105-21.

Stern, P. C. (2000). Toward a coherent theory of environmentally significant behavior. *Journal of Social Issues*, 56 (3), 407-24.

Stern, P. C. (1992). What psychology knows about energy conservation. *American Psychologist*, 47 (10), 1224-32.

Stern, P. C. & Gardner, G. T. (1981). Psychological research and energy policy. *American Psychologist*, 36 (4), 329-42.

Thøgersen, J. (1999). The ethical consumer: Moral norms and packaging choice. *Journal of Consumer Policy*, 22 (4), 439-60.

Thøgersen, J. & Ölander, F. (2003). Spillover of environment-friendly consumer behaviour. *Journal of Environmental Psychology*, 23 (3), 225-36.

UN. (2009). The ten principles of the United Nation's global compact: UN, United Nations, URL: http://www.unglobalcompact.org/AbouttheGC/TheTenPrinciples/index.html, Accessed: August 13, 2009.

Wang, G. P., Dou, W. Y., & Zhou, N. (2008). Consumption attitudes and adoption of new consumer products: A contingency approach. *European Journal of Marketing*, 42 (1-2), 238-54.

Völlink, T., Meertens, R. E. E., & Midden, C. J. H. (2002). Innovating 'diffusion of innovation' theory: Innovation characteristics and the intention of utility companies to adopt energy conservation interventions. *Journal of Environmental Psychology*, 22 (4), 333-44.

Chapter 8

Cases

Female adolescents' green purchasing behaviour: A study in Hong Kong

Lee Kaman

Abstract

This study extends Grunig's situational theory to examine to what extent problem recognition, constraint recognition, involvement, information seeking and information processing could predict green purchasing behaviour. It reports on a case study that used a sample of 3,035 female adolescents. Analyses confirm that the green purchasing behaviour of the study subjects can be predicted by factors in the following descending order of effectiveness: environmental information seeking, environmental involvement, environmental information processing, environmental constraint recognition and environmental problem recognition. Theoretical and practical implications of the findings are discussed at the end of the case study.

Key words

green marketing communications, green purchasing behaviour, female adolescents, consumers, Hong Kong.

The greening force in Asia

Studies confirm that Western consumers have become more environmentally conscious in the past decade (Curlo 1999). Recently, green consumerism has started to emerge in Asian regions, where environmental threats are alarming local governments and citizens (Gurău & Ranchhod 2005; Pugh & Fletcher 2002). The growing interest in culture among marketing communications scholars and practitioners notwithstanding, surprisingly little research has been conducted to understand Asian consumers' green purchasing decisions. To truly understand audiences of another culture, marketing communications research necessitates an audience-oriented approach.

The present case study reports on a study that examined factors that predict green purchasing behaviour among Hong Kong female adolescent consumers. The primary objective of this case study is to extend the situational theory (Grunig & Hunt 1984) by examining the extent to which, level of involvement, problem recognition, constraint recognition, information seeking and information processing could be applied to predict green purchasing behaviour. In a theoretical sense, by examining the predictability of the situational variables on green purchasing behaviour in Hong Kong's female adolescent consumers, this case study may contribute to the extension and application of the theory to (1) the green marketing communications context and (2) a non-Western context. In a practical sense, international green marketing communications may emerge as an inevitable force in the near future. Thus, there is an urgent need to understand what factors motivate green-purchasing behaviours among members of Asian societies.

With 'sustainable development' being pressed as the dominating theme in 21st century commerce, two trends are predicted as inevitable in the near future. First, the concept of an eco-friendly approach to doing business will be pushed into the mainstream (Hanas 2007). Second, the greening force will be expanded from developed countries to developing countries (especially in Asia) (Gurău & Ranchhod 2005; Pugh & Fletcher 2002). All these anticipated changes imply that green marketing communications necessitate two-way communication and understanding with consumers in a cross-cultural setting.

Female adolescent consumers

Past studies found that supporters of environmental protection tend to be younger in age (Martinsons *et al.* 1997). Compared to older generations, young people are more concerned about the deterioration of environmental quality (Connell *et al.* 1999) and are more likely to accept new and innovative ideas (Ottman, Stafford & Hartman 2006).

Among groups of young consumers, 'female adolescents' should be one of the most promising potential supporters of green products. Past studies have shown that females in general report stronger environmental attitudes, concern, and behavioural intention to improve the environment than males (Zelezny & Bailey 2006). Agarwal (2000) contends that the distinctive social networking behaviour of females constitutes an important basis for engaging sustainable environmental collective action. Given the strong eco-centric orientation, the long life span and the anticipated role of household decision makers of female adolescent consumers, it is worthwhile investigating what motivates them to make green purchasing decisions.

Situational variables and green purchasing behaviour

Aldoory (2001) describes that Grunig's situational theory (Grunig & Hunt 1984) comes closest to Moffitt's (1992) call for audience understanding in the field of public relations and marketing communications. To predict whether or not stakeholders will engage in active or passive communication behaviour, the theory offers three independent variables: problem recognition, constraint recognition and level of involvement. The theory posits that the different combinations of the three independent variables will predict two dependent variables: information seeking and information processing. For instance, a high level of problem recognition and involvement will correlate positively, and constraint recognition will correlate negatively with information-seeking behaviour (Grunig 1989).

This case study examines the level to which, green purchasing behaviour could be predicted by problem recognition, constraint recognition, level of involvement, information seeking and information processing in Hong Kong female adolescent consumers. Although information seeking and processing were regarded as dependent variables in the original situational theory, this case study has attempted to examine the question of 'what happens after information seeking and processing?' Existing studies have confirmed correlations between information seeking and purchases of daily commodities (e.g. Girish 1987). As such, this case study investigates whether the same connection exists between information seeking/processing and green purchasing behaviour among Hong Kong female adolescent consumers.

In this case study, a total of 3,035 female adolescents were surveyed. They were Hong Kong high school students from grade 7 to grade 13. Their ages ranged from 12 to 18 years with a mean age of 14.05 years (SD = 2.30 years). Fifty-four per cent of them were in grades 7 to 9, 34% of them were in grades 10 to 11 and 12% of them were in grades 12 to 13. The students were recruited through random sampling of all high schools in Hong Kong. To measure the five situational variables and green purchasing behaviour, 5-point Likert-types scales were used. Reliabilities of the scales of environmental problem recognition, environmental constraint recognition, environmental involvement, environmental information seeking, environmental information processing and green purchase behaviour were .86, .80, .84, .84, .76 and .75. Burns and Bush (2000) suggest a minimum value of .65 as an acceptable reliability value for a newly developed measure. Considering their suggestion, the new scales developed in this study were acceptable in terms of reliability.

Environmental problem recognition

Problem recognition in Grunig and Hunt's situational theory (1984) is defined as a state whereby an individual becomes aware of a problem and considers what can be done to resolve it. Bord and O'Connor (1997) found that women were more concerned about the negative outcomes of environmental damage than were men. Dunlap (1994) compared Asian and Western citizens and indicated that Asian residents tended to perceive their local environmental problems much more negatively than did their Western and European counterparts (Dunlap 1994). However, what remains undetermined is the effect of problem recognition on individuals' behaviour/behavioural change. As such, this case study attempts to examine how much individuals' environmental problem recognition could predict their green purchasing behaviour. Hierarchical multiple regression showed the predictive power of problem recognition on Hong Kong female adolescent consumers' green purchasing behaviour was $\beta = .11$, $p < .001$.

Environmental constraint recognition

Constraint recognition refers to the extent to which a person feels that he or she is constrained by the situation to do something to solve the problem (Grunig & Hunt 1984). It indicates when the locus of control becomes internal or external (Grunig 1983). Several studies have found that having a sense of self-efficacy differentiates those who are environmentally active and those who are not (Manzo & Weinstein 1987). Specifically, those who hold strong beliefs that their environmental behaviour will make a difference to the environment (i.e. a low level of constraint recognition) will become more environmentally active than those who perceive that they have limited ability to change the environment (i.e. a high level of constraint recognition). Following this logic, environmental constraint recognition should, to some extent, predict individuals' green purchasing behaviour. This case study examines whether such a relationship exists. Hierarchical multiple regression revealed that the predictive power of problem recognition on Hong Kong female adolescent consumers' green purchasing behaviour was $\beta = -.12$, $p < .001$.

Environmental involvement

Level of involvement is defined as the extent to which an individual perceives a connection between himself or herself and a situation (Grunig 1983). Grunig (1983) posits that the stronger the connection with a situation, the more probable it is that the person will communicate about it. Environmental involvement therefore refers to the degree to which individuals perceive that the environment's problems and issues are relevant to them. Early studies have found that age, level of education, political ideology, ethnicity, gender and value orientation influence people's concern over environmental quality and its effects on human beings and nature (Xiao & McCright 2007). Bang and his associates (2000) found that consumers who were more personally involved in the environmental problems expressed more commitment to pay more for renewable energy than those who were less involved.

Referencing existing literature, it is reasonable to posit that individuals' level of environmental involvement may influence their green purchasing behaviour. In this case study, environmental involvement yielded a predictive value of ß= .18, p<.001 in the hierarchical multiple regression.

Environmental information seeking

Information seeking is referred to as the deliberate search for information on a particular issue (Aldoory 2001). According to Brown (1991), information-seeking behaviour is a goal-driven activity. Grunig (1989) contends that communication behaviour can be active or passive, and that consumers' active communication is typified by high levels of information seeking. Past research efforts have identified problem recognition, constraint recognition and level of involvement as independent variables of individuals' information-seeking behaviour. High problem recognition, low constraint recognition and a high level of involvement are found to motivate individuals to actively seek information (Grunig 1983).

While existing literature provides a framework for predicting and analysing information seeking, little is known about what happens after individuals seek information. Existing consumer research has found that consumers' information seeking is followed by them purchasing new cars, major household appliances, durables or fashion items (e.g. Girish 1987). The present case study showed that same connection between information seeking and purchasing behaviour could be found in green products among Hong Kong female adolescent consumers, ß= .28, p<.001.

Environmental information processing

In contrast to information seeking, whereby individuals deliberately search for information, information processing often takes place randomly (Grunig 1989). According to Kahlor *et al.* (2006), the seeking and processing strategies that people apply to information can influence what they take away from messages. Specifically, active information seeking, which is goal-directed and driven, is more likely to lead to effortful, systematic processing of the information acquired than habitual/random information processing (Eagly & Kulesa 1997). Thus, information processing is used to denote passive communication behaviour in the situational theory (Grunig 1989).

While past efforts have been devoted to examining what affects information processing, little has been done to investigate what information processing affects. According to the consumer information processing model, consumers pass through a series of stages in making choices about which products to purchase (Reicks *et al.* 2003).These stages include: perceiving a need, scanning memory for previous experiences with the product, using evaluative criteria to process value and making the purchasing decision. That is to say, information processing often exists when consumers are considering a purchase. What is yet to be determined is how close the relationship is. This case study thus attempts to contribute by examining to what extent information processing can predict green purchasing behaviour.

Hierarchical multiple regression showed the predictive power of environmental information processing on Hong Kong female adolescent consumers' green purchasing behaviour was ß= .18, p<.001.

Implications

Information seeking and information processing, which are the original dependent variables in the situational theory, have been found to be two of the top three predictors of green purchasing behaviour in the present study. This finding shows (1) the applicability of Grunig's situational theory to the context of green marketing communications and (2) the plausibility of extending the original situational theory to include behavioural variables in future studies.

Among the five situational variables, environmental information seeking is the top predictor of green purchasing behaviour. Grunig (Grunig & Hunt 1984; Grunig 1989) contends that active consumers are typified by high levels of information seeking. The underlying assumption of the situational theory is that voluntary information seeking already reflects individuals' interest in a particular issue. This paper supplements the original theory by offering evidence that high levels of information seeking by active consumers are followed by purchasing behaviour.

There are two reasons that might help explain the positive relationship between information seeking and green purchasing behaviour. Firstly, information seeking is already, in itself, a behaviour that reflects an individual's interest in or consideration of purchasing a particular product or kind of product (Grunig & Hunt 1984). Uncertainty about and perceived risk of a product often deters a consumer from making a purchase decision (Midgley 1983). As an individual seeks more information about the product or product category, his or her sense of uncertainty or perceived risk might gradually be alleviated (Moorthy, Ratchford & Talukdar 1997). Consequently, the consumer feels safe to proceed with the purchase.

Secondly, the act of green purchasing could carry both functional meanings (e.g. purchasing products that contain healthier or less harmful ingredients) and symbolic meanings (e.g. acquiring the identity of being a moral, ethical or environmentally responsible citizen) (Midgley 1983). Through the information-seeking process, an individual's perceived symbolic identity is further reinforced. Such reinforcement might facilitate the individual's commitment to green living and green purchasing.

Environmental involvement is the second top predictor of green purchasing behaviour in Hong Kong female adolescent consumers. Studies have confirmed that individuals' perceived personal relevance of a topic is positively associated with information seeking and information selection (e.g. Grunig 1983; Kim 2007). Kim (2007) elucidates how perceived personal relevance acts as an intrinsic motivational force on information seeking and selection. This paper further evidences that when individuals are emotionally involved in, and concerned about, environmental issues, they are motivated to support environmental protection through green purchasing behaviour. Thus, when dealing with this group of consumers, green marketing communications practitioners are advised to use more emotion-involving and passion-triggering cues to cultivate personal concern and relevance in their green campaigns in the future (Petty & Cacioppo 1996).

Information processing is the third top predictor of green purchasing behaviour. Grunig (1983) distinguishes two primary means of encountering a campaign message: active information seeking (or the deliberate search for information on a topic) and passive information processing (the happenstance encounter with a message appearing on TV, newspaper, Internet, etc.). Because information processing is assumed to represent passive consumers, its importance has often been dwarfed by information seeking in past studies (Kim 2007). The present study shows that this more passive information processing is one of the top three predictors of green purchasing behaviour. It indicates that information processing has its own considerable importance in the context of environmental communication.

The early work of Cacioppo, Harkins, and Petty (1981) has already insinuated that although the state of information processing seems to appear passive in terms of seeking behaviour, it could involve active cognitive responses such as comprehension, recall, rejection or integration of new information into existing beliefs. This paper suggests that such cognitive responses could enact behavioural outcomes of green purchasing among Hong Kong female adolescent consumers. Thus, this finding gives some additional insight to the existing situational studies —that in the context of environmental communication, those who have been characterised as 'passive consumers' by their information processing display active behavioural support of green consumerism through their purchasing behaviours.

The deficit model (Bodmer 1985) helps explain the finding of the present study— that environmental information conveyed through different channels to the audience fills in their knowledge deficit gap. When audiences receive and absorb more environmental knowledge, (even though they do not initiate the search for it), they will enact more pro-environmental behaviours. This finding suggests to green marketing communications practitioners that future environmental campaigns should use various channels to disseminate/teach environmental knowledge/concepts to female adolescent consumers.

Constraint recognition was found to be the fourth predictor of green purchasing behaviour. Specifically, a lower degree of perceived constraint recognition predicts a higher degree of green purchasing behaviour in Hong Kong female adolescent consumers. This finding echoes the theory of efficacy expectation; whereby, it predicts that people process, weigh and integrate different sources of information with regard to their abilities and the outcomes of a behaviour, and then use this information to guide their behaviour and efforts (Bandura 1977). Those who believe they can make a change to their environment perceive less external constraints and are more motivated to take action to achieve certain goals than those who believe they cannot.

Several studies have found that having a sense of efficacy differentiates those who are environmentally active from those who are not (Manzo & Weinstein 1987). The present finding suggests that green marketing communications practitioners need to reduce consumers' sense of constraints on the issue of environmental protection. Green marketing communications efforts in the future should convey messages such as: 'each of our efforts counts', 'together we can make a difference' or 'we can make our world a better world'.

Among the five situational variables, environmental problem recognition appears to be the weakest predictor of green purchasing behaviour. This result suggests that the common approach of emphasising the seriousness of our environmental problems in environmental communication may not be sufficient to motivate Hong Kong female adolescents to make an environmental purchase. That is to say, environmental problem recognition has little effect on behaviour in Hong Kong female adolescent consumers. This finding poses a challenge to the general assumption that the more seriously the environmental problems are presented to the people, the more motivated they would be to act pro-environmentally.

Conclusion

It is anticipated that green marketing communications will play an important role in the near future in facilitating understanding between corporations and their international publics. Despite an increase in green consumerism in Asia, there is a scarcity of information about Asian consumers in this regard. In light of this, this paper applies Grunig's situational theory (Grunig 1997) to examine the predictability of the five situational variables on green purchasing behaviour in Hong Kong female adolescent consumers.

This paper serves as an exploratory study that examines the predictability of Grunig's situational variables on green purchasing behaviour in Hong Kong female adolescent consumers. The study was conducted in response to: (1) the gradually rising phenomenon of green consumerism in Asia and (2) the call by researchers for new variables to address the insufficiency of the reasoned action theory to predict green behaviours (e.g. Kaiser, Wolfing & Fuhrer 1999). This paper demonstrates the applicability of Grunig's situational variables to the field of green marketing communications. It also extends the theory to examine the effects of the variables on behavioural outcomes (here, green purchasing behaviours). The two dependent variables in the original situational theory—namely, information processing and information seeking—constitute two of the top three predictors of green purchasing behaviour in the present study. This finding might point to a need to re-examine the previous categorisation and definition of active and passive consumers in the situational theory.

The results of the present study also proffer some practical guidelines to green marketing communications practitioners. To produce effective environmental messages, an environmental campaign should focus more on: (1) triggering the emotional involvement and perceived personal relevance in environmental issues of female adolescent consumers; (2) exposing those consumers to more knowledge about environmental protection through various communication channels and (3) stressing how individual efforts could make a difference. Without cognitive engagement (through information seeking and/or processing), a sense of personal relatedness and a sense of self-efficacy, female adolescents will not engage in green purchasing behaviour even if they are aware of Hong Kong's environmental problems.

Reference

Agarwal, B. 2000. Conceptualizing environmental collective action: why gender matters. Cambridge Journal of Economics 24, no.3: 283-310.

Aldoory, L. 2001. Making health communications meaningful for women: factors that influence involvement. Journal of Public Relations Research 13, no.2: 163-185.

Bandura, A. 1977. Self-efficacy: Toward a unifying theory of behavioral change. Psychological Review 84, no.2: 191-215.

Bang, H., A.E. Ellinger, J. Hadjimarcou, and P.A. Traichal. 2000. Consumer concern, knowledge, belief, and attitude toward renewable energy: An application of the reasoned action theory. Psychology and Marketing 17, no.1: 6-26.

Bodmer, W. 1985. The public understanding of science. London: Royal Society.

Bord, R.I., and R.E. O'Connor. 1997. The gender gap in environmental attitudes: the case of perceived vulnerability to risk. Social Science Quarterly 78, no. 4: 830-840.

Brown, M.E. 1991. A general model of information-seeking behavior. Proceedings of the 54th ASIS Annual Meeting, 9-14.

Burns, A.C., and R. F. Bush. 2000. Marketing research 3rd ed. Upper Saddle River, NJ: Prentice Hall.

Cacioppo, J.T., S.G. Harkins, and P.E. Petty. 1981. The nature of attitudes, cognitive responses, and their relationships to behavior. In Cognitive responses in persuasion, ed. R. Petty, T. Ostrom, and T. Brock, 31-54. Hillsdale, NJ: Lawrence Erlbaum Associates, Inc.

Connell, S., J. Fien, J. Lee, H. Sykes, and D. Yencken. 1999. If it doesn't directly affect you, you don't think about it: A qualitative study of young people's environmental attitudes in two Australian cities. Environmental Education Research 5: 95-113.

Curlo, E. 1999. Marketing strategy, product safety, and ethical factors in consumer choice. Journal of Business Ethics 21, no.1: 37-48.

Dunlap, R.E. 1994. International attitudes towards environment and development. In Green globe yearbook of international co-operation on environment and development 1994, ed. H.O. Bergesen and G. Parmann, 115-126. Oxford: Oxford University Press.

Eagly, A., and P. Kulesa. 1997. Attitudes, attitude structure, and resistance to change: Implications for persuasion on environmental issues. In Environment, ethics, and behavior: The psychology of environmental valuation and degradation, ed. M. Bazerman and D. Messick, 122-153. San Francisco, DA: The New Lexington Press social and behavioral science series.

Girish, P. 1987. Presearch decision making in consumer durable purchases. Journal of Consumer Marketing 4, no.1: 71-83.

Grunig, J.E. 1997. A situational theory of publics: Conceptual history, recent challenges and new research. In Public relations research: An international perspective, ed. D.

Moss, T. MacManus, and D. Vercic, 3-48. London: International Thomson Business Press.

Grunig, J.E. 1983. Communication behaviors and attitudes of environmental publics: Two studies. Journalism Monograph 8, no.1: 1-47.

Grunig, J.E. 1989. Sierra Club study shows who become activists. Public Relations Review 15, no.1: 3-24.

Grunig, J.E., and T. Hunt. 1984. Managing public relations. Fort Worth: Harcourt Brace Jovanovich College Publisher.

Gurău, C. and A. Ranchhod. 2005. International green marketing: A comparative study of British and Romanian firms. International Marketing Review 22, no. 5: 547-561.

Hanas, J. 2007. A world gone green; Environmental awareness has not only yipped in the media: It's hit corporate boardrooms as well. http://adage.com/eco-marketing/article?article_id=117113.

Kahlor, L., S. Dunwoody, R.J. Griffin, and K. Neuwirth 2006. Seeking and processing information about impersonal risk. Science Communication 28, no.2: 163-194.

Kaiser, F. G., S. Wolfing, and U. Fuhrer. 1999. Environmental attitude and ecological behavior. Journal of Environmental Psychology 19, no.1: 1-19.

Kim, Y.M. 2007. How intrinsic and extrinsic motivations interact in selectivity: Investigating the moderating effects of situational information processing goals in issue publics' web behavior. Communication Research 34, no. 2: 185-211.

Manzo, L. C., and N.D. Weinstein. 1987. Behavioral commitment to environmental protection: A study of active and nonactive members of the Sierra Club. Environmental and Behavior 19, no.6: 673-694.

Martinsons, M.G., S.K.K. So, C. Tin, and D. Wong, D. 1997. Hong Kong and China: Emerging markets for environmental products and technologies. Long Range Planning 30, no.2: 277-290.

Midgley, D. 1983. Patterns of interpersonal information seeking for the purchase of a symbolic product. Journal of Marketing Research 20, no.1: 74-83.

Moffitt, M.A. 1992. Bringing critical theory and ethical considerations to definitions of a "public." Public Relations Review 18, no.1: 17-29.

Moorthy, S., B.T. Ratchford, and D. Talukdar. 1997. Consumer information search revisited: Theory and empirical analysis. Journal of Consumer Research 23, no.4: 263-277.

Ottman, J. A., E.R. Stafford, and C.L. Hartman 2006. Avoiding green marketing myopia: ways to improve consumer appeal for environmentally preferable products. Environment 48, no.5: 22-36.

Petty, R.E., and J.T. Cacioppo. 1996. Attitudes and persuasion: Classic and contemporary approaches. Boulder, CO: Westview Press.

Pugh, M., and R. Fletcher, R. 2002. Green international wine marketing, Australasian Marketing Journal 10, no.1: 76-85.

Reicks, M., C. Smith, H. Henry, K. Reimer, J. Atwell, and R. Thomas. 2003. Use of the think aloud method to examine fruit and vegetable purchasing behaviors among low-income African American women. Journal of Nutrition Education and Behavior, 35, no.3: 154-160.

Xiao, C., and A.M. McCright. 2007. Environmental concern and sociodemographic variables: A study of statistical models. Journal of Environmental Education 38, no.1: 3-14.

Zelezny, L., and M. Bailey. 2006. A call for women to lead a different environmental movement. Organization and Environment 19, no.1: 103-109.

Environmental versus convenience purchases and the role of online community champions: My Pizza Personality

Chad Renando

Abstract

Barriers exist for environmental purchases; whereas convenience purchases benefit from a self-sustaining habitual gratification cycle. Communities build trust and remove barriers to purchasing – particularly in online communities that allow rapid feedback on personal identity. The My Pizza Personality project assessed the extent of environmental beliefs for convenience consumers using fast food retail pizza purchasing. The results demonstrate that pizza purchasers are not generally green consumers. Pizza purchasers who do align with environmental beliefs, however, are less likely to make a purchasing decision based solely on price. Consumers with environmental beliefs are also more likely to share information with their communities.

This research demonstrates that consumers who engage in frequent activity involving convenience products may not hold strong environmental beliefs. Consumers that do hold environmental beliefs, however, are willing to pay higher prices and give brand loyalty to companies that support those beliefs. These green consumers are also more likely to champion the cause of the company within their community. These outcomes are relevant to managers responsible for marketing to the green consumer.

Environmental convenience

Businesses can respond to the 'business case for sustainability' based upon a belief that the green consumer will give brand loyalty and pay higher prices for environmentally friendly products. Differentiating products based on the green purchase can be difficult in a crowded market as there is general consumer dissatisfaction with environmental product label clarity (D'Souza *et al.* 2006). Environmental purchases face additional barriers that include the difficulty of the purchase, varying degrees of consumer self-determination, and cognitive barriers of trust (Green-Demers, Pelletier & Menard 1997).

Convenience purchases by comparison create a self-fulfilling loop. First, the marketing material targets the consumer's anticipation of immediate gratification (Herabadi, Verplanken & Knippenberg 2009). This results in short-term satisfaction (Seiders *et al.* 2005) followed by low self-esteem, to later be resolved by future purchases (Verplanken *et al.* 2005). This cycle can become habitual, resistant to informational interventions and reinforced by the consumer's physical environment (Verplanken & Wood 2006). The consumer's dissatisfaction is especially prominent when the consumer is forced to compromise environmental, nutritional and other concerns for the benefit of convenience (Gehrt & Yale 1993).

Community plays a role in both environmental and convenience purchases. Most customers will not cognitively process an inclination to change brands unless the motivation to change is sufficient (Feichtinger, Luhmer & Sorger 1988). As the consumer aligns themselves with the brand, they will have a greater degree of socialisation with the organisation and be less sensitive to price variations based on having their psychological needs met over their financial needs (Hsieh & Chang 2004). Once a sense of community with the supplier is established, the customer is able to move more quickly through the purchasing decision-making process due to having faster responses to affective (feeling) attitudes over cognitive (thinking) attitudes (Verplanken, Hofstee & Janssen 1998). Online communities, in particular, allow the consumer a framework to express and define their notion of ecological citizenship and control their degree of engagement (Rokka & Moisander 2009).

Environmental versus convenience purchases and the moderating role of community was explored in the My Pizza Personality project, which set out to find answers to the questions: 'Do people who buy fast food retail pizza care about the environment?' 'Does the environmental position of the pizza company impact the consumer's decision-making process?', and 'Can online communities help bridge an environment/convenience gap?'

My Pizza Personality

The My Pizza Personality online survey project (www.mypizzapersonality.com) used personality questions as an incentive, presenting the respondent with a 'pizza type' mapped to one of the sixteen Myers-Briggs personality types. Through the process of obtaining their 'pizza personality', the survey assessed each respondent's environmental beliefs using a modified New Ecological Paradigm scale (Dunlap *et al.* 2000). In addition, the survey established the respondents' beliefs about a company's responsibility towards the environment and environmental product price and quality (D'Souza, Taghian & Khosla 2007). The respondents were also asked about their purchasing intentions across six factors: 1) price, 2) product quality, 3) service, 4) convenience, 5) brand loyalty, and 6) the company's environmental position. Additional questions were included relating to online behaviour and perceived ability to influence a company's product direction.

The ongoing research had solicited 735 respondents at the time of writing, of which 50% resided in Australia, 20% in the US, 15% in Canada, and 6% in the UK. Sixty-four per cent of the respondents were female, 49% were between 25 to 44 years old, and 53% indicated an education of University or above. The sample was broken up into two groups: those who identified themselves as fast food retail pizza purchasers (48%) and those responding positively to all environmental behaviour measures (25%). A greater proportion of the environmental group was 25 to 44 years old (59%), female (69%), and educated at university (61%).

Looking at intentions for both groups (Table 8.1), taste and service were important, and there was a sense of general appreciation for their pizza provider. The research supports past studies that demonstrate that liking a fast food company does not translate to brand loyalty (Reich *et al.* 2005). Even with the intentions targeted towards fast food retail, price rated lowest of all the intentions to purchase.

Table 8.1 Intentions to purchase

Intention	Pizza (48% of total)	Environment (25% of total)
Service (delivery)	72.08%	69.89%
Service (general)	70.08%	75.81%
Taste (I would go out of my way)	64.68%	68.81%
Taste (best tasting)	84.90%	81.19%
Environment (I would pay more)	41.02%	65.59%
Environment (I would switch)	35.05%	64.52%
Price (I would put up with poor service)	17.95%	12.90%
Price (I want to pay the lowest)	26.50%	20.96%
Brand (I like the company)	73.79%	65.59%
Brand (I purchase from the same company)	37.61%	31.18%
Convenience (nearest)	53.28%	46.78%
Convenience (internet)	40.17%	44.09%

The environmental group indicated they would pay more for pizza from, and switch their purchases to, an environmentally active pizza company. The environmental group cared less about taste, although they would be more willing to go out of their way for a great tasting pizza. General service levels were also more important to the environmental group while the frequent pizza purchasers were more inclined to stay with a provider that delivered the pizza on time.

The environmental group cared less about price than the average frequent pizza purchaser and were less inclined to like their pizza provider or be loyal to one provider. They were also less likely to purchase based on a store being the closest and were more likely to purchase using online ordering if it was available – which correlates to the group being more predisposed to ordering products online.

The environmental group reflected beliefs and intentions based on past behaviour that successfully reinforced their self-image. They believe they can influence a company's direction with their purchases and that environmental products do not need to be more expensive or lower quality. These beliefs are reinforced by past behaviour of purchasing environmental products, thus supporting future intentions to repeat the behaviour.

Champions to engage with community

For companies looking to take advantage of environmentally motivated behaviour, the environmental group is more likely to be on *Facebook* and less likely to be on *Twitter* (Table 8.2). When using these social media channels, this environmental group is also less likely to engage with commercial entities through 'liking' or 'following' a company. However, the results of the research project's distribution method show this group as more likely to champion a cause in which they believe.

Table 8.2 Past behavioural and perceived behaviour control

Behaviour	Pizza (48% of total)	Environment (25% of total)
Facebook	47.86%	51.62%
Twitter	19.66%	14.52%
'Friending'	16.53%	14.52%
Have purchased environment	47.58%	70.97%
Can influence company through purchases	50.71%	52.15%
Frequent online purchaser	37.60%	41.39%
Environmental products cost more	64.67%	53.76%
Environmental products are lower quality	20.22%	15.05%

Upon completing the survey, respondents were offered opportunities to pass their results to other users through email, *Facebook*, *Twitter* and online forums. Overall, 22% of all respondents used email, and 41% of all respondents posted their results on *Facebook* (Table 8.3). The conversion of these referrals contributed to 10% of the total responses.

These numbers were greater for the environmental group – particularly in results from 'email a friend'. Forty-seven per cent of the environmental group emailed their friends about the survey, with 26% of those emailed then completing the survey. This was substantially greater than the group of frequent pizza purchasers. The *Facebook* links for the environmental group were also higher, although not as substantially.

Table 8.3 Referral results

Method	Pizza		Environmental	
	Referred the survey	**Conversion as a result of the referral**	**Referred the survey**	**Conversion as a result of the referral**
Email a friend	9%	10%	47%	26%
Facebook referral	37%	7%	42%	8%
Twitter referral		6		9

Conclusion

The My Pizza Personality research set out to resolve if people who buy pizza care about the environment, and if so, what do they look like and how should companies engage with them. The short answer is 'No, they don't care about the environment', or at least not as much as other contributing intentions to purchase. While 25% of the respondents reflected strong positive environmental beliefs, only 11% of all respondents cared about the environment *and* frequently purchased pizza.

With 48% of the respondents identified as frequent purchasers, pizza companies will try to increase the purchasing behaviour of the remaining 52%. Within that 52% of non-frequent pizza purchasers, only 14% indicated strong environmental beliefs. Based on the results, it would appear that fast food pizza convenience customers do not hold strong environmental beliefs.

There is, however, a valuable segment of educated consumers willing to go out of their way, pay more and promote behaviours that align with their ideals. Consumers holding strong environmental beliefs were more likely to pass information to others within their communities. The results demonstrate that businesses with convenience-based products that also have an environmental differentiation can benefit from gaining the trust of consumer champions within online communities.

References

D'Souza, C, Taghian, M & Khosla, R 2007, 'Examination of environmental beliefs and its impact on the influence of price, quality and demographic characteristics with respect to green purchase intention', *Journal of Targeting, Measurement and Analysis for Marketing*, 15(2), 69-78.

D'Souza, C, Taghian, M, Lamb, P & Peretiatko, R 2006, 'Green decisions: demographics and consumer understanding of environmental labels', *International Journal of Consumer Studies*, 31, 371-376.

Dunlap, RE, Van, KD, Mertig AG & Jones, RE 2000, 'Measuring endorsement of the new ecological paradigm: A revised NEP scale', *Journal of Social Issues*, 56(3), 425–442.

Feichtinger, G, Luhmer, A & Sorger, G 1988, 'Optimal price and advertising policy for a convenience goods retailer', *Marketing Science*, 7(2), 187-201.

Gehrt, KC & Yale, LJ 1993, 'The dimensionality of the convenience phenomenon: a qualitative examination', *Journal of Business and Psychology*, 8(2). 163-180.

Green-Demers, I, Pelletier, L G, & Menard, S 1997, 'The Impact of behavioural difficulty on the saliency of the association between self-determined motivation and environmental behaviours', *Canadian Journal of Behavioural Science*, 29(3),157-166.

Herabadi, AG, Verplanken, B & Knippenberg, AV 2009, 'Consumption experience of impulse buying in Indonesia: emotional arousal and hedonistic considerations', *Asian Journal of Social Psychology*, 12, 20-31.

Hsieh, AT & Chang, WT 2004, The effect of consumer participation on price sensitivity, The Journal of Consumer Affairs, 38(2), 282-296.

Reich, AZ, McCleary, KW, Tepanon, Y & Weaver, PA 2005, 'The impact of product and service quality on brand loyalty: an exploratory investigation of quick-service restaurants', *Journal of Foodservice Business Research*, 8(3), 35-53.

Rokka, J & Moisander, J 2009, 'Environmental dialogue in online communities: Negotiating ecological citizenship among global travellers', *International Journal of Consumer Studies*, 33(2009), 199–205.

Seiders, K, Voss, GB, Grewal, D & Godfrey, AL 2005, 'Do satisfied customers buy more? Examining moderating influences in a retailing context', *Journal of Marketing*, 69, 26-43.

Verplanken, B & Wood, W 2006, 'Interventions to break and create consumer habits'. *American Marketing Association*, 25(1), 90-103.

Verplanken, B, Herabadi, AG, Perry, JA, & Silvera, DH 2005, 'Consumer style and health: The role of impulsive buying in unhealthy eating', *Psychology and Health*, 20(4), 429-441.

Verplanken, B, Hofstee, G, & Janssen, HJW 1998, 'Accessibility of affective versus cognitive components of attitudes', *European Journal of Social Psychology*, 28, 23-35.

The last mile: Pricing for life

NICHOLAS SHIPLEY

ABSTRACT

Despite the concerted efforts of the development community and donors, access to clean water remains a problem for large numbers of rural Cambodians. The health impacts of this are often significant, and Cambodia has one of the highest infant and under-five mortality rates in the region (UNICEF Cambodia 2006).

NGO Inc. is a not-for-profit organisation seeking to promote *sustainable social, economic and environmental* change in Cambodia through the provision of point-of-use water purification. The ceramic water purifier (CWP) is a low-cost and highly effective product capable of producing potable water. NGO Inc. has adopted social marketing practices to disseminate the product and to ensure the program is financially sustainable. It has been identified, however, that when using social marketing practices to serve the socially disadvantaged, setting and maintaining a consistent and affordable price is a critical success factor (Kotler & Roberto 1989, Ch. 9). This is particularly true when considering the adoption of the CWP by Cambodia's rural poor, many of whom live on less than the equivalent of US$1 per day.

Attempts to increase CWP adoption through market channels have been limited by an inability to maintain a consistently low retail price. This has been caused, in part, by the high variability in regional distribution and transportation costs. In particular, the high cost of transporting CWPs that 'last mile' between regional storage facilities and retailers is ultimately passed on to buyers through higher prices. Consequently, there exists an inequity in price accessibility where the poorest people in more remote and difficult to access regions are unable to pay the price. This in turn adversely affects the organisation's goal to increase market adoption and consumer access to affordable point-of-use water purification.

The Last Mile explores the factors leading to the need for affordable water purification in Cambodia and the issues faced by NGO Inc. when considering whether price discrimination can be used to help achieve socially, economically and environmentally sustainable outcomes.

After the war

Cambodia is a nation recovering from widespread devastation caused by thirty years of conflict. Following prolonged civil war and intensive bombing by US forces during the war with Vietnam, between 1975 and 1979 the country was delivered its most severe blow from within by the genocidal Khmer Rouge (Shawcross 1986). During a rule of just under four years, the Khmer Rouge's Democratic Kampuchea regimen systematically dismantled the country's developing economy and culture in a bid to return society to 'Year Zero' and to establish a Maoist agrarian society (Ponchaud 1978). By 1979, Khmer Rouge policies had led to the death of two million or more people and left the country devoid of a functioning government, civil infrastructure, health care and education systems. Khmer Rouge aggressions towards neighbouring Vietnam led to ten years of occupation by Vietnamese armed forces (Chandler 2008) and further civil conflict until 1997.

Today, the people of Cambodia continue to grapple with their country's social and economic reconstruction. The Royal Government of Cambodia (RGC) has been dependant on significant overseas development assistance (ODA) since the Vietnamese military withdrawal in 1989. Delivering essential health services has been a key goal of ODA, with the challenges of reaching 80% of the population living in rural and remote areas and over a third attempting to live on less than one dollar per day (UNICEF 2006).

Increasingly, donors, international non-government organisations and other players partnering with the RGC to support the country's rehabilitation are challenged with ensuring the economic and social sustainability of development initiatives and reducing Cambodia's dependence on ODA (CDC 2010). An important part of achieving this goal is engendering behavioural change amongst rural Cambodians with low levels of education and very limited, if any, disposable income. Influencing cultural beliefs, behaviours and accepted practices that can put health at risk, and increasing access to affordable and preventative health care, is an essential part of improving development outcomes.

Donating people out of poverty

Since the early 1990s, some public health programs have focussed on the provision of free or highly subsidised health products such as condoms and mosquito nets to the rural poor (PSI 2011). However, there is increasing evidence that 'donating people out of poverty' does not always create the conditions that support the long-term adoption and effective usage of preventative health care products (Pollack 2007). Rather, users who make a personal investment in their family's preventative healthcare are more likely to exhibit sustained and improved practices and consequently achieve improvements in their health. Development practitioners and NGOs are therefore turning to social marketing techniques to help to improve awareness, change behaviour and disseminate products that contribute to improvements in health and hygiene. One of the primary goals of this approach is to leverage market forces and existing distribution channels to establish sustainable, market-based, distribution systems (Heierli 2000).

NGO Inc. is one such not-for-profit organisation specialising in the establishment of market-based social development programs. Their approach aims to leverage market systems and ensure the long-term adoption of health-related products that improve people's quality of life. In Cambodia, the organisation has developed a donor-supported social marketing program to help improve the quality of point-of-use water.

Access to clean water: Environmental, social and economic sustainability

It is estimated that 66% of Cambodians are without access to improved drinking water (NIS 2004). Traditional water sources in Cambodia include rivers, ponds, lakes, hand-dug wells, drilled wells and rainwater stored in open containers. All of these pose potential health risks due to bacterial contamination. According to UNICEF Cambodia (2006), diarrhoea along with respiratory infections and vaccine-preventable illness is responsible for Cambodia having the highest infant and under-five mortality rates in the region. The ceramic water purifier (CWP) is a simple and effective product that eliminates roughly 99% of the bacteria that can lead to diarrhoea and chronic illness. It can be simply installed, operated and maintained and field studies have proven that use of the product leads to a measurable reduction in the incidence of water-related disease (Brown 2007, p. 32).

In addition to health benefits, using CWPs can also contribute to a reduction in deforestation and degradation of the natural environment. Since in rural Cambodia it is common practice for people to burn wood to boil water as a means of eradicating bacteria from drinking water, use of the CWP reduces the extent to which households are dependent on collecting wood for fires. This practice is widespread, requiring villagers to spend significant time collecting wood – an increasingly scarce natural resource. Cambodia has the third highest rate of deforestation in the world, with the primary rainforest cover declining from 70% in 1970 to only 3.1% today (Butler 2011).

However, NGO Inc. is all too aware that achieving social and economic sustainability are critical factors in ensuring that the environmental and health benefits offered by CWPs can be achieved. Social sustainability involves effecting attitudinal and behavioural shifts that will result in the adoption of CWPs as a point-of-use filtration device. Economic sustainability involves reducing the subsidisation of acquisition costs to buyers through donor funding. This can be achieved by ensuring the CWP program is financially self-sufficient through the development of profitable and motivated distribution channels, and by pricing the CWP at levels accessible to target users – the rural poor. Maintaining low retail prices is critical in enabling the poorest and most vulnerable Cambodians to acquire a CWP. NGO. Inc. is therefore committed to continually seeking ways to reduce the cost of producing and distributing the CWP.

Reducing the cost of adoption

The challenge of maintaining price accessibility was tackled in three ways: continually controlling and managing production costs; maintaining channel motivation and participation through profit incentives; and, maintaining an affordable retail price.

Manufacturing cost

NGO Inc. introduced the CWP into Cambodia in 2004. A small manufacturing facility was established in Kampong Chhnang province, about 100kms north of the organisation's national office in Phnom Penh. The factory is managed by a workers' cooperative and has a theoretical capacity to produce 30,000 CWP units per annum. Due to glitches in the production process and poor organisation of the workforce, annual production has so far not exceeded 23,000 units, despite market demand significantly exceeding this existing production level. A significant amount of research has been conducted into improving the effectiveness of manufacturing techniques for the clay filtration pot, the only locally produced component. The management team concluded that they had explored all possibilities for reducing the unit cost of production and the factory door price of $6.50 could not be lowered. This ex-factory price enabled NGO Inc. to retain a surplus of 50 cents per CWP which was reinvested into the program. NGO Inc.'s ultimate objective was to obtain sufficient surplus in the ex-factory price to cover the cost of program operations and the national marketing communication campaign, which at the time was being subsidised by donors.

Channel participation and price accessibility

A key goal of NGO. Inc's social marketing program was the achievement of intensive distribution to improve end-user opportunities for CWP adoption. Retailers were established in seventeen of Cambodia's twenty four provinces and they expected to be able to make a fair return from the sale price. CWPs were sold to retailers at a price equal to the fixed manufacturing cost (ex-factory price of $6.50) plus the cost of transportation to the store. The transportation cost consists of a fixed and variable component. The fixed component comprises the unit cost per kilometre of transportation to one of five regional storage warehouses in Phnom Penh, Kampong Cham, Siem Reap, Battambang and Pursat. An additional variable component represents the 'last mile'; the unit kilometre cost of transporting the CWP from NGO Inc. regional warehouses to the retailer. The variability of this cost from one region to another could be a significant in contributing to variations in the actual sale price to retailers (see Table 8.4).

Since stock orders for CWPs were placed by retailers on an ad hoc basis (either triggered by a visit by an NGO Inc. representative or by the retailer's initiation of an order) each last mile delivery was organised through a local transport provider at the time delivery was required. It was felt by the staff of NGO Inc. that this method provided greater flexibility to respond in a timely manner to ad hoc order placement. In the absence of any coordinated national logistics and distribution network, the selection transport service providers for the last mile was limited to local suppliers. These transport service providers included local taxis, tuk tucs and motorbike trailers, which were capable of negotiating the poor roads that larger trucks could not.

Table 8.4 Price to retailer based upon ex-factory plus transportation cost pricing

(All values are in USD) Province	Factory door price (A)	Transport to warehouse (B)	Transport last mile (C)	Cost = A+B+C	Actual sale price to retailer
Siem Reap	6.50	0.77	0.39	7.66	8.50
SvayRieng	6.50	0.53	0.20	7.22	8.20
PreyVeng	6.50	0.53	0.25	7.28	8.20
Kampot	6.50	0.23	0.62	7.35	8.00
Banteay Meanchey	6.50	0.77	0.63	7.90	8.50
KompongThom	6.50	0.77	0.63	7.90	8.50
Pursat	6.50	0.29	0.13	6.92	7.50
Kompong Chhnang	6.50	0.00	0.29	6.79	7.20
Sihanoukville	6.50	0.23	0.63	7.37	7.75
Battambang	6.50	0.29	0.34	7.13	7.50
Koh Kong	6.50	0.23	0.70	7.43	7.75
Kompong Cham	6.50	0.41	0.31	7.22	7.50
Kratie	6.50	0.41	0.93	7.84	8.00
Phnom Penh	6.50	0.23	0.15	6.88	7.00
Takeo	6.50	0.23	0.74	7.48	7.50
Kompong Speu	6.50	0.23	0.51	7.24	7.20
Kandal	6.50	0.23	0.62	7.36	7.20

However, using such local transport providers and accommodating the subsequent cost variations presented further challenges. Since ultimately these transportation costs were absorbed in the delivered-CWP price, it meant that retailers and end-users furthest from the factory were charged a higher price for the CWP.

Achievement of NGO Inc.'s price-equity and accessibility strategy was further challenged by the behaviour and attitudes of the resellers to the CWP. It was difficult to get retailers to participate in stocking the CWP because of the bulkiness of the product and due to the lack of space available in many small rural stores. Those who agreed to distribute the CWP would often sell it at a price higher than the recommended 'social' price of $9.00 in order to maximise their return. This put ownership of a CWP beyond the means of many of the rural poor.

Table 8.5 Retail selling process, margins and sales volume

(All values are in USD) Province	Range of prices to end customers		Min margin for retailer	Max margin for retailer	Average monthly unit sales
	Min	Max			
Takeo	8.50	10.00	1.00	2.50	12
Kampot	9.00	10.00	1.00	2.00	6
Kandal	8.00	9.00	0.80	1.80	13
Kompong Speu	8.00	9.00	0.80	1.80	46
Koh Kong	9.00	9.50	1.25	1.75	2
Sihanoukville	9.00	9.50	1.25	1.75	10
Siem Reap	9.00	10.00	0.50	1.50	102
Kratie	9.00	9.50	1.00	1.50	14
Battambang	8.50	9.00	1.00	1.50	192
Phnom Penh	8.00	8.50	1.00	1.50	147
Prey Veng	9.00	9.50	0.80	1.30	6
Svay Rieng	9.00	9.50	0.80	1.30	8
Kompong Chhnang	8.00	8.50	0.80	1.30	75
Banteay Meanchey	8.50	9.50	-	1.00	29
Kompong Thom	9.00	9.50	0.50	1.00	89
Pursat	8.00	8.50	0.50	1.00	50
Kompong Cham	8.00	8.50	0.50	1.00	55

The CWP was also perceived by retailers as offering a low profit margin when compared to, for example, the sale of pharmaceuticals and competing water purification devices. The social development goals of NGO Inc. were therefore commonly subordinated to the retailer's desire to maximise profit. However it was understood by NGO Inc. that target buyers were highly price-sensitive and that offering the CWP above the recommended price point resulted in diminished sales.

Evaluations suggested that these factors may have contributed to variation in levels of adoption in different provinces.

These factors negatively influenced retailer participation, combined to raise prices to the consumer and reduced the likelihood of improving adoption levels. In Cambodia, families with higher disposable incomes and better education (and therefore greater propensity to buy CWPs) tend to reside in Phnom Penh or closer to provincial centres where the selling price was generally lowest. Conversely, populations with less disposable income and lower levels of education (therefore less likely to purchase a CWP) live in more remote rural locations where transport costs, and therefore the retail price, were higher. These factors created barriers to the achievement of price equity and accessibility. The issues presented are twofold and are summarised as follows:

1. Channel participation – Transportation costs resulted in higher delivered prices to retailers in remote areas. Channel participation could only be maintained by preserving reseller margins which in turn meant raising the sale price to consumers, thus making it difficult to maintain NGO Inc.'s price penetration strategy and maintain a consistent national shelf price of below US$9.

2. Price accessibility – The consequence of the above resulted in an inverse relationship between the selling price around the country and the capacity of target buyers to purchase the CWP.

A case for price discrimination?

The management team at NGO Inc. decided that the time was ripe to review their progress with the CWP National Distribution Programme. A review team was assembled to study the problem and to determine whether it would be possible to introduce a standard and affordable national price to retailers. Such a price would need to be set at around US$8.00 or equivalent, in order that retailers could maintain an acceptable retail price and margin of around $1.50. The team addressed the following questions:

1. Given the current factory door price of $6.50, was NGO. Inc. making a surplus and was this surplus adequate to sustain the program?

2. Was a standard nation-wide retail price of around $8.00 achievable and what might be the consequences of introducing this?

3. Could economies be achieved from the bulk transportation of CWPs (as opposed to the current ad hoc process) to achieve lower average costs to retailers (ex-factory door plus transportation)?

4. If lower average transportation costs could be passed on to retailers in remote locations would this result in lower retail prices to the rural poor?

The team determined that NGO Inc. was achieving a small monthly operating surplus from the ex-factory price of $6.50. However it was noted that total distribution and transportation costs in some provinces were not being fully recovered and that, in provinces where margins were high, sales were also consistently high. This suggested that a higher price to retailers (and subsequent decrease in margin) may impact negatively on retailer engagement and motivation to sell CWPs.

The introduction of a nation-wide price to retailers of US$8.00 would result in an increase in price in ten provinces, no change in two provinces and a decrease in five provinces. Whilst the decrease in prices achieved in five provinces was less than the increase incurred in the ten provinces identified, transportation costs would be covered across the board and a higher overall return would be achieved for NGO Inc.

Sale prices to consumers varied both within provinces and between provinces and ranged from between $8.00 and $10.00. Retailers, it was determined, were achieving margins of between $0.50 up to $2.50. It was unclear what the retailers' response to a reduced margin would be (assuming a maximum retail price of around $9.00) or weather retailers would be prepared to reduce their sale price and margins if sales reduced. This represented a significant risk since there were no mechanisms to assure retailers complied with NGO Inc's. desire to maintain a standard price.

The existing transportation system, it was concluded, generally suited the small scale of orders, the sporadic nature of their timing, condition of the roads and available modes of transport. Existing suppliers of transportation services proved unwilling to agree to contracts involving factory-to-retailer delivery, though they did indicate that economies may be achieved in scheduling bulk deliveries to key regional distribution points.

Pricing for life

Whilst it could be seen that some cost savings could be achieved from the utilisation of bulk transportation methods and by passing on savings achieved by way of lower prices to remote retailers, a critical question remained unanswered. How does this help the poor?

With the average national retail price of around $9.00, acquisition of a CWP represented more than a week's total income for over a third of Cambodia's fourteen million people. Even if a price reduction of 50% could be achieved, for these people the opportunity-cost associated with the purchase of a CWP could be that of an empty stomach. Social *and* economic marketing goals were evidently at odds with one another where this consumer segment was concerned. Clearly the rural poor comprised different segments and alternative pricing strategies needed to be considered for those who were poor but self-sufficient, and those who could be considered destitute. Discriminatory pricing at the levels described would be beneficial for the self-sufficient poor, but other forms of price discrimination, such as smart-subsidies and vouchers, would need consideration to effect an adequate reduction in price for the very poor. For these people, participation in a market-based system was simply not feasible, and NGO. Inc. were literally pricing for life.

References

Brown, J. and Sobesby, M. 2007, *Improving Household Drinking Water Quality – Use of Ceramic Water Filters in Cambodia*, UNICF Water and Sanitation Program, Cambodia

Butler, R.A. 2011. http://rainforests.mongabay.com/20cambodia.htm. Accessed: 19 May 2011.

CDC (Council for the Development of Cambodia), 2010, *The Cambodia Aid Effectiveness Report 2010*, Royal Government of Cambodia

Chandler, D. 2008. *A History of Cambodia*, Westview Publishers, Boulder Colorado.

Heierli, U. 2000, *Poverty Alleviation as a Business – The Market Creation Approach to Development*, Swiss Agency for Development and Cooperation, Switzerland.

Kotler, P. and Roberto, E.L. 1989, *Social Marketing – Strategies for Changing People's Behaviour*, The Free Press, New York.

NIS (National Institute of Statistic, Cambodia). 2000. Cambodia Demographic and Health Survey (CDHS) 2000. Phnom Penh: Ministry of Planning, Kingdom of Cambodia.

Pollack, P. 2007, Out of Poverty – *What Works When Traditional Approaches Fail?* Berrett-Koehler Publishers, San Francisco.

Ponchaud, .F. 1978, *Cambodia Year Zero,* Allen Lane, London

PSI (Population Services International) 2011, http://www.psi.org/cambodia. (Accessed: 19 April 2011)

Shawcross, W. (1986), Sideshow: Kissinger, Nixon and the Destruction of Cambodia, The Hogarth press, London.

UNICEF, Cambodia, 2006, http://www.unicef.org/infobycountry/cambodia_2190.html. Accessed: 1 April 2011.

Strategic brand promotions: Prospects for sustainability marketing

Mark J Kay

Abstract

This paper considers first-mover, niche firms that have developed effective and long term 'green' business models – primarily achieved by proactively educating consumers about sustainability. The Body Shop and other cases are examined to illustrate the risks and pitfalls of green marketing communications. The discussion considers the difficult issues facing firms in developing 'authentic' sustainability communication strategies that change the behaviour of consumers.

Introduction

As businesses make inroads to adopting sustainable business practices, managers logically try to promote an environmentally responsible and socially conscious corporate image. The usual goal is to expand the competitive market appeal for products by utilising 'green' or 'sustainability' promotional messages. Managers hope that these efforts can yield tangible competitive advantages by giving greater salience to their brands. However, there are risks to a singular or overly simple green marketing communications approach, particularly when utilised without forethought and planning.

This paper examines cases of first-mover, niche firms that have been green and sustainably focused for decades, and how the situation has changed as sustainability practices have become part of mainstream business processes. Current green marketing and sustainability efforts face new prospects, particularly as environmental problems increasingly come to light and new sustainability practices are developed. The paper discusses a broad-based, promotional model for effective green marketing efforts to achieve competitive advantages that are compatible with global sustainability concerns, consistent with new approaches to branding.

Sustainability promotions: The strategic problem

The primary problem is that terms such as 'green' and 'natural' can be ambiguous, elusive and even misleading to consumers. As Daniel Goleman (2009) notes, a product promoted as green along a single dimension usually ignores a multitude of adverse social and environmental impacts that are inherent in sourcing, production, product delivery and recycling. Firms may take a few meagre steps to become environmentally and socially responsible, yet these efforts often fall far short in making a firm authentically and fully sustainable.

Sustainability is a growing concern that reaches throughout the supply chain. Most businesses have yet to adequately address the many important challenges that can make sustainability a social reality. As reported in the *New York Times* (Krauss 2007), Home Depot, an American retailer of home improvement and construction products, invited manufactures to make their pitch to have products included in its new 'Eco Options' marketing campaign. The manufacturers that responded represented more than 60,000 products – about a third of the 176,000 products the chain sells. Many managers claimed to the retailer that their products could be considered 'environmentally friendly', but in fact, many of those green claims were inconsistent at best (if not deceptive). For example, plastic is not necessarily ecologically better than wood simply because it does not destroy trees; and wood products are not better just because it is a renewable material. As a result of the store's analysis, only about 2,500 products actually met Home Depot's green marketing criteria. This small number implies a widespread lack of proficiency in establishing green business practices among suppliers. However, the Home Depot's program was reported successful – sales of Eco Options products increased by an average of about 10 per cent in the initial months.

Consumers often show interest in green products, and many educated customers are aware that being sustainable is not a simple matter of a choice of materials. As new varieties of green product claims have proliferated, however, consumers have become suspicious, or at least highly sceptical (Mohr, Eroglu & Ellen 1998). As interest in sustainability grows, there are clearly business opportunities for sustainable firms. Yet many promotional efforts are being cynically dismissed by environmentalists as 'mere greenwash'.

In fact, firms that try to position their products as green may be subject to increased attention. Green product claims need to be real and substantial ones. Research shows that while the level of public concern for the environment has grown (Dunlap & Mertig 1992), support for the environment through pro-environmental purchasing by consumers is frequently lacking (Ottman 1998). The problem is that green marketing may not be very effective, particularly if benefits touted as green are not relevant or engaging to consumers (Pickett-Baker & Ozaki 2008). As a result, new green claims do not necessarily result in immediate sales revenue gains to targeted green customer segments, and green consumers may be suspicious of corporate motives (D'Souza *et al.* 2006; Kay 2006). To be effective, green marketing and promotional claims need to be perceived as contributing real value to the planet, thus providing an enhanced level of quality to customers.

More importantly, firms may get into trouble when they try to position their products as green. In a prominent case, Nike was charged with negligent misrepresentation, fraud and deceit in promotional communications on its global labour practices during the 1990s. As a result, the Nike brand became the focus of a variety of controversies in the media, including problems in globalisation, truth in advertising, and worker treatment. These were repeatedly highlighted and amplified by the press during the five year duration (1997–2002) of the *Nike v. Kasky* case. As the legal case slowly worked its way through the US court system, it kept disturbing questions about Nike's corporate practices in the news.

Sustainability concerns have certainly become more widely recognised as having social value in many communities, particularly as severe environmental problems such as the BP disaster surface in the media. There remain many questions as to how to run effective green promotions as these problems surface. Corporate critics and watchdogs such as CorpWatch[3] have suggested that firms may merely 'pose' as friends of the environment by employing greenwash promotional tactics that are without any real or substantial basis in the activities, corporate cultures or values of those firms. CorpWatch further warns that behind such green public relations efforts may lurk an even more pernicious corporate strategy that is primarily

---

[3] CorpWatch is a US non-profit investigative research group that uses journalism to expose corporate malfeasance and to advocate for corporate accountability and transparency (see www.corpwatch.org).

political (they call it 'deep greenwash'), namely to avoid the enactment of binding legislation and appropriate regulation (see Karliner 2001).

Firms need to be able to proactively consider the possible counter-arguments and attacks that may develop in formulating authentic green communication strategies. When increased attention is drawn to weak industry environmental standards or poor corporate norms, the behaviour of every firm in the industry may be collaterally affected. For example, PETA (People for the Ethical Treatment of Animals) campaigned first against McDonald's and later KFC, over the inhumane treatment of animals (Seijts & Sneider 2003, 2005). The PETA campaign was intended to raise issues for all other fast food companies with similar practices; the NGO simply choose the biggest targets. Firms need to change their organisational practices in response to these NGO change agents and become more alert to the growing salience of sustainability concerns and issues – even when the firm is not the immediate subject of public scrutiny.

In short, firms now have much more to worry about than just the competition. If important sustainability issues are highlighted to consumers by NGOs, this can legitimately draw attention to real social and environmental problems. For companies, game-changing shifts in consumer perceptions can occur. Firms need to proactively assess their vulnerabilities and develop strategies to cope with public reactions to a range of issues that are becoming increasingly relevant, including supply chain sourcing, energy use, toxic material use, waste disposal and recycling.

Firms that actively position themselves as responsibly green and sustainable can sharply raise public expectations of appropriate corporate behaviour, and ultimately change standards. However, firms that vigorously promote their environmental record or position themselves as leaders in social responsibility initiatives may be subject to much higher levels of public scrutiny. The Body Shop benefitted from publicity of its sourcing practices and materials, but an article published in *Business Ethics* asserted that the firm was misleading consumers, charging that they were selling products that were not 'all-natural' (Entine 1994). The resulting image sharply affected the firm's brand image.

Troubles have continued at The Body Shop. The provocatively vocal and controversial founder, Anita Roddick, left the executive ranks of the company, and it has continued to struggle with its corporate brand and position in the market. Among the pitfalls, these difficulties have allowed room for the store's competitor, Bath and Body Works, to imitate its products and marketing messages. Today, Bath and Body Works populates its stores with its branded 'All-Natural' and '100% Pure' product lines, effectively gaining market share through imitation with similar types of green appeal.

The risks and potential hazards of green or sustainable promotional approaches require special consideration since ecological and social sustainability practices can become particularly charged social concerns. Managers should proactively prepare themselves to develop and defend their corporate sustainability efforts to maintain the legitimacy of their enterprise. Sustainability needs to be part of systematic and company-wide efforts, authentically incorporated into values, work processes and business practices throughout the firm. As argued by McDonagh (1998), marketing communications need to be fundamentally and systematically integrated into a sustainable communications approach to marketing discourse.

Important organisational and branding issues are at stake in employing green promotional strategies. In fact, green product claims may be severely hindered by consumer perceptions of product effectiveness. For example, when it comes to detergents, the green attribute may be associated with less effective cleaning. Given that such perceptions are factually false, the situation forces many firms to become much more proactive in the process of educating consumers and overcoming their perceptual biases. Toyota achieved a notable reputation with the success of it hybrid cars, enhanced through their quality image. Yet executives managed to tarnish its sterling image with their belated and lame reactions to break system malfunctions.

A strategic branding model: The 'sustainability promoting' firm

A few firms have been able to develop stable, effective and relatively long-term, sustainable business models. Patagonia, Stonyfield Farms, The Body Shop and Ben & Jerry's each started as niche businesses that were based on values passionately held by their founders. Unlike other small businesses, the founders were driven by strong value commitments. They held strong beliefs about business practices and each carefully crafted mission and values statements to communicate their specific goals.

Rather than run their businesses solely as competitive enterprises and simply give a share of their profits to charity, the founders of these firms put forward a social mission and type of political agenda. Unlike other so-called 'values driven' organisations (Barrett 2006), these firms initiated programs to adopt socially responsible and sustainable practices well in advance of the 1992 United Nations Conference in Rio de Janeiro or other hallmark sustainability initiatives. The point is that these firms did not adopt green marketing or responsibility practices merely as one among several exploitive techniques for selling (Prakash 2002). Instead, they were committed to sustainability values as a core philosophy that shaped fundamental business practices.

These firms influenced consumers primarily by educating them, initiating an effort to shift the scale and pattern of consumption values. The resulting products and company efforts affected the expectations, choices, behaviours and lifestyles of consumers. Such educational efforts have grown to be key components of emerging 'sustainable consumption' promotional practices (see Fuchs & Lorek 2004; Jackson 2003).

'Sustainability promoting values' are the essence of these companies and are embodied in their business practices. These values are important in providing greater authenticity to these firms, particularly as they come to define and develop strong corporate brands (Kay 2006). Patagonia, for example, has remained at the leading edge of sustainability marketing by being authentically engaged in shaping environmental perceptions through educating customers about the benefits of organic fibres. Being well established as a brand, the Patagonia case example illustrates that correctly executed sustainable marketing promotions can help to establish social legitimacy and yield important corporate branding advantages. Firms such as The Body Shop and Ben & Jerry's have also retained some sustainability branding advantages, even in the context of their changed corporate ownership.

Changing consumer consumption behaviours, particularly those in advanced economies, is highly important to achieving global sustainability goals. The efforts of these sustainability promoting firms have become particularly noteworthy. Stimulating the development of market-oriented mechanisms to achieve the global sustainability initiatives (including those being endorsed by the United Nations Development Program) requires the support of effective branding used to influence behaviour. While promotional branding strategies are now understood to be critically important to businesses, information and education-based promotional strategies deserve additional consideration in the context of global sustainability initiatives. Global attitudes to environmental and social sustainability issues can be affected by the effective use of branding.

Conclusions

Green brands can effectively and authentically promote sustainable consumption practices. Established green brands have primarily been successful by educating consumers about sustainability concerns and practices. In the process, this effort has strengthened their brand franchise and gradually grown their niche to reach mainstream consumers. These companies have strategically promoted the quality of their brands as sustainability enhancing organisations, while changing consumption practices. This is an effective business 'brand promotional model' that will have increasing relevance as sustainability concerns expand in the coming decades.

References

Barrett. Richard (2006), *Building a Values-Driven Organization: A Whole System Approach to Cultural Transformation*, Oxford: Butterworth-Heinemann Publishers.

Dunlap, Riley and Angela Mertig, 1992, *American environmentalism: the U.S. environmental movement, 1970-1990*, New York: Tayor and Francis.

D'Souza, Clare Mehdi Taghian, Peter Lamb, Roman Peretiatkos, 2006, "Green products and corporate strategy: an empirical investigation," *Society and Business Review*, Vol. 1, 2, pp.144 – 157.

Entine, Jon, (1994) "Shattered Image," *Business Ethics*, London.

Fuchs, Doris and Sylvia Lorek (2004), "Sustainable Consumption", Nr. 4, March 2004, Sustainable Europe Research Institute (SERI).

Goleman, Daniel, 2009, *Ecological Intelligence*, NY: Random House (the excerpt from the book, "Green" Is a Mirage," can also be accessed at: http://www.danielgoleman.info/2009/04/28/green-is-a-mirage).

Jackson, Tim, 2003, "Policies for Sustainable Consumption: A report to the Sustainable Development Commission, Centre for Environmental Strategy, University of Surrey.

Kay, Mark J., 2006, Strong Brands and Corporate Brands, *The European Journal of Marketing*, Vol. 40, No. 7/8, pp. 742-760.

Karliner, Joshua, 2001, A Brief History of Greenwash, accessed at http://www.corpwatch.org/article.php?id=243

Krauss, Clifford, 2007, *New York Times*, "Can They Really Call the Chainsaw Eco-Friendly?" June 25.

Kasky v. Nike, Inc., 45 P.3d 243, 247, 256 (Cal. 2002).

McDonagh, Pierre, 1998, "Towards a theory of sustainable communications in risk society," *Journal of Marketing Management*, 14(6): 591-622.

Mohr, L., D. Eroglu, and P. Ellen, 1998, "The development and testing of a measure of skepticism towards environmental claims in marketers' communications," *Journal of Consumer Affairs*, 32: 30–55.

Ottman, J., 1998, *Green Marketing: Opportunity for Innovation*, NTC-McGraw-Hill, New York, NY.

Pickett-Baker, Josephine and Ritsuko Ozaki, 2008, "Pro-environmental products: marketing influence on consumer purchase decision," *Journal of Consumer Marketing*, Vol. 25, 5, pp. 281 – 293.

Prakash, Aseem, 2002, "Green Marketing, Public Policy, and Managerial Strategies," *Business Strategy and the Environment*, vol. 11, pp. 285–297

Seijts, Gerard and Michael Sneider, 2003, PETA's "Kentuck Fried Cruelty, Inc." Campaign, Ivey Case # 903C45, University of Western Ontario.

Seijts, Gerard and Michael Sneider, 2005, PETA Escalation, Ivey Case # 905C16, University of Western Ontario.

A sustainability perspective on domestic electricity usage: Distribution, consumption, behavioural and marketing issues

CHRISTOPHER HODKINSON

ABSTRACT

Electricity is a convenient household energy source but there is increasing environmental concern and awareness about the resultant household carbon footprint. Because most consumers understand relatively little about the electrical system and the consumption levels of the devices that provide them with such convenience, they are at a loss to understand how to reduce their energy usage and/or costs while maintaining their lifestyle. This situation is compounded by the current lack of an effective feedback system that could be used to identify energy wasting behaviours. This paper addresses these issues and identifies social and general marketing strategies that, in combination with recent technical advances, may provide household consumers with the opportunity to review and modify their consumption behaviour to benefit themselves and the environment.

Introduction

'Reduce, reuse and recycle' is the catchcry of many of today's green organisations. However, electricity is neither reusable nor recyclable in the domestic situation; thus, for most consumers reducing domestic electricity consumption is the remaining option for improving household sustainability. Despite the widespread household acceptance of that goal, a major reduction in domestic electricity consumption has not occurred in Australia. There are many reasons for this, including a general lack of understanding of the electricity distribution system, electricity tariff structures, power usage in the home, and a lack of effective feedback mechanisms to assist motivated consumers to monitor and reduce their consumption. This paper discusses these issues and identifies relevant marketing strategies to assist in achieving a reduction in household electricity usage.

Australia's per capita emissions are the highest in the OECD and among the highest in the world, and per head electricity consumption is 22% above the OECD average (Garnaut 2008). The high rate of emissions is largely due to the emission intensity of Australian electricity generation which accounts for almost 40% of Australia's greenhouse gas emissions (DCCEE 2010). Because of this, Australia faces a considerable challenge in reducing its emissions of greenhouse gases. The reduction may be accomplished via two tactics, namely (1) reducing the emissions caused by electricity generation, and (2) reducing electricity usage. The former may be achieved by a combination of measures including reducing the reliance on fossil fuels for power generation, using less emission-intensive fossil fuels, and utilising new technologies such as carbon sequestration if it proves viable. This paper addresses the latter, that is, controlling and/or reducing electricity usage specifically in the home.

The domestic (in-home) consumption of energy comprises some 13% of Australia's total energy consumption and it is a significant contributor to Australia's carbon footprint. Approximately 49% of household energy used is supplied by electricity (ABS 2010). Since 1961, electricity usage per capita has increased by 555%, and this figure would be higher but for the increased usage of gas as a form of energy in home and industry (Sachdeva & Wallis 2010). While total household energy use marginally decreased (~1%) between 2001 and 2002, and 2006 and 2007, domestic electricity usage per head has increased by around 15% during the same period (ABS 2010). Contributing factors include the increased use of air conditioning in the home and an increase in the number, type, and use of other electrical appliances. Multiple PCs in homes are now regarded almost as a necessity, especially for education, and other items previously regarded as luxuries such as dishwashers and home theatre systems have become more common. By way of example, since 2005, 33% of Australian homes have had more than one refrigerator, 42% have a dishwasher and 68% at least one personal computer (ABS 2010). While to a certain extent technical advances in appliance efficiency and home insulation offset the proliferation of appliances and usage, consumption tends to outweigh these improvements (Midden, Kaiser & McCalley 2007). While the introduction of national house energy rating schemes is making consumers and builders aware of the energy consumption of dwellings, this initiative can only influence new constructions or major rebuilds. Thus, the impact of such rating schemes on household energy usage will not become evident for some years as more efficient homes become part of the housing stock. By contrast, for householders in existing dwellings, there are relatively few options available apart from considering their current energy usage.

On first consideration, because householders wish to maintain their level of comfort and convenience, attempts to reduce domestic electricity consumption may appear to be futile and of limited social benefit. However, such is not the case. In fact, the characteristics of domestic electricity consumption make it problematic in terms of power generation and supply. There are a number of reasons for this which, when explained, show that using power more wisely in the home provides benefits extending beyond its walls.

The characteristics of domestic electricity consumption

Because much of Australia is urbanised, the daily cycle of urban living is a major driver of the uneven demand for electricity. The cycle of daily activity typically commences with making tea (e.g. boiling an electric kettle) and cooking breakfast (using a stove or microwave), showering (water heating), and perhaps running the dishwasher and/or the washing machine and thence departing for work. The simultaneous or concentrated use of these appliances in this relatively brief time period of typically around two hours incurs a high electrical demand, in other words, a high *rate* of use of electricity. During the day, the house of the typical family is empty with little electrical load apart from that required by the refrigerator to maintain its temperature.

The second peak electricity consumption period commences when the family returns later in the afternoon. The television may be turned on, and the refrigerator is typically opened more frequently thus requiring more energy to re-cool its contents. In addition, the washing machine again may be run and cooking commenced for the evening meal. Lights will also be turned on as darkness approaches and PCs and a range of entertainment devices including televisions will be in use at the traditional peak family viewing times. Depending on the season and the energy sources used in the household, space heating may also be used. Water heating will be at a premium in the evening with washing up and bathing adding to the energy demand. This high level of energy usage will continue until later in the evening. On cold winter days the higher household demand tends to occur in the evening because the afternoon-evening activity period is of longer duration, and often involves more activities (and appliances) than the shorter morning domestic peak. By contrast, in the summer months the time of peak electrical demand for the whole electricity system (i.e. domestic and industrial) tends to be in the middle of the day due to the air conditioning load. Whether this is also true for an individual household depends upon the ambient temperature, the occupancy of the house during the day, the extent of its air conditioning, insulation, and other variables. The rapid increase in the market penetration of domestic air conditioners has contributed to supply system overloads (i.e. demand exceeding supply) and resulted in power 'outages' (i.e. power cuts) and 'brown-outs' in which the supply system struggles to maintain the correct voltage under the excessive load.

It can be seen from this that most households have two energy usage peak periods during their daily cycle. For any given household, season, climate, geographic location, daylight saving, and day of week (i.e. work/weekend) all have an effect on the cycle and the electrical demand. The electricity generating companies and the electricity retailers have to accommodate the simultaneous demand of many thousands of homes with similar daily cycles. In addition, households have a relatively high cost of supply because they use relatively little energy for each supply connection and tend to have high peak energy usage at much the same time. At present there is little that the average householder can do to move their peak electrical usage to another time. Domestic supplies also tend to have high administrative costs due to frequent changes in tenancy and account holder and high levels of customer 'churn' caused by competition between the large number of new retailers. In addition, there is the financial impact of the tardy payment of accounts. For all of these reasons, domestic consumers are problematic for electricity suppliers. By contrast, industrial power users consume larger amounts of power per connection and often have a more even consumption pattern due to 24 hour operation or sophisticated control systems which schedule operations to achieve a steadier demand, that is, a more even rate of use.

The cyclic domestic load places significant demands upon the whole electricity supply system from the power stations through to power outlets in the home. The provision of extra power generation capacity and the extra capacity in substations and power lines is costly to the electricity suppliers, their consumers and the society. Nationally, the peak demand periods comprise just 0.29% of each entire year of electricity supply (i.e. about 25 hours per year), yet the expenditure required to strengthen the system to safely accommodate these peaks accounts for some 18% of the wholesale cost of electricity (Sachdeva & Wallis 2010). In addition, peak demand is supplied by more expensive forms of electricity generation such as hydroelectric and gas fired power stations. These higher costs for generation and system reinforcement are of course passed on to the householder and other users. If the domestic *peak* loads could be moderated, the cost of the electricity infrastructure would be significantly reduced. If, in addition, domestic electricity usage could also be reduced, there would be additional savings in household revenue and most importantly greenhouse gas emissions via a reduction in each household's carbon footprint[4].

---

[4] At present in Australia most of the gas fired power stations, which are generally more expensive to run, are used to boost generation in peak load times. This leaves the more emission-intensive coal fired power stations to supply the base load. Thus, at present any reduction in peak load that reduces the need for the gas fired power stations in fact creates a *greater* rate of emissions per unit used. Even with considerable governmental investment in renewable energy technologies, coal would still be used for some time to supply the base electrical load due to the increased expense and often intermittent nature of renewable energy generation methods (refer Needham 2008).

Research into Australian household electricity consumption shows that, for a variety of reasons, up to 90% of domestic users have taken some steps to limit their electricity consumption (ABS 2008). Despite this widespread sentiment, domestic electricity consumption continues to increase. While the already mentioned increase in the number of types of domestic appliances militates against decreased energy usage, there is certainly a will among consumers to use energy more efficiently in the home.

Electricity conservation is a complex matter that begins with the selection of appliances for the home from a range of appliances with varying energy efficiencies. Gardner and Stern (2008) refer to such choices as 'efficiency behaviours', which they define as 'one-time actions with a lasting impact'. However, such terminology may be confusing to many who might regard 'efficiency behaviours' as referring to energy-saving techniques such as only boiling the minimum water required when using an electric jug. It may be more appropriate to consider low energy appliances as characteristics of an individual household's infrastructure to more clearly separate it from electricity consumption behaviours. Whatever the range of appliances present in a home, once a consumption history has been established, a reduction in electricity use will require a change in the usage behaviour of the domestic energy consumers.

It is here that the domestic solar generation of electricity should be discussed in relation to the objective of a reduction in a household's electricity usage. Over the past decade there has been a significant reduction in the cost of solar cells and their associated control systems. This together with the government incentives has led many consumers to install systems which 'feed back' electricity to the distribution system during daylight hours. While household solar installations generate small amounts of power with a lower carbon footprint, they only lower net household electricity usage[5] and they have no effect on the total or gross amount of electricity used by a household.

Issues facing consumers in reducing domestic electricity consumption

Electricity is an unusual good. It is invisible to the user (Darby 2006; Fischer 2008) and it is usually paid for in arrears i.e. after the usage. In addition, usage does not leave any consumption clues such as 'diminishing stock' (Fischer 2008). Electricity is not socially visible and therefore is not a visible lifestyle element (Birzle-Harder & Gotz 2001 – translated and cited in Fischer 2008). It is used to provide services such as cooling drinks or warming a room, the costs of which are not obvious to the

---

However, the establishment of a 'carbon price' would offset this situation making it less economic for the 'dirtier' power stations to continue production thus speeding their phasing out.

[5] 'Net' electricity usage for a household = energy 'imported' from the distribution system *minus* the energy 'exported' to the distribution system (from the solar cells array). By contrast, 'gross' electricity usage for a household = energy 'imported' from the distribution system *plus* any energy from the solar cells array utilised inside the house (i.e. not 'exported' to the distribution system).

householder. Thus, acts of electricity consumption take place essentially without knowledge of the cost. Kempton and Layne (1994) drew the parallel of a grocery store totally without price markings and with only a monthly bill. They asked how grocery shoppers could economise under such a billing regime. While consumers may have in mind a rough dollar value of their seasonal account, they know little else apart from the amount of their typical usage. It is little wonder that consumers find their total usage hard to estimate subjectively.

With respect to changing environmental behaviour, householders clearly want to reduce their electricity consumption for environmental or economic reasons (or both) but may be uncertain how to do so. There are many reasons for this. Most people lack awareness and understanding about how their everyday behaviours affect the environment (Froehlich, Findlater & Landay 2010). To proactively and effectively address household electricity usage requires an understanding of the electricity distribution system, electricity tariffs and their implications, and above all, the provision of effective consumer feedback mechanisms which are currently lacking. These deficiencies become evident when one considers the existing feedback system available to consumers when seeking to change their electricity consumption habits.

In most cases, the only feedback the account holder receives is the electricity retailer's account, in which the dollar amount and the due date tend to be the primary items of concern. In most cases the account refers to consumption at least 90 days in the past. In some countries it is only obligatory for the supplier to read the meter every two years, with the intervening accounts being estimated and providing no usable feedback at all (Darby 2006). Even if the householder takes the trouble to read their (traditional/conventional) meter, it does not reveal *which* specific behaviours contributed most to electricity use (Steg & Vlek 2009). The newer smart meters have the potential to improve this situation, but only if they are paired with a convenient readout available inside the house. Even then, it requires a motivated and diligent consumer to monitor consumption to learn which behaviours are energy intensive and which should be avoided or modified to minimise usage or cost under a particular tariff. Furthermore, most consumers have little understanding of the meaning of the units of electrical consumption and this tends to be further compounded by little understanding of the various tariffs (i.e. the hierarchy of consumption charges) under which their electricity is supplied and charges accrued. In summary, the electricity account is typically an 'indirect' feedback method (Darby 2006) which is of little assistance to the account holder in modifying their electricity consumption behaviour. Even if the electricity bill includes histograms of the consumption over the last three quarters, at best the consumer can only make a general mental note of their typical energy usage behaviour in relation to particular appliances. This may result in resolutions to 'use the air conditioner less' or 'not watch so much television'.

In many cases the bill-reducing resolutions formed are misguided, because the majority of consumers do not understand the electrical load incurred by their different appliances and have only a vague idea of how much energy they are using for different purposes (Darby 2006). Depending on the type of television, its contribution to the total energy usage may not be large. Even if the consumer takes the trouble to read the electrical ratings plate on each device there may be an additional confounding factor, namely that of the duty cycle of the appliance. By way of example, while an electric kettle may have a high energy rating it consumes power for only a short time when boiling the required amount of water. By contrast, fan heaters which make a consistent 'whirr' typically give no indication as to whether their heating element is on or off. In cold conditions they can consume prodigious amounts of energy, a fact which may not become specifically evident even when the next electricity account arrives. Thus the unmanaged electricity consumption cycle is perpetuated.

In summary, due to the lengthy retrospectivity of the electricity account, the relative mystery of the basis of the charges and differences in appliances' consumption, consumers have little opportunity to modify their electricity consumption behaviour because there is no effective feedback system. Consumers who seek to modify energy consumption behaviour on the basis of their memory of activities undertaken ninety or more days previously are met with a virtually impossible task. Similar observations have been made with regard to domestic water use (e.g. Midden, Kaiser & McCalley 2007; Willis *et al.* 2010).

Given the ABS (2008) survey finding that up to 90% of domestic users took some steps to limit their electricity consumption, it is reasonable to assume that the goal of most householders is to live comfortably while minimising their electricity usage and cost. On this basis, if a consumer and their household comprise a system for controlling electricity consumption across a diverse range of applications then it would be what engineers term an 'open loop' system because it does not use feedback to determine if its output goal has been achieved. This situation remains the same whether consumers are driven to reduce their electricity consumption for economic reasons or whether they are driven by green sentiments and the wish to reduce their carbon footprint.

Electricity tariffs and 'smart meters'

Electricity tariffs (i.e. the scale of charges) are an integral part of the electricity distribution system. Economists consider that they provide price 'signals' to the marketplace but these are not sufficient measures by themselves to reduce energy use (Sachdeva & Wallis 2010). However, as previously discussed, many consumers have little understanding of the tariff structures under which they are charged, and the feedback obtained from current electricity bills is typically ineffective in changing either usage or demand. Such cost signals are supposed to discourage high consumption, limit demand or time-shift high demand periods. However, there are practical difficulties with such expectations as the following discussion of tariff structures will show.

Until recently, the most common domestic tariff for general power usage was the block tariff structure. In block tariff structures, the first units (e.g. the first 100 KWh) per month are charged at a specific rate and typically the next block (e.g. 101-10000 KWh) will be charged at another rate. In addition there will be a minimum charge per month or a fixed supply charge. Arguments rage over the social equity of block tariffs with some retailers charging a lower subsidised rate per unit for the first block compared to the second. This is typically set at a 'lifeline' level of electricity consumption. This approach assumes that low income earners are low users, which is not necessarily the case (Filipović & Tanić 2009). In cases where the second consumption block is charged at a *higher* unit rate, this could conceivably discourage higher consumption but only if the user: (a) cares about their level of consumption, (b) understands the tariff, (c) understands the account, and (d) obtains sufficient feedback from the bill to understand their usage behaviour and modify it. However, many electricity retailers have *reducing* charges for successively higher blocks of usage; thus as a household's consumption rises, the average charge per unit drops. This can be seen as either a disincentive to moderate power consumption or as an iniquitous measure because those with a wealthier lifestyle effectively receive a discount compared with others on a lifeline level of electricity consumption. In summary, block tariffs are generally not seen as an effective mechanism for modifying household electricity consumption (for an overview see: Monash Centre for Regulatory Studies 2009).

Houses with solar cell arrays exporting electricity to the distribution system require a special Feed-in Tariff (FiT)[6] which allows for the amount of energy exported to the distribution system. Ideally, the householder should receive a credit for every unit of electricity generated by their solar cells. Such a tariff is referred to as a *gross* FiT. However, in many states the tariffs only allow the householder a credit for any *net* energy generated over and above their usage at that point in time, that is, a *net* FiT. The effect of net FiTs is that solar arrays are less beneficial to businesses and homes which use electricity during daylight hours. This has angered green groups who claim that makes it more difficult to calculate the payoff for a solar array, discourages uptake, and inhibits the growth of the solar industry which would in turn lower equipment costs. It also 'raises equity issues as it disadvantages stay at home parents, people who work from home (who are reducing travel related carbon emissions) and also retirees... these people are disadvantaged as they will be using a larger portion (if not all) of the electricity they generate, compared to those households where everyone leaves their home for work during the day' (Local Power 2011).

Traditionally domestic electricity meters have only recorded the *amount* of electricity consumed without any record of the time of use. Thus, they total the amount of energy rather than recording the rate at which it was used, or when it was used. Most of the new 'smart meters' can meter and supply data on more than one supply; for example, many houses have separate supplies for general power usage and (electric) water heating. They also have the ability to control (i.e. switch

---

[6] Interestingly, in many Australian states, feeding electricity back into the distribution system was prohibited and penalised in the electricity regulations. The exception was cases where institutions such as sugar mills and sewerage plants generated excess power typically from by-products (bagasse and biomass respectively) in which formal energy export agreements were established with the electrical supplier. However, these were a rarity.

off) non-essential load such as storage-type water heating during periods of peak system load such as the morning and/or evening domestic peaks. This benefits the whole electrical network, and tariffs allowing for such supply interruption to non-essential equipment are traditionally cheaper than the continuous supply tariffs used in the rest of the house. The introduction of new electronic smart meters for domestic premises also presents an opportunity to introduce more sophisticated tariffs that have the potential to modify consumption and demand. However, it should be emphasised that this can only occur in coordination with proactive householder behaviour and only in households where it is possible to defer or modify electricity consuming activities. In other words, the benefit of such meters in modifying aggregated system demand relies upon a change in the behaviour of literally millions of households. This in turn requires the usage data to be available at a convenient location within the house. Since most electricity meters are still located outside, and few householders have internal usage displays, necessarily convenient real-time feedback is still not available despite the very significant expenditure incurred to date in the installation of domestic smart meters.

The tariff structure favoured for modifying the pattern of household electricity demand is the 'Time-of-Use' (TOU) tariff structure. However, TOU tariff implementation requires the installation of smart meters on every household supply in a retailer's area. Whilst the previous generation of electricity meters made no distinction between the times of day when power was consumed, the smart meters can be programmed to segment usage into various time periods of the day. Typically such domestic TOU tariffs designate three charge levels with the high to low unit cost periods referred to respectively as 'peak', shoulder' and 'off-peak'. Although the times may vary between electricity retailers, typically peak rates cover at least the morning high demand period of domestic use and the cheapest rate is typically overnight from about 10–11 pm to 6–7 am. Demand moderation via TOU implementation relies upon aware householders who are able to defer their usage, moving elements of their consumption from high price-per-unit periods to lower price-per-unit periods. While residential trials of TOU tariffs have been shown to flatten the load cycle (e.g. Herter 2007) by approximately 5% (Newsham & Bowker 2010) on their own, they have not been shown to reduce total domestic electricity usage (Newsham & Bowker 2010)[7].

In most regions of Australia domestic TOU tariffs are yet to be implemented and most electricity suppliers are in the roll-out phase of fitting the new smart meters to the homes of millions of customers. These smart meters can be read remotely by the electricity retailer thus making potential savings on meter reading staff (and thus costs) and obviating the need to regularly enter premises for that purpose. In addition, if provision is made by the retailer, the new meters can supply real-time

---

[7] These new metering technologies also make possible the introduction of 'live' variable cost tariffs in which the cost of domestic energy reflects the generation and supply system's actual cost from minute to minute. The effective use of such domestic tariff structures raises technical, application, and behavioural issues beyond the scope of this paper.

or near real-time usage data to the householder via a web page or by a portable or fixed readout unit inside the house. The utility of web page-based energy monitoring is questionable, especially if the data are not real time. The householder also requires a laptop or mobile device to make it useably convenient. By contrast, householders will generally be charged for the portable remote readouts which can be moved conveniently around the home – if indeed they are made available by the electricity retailer. While many electricity retailers are indicating that they will introduce an opt-in web-based system of usage information supply to the householder, others have as yet to make policy decisions about the type, cost, availability and responsibility for distributing and maintaining the in-home readout units. The provision of such feedback devices has been found to reduce overall usage by 5–15%. This illustrates the valuable role of feedback in enabling householders to change their energy use patterns (Sachdeva & Wallis 2010).

Changing energy usage behaviour – a marketing task

The current activity phase concentrates largely on smart meter installation (i.e. roll-out), and while there is some customer information available, much of the material makes little reference to the changes in customer behaviour that may be required under such tariff regimes if the householder is to avoid additional expense. The word 'may' is used here because not all customers will have a usage pattern that leads to higher charges under TOU tariffs. However, many customers will unknowingly have such patterns because *when* they use electricity has never been an issue, only the amount of power consumed over a lengthy period. In many cases maximising TOU tariff benefits or avoiding higher aggregate charges would require consumers to address the usage habits of a lifetime. The availability of convenient in-home readouts would seem to be an instrumental first step in providing the necessary feedback by which consumers could familiarise themselves with the financial and other impacts of their electricity usage behaviours. The foregoing discussions show that considerable customer education would be required to achieve the peak and/or usage reduction objectives desired by the electricity retailers.

From the marketing viewpoint, if usage reduction is the objective, it could be regarded as a de-marketing task. However, since household equipment diversification and usage historically appear to overcome gains in appliance efficiency, it is likely that the environmental objective of reduced domestic consumption will not be achieved. By contrast, a more achievable goal is the flattening of peak demand to create a more even system demand. Certainly the marketing challenge with regard to smart meters and TOU domestic tariffs is significant and to be effective it must transcend ethnic, educational, literacy, age and other limitations present in the customer base. If these marketing and educational barriers are not overcome, the effect of the introduction of smart meters and TOU domestic tariffs will be little more than a tariff increase which may have social and political ramifications. To date, perhaps because the metering and tariff arrangements have been the purview of engineers, the focus has tended to be on technical rather than human issues. This is ironic because the potential changes in household energy consumption made possible by recent technical advances rely for their success upon changing human behaviour. Inducing this change is the key to advancement (e.g. Sachdeva & Wallis 2010). Environmental psychologists have been working in the area of behavioural change for a number of years. It is informative to consider their body of research findings when designing what is essentially a social marketing program aiming to improve society's wellbeing.

Possible bases of behavioural change

Since the 1970s (e.g. Ellis & Gaskell 1978) psychologists and others addressing the issue of reducing household energy consumption realised that much of the behaviour that led to higher than needed consumption was habitual (e.g. Stephenson *et al.* 2010). Given that a habit refers to the way a behavioural choice is made (Steg & Vlek 2009) behavioural change is required (Geller 2002). In order to change existing energy consumption habits, consumers need to learn new ones. Habitual behaviours are guided by '...automated cognitive processes, rather than being preceded by elaborate reasoning' (Steg & Vlek 2009, p. 312). Those automated cognitive processes may also be based upon misperceptions and selective attention. However, habits generally stay in place until the outcome they produce is judged unsatisfactory. Thus, behavioural change can only be accomplished if the previously automated behavioural choices are cognitively reconsidered, perhaps in light of new goals and as a result new choices (i.e. behaviours), implemented to the point where they themselves become automatic. In that way new habits may overcome old.

Understanding why people engage in environmentally responsible behaviour is a complex topic spanning many disciplines (Stephenson *et al.* 2010) including education, economics, sociology, psychology and philosophy (Froehlich, Findlater & Landay 2010). For this reason, this section considers the diverse and inter-related mechanisms, strategies, and techniques that may be employed to encourage behavioural change. These may serve as a checklist for the design of an effective marketing campaign.

The provision of new information is instrumental in allowing consumers to make new choices from both learning and motivation perspectives. It is only by becoming aware of another possible (and desirable) outcome and the difference between it and the existing state that a motivation (i.e. drive) can be created. The greater the difference between the two states, the greater the potential motivation that may exist. Of course, individuals may be driven by more than one motive and possess a unique selection of motives. In addition, their motives, perceived relevance and their valence may also vary over time.

Motivation

Factors underlying behavioural change have been studied from many different behavioural perspectives (e.g. Steg & Vlek 2009; Vining & Ebreo 1992). Motivational bases include: perceived costs and benefits, moral and normative concerns and contextual factors.

In relation to perceived costs it has often been assumed that individuals make reasoned choices and as a result weigh costs and benefits and consider the probable or expected payoff – this is essentially a self-interested or 'what's in it for me' approach. Ajzen and Fishbein's (1970) Theory of Planned Behaviour (TPB) has proved successful in explaining various types of pro-environmental behaviour (Steg & Vlek 2009), including waste composting (Taylor & Todd 1995), household recycling (Kaiser & Gutscher 2003), and general pro-environmental behaviour (Kaiser, Wolfing & Fuhrer 1999). Thus, increasing motivation by emphasising the benefits available through a certain course of action is one marketing option.

By contrast, other approaches revolve around moral and normative concerns and values. A number of studies have found that the more strongly an individual subscribes to values beyond their self-interest, the more likely they are to engage in pro-environmental behaviour (De Groot & Steg 2007, 2008; Nordlund & Garvill 2002; Steg & Vlek 2009; Schultz & Zelezny 1999; Stern *et al.* 1999; Stern & Dietz 1994; Stern, Dietz & Kalof 1993).

Similarly, the higher the individual's level of environmental concern, typically measured using the New Environmental Paradigm (NEP) scale (Dunlap *et al.* 2000; Dunlap & Van Liere 1978), the more environmentally responsible they tended to act. However this relationship was generally not found to be strong (Poortinga, Steg & Vlek 2004; Schultz & Zelezny 1998; Vining & Ebreo 1992).

A third line of research identified by Steg and Vlek (2009) was based upon a perceived moral obligation to act pro-environmentally, for example, the norm-activation model (NAM) (Schwartz 1977; Schwartz & Howard 1981) and the value-norm-belief (VNB) theory (Stern *et al.* 1999; Stern 2000). Each of these moral and norm-based models, while having some explanatory value, tended to be more successful in situations where the behavioural change involved a relatively low cost (in the wider sense) to the individual. There was thus a gap between held values and concerns and their actual operationalisation.

From the point of view of employing these three motivational bases (perceived costs and benefits, and moral and normative concerns), they are of mixed benefit. Values are deeply-held and are thus notoriously hard to change or instil. By contrast, while environmental concerns can be raised, they may not lead to operationalisation via a change in behaviour. Thus, the motivational approach may be of limited utility. Finally, moral norms of obligation to act pro-environmentally tend to work only in low cost situations and in any case may be dependent upon the collectivist/individualist nature of a culture or sub-culture (e.g. Hoffstede 2001). Indeed, energy usage behaviours at a commercial or individual level have been conceptualised as a cultural issue, for example refer Lutzenhiser (1992) and Stephenson *et al.* (2010). Thus, corporate, social, local, family and individual energy usage norms affect habitual energy usage behaviours to the point where 'practices that lie outside their habitus may be excluded from consideration as unthinkable' (Stephenson *et al.* 2010 p. 6123). Certainly if motivational approaches are used in an attempt to transform an existing and often resistive 'energy culture' by promoting new morals or norms, then the proposed consumer actions must be practical or convenient and preferably supported by financial or other user-significant arguments.

A significant contribution by Steg and Vlek (2009) when discussing these issues was their insights into the effect of contextual factors. They recognised that such factors '...may facilitate or constrain environmental behaviour and influence individual motivations' (p. 312) and cited studies by Olander and Thøgerson (1995), Stern (1999) and Van Raaij (2002). Such constraints may make behavioural change very costly despite positive motivations (refer Coraliza & Berenguer 2000; Guagnano, Stern & Dietz 1995; Ludemann 1998). Thus, contexts may (1) directly affect behaviour (positively or negatively) by making pro-environmental behaviours either directly possible or impossible, (2) motivate by providing convenient opportunities for pro-environmental behaviour which then lead to positive (and reinforcing) attitudinal change, (3) moderate pro-environmental behavioural tendencies because of the difficulty of operationalising them which may also affect goal/reward motivations (for a detailed discussion refer to Guagnano, Stern & Dietz 1995; Steg & Vlek 2009).

In summary, on the basis of the literature, motivational approaches to changing household energy consumption behaviour should present information that suggests that an easily achievable cost benefit is available to the consumer for the proposed change in behaviour. In the case of TOU tariffs, the 'what's in it for me?' response could be acknowledged by emphasising the minimisation of electricity charges by simply rescheduling some household activities outside the peak period. In addition, the behavioural actions should be shown as convenient and practical and supported by suitable user-friendly facilities and infrastructure, for example by the provision of web-based feedback or better still the type of in-house real-time energy usage display described earlier. While there has been considerable research into feedback methods, the most effective format of feedback, for example, kilowatt hours (KWh), dollar costs, or GHG emissions, has yet to be determined (Fischer 2008). There are some indications that the preferred format may be culture-specific (e.g. Egan 1999; Wilhite, Fischer 2008; Høivik, & Olsen 1999) and possibly motive-specific. The provision of formats variable by the consumer would seem to be a logical choice to obviate expensive research. These motivational appeals can be reinforced by enhancing general environmental concerns, a task relatively easily achieved with all but climate change cynics and those who subscribe to the 'Human Exception Paradigm' (Bechtel, Corral-Verdugo & Pinheiro 1999) – a basic belief that humans are above nature and therefore do not have to regard it as they consume resources. These approaches may be supported by appeals to go beyond self-interest and they in turn may be effectively supported by moral and norm-based appeals. Such a range of appeals would most likely be effective in relation to altruistic and collectivistic-oriented householders. That segment could include certain ethic groups and those with certain forms of religiosity, especially those religions which have included environmental concerns in their pastoral ministry. This combination of appeals demands care when designing a motivational campaign to ensure that the themes are presented in such a way as to allow diverse consumers to absorb elements of the message that are immediately relevant to them while gently exposing them to information that could further enhance pro-environmental sentiments and any existing pro-environmental behaviours.

Interventions

Over the years many interventions have been used to encourage households to reduce their energy usage on a voluntary basis (Abrahamse *et al.* 2007). On the basis of learning leading to behavioural change, while information leads to improvements in knowledge, informational strategies alone rarely result in the desired changes (e.g. Abrahamse *et al.* 2005; Lehman & Geller 2004; Schultz, Oskamp & Mainieri 1995). As a result, 'tailored information', goal setting and feedback have generally been elements of schemes that have achieved their objectives (Abrahamse *et al.* 2005; Dwyer *et al.* 1993; Stern 1992).

The informational element of interventions may include topics that are general in nature, for example global warming (e.g. Staats, Wit & Midden 1996). An example of a more specific topic would be a workshop on energy conservation. Research suggests that while the latter produces measurably higher knowledge of energy conservation it does not of itself produce behavioural change (Geller 1981). Thus, the mere provision of information does not necessarily lead to behavioural change (Abrahamse *et al.* 2007). However, informational strategies can be effective when pro-environmental behaviour is relatively convenient and not very costly in terms of money, time, effort or social disapproval (Steg 2008). By contrast, tailored information, which better meets the needs of the individual, has been shown to be effective in health interventions (e.g. Kreuter *et al.* 1999; Rimer & Kreuter 2006). This individualised social marketing approach is one in which information is tailored to the needs, wants and most importantly the perceived barriers of individual segments of the population (e.g. Abrahamse *et al.* 2007; Daamen *et al.* 2001; Thøgersen 2007). This approach has been found to yield promising results in relation to workplace energy conservation (Daamen *et al.* 2001). In the domestic context tailored information often includes home audits, which can also be considered a form of feedback (Darby 2006). Home audits tend to result in behavioural changes especially when energy saving measures for their specific situation are included (e.g. Gonzales, Aronson & Costanzo 1988; Winnet, Love & Kidd 1982-83).

Goal setting is another approach that can yield benefits with savings of 5–10% (Abrahamse *et al.* 2007). This tends to be more effective when combined with a commitment (i.e. promise or undertaking) to save energy (e.g. Katzev & Johnson 1983) or in coordination with effective feedback (McCalley & Midden 2002). McCalley and Midden also found that it did not matter whether it was the individual householder or an external agent who set the goal, as long as one was set. However, Becker (1978) found that the combination of a difficult (individual) goal and effective feedback was particularly effective. By contrast, group goals, for example by comparing individual household consumption with that of others, while successful in some cases (e.g. Slavin, Wodarski & Blackburn 1981) were found to be very culture-specific (for a discussion refer, Egan 1999; Fischer 2008; IEA 2005; Sernhed, Pyrko & Abaravicius 2003; Wilhite, Høivik, & Olsen 1999). In some cases such comparison resulted in householders realising they used less than others and as a result they actually increased their consumption (Gaskell, Ellis & Pike 1982).

Feedback is another characteristic of interventions successful in achieving behavioural change. In view of the limited feedback typically available to householders, it is valuable to consider the types of feedback that have been found to be most beneficial. Existing types of feedback have revolved around the type of information included in conventional electricity accounts such as previous consumption for the same season of the year and comparisons with neighbouring households. However there is ongoing development of innovative eco-feedback devices including the Power-Aware power cord, garbage/trash monitors and mobile displays (for a discussion see Froehlich, Findlater & Landay 2010). Other technical approaches include 'product integrated energy feedback' (McCalley, de Vries & Midden 2010) via appliances which indicate energy usage levels. Many studies have found that the frequency of feedback is important and that continuous electronic real-time feedback is the most beneficial (Hutton *et al.* 1986; Van Houwelingen & Van Raaij 1989). Comparative or group feedback has also been effective in promoting energy conservation at work (Siero *et al.* 1996). However, the results have been mixed in relation to the effectiveness of individual versus comparative feedback for households. Group feedback appears to be effective when the groups communicate with each other directly because it makes the social norm salient to the individual (Abrahamse *et al.* 2007).

In summary, interventions that seek low cost behavioural changes to household energy consumption tend to be more effective than others and interventions which provide tailored information are more effective than those that provide general information. However, the tailoring of information is effortful as it may involve household audits and the devising of household-specific strategies. Most importantly, to be effective the tailored information should address the perceived barriers to action. It should also be noted that many of the studies reported have been of a relatively small scale and thus the scaling up of such techniques would require careful research and market segmentation if the approach was to be used on a large scale. Goal setting is similar in that it is household-individual and labour intensive from the point of view of running a large campaign especially if it is coordinated with household audits and specific tactics. These labour-intensive measures evident in earlier studies appear largely designed to address the existing disconnect between specific energy consumption behaviours and their financial and environmental impact. They may be less essential if continuous electronic feedback is available at a convenient location within the home because it essentially functions as an ongoing home energy audit. This could focus the attention of the household on specific energy consuming behaviours and enable the householders to operationalise any desire to reduce energy consumption. The role of such feedback devices in assisting householders to modify their behaviour was emphasised in a recent Australian study of household water consumption on the Gold Coast in which a long term trial of feedback devices resulted in an average 27% water saving for household showering (Willis *et al.* 2010).

To date, campaigns targeting householders' energy usage have consisted of little more than exhortations to use less. However, the means (i.e. effective feedback) that householders could use to relate their specific behaviours to their consumption and thence change their behaviour have not been provided. Given the extensive research that has already been undertaken in many fields of knowledge, the challenge exists for government to provide the technical (e.g. feedback readouts), informational (e.g. tailored information) and educational infrastructure (e.g. general environmental and energy information) necessary to harness the desire of householders to use energy efficiently while maintaining their level of comfort. Once this has been achieved, the crafting of appropriate social marketing campaigns will be required to assist householders in translating their energy saving or usage efficiency sentiments into effective actions.

Appendix A

The electricity generation and distribution system

Electricity has been dubbed the 'silent servant' (Nye 1990) and its convenience and silence conceal the large volumes of energy that are used in homes and businesses. Electricity as a home resource tends to be taken for granted and many people have limited understanding of the energy delivery system that silently enhances their lives. Apart from the occasional view of transmission towers and power poles, the generation system that produces and distributes our electricity largely goes unnoticed to anyone not living near a power station. Yet an understanding of electricity and its distribution system is a prerequisite to learning how users can reduce their usage of electricity and thus their carbon footprint. This lack of consumer understanding belies the large amount of fossil fuel that is required to power our modern lifestyle. Seventy-seven per cent of Australia's electricity is generated by the burning of coal (ABS 2008) in thermal power stations and this is a major emitter of carbon dioxide and other gases which contribute to global warming. Other fossil fuel energy sources are also viable inputs such as oil and natural gas. To produce the same amount of energy, burning natural gas typically produces about 30% less carbon dioxide than burning oil and about 45% less than burning coal (naturalgas.org 2010). The output of power stations consists of water vapour, gases and ash particles, but because the chimneys are equipped with sophisticated particle filtering systems generally there is little visible in the way of emissions apart from a heat haze or vapour trail above the chimney.

Unlike gas, coal is expensive and problematic to transport in large quantities. For this and other reasons, in Australia most coal-fired power stations are in rural areas, typically near their coal source. By contrast, because gas can be transported relatively easily by pipeline there tends to be a wider range of options for the convenient location of gas-fired power stations nearer to their centre of electrical load, generally major cities. Due to the location of thermal power stations and their filtered output, city dwellers rarely have any visual clues as to the magnitude of their throughput/output. Coal burning thermal power stations generally have an efficiency of about 33% whereas gas fired power stations convert up to 50% of the energy available in a unit of gas into electricity (NPC 2007).

Once the electricity is generated it has to be brought to the point of use. Because coal powered power stations tend to be located near their supplying coal mines there is typically a considerable distance between them and the geographic centres of electrical load such as major cities. In Australia this is typically accomplished by high voltage overhead transmission power lines strung across the countryside on large electricity pylons. For those not familiar with the term 'voltage', it is a measure of electrical pressure the best analogy of which is the pressure of water. 'High' voltage is used for power transmission to minimise energy losses and it is typically up to 500,000 volts. The electricity is then successively reduced in voltage by electrical transformers located in 'substations' (essentially electrical switching stations) and fed into a city's distribution system consisting of overhead conductors (i.e. power lines) and underground cables. The substations are interconnected for reliability and to provide a flexibility of distribution paths in the event of cable failures, system problems or necessary maintenance. In terms of energy efficiency, apart from the already mentioned energy losses during generation, the transmission and distribution system itself incurs a number of losses generally estimated at about 7% (USEIA 2010). These substations and conductors safely distribute the power at successively lower voltages until it reaches the above or below ground cables in suburban streets at the regulated voltage for Australiandomestic supply (240 Volts). At this point, individual connections provide power to houses and blocks of apartments and electricity meters measure the consumption of individual account holders.

References

Abrahamse, W Steg, L Vlek, C & Rothengatter, T 2005, 'A review of intervention studies aimed at household energy conservation', *Journal of Environmental Psychology*, vol. 25, pp. 273-291.

Abrahamse W, Steg L, Vlek C & Rothengatter T. 2007, 'The effect of tailored information, goal setting, and tailored feedback on household energy use, energy-related behaviors, and behavioral antecedents', *Journal of Environmental Psychology*, vol. 27, pp. 265-276.

ABS – see – Australian Bureau of Statistics

Ajzen, I & Fishbein, M 1970, 'The prediction of behavior from attitudinal and normative variables', *Journal of Experimental Social Psychology*, vol. 6, pp. 466-487.

Australian Bureau of Statistics 2010, Australian Social Trends - Energy in Focus: Energy Use in Australian Homes, cat. no. 4614.0.55.001, ABS, Canberra.

Australian Bureau of Statistics, 2008, Environmental Issues: Energy Use and Conservation, cat. no. 4602.0.55.001 ABS, Canberra.

Bechtel, RB Corral-Verdugo, V Pinheiro, JQ 1999, 'Environmental belief systems: United States, Brazil, and Mexico', *Journal of Crosscultural Psychology*, vol. 30, pp. 122-128.

Becker, LJ 1978, 'Joint effect of feedback and goal setting on performance: a field study of residential energy conservation', *Journal of Applied Psychology*, vol. 63, pp. 428-433.

Birzle-Harder, B, & Götz, K 2001, 'Grüner Strom—eine sozialwissenschaftliche Marktanalyse'. [Green Power - a sociological market analysis]. Frankfurt/M: Institut für sozial-ökologische Forschung.

Corraliza, JA & Berenguer, J 2000, 'Environmental values, beliefs and actions', Environment and Behavior, vol. 32, pp. 832-848.

Daamen, DDL Staats, H Wilke, HAM & Engelen, M 2001, 'Improving environmental behavior in companies. The effectiveness of tailored versus non-tailored interventions', Environment and Behavior, vol. 33, pp. 229-248.

Darby, S 2006, 'The Effectiveness of feedback on energy consumption: a Review for DEFRA of the literature on metering, billing and direct displays', Environmental Change Institute University of Oxford, Oxford.

DCCEE – see - *Department of Climate Change and Energy Efficiency*

De Groot, J & Steg, L 2007, 'Value orientations and environmental beliefs in five countries: validity of an instrument to measure egoistic, altruistic and biospheric value orientations', Journal of Cross-Cultural Psychology, vol. 38, pp. 318-332.

De Groot, J & Steg, L 2008, 'Value orientations to explain beliefs related to environmental significant behavior: how to measure egoistic, altruistic, and biospheric value orientations, Environment and Behavior, vol. 40, pp. 330-354.

Department of Climate Change and Energy Efficiency 2010, Australian National Greenhouse Gas Inventory 2008, Department of Climate Change and Energy Efficiency, Canberra.

Dunlap, RE & Van Liere, KD 1978, 'The 'new environmental paradigm': a proposed measuring instrument and preliminary results', Journal of Environmental Education, vol. 9, pp.10-19.

Dunlap, RE Van Liere, KD Mertig, AG & Jones, RE 2000, 'Measuring endorsement of the new ecological paradigm: a revised NEP scale' Journal of Social Issues, vol. 56, pp. 425-442.

Dwyer, WO Leeming, FC Cobern, MK Porter, BE & Jackson, JM 1993, 'Critical review of behavioral interventions to preserve the environment: research since 1980', Environment and Behavior, vol. 25, pp. 275-321.

Egan, C 1999. 'Graphical displays and comparative energy information: What do people understand and prefer?' Paper presented at the Summer Study of the European Council for an Energy Efficient Economy, 1999, paper no. 2–12, viewed 3 November 2010, <http://www.eceee.org/conference_proceedings/eceee/ 1999/Panel_2/p2_12/>.

Ellis, P & Gaskell, G 1978, 'A review of social research on the individual energy consumer', Unpublished manuscript, Department of Social Psychology, London School of Economics, London.

Filipović, S., and Tanić, G., 2009, "The Policy of Consumer Protection in the Electricity Market", *Economic Annals*, vol. 189-179, University of Belgrade, Faculty of Economics, viewed 3 November, 2010, <http://ea.ekof.bg.ac.rs/annals_178-179.php>

Fischer, C 2008, 'Feedback on household electricity consumption: a tool for saving energy?', *Energy Efficiency*, vol. 1, pp. 79-104.

Froehlich J, Findlater L & Landay, J 2010, 'The Design of Eco-Feedback Technology', CHI 2010 April10-15, Atlanta GA.

Gardner, GT & Stern, PC 2008, 'The Short List: The Most Effective Actions US Households Can Take to Curb Climate Change'. Environment, vol. 50, pp. 12-25.

Garnaut, R 2008, The Garnaut climate change review, Australian National University, Canberra.

Gaskell, G Ellis, P & Pike, R 1982, 'The energy literate consumer: the effects of consumption feedback and information on beliefs, knowledge and behaviour'. Dept of Social Psychology, London School of Economics, London.

Geller, ES 1981, 'Evaluating energy conservation programs: is verbal report enough?', Journal of Consumer Research, vol. 8, pp. 331-335.

Geller, ES 2002, 'The challenge of increasing proenvironmental behavior', in RB Bechtel, & A Churchman (eds.), Handbook of environmental psychology, New York, Wiley, pp. 525-540.

Geller, ES Berry, TD Ludwig, TD Evans, RE Gilmore, MR & Clarke SW 1990, 'A conceptual framework for developing and evaluating behavior change interventions for injury control', Health Education Research, vol. 5, pp. 125-137.

Geller, ES Winett, RA & Everett, P.B 1982, Preserving the environment: new strategies for behavior change, Pergamon Press, New York.

Gonzales, MH Aronson, E & Costanzo, MA 1988, 'Using social cognition and persuasion to promote energy conservation: a quasi-experiment', Journal of Applied Social Psychology, vol. 18, pp. 1049-1066.

Guagnano, GA Stern, PC & Dietz, T 1995, 'Influences on attitude-behavior relationships: a natural experiment with curbside recycling', Environment and Behavior, vol. 27, pp. 699-718.

Herter, K 2007, 'Residential implementation of critical-peak pricing of electricity', Energy Policy, vol. 35, pp. 2121-2130.

Hofstede, G 2001, Culture's Consequences, Comparing Values, Behaviors, Institutions, and Organizations Across Nations, Sage Publications, Thousand Oaks, CA.

Hutton, RB Mauser, GA, Filiatrault, P & Ahtola, OT 1986, 'Effects of cost-related feedback on consumer knowledge and consumption behaviour: a field experimental approach', Journal of Consumer Research, vol. 13, pp. 327-336.

IEA – see - International Energy Agency

International Energy Agency, 2005, 'International Energy Agency demand-side management programme, Task XI: Time of use pricing and energy use for demand management delivery, Subtask 1 Report: Smaller customer energy saving by end use monitoring and feedback, viewed 3 November, 2010,<http://dsm.iea.org/Files/Tasks/Task%20XI%20-%20Time%20of%20Use%20Pricing%20and%20Energy%20Use%20for%20Demand%20Management%20Delivery/Reports/Subtask1Report12May05.pdf>.

Kaiser, FG & Gutscher, H 2003, 'The proposition of a general version of the theory of planned behaviour (TPB): predicting ecological behaviour', Journal of Applied Social Psychology, vol. 33, pp. 586-603.

Kaiser, FG Wolfing, S & Fuhrer, U 1999, 'Environmental attitude and ecological Behaviour', Journal of Environmental Psychology, vol.19, pp. 1-19.

Katzev, RD & Johnson, TR 1983, 'A social-psychological analysis of residential electricity consumption: the impact of minimal justification techniques', *Journal of Economic Psychology*, vol. 3, pp. 267-284.

Kempton, W & Layne, LL 1994, 'The consumer's energy analysis environment', *Energy Policy*, vol. 22, pp. 857-866.

Kreuter, MW Farrell, D Olevitch, L & Brennan, L 1999, *Tailored health messages: customizing communication with computer technology*, Lawrence Erlbaum, Mahwah, NJ.

Lehman, PK & Geller, ES 2004, 'Behavioral analysis and environmental protection: accomplishments and potential for more', *Behavior and Social Issues*, vol. 13, pp. 13-32.

Local Power, '12 Reasons Why the Proposed "Solar Bonus Scheme" using an Import-Export Feed in Tariff (FiT) is not the Best Outcome for Queensland nor the Climate. Viewed 10 May, 2011 <www.localpower.net.au/images/12reasons.pdf>

Ludemann, C 1998, 'Framing and choice of transportation mode: testing the discrimination model vs SEU theory', *Rationality and Society*, vol. 10, pp. 253-270.

Lutzenhiser, L., 1992, 'A Cultural Model of Household Energy Consumption, *Energy* vol. 17, pp. 47–60.

McCalley, L & Midden, C 2002, 'Energy conservation through product-integrated feedback: the roles of goal-setting and social orientation', *Journal of Economic Psychology*, vol. 23, pp. 589-603.

McCalley, LT De Vries, PW & Midden, CJH 2010, 'Consumer Response to Product-Integrated Energy Feedback Behaviour, Goal Level Shifts, and Energy Conservation', *Environment and Behavior*, viewed 3 November, 2010 <http://eab.sagepub.com/content/early/2010/09/16/0013916510371053.abstract>

Midden, C, Kaiser, F & McCalley, T 2007, 'Technology's four roles in understanding individuals' conservation of natural resources'. *Journal of Social Issues,* vol. 63, pp. 155-174.

Monash Centre for Regulatory Studies, 2009 Foundation for Effective

Markets and Governance Project. '*Attaining optimal carbon abatement rules through consumer advocacy: Learning from European Experience on the Regulation of Energy*', at: www.advocacypanel.com.au/documents/ProgressReportSeptember09.pdf

[Accessed 3 November, 2010,

National Petroleum Council, 2007, 'Topic Paper#4 Electric generation efficiency' Working document of the NPC Global Oil & Gas Study, viewed 3 November, 2010, <http://www.npc.org/Study_Topic_Papers/4-DTG-ElectricEfficiency.pdf>

NaturalGas.org, 'Natural gas and the environment', 2010, viewed 3 November, 2010, <http://www.naturalgas.org/environment/naturalgas.asp#greenhouse/>.

Needham, S, 2008, "The potential for renewable energy to provide baseload power in Australia", Department of Parliamentary Services: Science, Technology, Environment and Resources Section, Australia, Report no. 9 - 2008-09.

Newsham, G R & Bowker, B G 2010, 'The effect of utility time-varying pricing and load control strategies on residential summer peak electricity use: a review', *Energy Policy*, vol. 38, pp. 3289-3296.

Nordlund, AM & Garvill, J 2002, 'Value structures behind pro-environmental Behavior', *Environment and Behavior*, vol. 34, pp. 740-756.

Nye, DE 1990, Electrifying America: social meanings of a new technology , MIT Press, Cambridge Mass.

Olander, F & Thøgersen, J 1995, 'Understanding of consumer behaviour as a prerequisite for environmental protection', *Journal of Consumer Policy*, vol. 18, pp. 345-385.

Poortinga, W Steg, L & Vlek, C 2004, 'Values, environmental concern and environmental behavior: a study into household energy use', *Environment and Behavior*, vol. 36, pp. 70-93.

Rimer, BK & Kreuter, MW 2006, 'Advancing tailored health communication: a persuasion and message effects perspective', Journal of Communication, vol. 56, pp. 184-201.

Sachdeva, A & Wallis, P 2010, 'Our demand: reducing electricity use in Victoria through demand management', Monash Sustainability Institute, Melbourne.

Schultz, PW & Zelezny, LC 1998, 'Values and proenvironmental behaviour. A five-country study', Journal of Cross-Cultural Psychology, vol. 29, pp. 540-558.

Schultz, PW & Zelezny, LC 1999, 'Values as predictors of environmental attitudes: evidence for consistency across 14 countries', Journal of Environmental Psychology, vol. 19, pp. 255-265.

Schultz, PW Oskamp, S & Mainieri, T 1995, 'Who recycles and when? A review of personal and situational factors', Journal of Environmental Psychology, vol. 15, pp. 105-121.

Schwartz, SH & Howard, JA 1981, 'A normative decision-making model of Altruism', in JP Rushton (ed.), Altruism and Helping Behaviour: Social, Personality and Developmental Perspectives, Erlbaum, Hillsdale, NJ, pp. 189-211.

Schwartz, SH 1977, ' Normative influences on altruism' in L Berkowitz (ed.), Advances in Experimental Social Psychology, vol. 10, pp. 221-279.

Sernhed, K Pyrko, J & Abaravicius, J 2003, 'Bill me this way!—customer preferences regarding electricity bills in Sweden', in Proceedings of the 2003 summer study of the European Council for an energy efficient economy, ECEEE, Stockholm, pp. 1147-1150.

Siero, FW Bakker, AB Dekker, GB & Van den Burg, TC, 1996, 'Changing organizational energy consumption behavior through comparative feedback', *Journal of Environmental Psychology*, vol. 16, pp. 235-246.

Slavin, RE Wodarski, JS & Blackburn, BL 1981, 'A group contingency for electricity conservation in master-metered apartments', *Journal of Applied Behavior Analysis*, vol. 14, pp. 357-363.

Staats, HJ Wit, AP & Midden, CYH 1996. ' Communicating the greenhouse effect to the public: evaluation of a mass media campaign from a social dilemma perspective', *Journal of Environmental Management*, vol. 45, pp. 189-203.

Steg, L & Vlek C, 2009, 'Encouraging pro-environmental behaviour: an Integrative review and research agenda', *Journal of Environmental Psychology* vol. 29, 309-317.

Steg, L 2008, 'Promoting household energy conservation', *Energy Policy*, vol. 36, pp. 4449-4453.

Stephenson, J., Barton, B., Carrington, G., Gnoth, D., Lawson, R., & Thorsnes, P. 2010, 'Energy cultures', *Energy Policy*, vol. 38, pp. 6120-6129.

Stern, PC & Dietz, T 1994, 'The value basis of environmental concern', *Journal of Social Issues*, vol. 50, pp. 65-84.

Stern, PC 1992, 'What psychology knows about energy conservation', *American Psychologist*, vol. 47, pp. 1224-1232.

Stern, PC 1999, 'Information, incentives, and proenvironmental consumer Behavior', *Journal of Consumer Policy*, vol. 22, pp. 461-478.

Stern, PC 2000, 'Toward a coherent theory of environmentally significant Behavior', *Journal of Social Issues*, vol. 56, pp. 407-424.

Stern, PC Dietz, T & Kalof, L 1993, 'Value orientations, gender, and environmental concern', *Environment and Behavior*, vol. 25, pp. 322-348.

Stern, PC Dietz, T Abel, T Guagnano, GA & Kalof, L 1999, 'A value-belief-norm theory of support for social movements: the case of environmentalism', *Human Ecology Review*, vol. 6, pp. 81-97.

Taylor, S & Todd, P 1995, 'An integrated model of waste management behavior: a test of household recycling and composting intentions', *Environment and Behavior*, vol. 27, pp. 603-630.

Thøgersen, J 2005, 'How may consumer policy empower consumers for sustainable lifestyles?', *Journal of Consumer Policy*, vol. 28, pp. 143-178.

Thøgersen, J 2007, 'Social marketing of alternative transportation modes, in T Garling, & L Steg (eds.), *Threats to the quality of urban life from car traffic: Problems, causes, and solutions*, Elsevier, Amsterdam, pp.367-381.

United States Energy Information Administration, 2010, 'FAQ: Where can I find data on electricity transmission and distribution losses?', viewed 3 November, 2010, <http://tonto.eia.doe.gov/ask/electricity_faqs.asp#electric_rates2>.

USEIA – see - United States Energy Information Administration

Van Houwlingen, JH & Van Raaij, W 1989, 'The effect of goal-setting and daily electronic feedback on in-home energy use', *Journal of Consumer Research*, vol. 16, pp. 98-105.

Van Raaij, W 2002, 'Stages of behavioural change: motivation, ability and Opportunity'. In G Bartels & W Nelissen (eds.), *Marketing for Sustainability; Towards Transactional Policy-making*, IOS Press, Amsterdam, pp. 321-333.

Vining, J & Ebreo, A, 1992, 'Predicting recycling behavior form global and specific environmental attitudes and changes in recycling opportunities', *Journal of Applied Social Psychology*, vol. 22, pp. 1580-1607.

Wilhite, H Høivik, A & Olsen, J-G 1999, 'Advances in the use of consumption feedback information in energy billing: The experiences of a Norwegian energy utility. Paper presented at the Summer Study of the European Council for an Energy Efficient Economy, 1999, paper no. 3-2, viewed 3 November 2010, <http://proceedings.eceee.org/library_links/proceedings/1999/pdf99/Panel3/3-02.pdf>.

Willis, RM Stewart, RA, Panuwatwanich, K Jones, S & Kyriakides, A 2010, 'Alarming visual display monitors affecting shower end use water and energy conservation in

Australian residential households resources', *Conservation and Recycling*, vol. 54, pp. 1117-1127.

Winett, RA Love, SQ & Kidd, C 1982-1983, 'The effectiveness of an energy specialist and extension agents in promoting summer energy conservation by home visits', *Journal of Environmental Systems*, vol. 12, pp. 61-70.

Rosia Montana: Building marketing communication for influencing stakeholders

RODICA MILENA ZAHARIA AND ALIN STANCU

ABSTRACT

This chapter uses a case study to illustrate the importance that marketing communication plays in managing the influence of stakeholders regarding a project. Ideally, the marketing communication will enhance the positive attitude and diminish the negative reactions that stakeholders can have.

The chapter's objectives are: (1) to demonstrate the complex role that stakeholders play in establishing an organisation's strategy, (2) to exemplify the importance of stakeholders in a particular case, and (3) to explain how marketing communication has been used in this case to minimise the influence of hostile stakeholders.

Stakeholders are of vital importance to a company. Starting with the influential work of Freeman in 1984, the stakeholder concept developed into so-called 'stakeholders theory', a massive body of work that covers the multi-faceted approaches towards these groups of entities that have interests over the companies.

Companies develop different communication strategies in order to address different group of stakeholders in the best way. These groups can be a threat to the company or they can cooperate and be supporters. And, according to their interests, stakeholders from a group can change their potential for posing a threat or for collaboration (Savage *et al.* 1991), and companies have to adapt their communication policy in relation to this potential.

This case study illustrates the evolution of an investment in the gold exploration industry in Romania (Rosia Montana), shaped by the confrontation between the company and different stakeholders – some of them opposing to the project, others sustaining the company. In this confrontation, which took more than a decade, marketing communication was the most important tool in determining the final decision regarding the implementation of the project.

The case study analyses how the company developed its marketing communication. Rosia Montana Gold Corporation (RMGC) used economic arguments as tools in its communication campaign, sustained by outstanding specialist and safety arguments which were confirmed by international specialists. NGOs opposing the project highlighted environmental protection and cultural heritage factors, touching the sensitivities and feelings of the public in relation to national treasures that shouldn't be alienated.

Introduction

The classical vision of business focuses on the interests of shareholders as the guiding line in determining the relationship between the company and its environment.

Unlike the classical view, the stakeholder theory argues that the company target 'is or should be the flourishing of the firm and all its stakeholders' (Werhane & Freeman 1999). It contends that companies have a social responsibility that goes beyond creation of profitability, growth and added value for shareholders. The company has the obligation to include all parties affected by its actions in decision making, both directly and indirectly.

The stakeholder theory was infrequently used in classical marketing literature. In recent years, the evolution of the marketing concept was rapid and one of the areas of development was in the sphere of corporate social responsibility. The American Marketing Association (AMA) incorporated the stakeholder concept into the definition of marketing in 2004, when marketing was defined as 'an organisational function and a set of processes for creating, communicating and delivering value to customers and for managing customer relationships in ways that benefit the organisation and its stakeholders'. (American Marketing Association 2004)

Wolfe and Putler (2002) argue that stakeholder analysis facilitates the understanding of the more unpredictable company's dynamic environment, and that by doing this the company increases its capacity to face the changes. The stakeholder concept is defined as those individuals or groups towards whom the company is responsible - including here the clients, the investors and shareholders, employees, suppliers, authorities, local community, etc.

To clarify, Clarkson (1995) makes a distinction between two types of stakeholders, taking into account their role in the company: primary stakeholders and secondary stakeholders. Primary stakeholders are those that influence or are influenced by the company constantly, their participation being vital for the functioning of the company. In this category we include shareholders and investors, employees, clients and suppliers but also governments and communities. The secondary stakeholders are those entities affected by the company's shares, but not involved in direct transactions with it and whose participation does not depend on the existence and survival of the company. From this point of view a stakeholder can influence and can be influenced by companies' activities, and can have a positive or a negative impact upon the company.

Werther Jr. and Chandler (2006) classify the stakeholders into three main categories: (1) organisational stakeholders (internal stakeholders), (2) economical stakeholders and (3) societal ones (external stakeholders). Included in the 'organisational stakeholders' category are the employees, managers, unions and shareholders. The 'economical stakeholders' are the clients, suppliers and distributors, and the 'societal stakeholders' include NGOs, government and authorities, local communities and the environment.

After a review of the literature, Bunn, Savage and Holloway (2002) developed a model of stakeholder analysis encompassing five stages. At the beginning, the company should (a) identify key sectors and relevant stakeholders, (b) describe the most important characteristics of each stakeholder group, and then (c) analyse and classify the stakeholders according to their attributes, (d) examine the dynamic relationships among stakeholders and finally (e) evaluate generic stakeholder management strategies. This model should be viewed as a process, each step being an important element in shaping the company's analysis.

The recent development of the marketing literature underlines the importance of the different categories of stakeholders (Mitchell, Bradley & Wood 1997; Savage *et al.* 1991). Their importance, influence and power over the company are not similar and are changing over the time, forcing companies to evaluate permanently the stakeholders' potential. In this regard, marketing specialists should be very careful about the types of stakeholders the company interacts with. Therefore, it is necessary to conduct an analysis on the formal structure of the organisation, to identify the direct interactions of stakeholders with the company, and also to undertake an informal analysis of the structure of the organisation, to study its indirect relations (Recklies 2001). After identifying all categories of current and potential stakeholders, the company should understand the nature of them. At this point a description from the perspective of their impact (local, regional and international), their expectations, the assumed risks and the resources owned is necessary.

The analysis and classification of stakeholders according to their attributes involves taking into account their power, legitimacy and urgency (Mitchell, Bradley & Wood 1997). Stakeholders have power as far they have access to coercive power and utility or symbolic means to impose their views or communicate to an organisation (Etzioni 1964). Coercive power involves the use of physical force, violence or any type of restriction. Utility power involves a financial or material control, such as boycotts or legal actions. Symbolic power refers to the use symbols that suggest social acceptance, prestige, or other attribute. It is the most common way in which stakeholders behave and in recent times it has been the most effective way stakeholders have gained the influence and most power over company decision making. In this category are included complaints campaigns, advertising messages and websites that can generate solidarity among stakeholders and thus the message gets a greater power.

The legitimacy of stakeholders considers the extent to which they are accepted by the relational network. Suchman (1995) argues that legitimacy is the perception that the actions of stakeholders are desired, appropriate or suitable for a system of social norms, values, beliefs and definitions. The definition states that an action is legitimate when other stakeholders and society at large consider it a reasonable approach to the one who initiated it. Therefore, extreme measures are not very well received by society, even when they are the most appropriate.

Urgency is based on two characteristics of stakeholder requirements: time pressure and the importance of the request. Time pressure increases stakeholders' effort and it can overcome the company's ability to investigate and respond to their requirements. Urgency means that something really must be done.

Because the company acts in a changing environment, the next step is to focus its effort to identify dynamic relationships with stakeholders and create scenarios for their future development. Because stakeholder attributes (power, legitimacy, urgency) can evolve over time among stakeholders, the company may at this stage initiate steps to change the position of one or a group of stakeholders.

This case study is an example of the importance of marketing communication in managing the influence of stakeholders in order to enhance the positive attitude and diminishing the negative reactions regarding a project. The case illustrates the evolution of an investment in gold exploration industry in Romania (Rosia Montana), shaped by the confrontation between the company and different stakeholders that opposed to the project. In this confrontation that took more than a decade, marketing communication was the most important tool in determining the final decision regarding the implementation of the project.

Rosia Montana case study

Rosia Montana is a small village in the Apuseni Mountains, one of the oldest gold and silver exploitations in Europe. The place is rich in minerals, especially iron oxides which cause the red colour of the water. The small community is also an important archaeological site, with ruins of Romans mines, unique geological areas and a valuable ethnographical region (with houses from XVIII-XIX century and monuments of traditional architecture).

The disputed project is related to the newly established company (1997), S.C. Rosia Montana Gold Corporation S.A. (RMGC), owned by: Gabriel Resources Ltd. (80%), a Canadian company specialised in mining; the Romanian government represented by the mining company C.N.C.A.F. Minvest S.A. Deva (19.3%); and minority shareholders (0.7%). RMGC wants to mine gold and silver at Rosia Montana, estimating that 300 tons of gold and 1600 tons of silver will be extracted. The Rosia Montana Project is located within the Golden Quadrilateral which is situated within the Apuseni and Metaliferi Mountains of Transylvania and covers an area of approximately 900 square kilometres immediately to the north of the city of Deva. The exploitation involves, physical displacement of about 974 households, most of which are currently in the localities of Rosia Montana, and also the use of cyanide for gold extraction. For more than ten years the project has been highly debated, and as a result, the exploitation in Rosia Montana hasn't started.

Table 8.6 The stakeholders' importance to and influence on project Rosia Montana

	High Influence/high potential to threaten	Low Influence/low potential to threaten
High importance/ high potential to cooperate	In this group there are stakeholders that have a high degree of influence on the project, and are highly important for its success. The project will need to construct good relationships with these stakeholders to ensure an effective coalition of support for the project. **Local community, local administration, central administration.** Strategy recommended: collaboration Strategy followed: collaboration	Stakeholders are of high importance to the project, but have low influence. Special initiatives have been created in order to keep these stakeholders in favour of the project. **Land owners (have to be convinced to move from the area and to sell the land to the RMGC); trade union 'The future of mining' and Roma Community (attracted by the employment opportunities created by the project).** Strategy recommended: exploit/involve Strategy followed: involve and exploit
Low importance/ low potential to cooperate	Stakeholders with high influence, who can therefore affect the project outcomes, but whose interests are not the target of the project. These stakeholders may be a source of significant risk, and they will need careful monitoring and management. **NGOs such as Alburnus Maior formed the coalition Save Rosia Montana that action against the project. There are, also, supporters of the project, as technical specialists or other personalities.** Strategy recommended: defend Strategy followed: defend/offensive/exploit	Stakeholders with low influence on or importance to project objectives may require limited monitoring or evaluation but are of low priority. They are unlikely to be the subject of project activities or management **In this category can be included Canadian Embassy representatives that supported the project, Hungarian Prime Minister, who declared serious concerns regarding the project safety for the environment.** Strategy recommended: hold current position/monitor Strategy followed: involve/exploit/defend

Adapted from Moorhouse Consulting (2007) and Polonsky (2005), p. 1201

Following the Mendelow's Power-interest grid (Moorhouse Consulting 2007) and Polonsky's matrix (Polonsky 2005), the stakeholders of the project of Rosia Montana are local community, local and central authorities, individuals (land owners in the area) and civil society representatives. Each of these groups of stakeholders attempts to influence the state to act according to their interests. A matrix that shows the influence/interest of stakeholders in the Rosia Montana project reveals the following situation.

The main instrument used by different groups of stakeholders in influencing the decision-making structures was marketing communication. Having a strong impact on the environment and on the local community, each group used media in order to attract more supporters and, in this way, to influence the decision-making authorities to act in their favour.

Disputed aspects and reactions of stakeholders

Soon after the details about the mining project were issued in the media, a local NGO, named after the roman name of the village, Alburnus Maior Association, emerged to promote sustainable development that preserves Rosia Montana's natural and historical heritage. Alburnus Maior opposes the resettlement plan that will affect 974 small farms, destruction of valuable historical and archaeological patrimony, use of the cyanide leaching technology and large scale extraction of gold via open cast mining.

The stakeholders related to this project are local community, local and central authorities, and civil society representatives. The stake in this case was to influence public opinion in favour of one side (those that opposed to the project or the RMGC) and, thus, to orient the decision in favour of those that have more credibility. The two groups that have formed are led by (1) Alburnus Maior and (2) the Rosia Montana Gold Corporation. Each of them tried to convince as many personalities as possible that what they sustain is the best solution for Rosia Montana, for the community, and for the state.

Alburnus Maior initiated one of the highest environmental and social movements in the country, the Save Rosia Montana Campaign, which represented the opposition to the opening of the largest surface mines in Europe. In the last five years, almost 40 NGOs from Romania and abroad (as Green Peace), different personalities, universities, Romanian Academy, Romanian Orthodox Church and even the Prime Minister of Hungary, dedicated a lot of energy into gaining as much support as possible in opposing the acceptance of the project. The decision-making institutions have been put under a lot of pressure by the activities of this coalition. The tragic pollution accident in 2000, when the river Tisa was contaminated with cyanide, was used by the Save Rosia Montana Coalition as a reason to block the mining project.

In the meantime, Rosia Montana Gold Corporation (RMGC) initiated a public campaign stressing the benefits that the project brings in the community: large investments, job creation, programs for environment protection, consideration for archaeological sites and budget contribution. However, the efforts made by the RMGC remained proved ineffective for the company. In 2008, Leo Burnett was hired to handle the image of the mining project, starting an aggressive new campaign to promote the mining company to raise the awareness of the Romanian population regarding the social and financial benefits of the Rosia Montana project.

After two years of an offensive campaigning, RMGC started to gain the results. Important and outstanding personalities testified in favour of the project. The O'Hara Report from 2004 (the General Reporter for Cultural Patrimony of the Parliamentary Assembly of the Council of Europe) appreciated the project as an example of responsibility regarding archaeological, ethnographical and architectural development. Further, an evaluation from the University of Alba Iulia in a study on the economic and social impacts of the mining project on the area concluded: 'The Project does not contradict with other economic development projects, but rather may act as a catalyst for them' (http://www.rmgc.ro/proiectul-rosia-montana/opiniile-expertilor-despre-din-rosia-montana.html). Other evaluations that sustained the benefits of the project appeared on the front page of the newspapers. All these reports contradicted the concerns of the Save Rosia Montana Campaign. An international independent group of experts, IGIC, concluded in 2007 that the cyanide is widely used and is a safe technique. In 2009, the Norway Geotechnical Institute concluded that the investigation and monitoring conducted during construction and operation of the dam were probably the most effective ways to further reduce the risk of associated with this construction. And in 2010, Oxford Policy Management confirmed that the mining project of Rosia Montana Gold Corporation (RMGC) has a potential contribution of 19 billion to the GDP of Romania, through the multiplier effect generated by the project over its lifetime. Other personalities, such as Joel Bell (representing the Canadian Government support), Alex Burger, strategic counsellor of the NGO TechnoServe Extractive Partnership, NGO Pro Dreptatea, the Trade Union 'The future of Mining', the Roma Community from Rosia Montana, the CEO of the Project Mining Institute IPROMIN, also raised their voices in support of sustaining the project.

It should be added that financial crisis is a silent, but very powerful, ally of the RMGC. In a region that has chronic unemployment, where opportunities are non-existent, financial and economic arguments are very strong. And if the company brings additional arguments in favour of safe business, and some of the opponents are less than credible, then the decision of central and local authorities will be easy.

As a result of a battle that seemed to be won by the RMGC, the Environment Ministry announced that the Project of Rosia Montana will be re-opened and re-discussed, and if it complies with the legislation and safety measures, it will be approved.

Following the principles of sustainable communication (McDonagh 1998), it can be argued that the communication strategy of Rosia Montana project followed the principles of ecological trust, ecological access, ecological disclosure, ecological dialogue and promotion, and has attracted mostly non-profit organisations and relevant agencies and personalities specialised in sustainable mining operations.

According to ecological trust, both sides tried to convince the general public that their versions of the situation were true. They brought into discussions the preservation aspects (whether it was about damages brought to the environment or conservation of the natural potential of the area) in order to underline the safety (or lack of safety) of business operations that would be developed in the Rosia Montana region.

Ecological access and ecological disclosures were embodied in the reports, which were produced to demonstrate ecological trust. Data about operations, the risks of those operations, damages to the environment or to the archaeological sites have been release in the media with the same purpose: to create a favourable image of one of the sides' opinion in order to influence decision-making bodies to approve or to reject the project. Again, the focus has been on environmental and cultural preservation.

Few public debates have been initiated by stakeholders involved in the projects, or by the company RMGC. Instead, disclosing the data from different reports, and using the promotion principle by advertising the benefits of the projects (supported mainly by RMGC) or the damages involved by the gold exploitation, were important aspects of the communication strategy. RMGC adopted a mainly offensive campaign focusing on the advantages of the projects, using mostly non-profit organisations: investments in cleaning the region, preserving the natural and cultural potential of the area, educational and cultural benefits, sustainable jobs creation and, as a corollary, human dignity reconstruction for the people in that area.

Conclusion

This case study can be considered a demonstration of the importance of marketing communication in reducing or enhancing the influence of some groups of stakeholders over the authorities. The subject of environment protection, combined with mining activities in the field of rare natural resources (such as gold) is a contentious issue for politicians, environmentalists, nationalists and businesses.

RMGC used economic arguments as tools in its communication campaign. These were sustained by outstanding specialist and safety arguments and confirmed by international specialists.

NGOs that opposed to the project followed the way of environment protection and cultural heritage, touching the sensitive feelings of national treasures that shouldn't be alienated.

We can argue that non-profit organisations and other relevant stakeholders initiated sustainable communication strategies focused on the paradigm of preservation rather than domination of nature. This campaign took into account the switch to sustainable consumption and pointed out the importance of the environmental and cultural aspects.

References

American Marketing Association (2004), *AMA Dictionary*, http://www. marketingpower .com/_layouts/Dictionary.aspx?dLetter=M.

Bunn, M., Savage, G.T., Holloway, B.B. (2002) *Stakeholder analysis for multi-sector innovations*, Journal of Business & Industrial Marketing, volume: 17 Issue: 2/3 Page: 181 – 203.

Clarkson, M.B.E (1995) *A Stakeholder Framework for Analyzing and Evaluating Corporate Social Performance,* Academy of Management Review, volume: 20, No1, Page: 92-117

Etzioni, A. (1964) *Modern Organisations*, Upper Saddle River, NJ, Prentice Hall.

Freeman, R.E., (1984) *Strategic Management: a Stakeholder Approach*, Marshfield, MA: Pitman.

McAlister, D.T., Ferrell, O.C., Ferrell, L. (2005) *Business and Society A Strategic Approach to Social Responsibility*, 2nd Edn, Houghon Mifflin Company, New York.

McDonagh, P. (1998) *Towards a Theory of Sustainable Communication in Risk Society: Relating Issues of Sustainability to Marketing Communications*, Journal of Marketing Management, volume: 14, Issues: 6 Page: 591–622.

Mitchell, R., Bradley, R.A., Wood, J.D. (1997) Toward a Theory of Stakeholder Identification and Salience: Defining the Principle of Who and what Really Counts, Academy of Management Review; Oct 97, Volume: 22 Issue: 4, Page: 853-886.

Moorhouse Consulting (2007), Beyond conventional stakeholder management: developing PRIME intelligence on complex programs, in Chinyio E. and Olomolayie P. (edits.), 2010, *Construction Stakeholders Management*, Blackwell Publishing, available at http://books.google.ro/books?id=ptPD8zz-vTcC&pg=PA1&lpg=PA1&dq=Chinyio+E+Construction+stakeholders+managem ent&source=bl&ots=BKMnYGYXtv&sig=5pRnHRVsrPIfWFbzfpnkP2pH57o&hl=r o&ei=tR9ITIGaLsvdsAbsuuCVDg&sa=X&oi=book_result&ct=result&resnum=1&v ed=0CAwQ6AEwAA#v=onepage&q=Chinyio%20E%20Construction%20stakehold ers%20management&f=false.

NGO statement in support of Roşia Montană community, January 22, 2007, available at http://www.earthworksaction.org/pubs/RM_NGOstatement.pdf.

Nistorescu, C., 2010, *Afacere guvernamentală cu aur de Roşia*, available at http://www.rosiamontana.org/.

Polonsky, M.J., 2005, *Stakeholders thinking in marketing*, European Journal of Marketing, volume: 39 Issue 9/10, Page: 1199-1216.

Proiectul Rosia Montana este un proiect pentru Romania, available at http://www.rmgc.ro/proiectul-rosia-montana/economie.

Recklies, D., 2001, *Stakeholder Management*, Recklies Management Project GmbH, available at www.themanager.org.

Richards, J., 2005, Rosia Montana gold controversy, *Mining Environmental Management*, January 2005 pp. 5-13, available at http://www.dundee.ac.uk/cepmlp/ journal/html/Vol15/Vol15_13.pdf.

Savage, G. T. , Nix, T. W., Whitehead, C. J., & Blair, J. D., 1991, *Strategies for assessing and managing organizational stakeholders.* Academy of Management Executive, 5, pp. 61-75.

Suchman, M.C., 1995, *Managing legitimacy: strategic and institutional approaches*, Academy of Management Review, Volume: 20 Page: 571-610.

Universitatea "1 Decembrie 1918" Alba Iulia (2007) *Studiu privind impactul economic si social al al proiectului minier propus de catre Rosia Montana Gold Corporation*, available at http://www.rmgc.ro/sites/default/files/opiniile-expertilor/UAB-Studiu-economic-SUMAR-EXTINS-2007.pdf, accessed at 22 August 2011

Werhane, P.H., Freeman, R.E. (1999). *Business ethics: the state of the art International Journal of Management Reviews*, Volume: 1 Issue:1, Page:1-16.

Werther Jr., W.B., Chandler, D. (2006) *Strategic Corporate Social Responsibility Stakeholders in a Global Environment*, USA, Sage Publications, p. 4.

Wolfe, R.A., Putler, D.S. (2002), *How tight are the ties that bind stakeholder groups?*, Organization Science, Volume: 13 No. 1, Page: 64-80.

Acknowledgment

This study was carried out under the project no. 1888 IDEI, financed by CNCSIS.

Towards sustainable marketing systems

SUMESH R NAIR

ABSTRACT

Sustainable marketing is an important business practice in the wake of the environmental troubles of recent times. However, a very comprehensive framework for the practice of the same is missing in the literature. This chapter is an attempt to offer a basic framework of sustainable marketing, aiding practitioners and academics in gaining a better understanding – and for further development of the concept. The framework uses the conventions of systems thinking, holistic marketing and green marketing for the development of the framework. The chapter concludes that sustainable organisations precede sustainable marketing and green practices, therefore, the focus should be to develop sustainable organisations. And, because of its all-pervading nature in organisations, marketing can take a central role in spearheading green practices in sustainable organisations.

KEY WORDS

sustainable marketing, green marketing, holistic marketing, systems thinking

Introduction

Sustainable business initiatives, like sustainable marketing, are reported to impact firm performance and reputation (Baker & Sinkula 2005; Miles & Covin 2000). However, the exact nature and extent of sustainable marketing has not been explored enough in the extant literature (Nair & Menon 2008). This chapter proposes a comprehensive sustainable marketing framework that encompasses various levels and functions of organisations' performance. Nothing less than a systems perspective of an organisation is essential for the effective development and implementation of sustainable initiatives; hence the framework is called a Sustainable Marketing System (SMS). A systems perspective of an organisation is important given the recent findings that marketing as a business function is losing its importance and influence within firms (Verhoeef & Leeflang 2009), largely due to its narrow focus.

'Sustainable marketing' (Van Dam & Apeldoorn 1996) in this chapter will be treated along the lines of concepts like 'environmental marketing' (Peattie 1995; Polonsky 1995), 'green marketing' (Charter 1992; Ottman 1993) and 'ecological marketing' (Apaiwongse 1994). Peattie (2001) has observed that that sustainable marketing is the latest incarnation of green marketing practice, which had started off as ecological marketing in 1970s and then had an environmental marketing perspective in 1980s. However, it is assumed that at a fundamental level all these practices embody the same philosophy and pursue the same commitment, that is, trying to improve the environmental performance of firm and their stakeholders. Therefore, this paper proposes a fundamental approach in developing a sustainable marketing system with the help of a holistic or systems organisational perspective.

Holistic marketing and sustainable marketing

To develop the theoretical constructs of holistic sustainable marketing, this paper uses literature from two major areas: (1) holistic marketing, and (2) sustainable and green marketing.

The holistic approach in business practices is rooted in theories of systems thinking (Checkland 1981; Forrester 1961, 1994; Senge 1990). According to the systems theory perspective, modern organisations are better understood as 'open systems'. An open system is often described in terms of systems thinking. Systems thinking would generally encourage organisational players to see the bigger picture when it comes to solving complicated problems. This perspective helps to deal with organisational problems in their totality.

Though not widely researched and reported in the literature, holistic marketing has slowly gained prominence in marketing text books recently. Kotler, Keller and Burton (2009, p. 18) have defined Holistic Marketing as

> ...development, design, and implementation of marketing programmes, processes, and activities that recognises their breadth and interdependencies. Holistic marketing recognises that 'everything matters' with marketing - and that broad, integrated perspective is often necessary.

Holistic marketing proposes four major processes namely, internal marketing, performance marketing, relationship marketing and integrated marketing (Kotler, Keller & Burton 2009) (Figure 8.1).

Figure 8.1 Holistic marketing

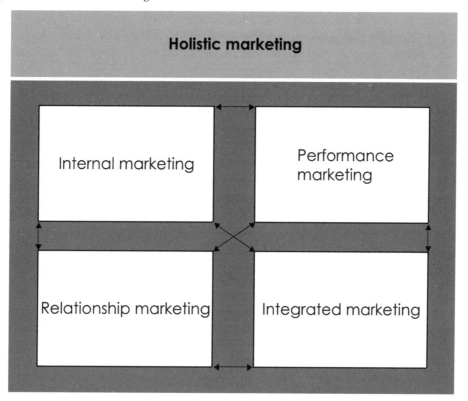

Internal marketing is primarily meant for the internal stakeholders of the company, to prepare them for effective external marketing interactions. 'Internal marketing ensuring that everyone in the organisation embraces appropriate marketing principles, especially senior management' (Kotler, Keller & Burton 2009, p. 22) Performance marketing on the other hand is meant for making the external stakeholders receptive to the marketing initiatives of the firm in '…understanding the returns to the business from marketing activities and programs, as well as addressing broader concerns and their legal, social and organisational effects'(Kotler, Keller & Burton 2009, p. 22). Relationship marketing proposes establishing a long-lasting relationship with firm's stakeholders and ensuring that lifelong value is delivered to them. Integrated marketing concentrates on developing 'fully integrated marketing programs to create, communicate, and deliver value for consumers' (Kotler *et al.* 2009, p. 21).

While expounding the environmental marketing concept, Coddington (1993, p. 1) has highlighted the holistic perspective of the concept and observed that 'environmental marketing is about more than environmental marketing'. Coddington's intention was to give emphasis to the depth of the practice, which goes beyond the boundaries of marketing as a business function. Peattie

(1995, p. 28) complemented this idea by defining green marketing as: 'the holistic management process responsible for identifying, anticipating, and satisfying the requirements of the consumers and society, in a profitable and sustainable way'. Charter (1992, p. 28) has proposed a strategic dimension to the concept. According to him,

> Greener marketing is a holistic and responsible strategic management process that identifies, anticipates, satisfies and fulfils stakeholder needs, for a reasonable reward, that does not adversely affect human or natural environmental well-being.

The majority of green/environmental/sustainable marketing literature was developed in late 80s and 90s. Most of the contributions to the conceptualisation of the practice happened during this time, primarily through the work of Charter (1992), Coddington (1993), Ottman (1993), Peattie (1995), Polonsky (1995) and Menon and Menon (1997). Peattie and Crane (2005) have observed that 'green marketing' practices in its early years attracted hype in the late 80s and early 90s that led to serious research and publication of green literature. However, the practice experienced a slump in the late 90s and early 2000s. Ottman, Stafford and Hartman (2006), while investigating the problem, identified short-sighted green marketing initiatives that they called 'green marketing myopia', which are partly to blame for the decline in interest.

Though literature agrees on the nature of green/environmental/sustainable marketing in general, a comprehensive framework for the practice of the same is largely absent.

Sustainable marketing system

Holistic and systems perspectives as mentioned previously are thought to be better tools to develop an absolute sustainable marketing practice. Following the conventions of systems thinking, the SMS philosophy assumes to work effectively in an 'eco-thinking' culture of an organisation (Nair & Menon 2008), everyone concerned is expected to think proactively for comprehensive environmental solutions. Eco-thinking should be interwoven into the culture of organisations, justifying the 'everyone and everything matters' philosophy in the making of a sustainable organisation.

A marketing framework of four interrelated processes is adopted for the SMS framework; however, SMS proposes some differences in the depth and details of the processes and introduces the theoretical framework shown in Figure 8.2. A detailed discussion follows.

Figure 8.2 Sustainable marketing systems framework

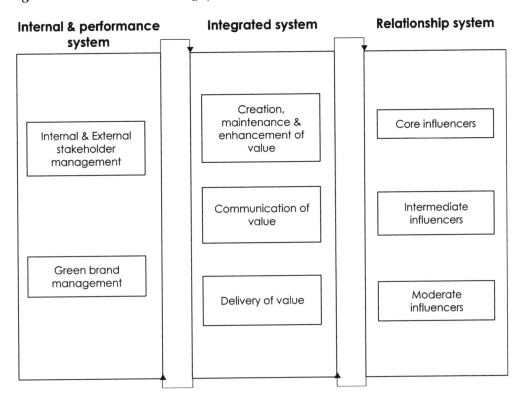

Internal and performance system

Internal and external stakeholder management

Clarkson (1995) argued that corporate social responsibility initiatives should be developed by taking into account the needs of all major stakeholder groups. Dissatisfaction in any primary stakeholder groups in this regard would lead to their lack of interest and support for the firm (Clarkson 1995). A primary stakeholder group according to Clarkson (1995) is one that interacts with the firm on a regular basis, and without its participation an organisation cannot survive. Examples of such groups are shareholders, investors, customers, suppliers, employees, governments and communities. Many similar studies have classified stakeholders based on different parameters and suggested strategies to deal with them (for example Mitchell, Agle & Wood 1997; Buysse & Verbeke 2003; Freeman 1984; Frooman 1999; Polonsky & Scott 2005; Touminen 1995).

Mitchell *et al.* (1997) identified many classes of stakeholders based on three attributes: power, legitimacy and urgency. Frooman (1999) argued that the stakeholder influence is determined by the dependency of the company on stakeholders and vice versa. Buysse and Verbeke (2003) introduced a stakeholder classification namely, primary and secondary stakeholders, based on the type of relationship they have with the firm. However, most studies have attempted to classify stakeholders on the basis of the frequency of their interactions and economic impact on organisations. For environmental and sustainable marketing, a new perspective and approach is desirable. The firm-stakeholder relationship cannot be entirely understood based on economic interactions as the relationship equations may differ in situations characterised by sustainable marketing.

This chapter proposes a new classification (Figure 8.3), which groups stakeholders into three categories depending on their influence on the sustainable marketing practices of an organisation. The 'core influencers' are the first category; they are not only closer to the organisation, they also impact sustainable initiatives of the firm more closely than the stakeholders in other two groups. For example, because of their closeness, the influence of the two internal stakeholders (employees and management) on environmental marketing might be stronger than external stakeholders. Besides, in most cases, management and employees are the ones who develop, implement and maintain a firm's environmental marketing strategies and at the same time safeguard the interests of other stakeholders. Government, customers and active public are believed to impact and be impacted by the sustainable initiatives of a firm more than other stakeholders; hence their inclusion in the core group. Business partners, competitors, media and non-government organisations (NGOs) are not usually concerned about the environmental orientation of the firm unless there are related issues that impact them. Hence they are part of 'intermediate inflecting group'. Courts/the legal system, financial institutions and the scientific community tend not to intervene in the environmental activities of a firm unless there are compelling reasons; hence they are classified as 'moderate influencers'. Sustainable marketing strategies intended for internal and external stakeholder management would find this classification useful (Nair & Ndubisi 2011).

Green corporate brand management

Green brand building and management is a complex and challenging area. Studies on green brand management are not extensively reported but brand management in general is widely studied and reported in the literature (Hartman, Ibáñez & Sainz 2005). The development of a green corporate brand image is a basic necessity in holistic sustainable marketing. This is definitely not the domain of a marketing department in the conventional sense of business. However, to fulfil the holistic ambitions of SMS, ideally the marketing department should spearhead the green corporate brand building process and the corporate think-tank (and everybody else in an organisation) work alongside in this initiative. van Reil and Balmer (1997) have suggested that 'corporate identity', which is also known as 'corporate branding' (van Reild & Maathuis 1993), needs the positioning of the entire organisation in the minds of its stakeholders. Coddington (1993) and Peattie (1995)

Figure 8.3 Stakeholder influence on sustainable marketing

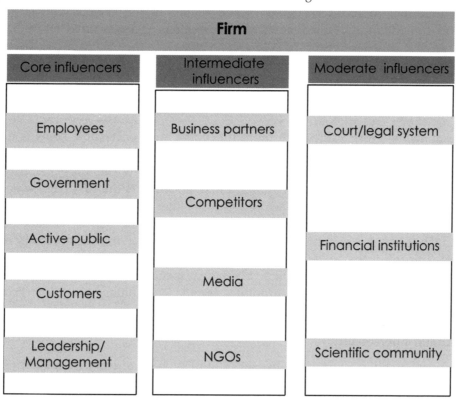

have proposed a few ideas in the green positioning strategy of a firm that are concerned with product line positioning rather than corporate brand positioning. However, following the convention of SMS, it is best to use the 'identity-reputation gap model' (Figure 8.4) of brand management proposed by de Chernatory and Harris (2000). Green corporate brand building needs a very systematic and proactive method of brand building like the identity-reputation gap model that also fuses well with the stakeholder theory approach elucidated in the previous section of SMS.

The identity-reputation gap model suggests the following components as part of the corporate brand building process: the brand's vision, the brand's culture, the brands positioning, the brand's personality, relationships, presentation and reputation (de Chernatory & Harris 2000). A detailed discussion on these components and relating them to the SMS framework follows.

The brand's vision

de Chernatory & Harris (2000) have suggested the brand's vision to be the starting point. It is the responsibility of the managers to develop the brand's green vision and communicate it clearly to the internal and external stakeholders of the firm. This is of paramount importance to SMS because of its green and sustainable orientation, which needs to stay clearly in the minds of the stakeholders for extended periods of time for desired effect.

The brand's culture

It is important to blend the green brand values of the organisation with the organisational culture. This also should be initiated as a concerted effort by top management in order to fuse the core green values into the collective psyche of the organisation. Eco-thinking initiatives of SMS discussed previously would be the ideal method in this regard.

The brand's positioning

Translating the green values into more functional and conceivable benefits to the major stakeholders is the essence of green brand positioning. Peattie (1995) has suggested a few eco-positioning strategies that a company can adopt for effective positioning of green products. 'Finding a new position' is the first part, which he believes is easy because of the newness of the environmental performance dimension of a product; hence an unabridged gap in the market is likely to be found. The second part is 'repositioning the product' which may be necessary in the future. The third one is 'repositioning the competition' and the fourth, 'position close to the market leader'. Peattie's (1995) ideas focus more at the functional level; however, while developing corporate brand positioning a much broader perspective is necessary.

The brand's personality

Brand personality is defined as 'the set of human characteristics associated with a brand' (Aaker 1997, p. 347). Green brand personality can project the personalities of typical green consumers. Green consumers take into account how their purchase decisions affect social and environmental issues (Follows & Jobber 2000). Laroche, Bergeron and Barbaro-Forleo (2001) have reported that green consumers were mostly females, married, with at least one child living at home. This image can be projected while developing the green brand personality of an organisation. However, this needs to be projected consistently through the media and the behaviour of the organisation's staff (van Reil & Balmer 1997) for effective results.

Relationships

Though the concept of relationship marketing is familiar to the business world, only in the late 80s and early 90s were serious academic efforts shown to offer a conceptual framework to the practice. The pioneering work of Berry, Shostack and Upah (1983), McKenna (1991) and Grönroos (1996) has helped to provide insights into relationship marketing practice; however, McKenna is widely acknowledged as the major contributor in this area (Aijo 1996). In the SMS framework, relationship building efforts do not stop with a firm's consumers. More about relationship building with stakeholders will be discussed in relation to relationship systems of the SMS framework in the next section.

Presentation

Presentation is about the communication of a brand's identity to its stakeholders. Sustainable communication is defined by McDonagh (1998, p. 599) as 'an interactive social process of unravelling and eradicating alienation that may occur between an

Figure 8.4 The 'identity-reputation gap' model of brand management

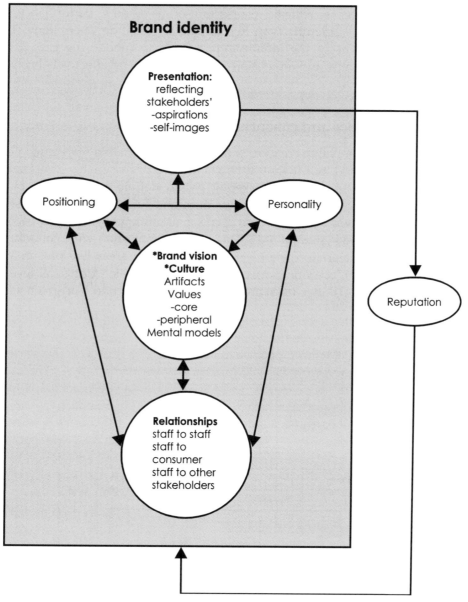

Source: de Chernatory and Harris (2000).

organisation and its publics or stakeholders'. However, presentation in this context is about carefully communicating the corporate sustainable brand image of the organisation. Clear messages and symbols that convey accurate and intended green brand identity and personality to its audience are important in corporate communication.

Reputation

Fombrun and van Rindova (1997, p. 10) have defined brand reputation as 'a collective representation of a brand's past actions and results that describes the brand's ability to deliver valued outcomes to multiple stakeholders'. Brand reputation would offer a realistic estimation of a brand's performance and perceptions of a brand's identity (van Reil & Balmer 1997). de Chernatony (1999) has reported that by using the identity-reputation gap model, the gap, if any, between the brand identity and reputation can be assessed and effectively bridged.

Integrated system

Creation, maintenance and enhancement of value

Environmental or green value-creation is the core of sustainable marketing. Green value is not only created, but it should be maintained at reasonable levels and be constantly enhanced. Sustainable marketing would definitely be judged by the quality of the green products and the process through which they are produced and marketed. Value-creation being the core of any marketing program thus becomes the focus the integrated system of SMS. This needs organisation-wide commitment and a high level of integration among various functional areas like procurement, inventory management, operations management, logistics, etc. Almost all levels of the value chain process (Porter 1985) are involved in this function. The green value-

Figure 8.5 The green value-added (gva) process

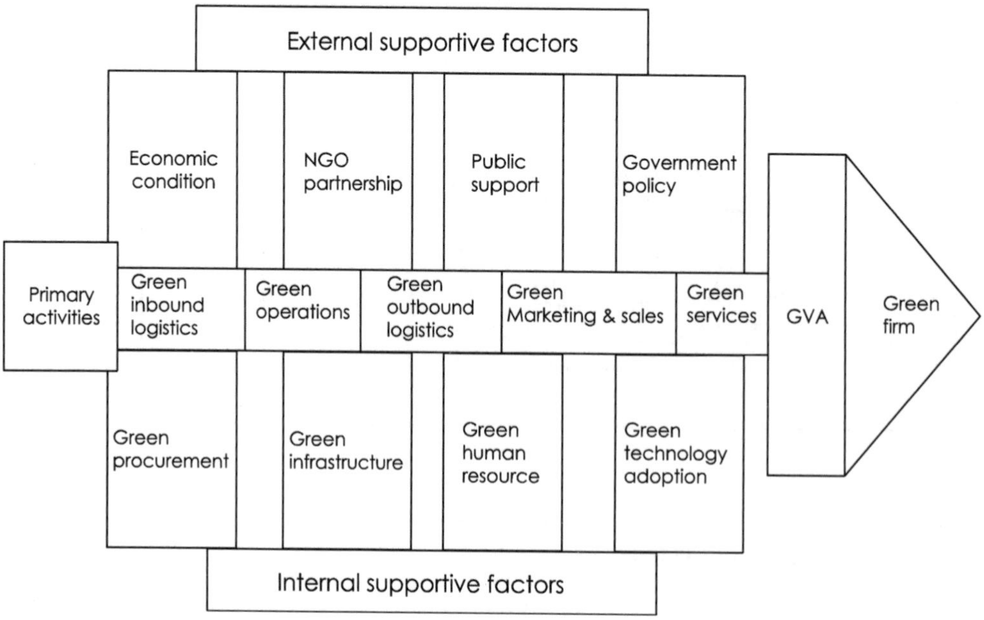

Sources: Ndubisi and Nair (2009); Porter (1985).

added framework (Figure 8.5) proposed by Ndubisi and Nair (2009) is useful here to create green value.

Green value-adding is a technically complex process. The firm should develop a broader perspective in the entire production process: from procurement of raw materials, to inbound logistics, to the manufacturing process, to outbound logistics, to waste disposal to services. Pun (2006) has identified six major tools that can be used for environmentally responsible operations (ERO): i) life cycle assessment; ii) green quality function deployment; iii) design for recycling and remanufacturing; iv) green purchasing; v) green material requirements planning; and vi) green supply chain. Pun's (2006) idea can be incorporated in the green value-added framework (Ndubisi & Nair 2009) to guide the value-creation, maintenance and enhancement process in the SMS.

Communication of value

At the functional level communication of green value methods and strategies are basically the same as any other marketing communication initiative. The objective of green communication is to inform, persuade or remind customers about the green products and initiatives of the company (Peattie 1995). However, SMS with its systems perspectives and scope would draw on corporate environmental communication literature to aid its development and implementation. According to van Reil (1995, p. 26), corporate communication is

> an instrument of management by means of which all consciously used forms of internal and external communication are harmonised as effectively and efficiently as possible, so as to create a favourable basis for relationships with groups upon which the company is dependent.

van Riel (1995) has suggested three communication methods (Figure 8.6) to establish contact with different groups of stakeholders. SMS can adopt van Riel's (1995) integrated corporate communication model for effective dialogue with its key stakeholders.

Figure 8.6 Partial adaptation of van Riel's (1995) integrated corporate communication model

Source: Welch and Jackson (2007).

Delivery of value

A value delivery system typically makes use of marketing channels and logistics networks (Kotler *et al.* 2010). A conventional distribution system considers aspects like speed and timely delivery of the goods, the distance travelled by the goods, the means of travel, locations of travel, the expenses and the risks involved. The Green value delivery system covers all these but considers eco-efficiency as the main focus. Kotler *et al.* (2010) have suggested a comprehensive framework (Figure 8.7) to understand how a marketing logistic network works in a manufacturing industry setting. However, in all possible value delivery processes, the focal point, as far as SMS is concerned, is eco-efficiency and green value to customers and other major stakeholder groups.

Figure 8.7 Manufactured goods marketing logistics

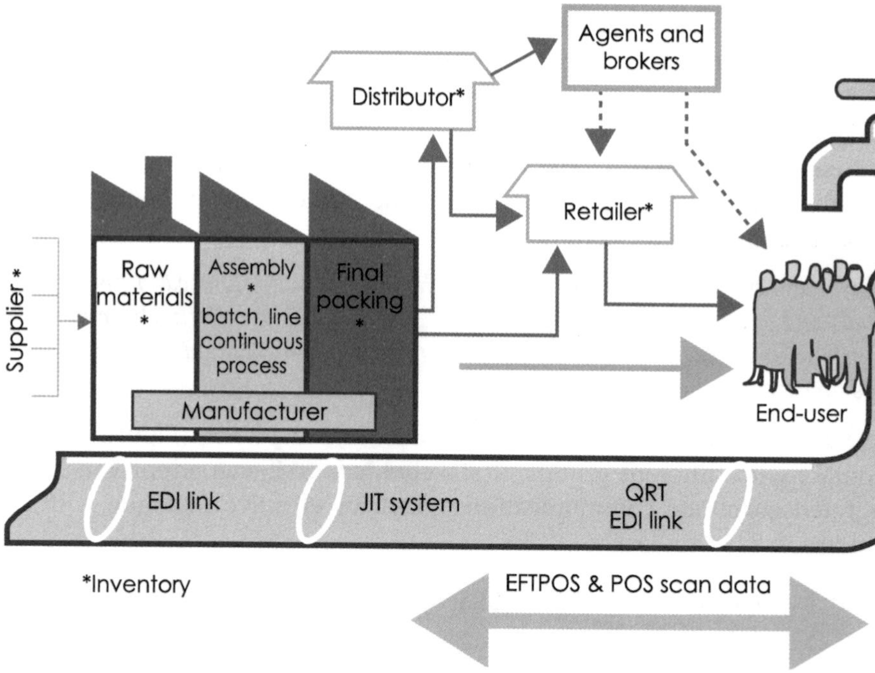

Source: Kotler *et al.* 2010.

Relationship system

Kotler, Keller and Burton (2009, p. 20) suggested that 'relationship marketing aims to build mutually satisfying long-term relationships with key constituents in order to earn and retain their business'.

Wasik (1996) identified three major components in a successful stakeholder partnering program: identify stakeholders; communicate with stakeholders and identify issues in common; and set up, monitor, and evaluate a partnering program.

Since environmental concerns are issues of special importance to the world, it is vital to identify the stakeholders who share the same concern and build up long-lasting, mutually beneficial relationships with them through the practice of SMS. The same three-step process is slightly modified for the purpose of the SMS framework. The revised steps are:

Identify the stakeholder groups based on its importance and influence

The SMS relationship system uses the same classification and logic given in Figure 8.2 for the purpose. Therefore, the stakeholder groups identified are core influencers, intermediate influencers and moderate influencers.

Communicate with green consumers and other stakeholders, identify the environmental issues in common

Establishing initial communication with the stakeholders is the key in SMS. It is indeed essential to identify and understand the common environmental concerns and demands of the stakeholders, especially with those in the core group. The issues identified may differ from organisation to organisation, and from stakeholder group to stakeholder group. However, it is important to address the major common concerns that need to be resolved urgently.

Developing the relationship

Wasik (1996) has suggested a few guidelines to follow while developing a partnering program with stakeholders. They are used for SMS with some modification to make them suitable for the framework. They are:

- Structure the company's clear environmental message to all different stakeholder groups.

- Review the organisation's sustainable marketing goals thoroughly.

- Verify the environmental claim and marketing methods.

- Establish an eco-literacy program to educate the stakeholders.

- Find out the reason for any possible customer confusion, poor credibility and cynicism and prepare plans to address these issues.

- Develop a comprehensive relationship program at the tactical and strategic levels. At the tactical level the emphasis should be to create and deliver superior green values to the consumers and other stakeholders. At the strategic level, effort should be made to establish and maintain a lifelong relationship with all stakeholders.

Conclusion

This chapter proposed a basic SMS framework that is capable of establishing an organisation's sustainable agenda in the most comprehensible and convincing fashion to the outside world – especially to the stakeholders. It is argued that sustainable marketing will contribute to the satisfaction of a firm's (green) consumers and other key stakeholders and this ultimately would lead to a long lasting relationship between the firm and its key stakeholders. The SMS framework uses a holistic and systems approach to emphasise the fact that sustainable commitments and practices should be developed as organisation-wide philosophies to meet the firm's desired goals. It is suggested in the chapter that it is not sustainable for green practices to build sustainable organisations; rather, sustainable organisations yield sustainable practices. In other words, sustainable organisations antecede sustainable practices. Therefore, the focus should be to develop sustainable and green organisations. Marketing activities with their very holistic impact in organisations can spearhead such initiatives. The SMS framework is intended to propose a basic structure to inspire thoughts and ideas in this direction, a more detailed framework should be developed to aid clear understanding and practices in this area.

References

Aaker, J.L. (1997). Dimensions of brand personality. *Journal of Marketing Research.* 34, 3.

Aijo, T. S. (1996). The Theoretical and Philosophical Underpinnings of Relationship Marketing. *European Journal of Marketing,*30, 8-18.

Apaiwongs. T.S. (1994). The Influence of Green Policies on a Dual Marketing Center - An Ecological Marketing Approach. *Journal of Business & Industrial Marketing,* 9, 41-50.

Baker, W., & Sinkula, J.M., (2005). Environmental strategy and Firm performance: Effects on New Product Performance and Market Share. *Journal of the Academy of Marketing Science.* 33, 4, 461-475.

Berry, L.L., Shostack, G.L., Upah, G.D. (Eds). (1983). *Emerging Perceptions on Service Marketing. Chicago* :American Marketing Association.

Buysse, R. & Verbeke A. (2003). Proactive Environmental Strategies: A stakeholder Management Perspective. *Strategic Management Journal.* 24, 453-470.

Charter, M. (1992). Green Marketing- A Responsible Approach to Business. U.K:Greenleaf Publishing.

Checkland, P. (1981), *Systems Thinking, Systems Practice,* Chichester, UK: Wiley.

Clarkson, M. B. E (1995). A stakeholder framework for analyzing and evaluating corporate social performance. *The Academy of Management Review;* 20, 1, 92-117.

Coddington, W. (1993). *Environmental Marketing - Positive Strategies for Reaching the Green Consumer.* N.Y :McGraw-Hill.

de Chernatony, L. (1999), ``Brand management through narrowing the gap between brand identity and brand reputation'', *Journal of Marketing Management,* Vol. 15, pp. 157-79.

de Chernatory, L. & Harris, F. (2000). Developing Corporate Brands through Considering Internal and External Stakeholders. *Corporate Reputation Review.* 3,3.

Follows, S. B. & Jobber, D. (2000). Environmentally Responsible Purchase Behaviour: A Test of a Consumer Model, *European Journal of Marketing,* 34, 723-746.

Fombrun, C. J. and van Rindova, C.B.M. (1997), The Reputational Landscape. *Corporate Reputation Review.* 1(1/2) 5-13

Frooman, J. (1999). Stakeholder Influence Strategies. *Academy of Management Review*. 24, 191-205.

Forrester, J. W. (1994) System dynamics, systems thinking, and soft OR System. *Dynamics Review*. 10, 2-3; 245-256

Forrester, J. W. (1961). *Industrial Dynamics*. Portland, Ore: Productivity Press.

Freeman, R. E. (1984). *Strategic management: A stakeholder approach*. Boston: Pitman.

Grönroos, C. (1996). Relationship Marketing: Strategic and Tactical Implications, *Management Decision*, 34, 5-14.

Hartman. P, Ibáñez, V.A., & Sainz, F.J.F., (2005). Green Branding effects on Attitude. *Marketing Intelligence & Planning*. 23, 1.

Kotler, P., Keller, K. L., & Burton, S. (2009) *Marketing Management*. Pearson Education; NSW.

Kotler, P., Brown, L., Burton, S., Deans. K., & Amstrong, G. (2010). *Marketing (8e)*. Pearson: NSW.

Laroche, M., Bergeron, J., & Barbaro-Forleo, G. (2001). Targeting Consumers Who are Willing to Pay More for Products. *Journal of Consumer Marketing*,18, 503-520.

McDonagh, P. (1998). Towards a Theory of Sustainable Communication in Risk Society: Relating Issues of Sustainability to Marketing Communications. *Journal of Marketing Management*. 14(6): 591–622

McKenna, R. (1991). Relationship Marketing: Successful Strategies for the Age of the Customer. Reading: Addison-Wesley.

Menon, A. & Menon, A. (1997). Enviropreneurial Marketing Strategy: The Emergence of Corporate Environmentalism as Market Strategy. Journal of Marketing. 61, 51-67.

Miles, M & Covin, G. (2000) Environmental Marketing: A Source of Reputational, Competitive, and Financial Advantage. Journal of Business Ethics, 23, 299–311.

Mitchell, R.K. Agle, B.R. & Wood, D.J. (1997) Towards a Theory of Stakeholder Identification and Salience: Defining the Principles of Who and What Really Matters. Academy of Management Review. 22, 853-886.

Nair, S.R. & Menon, G. (2008). Environmental Marketing System: A Proposed Model based on Indian Experience, Business Strategy & Environment, 17, 8. 467-479

Nair, S.R and Ndubisi, N.O. (2011), Stakeholder Influences on Environmental Marketing. Journal of Management Research. 11 (2): 67-76.

Ndubisi, N.O. & Nair, S.R. (2009) Green Entrepreneurship (GE) And Green Value Added (GVA): A Conceptual Framework. International Journal of Entrepreneurship, 13, Special Issue. pp 21-34

Ottman J.A., Stafford E.R., Hartman C.L. (2006). Green Marketing Myopia. Environment Science and Policy for Sustainable Development 48: 21–36.

Ottman, J. A. (1993). *Green Marketing - Opportunity for Innovation*. Illinois: NTC Business Books

Peattie, K (1995). *Environmental Marketing Management - Meeting the Green Challenge*. London: Pitman Publishing.

Peattie, K. (2001). Towards sustainability: The third age of green marketing. The Marketing Review, 2(2), 129–146.

Peattie, K. & Crane, A. (2005). Green marketing: legend, myth, farce or prophesy? Qualitative Market Research: An International Journal, 8, 357-370.

Polonsky, M. J. & Scott, D. (2005). An Empirical Examination of the stakeholder Strategy Matrix. *European Journal of Marketing*. 39. 9/10. 1119

Polonsky, M. J. (1995) A Stakeholder Theory Approach to Designing Environmental Marketing Strategy , *Journal of Business & Industrial Marketing*, 10, 29-46.

Porter, M. E. (1985). *Competitive Advantage*, The Free Press, New York.

Pun, K.F. (2006). Determinants of Environmentally Responsible Operations: A Review. *International Journal of Quality & Reliability Management*. 23, 279-297.

Senge, P. M. 1990. *The Fifth Discipline*. New York: Doubleday/Currency

Tuominen, P. (1995), *Relationship Marketing-A New Potential for Managing Corporate Investor Relations*. In: Nasi, J. (ed.), Understanding Stakeholder Thinking, pp. 165–183. Helsinki Finland: LSR-Publications.

Van Dam, & Apeldoorn Y.K., (1996), Sustainable Marketing. *Journal of Macromarketing*,16. 45-56.

van Reil, C.B.M. and Balmer, J.M.T. (1997). Corporate Identity: The Concept, its Measure, and Management. *European Journal of Marketing*. 31, 5/6, 340-355.

van Riel, C.B.M. (1995), *Principles of Corporate Communication*, Prentice-Hall, Hemel Hempstead, UK.

van Reild, C.B.M & Maathuis, O.J.M. (1993). *Corporate Branding*, Working Paper, Erasmus University Rotterdam.

Verhoef, P. & Leeflang, P.S.H. (2009). Understanding the Marketing Department's influence within the firm. *Journal of Marketing*, 73, 14-37

Wasik, J.F. (1996). *Green Marketing & Management: A Global Perspective*. Massachusetts :Blackwell Business.

Welch, M. and Jackson, P.R. (2007) Rethinking internal communication: a stakeholder approach. Corporate Communications: *An International Journal*. 12, 2. pp. 177-198

How should we dispose of the dead? Addressing the environmental issues

LOUISE CANNING AND ISABELLE SZMIGIN

ABSTRACT

As recognition grows regarding the need to move towards a more sustainable form of existence, so the way of thinking must change amongst individuals, organisations and governments. A move towards more mindful consumption can lead to reduced resource use and less environmentally damaging behaviour. However, demand in some markets is unlikely to drop, reduced surplus and reverse supply is less applicable, reuse and recycling is not an option, and the choices available are limited. The funeral industry and specifically the disposal of the dead are subject to such pressures. Removal of the dead is a common yet essential activity that is of personal and emotional significance. It is also something that cannot be avoided and therefore is of fundamental environmental consequence. We present a case study which examines the convergence of the consumer decision with key environmental issues associated with disposal of the dead: land use; material and resource consumption; and waste and emissions. The case study centres specifically on disposal practices in the United Kingdom which is an ethnically diverse country. Currently cremation dominates, but the United Kingdom is witnessing shifts in practices and an emerging demand amongst some for greater consumer choice and influence in the funeral ritual and disposal.

Introduction

The call for society to move towards more mindful consumption (Sheth, Sethia & Srinivas 2011) requires countries, governments, private and public sector organisations, as well as individuals, to consume fewer resources and to engage in activities that are as environmentally benign as possible (Polonsky 2011). So if we have to travel, we are encouraged to use methods of transport other than, for example, aeroplane or private automobile. If we do use the automobile then we might opt for a car-pooling scheme, select models with alternatives to the internal combustion engine, delay the point at which we might replace the vehicle, and when we do replace it, ensure that the old vehicle is processed via a recognised recycling and disposal scheme (Auld 2001).

There are products that we can choose not to consume, but for those that we do consume, we can search out forms of consumption that are less environmentally damaging. There is, however, one activity that is fundamental to man's existence, cannot be avoided and in which everyone around the world will participate: disposal of the dead. While removal of the dead might be considered in the broader context of other disposal activities like electrical goods, cars or other consumer products, it is a unique process. The normal options to repair, reuse or recycle end-of-life goods do not exist when we are faced with the task of arranging a funeral and thus the disposal of a relative or friend (Canning & Szmigin 2010). The purpose of this case study is to examine the convergence of the consumer decision with key environmental issues associated with disposal of the dead, namely land use, material and resource consumption, waste and emissions. By 2009 the United Kingdom (UK) population stood at 61.8 million (Office for National Statistics 2010) – an increase of over 4% since 2001, resulting from a higher number of births and a slowing in the mortality rate, the latter totalling 0.56 million in 2009. That people are living longer is clearly good news, but in some senses this delays and presents different capacity demands for those organisations providing disposal services to the public. Removal of the dead is a universal activity that has personal, emotional, social as well as environmental consequences and generally consists of two forms, burial or cremation. Which of these disposal methods is used is strongly influenced by the religious and cultural context surrounding the consumer. This case study centres specifically on disposal practices in the UK, an ethnically diverse country in which cremation dominates but which at the same time is witnessing shifts in practices and an emerging demand amongst some for greater consumer choice and influence in the funeral ritual, and disposal as part of this.

Cremation

Whilst cremation is not accepted amongst Jewish and Muslim religions, it was legalised in the United Kingdom in 1884, approved by the Roman Catholic Church in the 1960s, and is practised by the Sikh and Hindu faiths and a large majority of the British population (secular and religious). It is now so widely accepted as an accessible and affordable disposal method that it accounts for over 70 per cent of all deaths in the United Kingdom (Davies & Mates 2005). This acceptance aside, there are clearly environmental consequences of the use of cremation, both in terms of energy consumption and emissions. Modern industrial cremators require up to two hours and temperatures in excess of 800°C to reduce the body to bone fragments and to minimise the release of chemical compounds and particulate matter. Filtering systems help control these emissions and the installation of mercury abatement equipment is now a requirement in the United Kingdom (as in other EU countries) to mitigate against the release of mercury from dental fillings during cremation (DEFRA 2005).

UK operators of crematoria actively seek ways in which to make the process more energy efficient as part of good business practice, and some have started using carbon footprinting to help do this. So, for example, one local authority has brought about a 30% reduction in energy consumption via improved operational processes such as rethinking scheduling and capacity management of its cremators. Another has invested in new equipment that will allow excess heat (generated when gases resulting from the cremation processes are cooled prior to filtration) to be used to heat the chapel and other parts of the crematorium facility. In the longer term it plans to investigate whether this heat can be used to generate electricity (Walker 2009).

Aside from reducing the environmental impact of existing cremation processes, some organisations are developing alternative methods to deal with the deceased. The company Resomation (www.resomation.com) has created a water and alkali-based method to transform the body into ash, and whilst the time taken to do this is comparable to cremation (taking 2–3 hours), the firm claims that its process uses less energy, produces less CO_2 emissions and eliminates others, such as mercury, completely. An alternative technology being developed by Cryomation (www.cryomation.co.uk) uses liquid nitrogen to render the body brittle and freeze-dry the resulting fragments to remove moisture. Cryomation argues that its 'cryonic cremation alternative technology' will result in 75 per cent reduction in CO_2 footprint and zero mercury emissions. However, both firms are yet to commercially install the technology in existing crematoria facilities in the UK, and legislation requires amendment to allow these disposal practices to be added to burial and cremation. Although these technologies are not yet accepted in the United Kingdom, in summer 2010 Resomation shipped its first commercial installation for 'Bio Cremation' to Florida via its US partner Matthews International.

Burial

Land burial has been practised since the Stone Age and in the United Kingdom there are between 12-20,000 graveyards, cemeteries and burial grounds (CABE 2007). The actual disposal of the deceased via land burial presents different issues compared to cremation, centring principally on contamination of land from chemicals used in wood coffins (preservatives, varnishes, sealers), materials used in metal caskets (lead, zinc, copper, steel) and embalming chemicals – approximately 50% of all bodies buried in the United Kingdom are embalmed. Contamination of land in the vicinity of water supplies and residential areas is avoided by either situating cemeteries in areas where soil conditions are such that leachates cannot pollute the sensitive areas nearby, or by locating burial sites away from these areas all together. Indeed, as in many other countries, the traditional churchyard has been replaced in the United Kingdom with municipally run cemeteries located on the outskirts of towns and cities. Whilst burial and cremation are both associated with (albeit different) forms of pollution, using land for burial has particular environmental consequences because cemeteries require maintenance and have capacity constraints.

Space for cemeteries is a major concern, and to contain the amount of land used for burial, countries such as Greece require that a grave be exhumed after 3 years and the remains placed in private or communal ossuaries – thus allowing for the regular reuse of burial plots. In the United Kingdom, however, such requirements do not exist and graves remain undisturbed for 75 years, or longer. This means that whilst there are up to 20,000 burial sites in the country, many of these are faced with major capacity constraints or have run out of space completely. Only the City of London Cemetery has introduced a program of grave reuse and in doing so has generated burial capacity for the next 5 years. Where this problem has not been addressed, capacity shortfall results in families either having to pay higher fees for the remaining sections or locating plots at cemeteries some distance away.

Consumer engagement in disposal choices

For some, religious practice determines the method of removal, and in other cases it can be that customary burial or cremation practised from one generation to the next or amongst immediate family members becomes the default means by which the deceased are disposed. However in the last decade or so the United Kingdom has witnessed a growing number of people seeking alternatives to customary practice – this might be the bereaved organising the funeral of a loved one, or alternatively, individuals writing living wills (ahead of their death) in which they specify details of their own funeral arrangements. Themes emerging from this shifting behaviour include the desire to have more control and individual choice throughout the funeral, to participate in a ritual that is a truer reflection of the deceased and to engage in a process of consumption that is less environmentally damaging. With regard to reduced environmental impact, consumption decisions include preparation and containment of the corpse, as well as disposal. So for example, embalming of the deceased is eschewed, and where a coffin is used then traditional materials (metal, solid wood, chipboard) are replaced with alternatives such as papier mâché, cardboard, banana leaves, bamboo, seagrass and willow. In terms of disposal, the United Kingdom has witnessed considerable growth in demand for natural burial where individuals are not required (for religious reasons) to practice cremation. Currently there are over 220 natural burial sites in the United Kingdom and whilst there is no universal definition of what constitutes such a site, unifying principles are:

- the absence of gravemarkers or where these are used, they do not detract from the natural landscape, indeed the most common marker tends to be a tree of some sort

- site maintenance regimes free from pesticides, herbicides and irrigation

- locations in existing cemeteries, meadows or woodlands or newly created facilities

- site protection from change in usage or future development.

(Clayden & Dixon 2007)

Choosing alternative coffin materials or opting for natural rather than traditional burial or cremation may be motivated by ecological reasons or the desire for a ritual which more closely embodies the identity of the deceased. Yet enacting these choices can be challenging. For example, not all funeral directors in the United Kingdom readily supply caskets other than those made of traditional materials – a consumer may have to request further choice from their undertaker or even have to source a coffin of their preferred material independently. Although there are more than 220 natural burial sites in the United Kingdom, funeral directors do not necessarily feature these as part of their service provision and there may not be such locations within easy travelling distance of the deceased or the bereaved. So although there may be interest amongst UK consumers in less environmentally damaging disposal practices, obstacles can exist that make it difficult for the individual consumer to act on this desire.

An important aspect of current and future provision relates specifically to the actual environmental impact of disposal practices. Alternative casket materials are presented/perceived as being more environmentally benign, and natural burial as less environmentally damaging than traditional burial and certainly less so than cremation. However, there has been little scientific comparison (or dissemination of information to the public) between materials used to contain corpses or processes for disposing of the dead. For example, there has been lifecycle analysis comparing burial with cremation and alternative technologies, but this is based on disposal practices in Holland. If the UK consumer is to make a choice, then not only should he/she be able to act upon this, but it should also be an informed choice.

Some consumers might be attracted to natural burial for ecological or personal reasons, but unless legislation changes in the United Kingdom to allow grave re-use (at fairly regular intervals) then as a form of disposal it will not resolve capacity constraints and in the future it may simply become an option for those with higher levels of disposable income. This leaves us with newer technologies such as those being developed by Cryomation and Resomation. Assuming that these can be shown to be less environmentally damaging than cremation, then for them to gain a foothold in the UK funeral market requires acceptance amongst funeral directors, owners of crematoria, government bodies, religious groups and most importantly the consumer. If cremation was legalised in the United Kingdom in 1884 but only really saw dramatic growth from the 1940s onwards, how long might it be before new technologies are accepted? And what forms of education and information provision might be needed to facilitate this process?

Conclusion

This case study has examined the sustainability challenge in a marketplace that until now has been overlooked. Disposal as part of the funeral ritual is a market that will always exist and for which demand will only fall when the world population declines. In light of this, meeting the sustainability challenge through more environmentally benign disposal practices is critical. This requires market readiness with regards such practices both in terms of their acceptance and access to them. Responsibility to bring about market readiness for more sustainable disposal methods is a shared obligation amongst different stakeholder groups, amongst individual consumers, the funeral industry, faith communities and governments.

References

Auld, JW. (2001). "Consumers, cars and communities: the challenge of sustainability". *International Journal of Consumer Studies*, 25: 228-237.

CABE, (2007), *Briefing: Cemeteries, Churchyards and Burial Grounds* [online], Commission for Architecture and the Built Environment. Available at http://www.cabe.org.uk/AssetLibrary/10701.pdf, [Accessed 20th March 2008]

Canning, L.E. & Szmigin, I. (2010). "Death and disposal: the universal, environmental dilemma". *Journal of Marketing Management*, 26: 1129-11242.

Clayden, A. and Dixon, K. (2007). "Woodland burial: memorial arboretum versus native woodland?" *Mortality*, 12: 240-260.

Davies, DJ. and Mates, LH. (2005). *Encyclopaedia of Cremation*, London: Ashgate Publishing.

DEFRA (2005), Control of Mercury Emissions from Crematoria, AQ1 (05) [online], Department for Environment, Food and Rural Affairs. Available at: http://www.defra.gov.uk/environment/ppc/localauth/pubs/guidance/notes/a qnotes/aq01(05).htm [Accessed 22nd July 2008]

Office for National Statistics (2010). UK Population Approaches 62 million. News Release, 24 June,

National Statistics Online, www.statistics.gov.uk/statbase/Product.asp?vlnk=601, [Accessed 30th September 2010].

Polonsky, MJ. (2011). "Transformative green marketing: impediments and opportunities". *Journal of Business Research*, (in press).

Sheth, JN. Sethia, NK. and Srinivas, S. (2011). "Mindful consumption: a customer-centric approach to sustainability". *Journal of the Academy of Marketing Science*, 39: 21-39.

Walker. E. 2009, Sussex crematoriums to generate electricity, The Argus, 8th December.

http://www.theargus.co.uk/news/4779646.Sussex_crematoriums_to_generate_electric ity_from_ bodies/[Accessed 3rd October 2010].

Introduction

To implement sustainability oriented marketing and consequent consumption successfully requires improved understanding of consumer behaviour and attitudes. Consumers have different needs with respect to information and their potential to be influenced by instruments and tools varies. Most consumers have a positive but passive view of sustainability consumption (OECD 2008). Different policy tools, instruments and information systems may need to be used to target different types of households, individuals or groups in regard to their purchasing behaviour. Currently, information plays a major role in influencing consumer decision-making. Proportionately, however, the contribution of information of direct relevance to the environment is small. Of the environmental information that is available, some is factual, but most is confusing, misleading or not immediately relevant to consumer concerns.

A number of studies have found a positive correlation between increased environmental information and consumer purchasing behaviour (Grankvist, Dahlstrand & Biel 2005). Consumer behaviour is a field of study that embraces many models derived from a range of disciplines such as psychology, sociology, social psychology, ecology and economics. Evolution of consumer behaviour runs on par with marketing concepts and it runs from production orientation to consumer orientation and then to societal orientation. Amongst these new faces of marketing concept transitions, sustainability marketing has considerable value as it endures and delivers solutions to ecologically oriented, viable, ethical and relationship-based needs.

Theoretical perspectives of consumer behaviour in this case are based on consumer buying behaviour, economic psychology, behavioural economics and ecological behaviour. Framework 1 (Figure 8.8) explains how consumer behaviour decision-making is dependent upon the effects of sustainability derived labelling. Sustainability derived labelling is based on the flow of sustainability marketing and to proceed to each level an interlock with each factor in the process is required. The ultimate outcome is enhanced sustainable development as producers find a market for the products of sustainable development initiatives and consumers build trust in claims of these producers.

Consumer behaviour

As per the framework, consumer buying behaviour plays a central role in decision making towards sustainability consumption. Consumer buying behaviour can be defined as the analysis of how independent consumers or groups purchase, use and regulate the services according to their needs and preferences. Even if environmental information has only a small influence on behaviour, this may be sufficient to influence a consumer's purchasing choice. Such choices are guided by a complex variety of mental processes and are therefore affected by different kinds of factors (Krarup & Russel 2005). Consumer buying/purchasing behaviour is a complex, multi-faceted territory. The context in which consumers make their choices determines whether sustainability consumption can become a reality

(Brandt 2003). To implement sustainability consumption successfully requires improved understanding of consumer behaviour and attitudes. Consumers have different needs with respect to information and their potential to be influenced by instruments and tools varies.

Figure 8.8 Framework 1: Interlocking flow of sustainability marketing, sustainability derived labelling with consumer behaviour

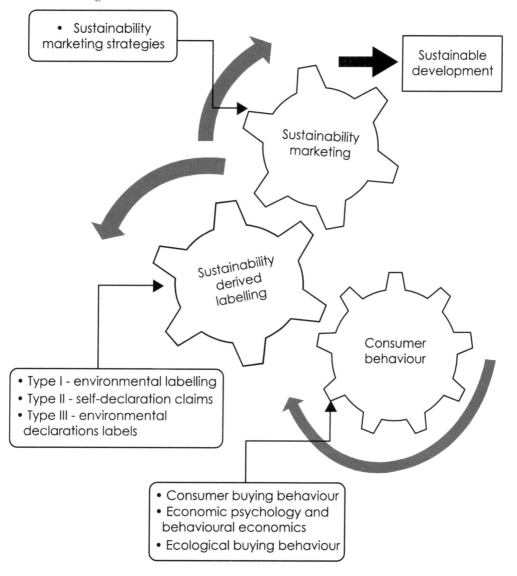

Most consumers have a positive but passive view of sustainability consumption (OECD 2008). Different policy tools and instruments and information systems may need to be targeted to different types of households, individuals or groups as per their purchasing behaviour. To assess opportunities that arise in the ecological market, interest is now focused on the consumer profile characteristics that best define a respectful behaviour towards the environment (Fraj & Martinez 2007).

Based on this, several studies have been developed to determine consumer buying behaviour.

These needs vary in different cultures, situations and depending on the characteristics of people (Kotler *et al.* 2009, p. 224). Therefore, those consumers whose purchasing behaviour is influenced by ecological environmental concerns will be considered as green consumers (Shrum, McCarty & Lowery 1995). Consumer research has focused on how individuals make purchasing decisions. The standard model of the purchase decision is a stage model (Kotler *et al.* 2009) in which the consumer recognises a need, collects information in some way to form product preferences, chooses specific product, consumes the product and finally considers satisfaction and other issues obtaining feedback that can be used in future decision-making.

In the last few decades, concerns about the environment have increased and the world has seen an exponential growth in campaigns and programs promoted by environmentalist groups who focus on environmental deterioration (Fraj & Martinez 2007; Thogerson 1996). As discussion goes on, involvement of government, organisations and consumers has resulted in increased protection and conservation of the environment and changes exerting an influence on consumer attitude and behaviour. Consumers are more aware of their responsibility to protect the environment, that it is not just the task of firms, institutions and government. Thus, a new type of consumer called 'the ecological consumer' has been identified and more companies have been interested to offer 'best satisfied' products to the ecological consumer.

Some (Grundey & Zaharia 2008) align 'green' and 'environmental' marketing as synonymous. They further define the concepts as the sum of activities to generate, facilitate and satisfy human needs or wants in such a way that it happens with minimal detrimental impact on the natural environment. Similarly, Peattie (1995) defined green marketing as a holistic management process that aims to recognise, understand and ultimately satisfy the needs of customers and also the overall society, in a profitable and sustainable way. Both definitions emphasise the ultimate aim of satisfying customer needs as a keystone of classical marketing, but with the addition of 'minimal detrimental impact' or 'in a sustainable manner' to make it green. Awareness of environmental issues and existing alternatives or solutions constitutes environmental knowledge and this affects the consumer's behaviour. Some of the research findings were contradictory in the analysis of how knowledge affects consumers' ecological behaviours. However, knowledge has long been known to relate significantly to how consumers gather, organise and evaluate products (Alba & Hutchinson 1987). Environmental knowledge provides the individual with the necessary action strategies to protect the environment, and that system of values also shapes the attitudes and intentions of consumers (Laroche *et al.* 1996). In recent literature, Fraj & Martinez (2007) stated that individuals with higher environmental concern had a higher level of ecological knowledge. It has also been found that a higher level of ecological knowledge intensifies the individuals' affective 'ecological behaviour'-'verbal ecological behaviour' relationship (Fraj & Martinez 2007).

A different perspective on consumer behaviour is provided by economic psychology. Economic psychology studies the economic behaviour of consumers and entrepreneurs. Economic behaviour involves decisions on money, time and efforts. Economic behaviour is the behaviour of consumers and clients that involves economic decisions and the determinations and consequences of economic decisions (Raaij 1999). Katona (1968) discussed the relationship between economics and psychology. He argued that it is not the objective economic conditions but the economic conditions that are perceived by the consumer/household that determine economic behaviour. To understand economic behaviour, psychological variables complement the economic variables. Economic psychology is both part of psychology and part of economics. As a part of psychology, it evaluates psychological principles of behaviour with the measurement in survey, interview and laboratory research. Economic psychology is applied in psychological theories and techniques. Studies of consumer expectations and aspirations lead to new theories in economic psychology and this applies to decision-making on sustainability labelling towards sustainability consumption. Related areas of psychology that are of importance for the development of economic psychology, are cognitive psychology, social psychology and experimental psychology (Raaij 1999). Economic psychology explores the psychological mechanisms behind economic behaviour (Pesendorfer 2006). Economic psychology is a dynamic and valuable division of psychology at the interfaces of general and business economics, marketing and psychology. As people are not irrational, there is regularity and systematic bias in their perceptions and reasoning. Behavioural economics has come to play a major role in economic psychology as economic psychologists discover and model economic behaviours and their antecedents and consequences. Within this approach, they obtain a better understanding of how people, in their roles as consumers, investors, savers or borrowers react to economic stimuli in their environment (Raaij 1999).

Behavioural economics is a subdivision of economics that draws strongly on psychology and other disciplines such as sociology. The difference is that behavioural economists use observations of real behaviour in their work.

> Behavioural economics is best characterised as not a single specific theory but as a commitment to empirical testing of the neoclassical assumptions of human behaviour and to modifying economic theory on the basis of what is found in the testing process. (Simon 1997, p. 278)

Behavioural economics refers to the attempt to increase the exploratory and predictive power of economic theory by providing it with more psychologically plausible foundations (Camerer & Loewensein 2003, Webner & Daws 2005). Behavioural economics is a relatively new concept in the regulation field, and it has not questioned the issue of whether the regulation of environmental marketing claims is necessary (Minneti 2009). Behavioural economics questions and empirically tests the concept of a rational consumer and is applicable within the environmental/sustainability marketing field. The consumer may have confusion or mistrust about the claims of producers, which can then result in consumers not making decisions in their own best interest. This concept blends with law, economics, psychology and behavioural analysis. Analysis has come to consider subject areas in cognitive psychology, thinking, decision-making and language (Foxall 2001). Behavioural economists have created models to provide more information on what exactly is happening in different areas of an economic activity. Observations have given a differential approach to this theory, which analyses the real behaviour of consumers. Behavioural economists believe that the more realistic observations they put into their models (NOT the assumptions of perfect rationality), the more powerful economic results they will get – because their models provide much better approximations of the real world (Sylvan 2009). As per behavioural economics, even in the simplest of economic environments, real human behaviour often deviates from theoretical assumptions as people make choices that do not result in the greatest possible benefits. With so many choices available, people are unlikely to make a fully informed choice and instead often rely on simple decision-making rules and habits (Reeson & Tisdell 2007).

The literature on behavioural economics generally discloses mixed conclusions on the value of environmental information and consumer information as well as the possibility to affect consumer behaviour. A number of studies have found a positive correlation between increased environmental information and consumer purchasing behaviour (Grankvist *et al.* 2005). Grankvist *et al.* found that positive consumer reaction depends on whether the eco-label is expressed in positive or negative terms. A positive label signifies the environmental benefits of a product. Alternately, a negative label informs the consumer about the negative environmental consequences of not using a product. The study found that those consumers who had shown a strong environmental concern were influenced by positive labelling. Consumers with a weaker environmental concern were primarily influenced by labels signalling negative environmental concerns. In view of that, it is necessary to consider the use of eco-labels in use around the world and that they are expressed in positive terms. It may thus be that the lack of impact on consumer behaviour of eco-labels results from the positive framing having no influence on the majority of consumers with weak environmental concerns. According to behavioural economics, the negative framing would be a definitive step in the introduction of labelling. The purpose of eco-labelling should shift from not only encouraging consumers to choose 'green friendly' products, but also encouraging them to avoid the environmental damage of not choosing the product.

Studies have found that consumers do not necessarily make sustainable purchase choices even when they are given greater environmental information (Grankvist *et al.* 2005). Two reasons were suggested as explanations for this behaviour. The first is that environmental problems are often complex and consumers are asked to perform difficult tasks. In this scenario, consumers usually decide not to change their behaviour or select an environmentally friendly product without enough information and guidance from external sources. The second is that consumers are not willing to pay extra for ecological products. The behaviour of consumers in the market has provided a solid foundation for the development of the behavioural economics as well law conditions. The assumption of economics is that consumers will make decisions by applying cost-benefit analysis and make the purchase decision that best matches with preferences and objectives. This rationality has been become subject to empirical testing. Empirical testing revealed substantial cracks in the rationality foundation and has inspired others to critically and empirically evaluate rational choices, assumptions and explanations (Kahneman 2003; Minneti 2009) through the lens of behavioural economics. As the rational choice theory model operates as a device to predict an objectively optimal response, the behavioural economics approach describes the actual capacities of the human mind (Minneti 2009). As per behavioural research literature, consumers are likely to employ a heuristic approach and make a satisfying decision in purchase choice, rather than rationally optimising decisions.

Sustainability derived product labelling can effectively influence sustainability decision-making and purchasing in two ways: by providing more information (as identified during consumer behaviour research) and considering framing of the labels, as well as by providing a simplified heuristic approach (as identified in behavioural economic models). Sustainability derived labelling therefore, is deserving of attention for its potential to positively influence consumer behaviour in an efficient and focused manner.

Sustainability derived labelling

Framework 1 shows the involvement of sustainability derived labelling in the process of sustainability marketing within an interlocking system with consumer buying behaviour. It is important to investigate the different types of labels and analyse each type of claim for effectiveness and how they might contribute to sustainable development. Eco-labelling is only one type of environmental performance labelling; it refers specifically to the provision of information to consumers about the relative environmental quality of a product (GEN-Global Eco labelling network). There are many different environmental performance labels and declarations being used or contemplated around the world. As per the International Organization for Standardization (ISO), types of labels that currently exist are categorised as voluntary environmental labelling types, Type I - environmental labelling (eco-labels), Type II - self-declaration claims and Type III - environmental declarations (e.g. report cards/information labels). Sustainability derived labelling has become a useful tool for governments to encourage sound environmental practices and for businesses in identifying and establishing markets (i.e. domestic and sometimes international) for their environmentally preferable products. Many countries now have some form of eco-labelling in place while others are considering program development. Labelling is directly communicated to the end customer while producers have direct control over sustainability derived labelling as well as packaging.

Type 1 labelling: Eco labelling

Type I environmental labelling, according to ISO-14024, is

> *a voluntary, multiple-criteria based, third party program that awards a license which authorizes the use of environmental labels on products indicating overall*

environmental preferability of a product within a particular product category based on life cycle considerations.

Nowadays, most reputable environmental labels for products and services are based on this ISO standard. This standard of labelling is the most desirable as it offers consumers assurance of claims and protects the producers from accusations of green-wash/sustainability-wash. A very recent study was conducted to investigate awareness of 'green energy' availability and awareness levels in Australia. The study provided input on the current effectiveness of Type I labelling. This research by Hartmann, Apaolaza Ibanez and D'Souza (2011), using consumer focus groups of those interested in solar energy, confirmed that most consumers are not environmentally sensitive when it comes to buying green solar panels. It was ascertained that price was the main factor involved and the benefits received in terms of cost savings were the main reason why consumers would invest in solar energy. Though most purchasers supported environmental and climate change causes, immediate price/cost was a factor that was considered most important. This indicates that if consumers are asked to put down a financial investment towards the environment, return on investment must be favourable in terms of costs.

During the focus groups, slides were shown on the effects of climate change as well as the Green Energy label. Only a minority in the group identified the Green Energy labelling. This was probably because most of the consumers in the group had not been previously exposed to this labelling. Some of the group members could hardly recall the label later when the label was shown to them in focus groups; neither the contents nor the details of the label could be remembered. The consumers who had experienced some sort of environmental catastrophe such as floods were highly sensitive about the environment; however, this did not bring about a behavioural change. This particular research supports most of the prior research conducted (D'Souza 2004; D'Souza, Taghian & Lamb 2006; Gallastegui 2002) and indicates that, even in the context of third party labelling, consumers may rely little on them in decision-making when the label is present without further aids in decision framing.

The success of any eco-labelling scheme depends to a large degree on the level of consumer awareness. According to the studies undertaken during the late 1990s, targeted awareness of the label exceeded 50 per cent each year and was increasing (Lewis *et al.* 2010). Consumers associated the eco-label with decreased environmental impact and generally considered the brand to be trustworthy (Nilsson, Tunçer & Thidell 2004). The most straightforward way in which an eco-label can be efficacious, is if it increases consumer awareness and results in a change in buying behaviour. Similar to the above case study, several further studies have been undertaken to identify purchasing practices after exposure to a particular eco-label (Leire & Thidell 2005; Loureiro & Lotade 2005). These surveys revealed that consumer awareness does not always result in changes in purchasing decisions and that positive attitudes towards an eco-label do not necessarily mean the product will be purchased (Leire & Thidell 2005; Reiser & Simmons 2005).

Type II labelling: Informative environmental self-declaration claims

Informative environmental self-declaration claims are environmental claims made about goods by their manufacturers, importers or distributors. They are not independently verified, do not use pre-determined and accepted criteria for reference and are arguably the least informative of the three types of environmental labels.

A good example of the self- declaration claims or labels is used in the Australian farmers' market labelling system. Farmers' markets have been growing in number and popularity over the past decade providing valuable opportunities for thousands of full and part-time farmers. At direct selling venues, farmers' markets customers have the ability to personally communicate with the growers and investigate their production practices over face-to-face discussions. This interaction provides the consumer with improved knowledge and appreciation of the agricultural processes used to grow their foods resulting in increased confidence, awareness in the food production systems and more efficient purchases (Guthrie, Dahlstrand, Biel, 2006). Literature analysing farmers' markets has found that consumers attend farmers markets for a variety of reasons. While some attend to purchase better and high quality foods, others are interested in the societal and environmental attributes of their food purchases (Guthrie *et al.* 2006)(Guthrie et al, 2006). Specifically, consumers also expressed interest in food production practices, safety issues and environmental impacts (Kremen, Green, Hanson, 2002).

New consumer insights research commissioned by Meat & Livestock Australia (2009) suggests that successful food brands will need to prove their nutrition and ethical credentials to consumers if they are to prosper in the future. The research finds a growing number of consumers are investing more of their time and money into buying fresh food and cooking from scratch. Meanwhile, 52% of consumers are buying more fruit and vegetables from markets or farmer's markets and 51% mainly shop for fresh fruit and vegetables at a greengrocer (Retail World 2008). In this research it was noted that a range of signage types were used by growers. There was individual labelling of products with the word 'organic' and the display of banners from certification agencies and farmer associations. Farm names also incorporated the word 'organic'. Some conventional producers have been using signs to specify which crops, like lettuce and selected fruit crops, were grown without synthetic inputs (Kreman, Greene & Hanson 2002). Other labels being used by organic farmers and others using alternative production methods were 'chemical-free', 'no chemical fertilizers', 'no harmful insecticides', 'natural growing conditions', 'naturally grown, 'free-range', 'pastured', 'grass fed', and 'no antibiotics or hormones'. There is little research to date on the comparative effectiveness of these labels and their claims.

Type III labelling: Environmental declarations

Type III labels, environmental declarations, consist of product information based on lifecycle impacts. Environmental parameters are fixed by a qualified third party, then companies compile environmental information into the reporting format and the data are independently verified. The environmental impacts are expressed in a way that makes it very easy to compare different products and sets of parameters for public procurement purposes. Type III labels do not assess or weigh the environmental performance of the products they describe. They simply show the objective data, and their evaluation is left to the buyer. Type III labels are found in only nine countries and required exhaustive lifecycle data sheets called 'environmental product declarations' (EPD).

EPDs are constituted in accordance with a set of standard Product Category Rules (PCR) to ensure that EPDs of products produced by different organisations in the same 'functional use category' use the same scope of data and metrics. EPDs developed by organisations are subjected to major stakeholder review processes and then published in the public domain by country-based registrars. For example, lifecycle assessments appraise environmental effects based on a functional unit, which measures the product's ability. A functional unit for a bottle of laundry detergent might be defined as the recommended amount to wash 32 loads of laundry (Bolon & Fujihira 2006). However, there is no single functional unit that can be applied across the entire range of consumer products. A single package functional unit may be suitable for certain product types, while other product types may require a serving-size or performance-based functional unit. Further research on the high demands for information processing of these types of labels is warranted.

Integrating labelling approaches

The three types of sustainability labelling provide differing approaches to facilitating consumer behaviour in shifting towards sustainability. Information on the environmental characteristics of products and services is communicated in the market through a range of labels (single issue, multi-criteria, place of origin, etc.) and a diverse and constantly evolving set of what can loosely be called 'environmental claims', often uncontrolled, and self-declared claims and images (OECD 2001). These labels are designed to provide relevant, accurate and up-to-date environmental information on products by promoting environmentally sustainable consumption and production. Sustainability derived labelling helps consumers to make an environmentally aware choice, provide industries and businesses with an environmental marketing communication tool, create markets for environmentally friendly goods, provide assistance for product development and design in a sustainable manner and help serve environmental and educational policy objectives.

Sustainability labelling and standards enable the selection of products and services according to specific environmental and social criteria, with the focus on immediate and long-term benefits to the consumer and to the producer by improving the overall performance of products throughout their lifecycle. Sustainability derived labelling helps consumers to gather information relevant to the protection of the environment in a complex marketplace, as it is a difficult task for consumers to determine the impact of their choices.

Labelling provides information about the hidden impacts of products and uses the social and environmental values of consumers to introduce incentives for producers to improve their manufacturing processes. Labels are not just a message about its product or a service but a claim stating that it has particular properties and features. In fact, even the instrument of labelling itself is a claim as it refers to certain characteristics of the procedure under which the label is awarded (Boer 2003).

Even though producers and marketers try to provide enough information about the product via labelling, the success of sustainability derived labelling can be diminished due to ineffective marketing, consumer distrust and consumer misinterpretation of data. Considering the implications of the role of information in making enhanced sustainability decisions and the information on framing and use of heuristics from behavioural economics, there are indications that the approach to sustainability labelling should be one that provides credible, audited and trustworthy information. And it must do so in a manner facilitates the use of the label as a heuristic and that frames the label as one of loss or damage if the sustainability based product is not chosen, as this influences decisions of the majority of consumers only weakly interested in sustainability concerns.

Environmental labelling is an effective mechanism to inform consumers, but at the same time they have been a source of confusion and miscommunication. One of the main problems of sustainability derived labelling and environmental claims in general is their perceived lack of transparency and credibility. The effectiveness of an environmental label is ultimately determined by how consumers perceive it, and how consumers use the information it conveys and then act on it. Some research has shown that consumers often do not distinguish between Type I and Type II claims, or between third-party verified and self-declared claims. They often assume that all environmental claims have some kind of official backing (Leubuscher 1998). Success of sustainability derived labelling depends on a relatively high level of consumer awareness of environmental issues and the availability of environmentally preferable products on store shelves (OECD 1997). These facts in turn reinforce the need for successful application of sustainability marketing. Therefore successful application of sustainability labelling as part of a sustainability marketing strategy is required to implement efficacious sustainable development.

Sustainability marketing strategies

Sustainability marketing requires an aware, open and targeted approach to environmental and social issues, which takes account of all direct and indirect stakeholders (Charter *et al.* 2002). Companies focus on environmentally and socially related strategies to cater to sustainability application when launching a sustainable product or service program.

As the marketing process runs through the raw materials to product usage and disposal stages, companies need to consider the environmental and social impacts of products and services from 'cradle-to-grave', from procurement of materials, manufacturing, distribution, consumption and disposal. The customisation of the marketing mix is always situation-specific reflecting the demands or needs of customers, the nature of the product, the technological setting, type of firm (i.e. manufacturer, supplier, distributor, retailer, etc.), and other unique local factors (Fuller 1999). Compatibility with ecosystems or sustainability are criteria to be used by the company to determine which marketing mix elements are most actionable and which decisions may be most appropriate in a specific situation.

Products and services offered need to be modified and adapted to changing customer attitudes and behaviour towards sustainability consumption. Some of the sustainable product or service characteristics are designed to satisfy a genuine human need without having harmful health effects and being green throughout the lifecycle. Such characteristics should be desirable in the 'Age of Sustainability'. They would be, for example, energy efficient, non-polluting, easily repairable, reusable and recyclable, and manufactured from renewable (Charter *et al.* 2002). Branding, packaging and labelling are all intrinsically involved in the sustainability marketing product process and heavily contribute to the increased consumer awareness regarding product characteristics. Price is a key element in sustainability marketing as a profit factor. However, green marketing looks at pricing beyond the traditional retail price of the product. New strategies include pricing products with service contracts. Some products are leased instead of sold. Green pricing is not about the dollars as much as it is about structuring the mutually beneficial exchange of results for rewards. Apart from monetary rewards, consumers are rewarded with credibility.

Logistics have exploded in volume since globalisation of manufacturing and the Internet, and this has also changed the way businesses operate. 'Place' is no longer just a wholesale chain or a company owned retail outlet. Place includes the Internet, global supply chains, multiple niche markets and local community. In sustainability marketing, place is about managing logistics to cut down on transportation emissions. Distributed manufacturing is one 'place' strategy that can improve a carbon footprint. Licensing technology and brand identity to distant partners can expand business without expanding transportation and logistics.

An integrated communications approach is the best approach to the sustainability marketing application of environmental and social aspects. Transparency is a focal point in communication strategy for sustainability marketing and consumers, pressure groups and the media form a critical audience. If claims are inaccurate, unsubstantiated negative publicity will be attracted and claims that are over-ambitious, vague or do not have a good sense of synergy with the product and company may damage customer perceptions. Advertising, public relations, sponsorships, personal selling, direct marketing, exhibitions and conferences are the main streams of the communication strategy.

Marketing strategy is traditionally based on the above discussed marketing mix. Recent literature, adds the triple bottom line approach (Elkington 1997) for sustainability marketing. The triple bottom line approach includes people, planet and profit. Part of marketing is analysing the numbers, the revenue and profits. Triple bottom line accounting expands the traditional analysis and communication reporting framework to take into account environmental and social performance in addition to financial performance. The people aspect refers to fair, ethical, and beneficial business practices toward employees, community, and the country in which a corporation conducts its business. Planet or natural capital is based on the goal of 21st century companies, that is, not only to help protect the environment by producing green or environmentally responsible products but also to have their own sustainable, environmentally sound business plan. Within a sustainability framework profit is viewed as the economic benefit enjoyed not just by the company but by the employees and community as a whole (Ashkin & Schultz 2009).

Conclusion

In conclusion, for sustainable development to be successful, companies need to understand consumer behaviour and its relationship to sustainable development, following the model as described within Framework 1. Two approaches to understanding consumers are useful. There are the more traditional five stages of consumer decision-making process as used in marketing for many years as well as the newer approaches of economic psychology/behavioural economics, which focus on amongst other areas, framing effects and heuristics as being beneficial to the success of sustainable development.

Companies aiming to be successful as a result of sustainable development practices need to be aware of the role of information, the processing of information and bounded rationality in consumer decision-making. They have an interest in not only appealing to the traditional and slowly expanding green segment, but in speeding the extension of the appeal of their sustainability based products beyond the green segment to the broader consumer market. Combined with the knowledge of the stages of consumer decision-making approach and the behavioural economics approach, the range of sustainability derived labelling provides an important tool in sustainability marketing and communication.

The use of sustainability derived labelling, Types I, II and III, should be developed and deployed within the extended marketing mix of sustainability marketing strategies. As an end result, the use of sustainability derived labels should become more differentiated, varying from marketing aids to quality assurance stamps embedded in both sustainability practices and communication strategies with enhanced focus on message framing, thus making a strong contribution to consumer decision-making and impacting the success of sustainable development initiatives.

References

Alba, J.W., & Hutchinson, J.W. (1987). *Dimensions of consumer expertise*, Journal of consumer Research, Vol. 13, (March, 1987), pp. 411 – 54. ISSN 0093-5301.

Ashkin S. & Schultz, C. (2009). *The Triple Bottom Line- The rise of the "sustainability" concept*, ISSA Today, viewed on 7th August 2011, http://www. green2sustainable.com/media/docs/TripleBottomLine.pdf.

Belz F. & Karstens B. (2005). *Strategic and Instrumental Sustainability Marketing in the Western European Food Processing Industry: Conceptual Framework and Hypotheses*, BSE Conference, Devonshire Hall, Leeds, UK, September 4-6, 2005.

Belz, F.M. & Peattie, K. (2009). *Sustainability Marketing: A Global Perspective*, John Wiley & Sons, *ISBN*-13 978-0470519226.

Boer, J.D. (2003). *Sustainability labelling schemes: The logic of their claims and their functions for Stakeholder*, Business strategy and the environment, Vol. 12, No. 4, (July, 2003). pp. 254 - 264, ISSN 0964-4733.

Bolon, K. & Fujihira, K. (2006*). Guidelines for the Creation of a Program for Type III-Environmental Declarations in the United States*, University of Michigan, Retrieved from http://deepblue.lib.umich.edu/bitstream/2027.42/35333/2/Guidelines%20for%20Type%20III%20Declarations%20-%20Full%20Report%20-%20by%20Bolo.pdf.

Brandt, B. (1995). *Whole Life Economics: Revaluing Daily Life*, New Society Publishers, Philadelphia, *ISBN* 0865712662.

Brandt, B. (2003). *Setting the Stage, The International Context of Certification and labelling-*the future of eco labelling conference, Canberra, October 2003.

Buenrostro. O, et al, (2002*) Forecasting generation of urban solid waste in developing countries. A case study in Mexico.* Journal of the Air & Waste Management Association, 51, pp. 86–93

Camerer, C & Loewensein G. (2003). Behavioral Economics: Past, Present, Future, In Advances in Behavioral Economics, ed., Princeton: Princeton University Press, ISBN 9780691116822.

Charter, M., Peattie, K., Ottman, J., & Polonsky, M.J., (2002*). Marketing and sustainability, Centre for Business Relationships*, Accountability, Sustainability and Society (BRASS), and The Centre for Sustainable Design, Retrieved from http://www.cfsd.org.uk/smart-know-net/smart-know-net.pdf.

D'Souza, C. (2004). *Eco label programmes: a stakeholder (consumer) perspective*, Corporate Communications: An International Journal, Vol. 9 No. 3, (August, 2004), pp.179 – 188, ISSN 1356-3289.

D'Souza, C., Taghian, M., & Lamb, P. (2006). *An empirical study on the influence of environmental labels on consumers*, Corporate Communications: An International Journal, Vol. 11, No. 2, (April, 2006), pp.162 – 173, ISSN 1356-3289.

D'Souza C. & Taghian M., (2010). *Integrating Precautionary Principle Approach in Sustainable Decision-Making Process: A Proposal for a Conceptual Framework*, Journal of Macro marketing, Vol. 30, No.2, (June, 2010), pp. 192-199, ISSN 0276-1467.

Elkington, J., (1997). *Cannibals with Forks: The triple bottom line of 21ˢᵗ century business*, Capstone: Oxford, *ISBN* 0865713928.

Fraj, E. & Martinez, E. (2007). *Impact of environmental knowledge on ecological consumer behaviour: an empirical analysis.* Journal of International Consumer Marketing, Vol.19, No.3, (September 2007), pp. 73-102, ISSN 0896-1530.

Fraj, E. & Martinez, E., (2007). *Ecological consumer behaviour: an empirical analysis*, International Journal of Consumer Studies, Vol. 31, No. 1, (January, 2007) pp. 26 – 33, ISSN 1470-6423.

Fuller, D., (1999). Marketing mix design-for-environment (DFE): A systems approach, Journal of Business Administration and Policy Analysis, Vol. 29, (November, 1999), p 309, ISSN 1701-9680.

Foxall, G.R. (2001*). Foundations of Consumer Behaviour Analysis,* Marketing Theory, Vol. 1, No. 2, pp. (June, 2001), 165 – 199, ISSN 1470-5931.

Gallastegui, I.G., (2002). *The use of eco labels-A review of the literature*, European Environment, Vol. 12, No. 6, (November, 2002), pp. 316 – 331, ISSN 0961-0405.

GEN (Global Eco labelling Network), *what is eco labelling*, Retrieved from http://www.globalecolabelling.net/what_is_ecolabelling/.

Grankvist, G., Dahlstrand, U., Biel, A., (2005). *The impact of Environmental Labelling on Consumer Preference: Negative vs. Positive Labels,* In S Krarup & C Russell (Eds), Environment, Information and Consumer Behaviour (2005) pg. 215-224, *ISBN* 184542011.

Grundey, D. & Zaharia, R.M. (2008). *Sustainable incentives in marketing and strategic greening.* Baltic Journal on Sustainability, Vol. 14, No. 2, pp.130–143, ISSN 1392-8619.

Guthrie, J., Guthrie, A., Lawson, R., & Cameron, A. (2006). *Farmers' Markets: The Small Business Counter-Revolution in Food Production and Retailing*, British Food Journal, Vol. 108, No. 7, pp. 560-57, ISSN 0007-070X.

Hartmann, P., Apaolaza Ibanez, V. & D'Souza, C. (2011) *Green energy motivations.* Unpublished report. *ISO-14024,* Retrieved from http://www.iso.org/iso/catalogue_detail?Csnumber =23145.

Kahneman, D. (2003). *Maps of Bounded Rationality: Psychology for Behavioural Economics.* The American Economic Review, Vol.93, No.5, pp1449-1475. ISSN 0002-8282.

Katona, G., (1968*). Consumer Behaviour: Theory and Findings on Expectations and Aspirations.* American Economic Review, Vol. 58, No.2, pp. 19–30. ISSN 0002-8282.

Kotler P. & Armstrong G., (2010). *Principles of Marketing*, 13th edition, Pearson publications, London, ISBN 0136079415.

Kotler P., Keller K., Brady M., Goodman M., & Hansen T., (2009). *Marketing Management.* 13th edition, Pearson publication, London, ISBN-10 0136009980.

Krarup, S. & Russell, C.S, (2005). *Environment, information and consumer behaviour*, Reference and Research Book News, Vol.20, No.3, (August, 2005), ISSN 0887-3763.

Kremen, A., Greene, C., & Hanson, J. (2002) *Organic Produce, Price Premiums, and Eco-Labelling in U.S. Farmers'* Markets, Retrieved from www.ers.usda.gov.

Laroche M., Toffoli, R., Kim, C. & Muller, T.E. (1996), The influence of culture on pro-environmental knowledge, attitudes, and behaviours: a Canadian perspective, in Corfman, K.P. Lynch, J.G. (Eds), *Advances in Consumer Research*, Association for Consumer Research, Provo, UT, Vol. 23, pp. 196-202. ISSN 0825-0383.

Leubuscher, S., Hager, W., Wattiez, C., Farmer, J.,Liaska, E., (1998). Study on Verification and Control of Environmental Product Claims. ProSpect, September

Leire, C. & Thidell, A. (2005). *Product-related environmental information to guide consumer purchases – A review and analysis of research on perceptions, understanding and use among Nordic consumers,* Journal of Cleaner Production, Vol. 13, No.10-11,pp. 1061-1070, ISSN 0959-6526.

Lewis K.A., Tzilivakis, J., Warner, D., & Green, A., McGeevo, K., (2010). *Effective approaches to environmental labelling of food products,* Agriculture and Environment Research Unit Science and Technology Research Institute, University of Hertfordshire, UK.

Loureiro, M.L., & Lotade, J. (2005). *Do fair trade and eco-labels in coffee wake up the consumer conscience? Ecological Economics,* Vol. 53, No.1, pp. 129-138, ISSN 0921-8009.

Meat and Livestock Australia 2009. Meat Standards Australia. Downloaded from: http://www.mla.com.au/TopicHierarchy/IndustryPrograms/MeatStandardsAustralia

Minneti J.J. (2009*). Is it Too Easy Being Green? A Behavioural Economics Approach to Determining Whether to Regulate Environmental Marketing Claims,* Retrieved from http://works.bepress.com/jeffrey_minneti/1.

Nilsson, H., Tunçer, B., & Thidell, Å. (2004). The use of eco-labelling like initiatives on food products to promote quality assurance—is there enough credibility? Journal of Cleaner Production, Vol. 12, No. 5, pp. 517-526, ISSN 0959-6526.

OECD Organization for Economic Cooperation and Development (1997). Eco-labelling: Actual Effects of Selected Programmes, Retrieved from http://www.oecd.org/officialdocuments/displaydocumentpdf/?cote=OCDE/GD (97)105&doclanguage=en.

OECD Organization for Economic Cooperation and Development, (2001). Experts Workshop on Information and Consumer Decision-Making for Sustainable Consumption, Retrieved from http://www.oecd.org/dataoecd/46/19/1895757.pdf.

OECD Organization for Economic Cooperation and Development, (2008*). Promoting Sustainable Consumption- Good practices in OECD countries,* Retrieved from http://www.oecd.org/dataoecd/1/59/40317373.pdf.

Ottman J.A. (1992*). Green Marketing: Challenges &Opportunities for the New Marketing Age.* NTC Business Book, Chicago, ISBN-10 1594570787.

Peattie, K. (1995). *Environmental marketing management: meeting the green challenge.* London: Pitman Publishing Company, ISBN 9780273602798.

Pesendorfer, W. (2006). *Behavioural Economics Comes of Age: A Review Essay on Advances in Behavioural Economics,* Journal of Economic Literature. Vol. 44, No. 3, (Aug 2006), pp. 712-721, ISSN 0022-0515.

Raaij W.F. (1999). *Economic psychology between psychology and economics: an introduction, applied psychology,* an international review, Applied Psychology, Vol. 48, No. 3, (July, 1999), pp. 263, ISSN 0269-994X

Research shows consumers returning to fresh, Retail World. Rozelle: Jul 21-Aug 1, 2008. Vol. 61, No. 13; pg. 10, ISSN 00346136.

Reeson, A.F., & Tisdell, J., (2007). *Markets, motivations and public goods: Experimental investigations on the impact of institutions.* Monash University Department of Economics Discussion Paper, Retrieved from www.buseco.monash.edu.au/eco/research/papers/2007/2207marketsreesontisdell.pdf.

Reiser, A., & Simmons, D.G. (2005). *A quasi-experimental method for testing the effectiveness of eco label promotion*, Journal of Sustainable Tourism, Vol. 13, No. 6, pp. 590-616, ISSN 0966-9582.

Shrum L.J., McCarty J.A., & Lowery T.M. (1995). *Buyer Characteristics of the Green Consumer and Their Implications for Advertising Strategy*, Journal of Advertising, Vol.24 No.2, summer, (July, 1995), PP.71-82, *ISSN* 0091-3367.

Simon, H.A. (1997) *Models of bounded rationality: Volume 3 empirically grounded economic reason.* Massachusetts Institute of Technology, Boston, p. 278.

Sylvan L. (2009). An examination of behavioural biases and implications for competition and consumers, Victorian Consumer Affairs Lecture, Retrieved from www.accc.gov.au/content/index.phtml/itemId/727562/fromItemId/8973.

Thogersen J (1996) *Recycling and morality: a critical review of the literature.* Environmental Behaviour 28:536–558

Thompson, P.B. (2010). *What Sustainability Is (And What It Isn't), in Pragmatic Sustainability: Theoretical and Practical Tools.* Steven A. Moore, ed.: New York: Rutledge, 15-29, ISBN-13 978-0415779388.

Veisten, K. (2007), "*Willingness to pay for eco-labelled wood furniture: choice based conjoined analysis versus open-ended contingent valuation*", Journal of forest economics, Vol. 13, No. 1, pp. 29-48Wilhelmson, T. (1998). *Consumer Law and the Environment: From Consumer to Citizen*, Journal of Consumer Policy, Vol. 21, No. 1, (March, 1998), pp. 45-70, ISSN is 0168-7034.

Weber, R. & Dawes, R. (2005). *Behavioural economics*, In Handbook of Economic Sociology, eds. Neil Smelser and Richard Swedberg, Princeton University Press, . Princeton, NJ, ISBN-10 0691121265.

Index

A

anti-consumers, 33, 44
anti-consumption, 3, 31, 33, 34, 38, 40, 41, 42, 43, 44
anti-consumption, second order, 39
attitude-behaviour link, 35
attitudinal factors, 42, 261, 263, 268, 269, 270

B

behavioural economics, 366, 370, 375, 377
brand loyalty, 23, 24, 288, 289, 290
branding framework, 3, 12, 14, 19
Brundtland Commission, 200, 201
business process outsourcing (BPO), 171
by-products, 85, 86, 89, 90, 99, 101

C

campaign message, 283
capabilities, organisational, 203
carbon footprint calculators, 93
carbon tax, 87, 247
ceramic water purifier (CWP), 294, 296, 297, 298, 299, 300, 301
channel management, 164
codes of conduct, 180
coercive power, 335
collaboration, 125, 127, 131, 136, 178, 204, 206, 210, 212, 213, 333
communication-as-advertising, 129
competitive advantage, 3, 13, 137, 153, 176, 182, 189, 193, 203, 223, 232
conspicuous consumption, 74, 77, 79, 110, 136
consumer advocacy, 126, 179
consumer change, drivers, 251
consumer durables, 60, 169
consumer expectations, 20, 369
consumer perceptions, 76, 146, 154, 178, 181, 306, 307
consumer segmentation methodology, 17
consumption values, 307
content analysis, 143, 144, 145, 147, 148, 153
continuous innovation, 203, 207
convenience purchases, 288, 289

corporate marketing initiatives, 226
corporate social behaviour, 23
corporate strategy, 226, 227, 305
cradle-to-cradle, 50, 54, 65
cradle-to-grave, 54, 87, 94, 103, 375
creating value, 246, 253
cremation alternatives, 361
cultural change model, 60

D

demand management, 130
dematerialisation, 56, 57
domestic electricity usage, 311, 313, 318
Dutch Green Funds Scheme (GFS), 61
Dyson, 56

E

eco-consciousness, 118
eco-innovation, 257, 258, 259, 260, 262, 263, 264, 266, 267, 268, 269, 270, 271
ecological behaviour analysis, 34
ecological consciousness, 124
ecological motivations, 4, 31, 33, 36, 38, 40, 41, 42, 43, 44
economic psychology, 366, 369, 377
economic theory argument, 1
economic wellbeing, 246
economies of scale, 58, 102, 247
eco-positioning strategies, 350
effective branding, 78, 308
electricity consumption, 311, 312, 314, 315, 316, 317
electricity consumption cycle, 316
emerging economies, 167, 168, 170
enterprise logic, 118, 126, 131, 132, 136
environmental advertising, 5, 143, 144, 145, 146, 147, 148, 149, 150, 152, 154
environmental costs, 86, 89, 246, 248, 252
environmental psychology, 75, 264
environmental quality, 21, 102, 278, 280, 371
environmental responsiveness, 226, 227, 228
enviro-preneurial marketing strategies, 223
ethical retailers, 180
ethics, 5, 117, 177, 178, 182, 191, 192, 218, 229
Eurobarometer data, 39, 43
expectancy-value models, 33, 35, 36